Research-Inspired Design

fb

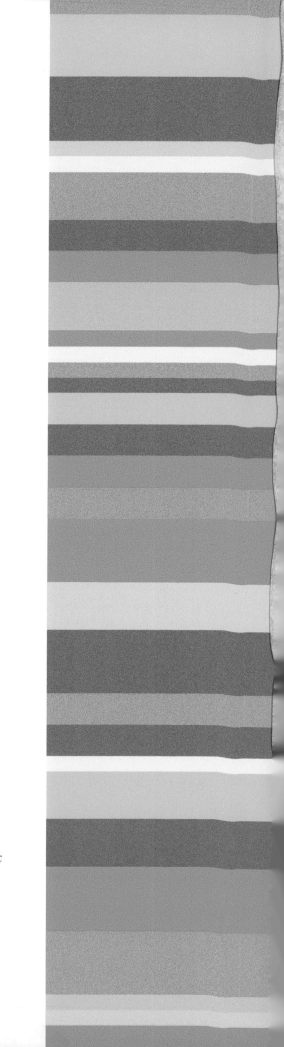

Fairchild Books ■ *New York*

Research-Inspired Design

A Step-by-Step Guide for Interior Designers

Lily B. Robinson

Design Institute of San Diego

Alexandra T. Parman

The Art Institute of California–San Diego

Executive Editor: Olga T. Kontzias
Assistant Acquisitions Editor: Amanda Breccia
Editorial Development Director: Jennifer Crane
Development Editor: Catherine DaPron
Associate Art Director: Erin Fitzsimmons
Production Director: Ginger Hillman
Associate Production Editor: Andrew Fargnoli
Copy Editor: Diane Shanley
Cover Design: Erin Fitzsimmons
Cover Art: iStockPhoto
Text Design: Chris Welch

Library of Congress Catalog Card Number: 2009925893
ISBN: 978-1-56367-721-2
GST R 133004424
Printed in the United States of America

TP08, CH14

Contents

Part One   Planning Your Research

Part Two   Information Gathering

Extended Contents

Part One
Planning Your Research

1 Why Research?

2 Systems of Inquiry

Part Four
Design

Preface

Research-Inspired Design began as a dialogue between two interior design educators who care about their students' experience in the design studio. The studio-based learning model operates on the premise that students learn by doing, while being directed or assisted by an expert within the framework of an accepted problem-solving method. It has been found that the design studio assists young designers in a structured, purposeful process, where they begin to see patterns of information and use these patterns to develop and refine their design solutions (Brunner, 2006). The idea is that this experience will help form the habits and strategies found in professionals' problem-solving methods (Phye, 1997).

Because we, the authors, teach upper-level, studio-based classes—the outcomes of which rely heavily on the students' ability to research independently: to collect data, analyze that data, and synthesize the findings into viable creative solutions—we found ourselves searching the school libraries, publishers' websites, academic and trade conferences, and our own bookshelves for a textbook that would be appropriate for the class. We kept coming up short. Semester after semester the syllabus would read "No Textbook Required"—not because there was none needed, but because there was none to be found.

This book is the one we've been searching for. We believe it fills a need in current studio-based courses to help students navigate through all aspects of the interior design process, from information-gathering to implementation, and that it will inspire those students along the way.

Whom Is This Book Written For?

Research-Inspired Design is written for the interior design student who is taking a studio course that involves independent or directed research prior to design, and it can be used for all levels, from introductory through advanced, for assignments such as a thesis or senior project. The book explores methods of data collection and analysis, organized in a manner that seeks to serve as a source of inspiration for studio design projects.

The book is divided into four parts, which are intended to be used sequentially but can be used singly.

"Part One: Planning Your Research" consists of chapters that explore the fundamentals underlying research for design. Each chapter contains activities to get students to understand why research is important and techniques for coming up with research topics—to think outside the box and to conceive overall research strategies.

"Part Two: Information Gathering" contains chapters that delve into the data collection methods, from the basics to innovative approaches. We have included many activities that encourage students to explore and document the built environment as it pertains to the design problems they have chosen to solve.

"Part Three: Programming" is a step-by-step approach to translating the collected information into a written program. It is a process that is the heart of this book, the pivotal document that, along with site analysis, seeks to encourage innovation in the design solution.

"Part Four: Design" is a summary of the continuous information-gathering that occurs during the design process as well as an overview of diagramming techniques, presentation techniques, and beyond. The final chapter seeks to address the cyclical nature of design: the idea that the final product, a built space, continues to be a source of feedback to inform the body of knowledge for interior design and spaces to be designed in the future.

We envision this book to be useful as part of an interior design studio or class in which students establish and conceptualize a project to design, explore a client and/or end user profile, choose (or are given) an existing building in which to incorporate the design, as well as present their project to jurors who offer professional feedback. For example, it can help establish in students of all levels a "strength of purpose" for their design process, and it offers enough insight to allow students to use it to a greater level of depth as they evolve as interior design students.

A Note to Students

An early conversation—a dialogue—with one of the book's editors revealed a common misperception about interior design. The editor said she would love to hire an interior designer for her home but was worried that she "had too much stuff" and the designer would want to get rid of it. She was fearful the designer would design something beautiful (like in a magazine) but that it wouldn't be a comfortable space to live in.

This belief may be widely held by potential clients: a belief that design is something that will be *imposed on* the client rather than *derived from* them. We explained to the editor that, as professional interior designers, we would first *collect information*: listen to her wants, observe the behavior in her home, document the pieces of furniture and other items that had sentimental value for her. Then we would *analyze the information*: define the problems to be solved—such as a need for storage, a lack of privacy, improved acoustics, circulation, as well as aesthetics. We would come to an agreement on the "problems to solve" (or the *program*) and base the design on these requirements. At no point would the design be disconnected from the *context* (her needs/location/budget) and *purpose* (the most ideal living environment for her).

The internationally known interior designer Tiiu Poldma, author of *Taking Up Space: Exploring the Design Process* (Fairchild Books, 2009), explains the designer's role and responsibilities well:

> Interior design is about thinking and doing. We as professionals consider all the aspects of a design issue or situation and look for ways of designing that provide useful and functionally aesthetic solutions for interior space. We do this using aesthetic ideas constructed in real time with real people. This process is a "moving target" socially, economically, politically, and culturally and requires complex considerations. Understanding the thinking of all of the stakeholders and how the designer orchestrates the various contexts and issues into viable solutions are all part of this process (Poldma, 2008).

About the Authors

Originally from New York, Lily Robinson is an architect, an interior designer, and a design educator living and working in San Diego. Lily received her Bachelor of Science in Design and Environmental Analysis from Cornell University and a Master of Architecture from Parsons School of Design. She enjoys teaching at Design Institute of San Diego, working on freelance projects, and acting as an architectural docent at the Salk Institute for Biological Studies, designed by Louis Kahn. Ms. Robinson's work has been published in magazines such as *Interior Design, San Diego Home & Garden, Better Homes and Gardens, Kitchen & Bath Ideas*, and *Dream Kitchens*.

Alexandra Parman is an interior designer and design educator specializing in "Healing Environments." She holds a Bachelor's degree in Anthropology from the University of Oklahoma and a Master of Interior Architecture from the University of Oregon. Alexandra has worked with businesses and organizations across the country to develop their professional image and create exciting and meaningful personal and professional spaces. Her graphic and interior design work has been displayed at the Smithsonian and featured on the Discovery Channel. She enjoys teaching at the Art Institute of California, San Diego, and encourages students to explore the powerful impact design can have on humanity—physically, emotionally, mentally, and spiritually.

Acknowledgments

The authors wish to thank . . .

From Lily B. Robinson—Thanks to my family and friends, Sherman and Sandy Robinson, Binnie Robinson, Sylvia Berson, Casey Green, and Ellen Zimmerman, who encouraged me through the writing process; to my mentors and fellow colleagues Jan Bast and Denise Homme; to all of the design professionals who have contributed to the book; to my students, who are continual sources of inspiration; and to Madison and Harley—the pets that make working at home more enjoyable. This book is dedicated to my grandfather Fred Berson, the original author in the family.

From Alexandra T. Parman—Thank you to all of my friends and to my family, Larry and Darlene Parman and Scott Parman, for being so supportive. I also am grateful to the late Harold Trammell for his constant enthusiasm and encouragement. Thank you to my academic and professional colleagues, who have contributed their encouragement, time, and expertise to the writing of this book; to my students, who have given me the heart of a habitual learner; and to Michael Pitts, who inspires me every day.

References

Brunner, L. A. (2006). *Are there lasting effects of a schema-based learning system in the interior design studio?* Proceedings of the 2006 IDEC Conference, Scottsdale, AZ.

Phye, G. D. (1997). Learning and remembering: The basis for personal knowledge construction. In G. D. Phye (ed.), *Handbook of academic learning: Construction of knowledge* (pp. 47–64). San Diego: Academic Press.

Poldma, T. (2008). Interior design at a crossroads: embracing specificity through process, research, and knowledge. *Journal of Interior Design, 33*(3), (pp. vi–xvi). Indianapolis: IDEC.

About the CD-ROM

Research-Inspired Design: A Step-by-Step Guide for Interior Designers is accompanied by a CD-ROM, which can be found inside the back cover of the book. The CD-ROM contains digital versions of many of the Activities found within the book as well as Additional Resources and images. Activity files can be used to record your ideas and solutions to the questions posed in the Activities, either electronically or printed out and written in by hand. Additional Resources are included to offer further examples, links to industry Web sites, and inspiration for your design process. Activities or other text printed in the book that are also included on the CD-ROM are indicated in the text with an icon (⊙). Also see the CD-ROM Contents.

How to Use This CD-ROM

The CD-ROM accompanying *Research-Inspired Design: A Step-by-Step Guide for Interior Designers* is compatible with both Windows PC and Mac platforms. The files contained on this CD-ROM are saved in Microsoft Word, Excel, and Adobe Acrobat Reader. The files on the CD-ROM should be saved to your desktop before you work on them, or you can print the files and write your information on the printouts.

- Microsoft Word
- Microsoft Excel
- Adobe Acrobat Reader (http://get.adobe.com/reader/)
- Microsoft Internet Explorer, Google Chrome, Apple Safari, or other browser
- CD-ROM or DVD-ROM drive

CD-ROM CONTENTS

Part One: Planning Your Research

Chapter 1. Why Research?

Activity

- Activity 1.1: Adapting a Space

Chapter 2. Systems of Inquiry

Activity

- Activity 2.1: Understanding Relationships and Relativity

Chapter 3. Meaningful Influences

Activities

- Activity 3.1: Researching the Design Philosophies of Three Famous Interior Designers
- Activity 3.2: Searching for Your Personal Design Philosophy
- Activity 3.3: Identifying Your Personal Design Philosophy

Additional Resources

- Additional Resource 3.1: Categories of Philosophical Inquiry (Table 3.1)
- Additional Resource 3.2: Identify Problems, Hypotheses, and Solutions (Table 3.4)

Chapter 4. Brainstorming

Activities

- Activity 4.2: Personal Collage
- Activity 4.3: Personal Interest Questionnaire
- Activity 4.4: Selecting Your Design Issue
- Activity 4.5: Selecting Your Space
- Activity 4.6: Selecting Your End User
- Activity 4.7: Build Your Own Concept Map
- Activity 4.8: Transforming Your Area of Interest into a Research Question

Additional Resources

- Additional Resource 4.1: Concept Mapping Tool: The Visual Thesaurus
- Additional Resource 4.2: Blank Matrix for Identifying a Focused Research Question
- Additional Resource 4.3: Sources of Inspiration (Table 4.4)

Part Two: Information Gathering

Chapter 5. Identifying Information Sources

Activities

- Activity 5.1: What Kind of Source Is It?

Chapter 6. Interviews

Activities

- Activity 6.1: Seeking Out the Experts
- Activity 6.2: Composing the Hypothetical Interview
- Activity 6.3: Distinguishing Truth from Falsehood
- Activity 6.4: The Practiced Art of Body Language (with additional resource links)
- Activity 6.5: Contacting the Experts

Additional Resources

- Additional Resource 6.1: ìStart-Up Agendaî for an Interview
- Additional Resource 6.2: Sample Document: Informed Consent

Chapter 7. Surveys

Activities

- Activity 7.1: Compose a Simple Survey
- Activity 7.2: Conducting a Simple Survey
- Activity 7.3: Representing the Data from a Survey (with additional resource links)

Additional Resources

- Additional Resource 7.1: Sample Questions (Exhibit Makeover)
- Additional Resource 7.2: Preliminary Checklist (Museum)
- Additional Resource 7.3: Sample End User Questionnaire (Faculty Workspace)
- Additional Resource 7.4 Open-Ended Question Survey (Funerary Services)

Chapter 8. Observation

Activities

- Activity 8.1: Defining the Public
- Activity 8.2: Developing a Data Sheet
- Activity 8.3: Looking Deeply
- Activity 8.4: Identifying Trace Evidence in the Field
- Activity 8.5: Mental Mapping
- Activity 8.6: Case Study Through Direct Observation

Additional Resource

- Additional Resource 8.1: Sample Case Study Outline

Part Three: Programming

Chapter 9. Research-Inspired Design: The Thesis Project

Activities

- Activity 9.1: Turning Your Research Question into a Thesis Statement
- Activity 9.2: Knowledge Visualization for Communicating in Imagery
- Activity 9.3: "Points of View"—Documenting and Interpreting the User's Wants and Needs Through a Photo Study

Introduction

For our readers, our intent in this brief introduction is to clarify three important ideas that help form the basis for our writing this book:

1. To explain the difference between research and information-gathering.
2. To define the profession of interior design and its relationship to research and information-gathering.
3. To explain how this book addresses both interior design programs housed in research-based Human Ecology Colleges and art-based interior design programs housed in Art and Architecture Departments.

What Is the Difference Between Research and Information-Gathering?

In the broadest sense of the word, *research* is a systematic way of finding answers to questions by gathering data, information, and facts to advance knowledge (Shuttleworth, 2008). According to Jain Malkin, in her book *A Visual Reference for Evidence-Based Design* (2008), well-intentioned designers should also be well informed. She further references healthcare architect D. Kirk Hamilton, who identifies four levels of interior design practitioners who incorporate research into their designs. Level One practitioners "stay current on literature" and "learn from others," while the highest-level practitioner, at Level Four, "creates hypotheses about intended outcomes," collaborates with other researchers, and attempts to publish his or her findings to advance the field of evidence (2003). We believe that there are several levels in which interior design students can participate in the collective "body of knowledge" of the interior design profession. Gathering information is a step in the research process. But the big question, as posed by the designer Roberto Rengel, is, "Are you a *consumer* of knowledge or are you a *generator* of knowledge?" (personal communication, July 15, 2008)

In graduate school, you may be called upon to design your own research study, which has a rigid prescribed methodology, similar to a scientific inquiry. In undergraduate education, however, you are required to use information in order to design. In this book, we'll examine the techniques that interior designers use to gather information and then we'll explore how to implement the information to produce well-informed interior spaces.

How Does Interior Design Use Information?

The answer to this question is best answered in the National Council for Interior Design Qualification's current definition of our profession:

> **Interior design** is a multifaceted profession in which creative and technical solutions are applied within a structure to achieve a built interior environment. These solutions are functional, enhance the quality of life and culture of the occupants, and are aesthetically attractive. Designs are created in response to and coordinated with the building shell, and acknowledge the physical location and social context of the project. Designs must adhere to code and regulatory requirements, and encourage the principles of environmental sustainability. The interior design process follows a systematic and coordinated methodology, including research, analysis, and integration of knowledge into the creative process, whereby the needs and resources of the client are satisfied to produce an interior space that fulfills the project goals.
>
> Interior design includes a scope of services performed by a professional design practitioner, qualified by means of education, experience, and examination, to protect and enhance the life, health, safety, and welfare of the public (NCIDQ, 2004).

Two Schools of Thought—One Profession

Is interior design a social science or an art? For many forward-thinking people, the boundary between art and science is blurred or nonexistent. The creative solution to a problem often lies in intense scrutiny of the problem. Researchers who are searching for cures to diseases often spend their lifetime examining "What is." The authors of this book are firmly committed to the idea that inspiration is derived from a state of immersion in information.

We take the position that Art + Science = Design. Interior Design programs fall onto a continuum, with some of them emphasizing art and some emphasizing science. This is due to the fact that, historically, the profession of interior design evolved from two different sources: (1) under the auspices of Art and Architecture or (2) housed in a College of Human Ecology (which evolved from Home Economics). Even the most art-based schools have an interest in technical data such as human factors. And even the most research-based design schools—which emphasize a scientific approach to design—address historic precedent, theory, and aesthetics.

The common thread of both programs is an emphasis on information to help solve design problems. Other similarities are noted: increased social responsibility, environmental awareness, and psychological as well as physiological wellness for the end user. Also important is the recognition that an elegant response—supported by knowledge of context, users, budget, and other constraints—would be pleasing to the senses.

While we authors possess a firm opinion, we are also open to dialogue. Our goal for this book is that it be used as a tool to accompany the interior design studio, to inspire, and to encourage the use of research in interior design.

References

Hamilton, K. (2003, November). The four levels of evidence-based design practice. *Healthcare Design*, 18–26.

Malkin, J. (2008). *A visual reference for evidence-based design*. Concord, CA: The Center for Health Design.

National Council for Interior Design Qualification. (2004). *Who we are: NCIDQ definition of interior design, July 2004*. Retrieved November 30, 2008, from http://www.ncidq.org/who/definition.htm

Shuttleworth, M. (2008). *Definition of research*. Retrieved November 30, 2008, from http://www.experiment-resources.com

Research-Inspired Design

Part One

Planning Your
Research

Part One of *Research-Inspired Design* consists of chapters that explore the fundamentals underlying research for design. Each chapter contains activities to help you understand why research is important and provides techniques for coming up with research topics, to "think outside the box," and to conceive overall research strategies.

1 Why Research?

CHAPTER OBJECTIVES

When you complete this chapter you should be able to do the following:

- Describe the five stages of the Interior Design Process.
- Understand how information can be used as a source of inspiration for interior design.
- Explain the research process, which includes (1) defining a problem, (2) gathering information, and (3) analyzing the data.
- Understand design as creative problem-solving that begins with defining a problem that can be solved through interior design.

KEY TERMS

Aesthetics
Art-based design concept
CIDA (Council for Interior Design Accreditation)
Client
Direct observation
End user (or user group)
Indirect observation
Interior design

Interior design concept
Interior design problem
Interior design process
Interior design programming
Interior design solution
NCIDQ (National Council for Interior Design Qualification)
Objectivity

The Information Age

Since the early 1960s, with the advent of the term *architectural programming* by Caudill and Pena (as cited in Cherry, 1999), data collection, research methods, analysis, and other aspects of the programming process have become integrated into the practice of **interior design** and **interior design programming**. More recently, the Council for Interior Design Accreditation (CIDA) and the National Council for Interior Design Qualification (NCIDQ) have put a greater emphasis on the role of the interior designer in the programming process—**CIDA** in interior design education, and **NCIDQ** in the profession. No longer considered outside the realm of professional services, conducting research and gathering information throughout the **Interior Design Process**, especially in the programming phase, is an activity that involves extensive creativity—and the active participation of client, designer, and users, as well as other points of view.

When interior design has a strong foundation of information, it yields designs in which substantial reason has gone into the making of each decision. We are living in an "information age," where clients demand to know the "why" behind the design decisions that shape their space (Guerin & Dohr, 2007). As a designer, when you approach a client with a foundation of research and articulated understanding of the issues at hand, the site conditions, and the nature of the client and the end user, your credibility and ability to sell your design ideas to the client are greatly enhanced (Guerin & Dohr).

There are also financial benefits to embracing a research-based design process. Your scope of practice is increased as you are able to participate in all phases of the design process, including programming. Also, research provides the information and resources necessary to offer expanding services to include a broader variety of space and occupancy types as well as design problems and issues that you can address successfully (Guerin & Dohr, 2007).

As an interior designer, you have choices about how you approach your own Interior Design Process. You can design spaces that are similar to all of the familiar ones that have come before. If you approach the design process this way, your design may or may not respond to the unique needs and problems posed by each new interior design project. Alternatively, you can be on the frontier of your field and design a space unlike anything that has come before, using research as a tool to help you successfully respond to the unique problems and needs that each new project, **client**, and **end user** bring to the table.

Research-Inspired Design

To embrace this philosophy of **research-based design**, the designer must also embrace a method of research that provides all the insight, information, and facts needed to make the complex problem-solving decisions required in successful interior design. Extensive and multifaceted research will allow you to make informed programming and design decisions and ensure design success from the very beginning. You can use your research to inform yourself about the problems to be solved, the challenges posed, how the space will be used, and what has and hasn't worked in the past, helping to ensure that mistakes are not repeated.

You could approach your **research methodology** as if you were taking on a mundane process of fact-finding and surveying. However, an interior designer can rise above this perspective and draw upon research as a source of motivation, innovation, and inspiration for the Interior Design Process. **Research-inspired design** expands the potential of interior design as your research becomes an exciting part of the design process. Research can open your eyes to possible innovations, solutions, and creations you might never have imagined otherwise.

As you begin to develop a **research strategy** for your design project, do not think of the research as something outside of yourself that must be completed for an assignment. Instead, make it a personal experience and think of yourself as an investigator seeking out questions and answers that will impact the greater good for those individuals who experience the spaces you design. Interior designers have the opportunity to create spaces that change the human experience for the better, but we cannot rely on our creativity alone. We must equally supplement it with knowledge, understanding, and exploration. As Figure 1.1 illustrates, it is the synthesis of all of these things that leads to design excellence.

Research as an Everyday Experience

A goal of this chapter is to help you understand that research is not a daunting new task or skill to be learned. In fact, it's a process that is part of everyone's daily life. Every day we seek out information, process it and analyze it, and make informed decisions about our life and the world around us. That familiar process is the foundation for how students go about developing a research or information-gathering strategy for any interior design project.

As it is applied in this book, *research* can be broadly defined as the gathering of information, data, and facts in order to advance your knowledge about

Figure 1.1 Creativity, Exploration, Knowledge. The criterion for evaluating a design project is the interrelation of research, design, and innovation—that gray area where the "known" intersects or overlaps the "unknown."

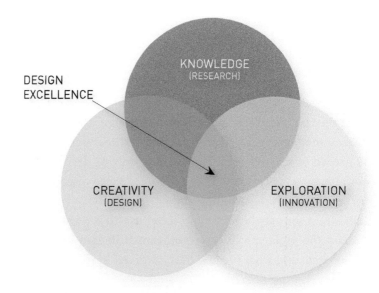

a design problem, the context surrounding it, or topics related to it. Research can be divided into four steps: (1) defining a problem, (2) gathering information about it, (3) analyzing and evaluating that information, and (4) presenting the information and citing your sources (Library at UOIT, 2008). Thus, information-gathering is the second step in your research process, as illustrated in the following example of searching for a new apartment.

As an interior designer—or any other type of designer, for that matter—you gather information as a continuous and conscientious process. This expansion of your knowledge becomes the foundation of expertise that allows you to program and design a new and unfamiliar project type for the very first time, or to revisit a project type you are already familiar with and make it better for future users.

In school, every design project should begin with research. In your professional life, every design project should begin with research. Remember that doing research is not always about finding answers. It is often about helping you find the right questions to ask. "Research allows you to know enough to ask the right questions" (V. Bissonnette, personal communication, December 2007).

Dissecting the Interior Design Process

Great interior design doesn't just happen. The Interior Design Process takes an interior designer's idea through various concentric steps and stages, all of which build upon each other, until at the end of the process a new space and experience emerges.

The Interior Design Process is a five-step journey that progresses from the identification of an **interior design problem**, usually by the interior de-

1. You've identified the problem: Your current living conditions are not suitable so you decide to take on the task of finding and moving to a new apartment.
2. You begin gathering information.

   - You might check the newspaper for advertisements of available places in the neighborhood that interests you (periodical research).
   - To help you narrow your search, you could set parameters such as a price limit or identify desired amenities like an assigned parking space or an automatic dishwasher.
   - You could talk to people who are familiar with the neighborhood (surveying) and visit several apartments to see the exterior and interior conditions of each (site visit).
   - You might even spend a couple of minutes walking around the block to scope out the neighborhood, watch who lives in the area, and find out what convenient businesses might be nearby (direct observation).

3. Before making a decision about signing a lease or contract to make the preferred apartment your new home, you follow up your information-gathering with an evaluation of what you have learned and the potential options or solutions available.
4. The process concludes with the final selection of a new apartment, evidenced by your official change of address.

Note: In this very common process of searching for a new apartment, your research method or strategy has employed four of the information-gathering techniques that we will discuss in Chapters 5 through 8 of this book: journal or periodical reading, interviewing, conducting building or site visits, and direct observation of an environment.

signer or the owner or end user of a space, through a complex series of steps that end in an implemented **interior design solution**. The five steps of the Interior Design Process are as follows:

1. Programming
2. Schematics
3. Design Development
4. Contract Documents
5. Contract Administration

Although there should be a balance of integrated research and information-gathering at every step along the way, the heart of the research process should be found in the foundational programming phase. This research approach at the commencement of a design project helps to ensure a solid and successful continuation of the Interior Design Process, and eventually it will lead to a creative and exciting solution that meets the needs of the client and/or end user and addresses the problems and parameters identified in the programming phase.

Design as a Circular Process

In looking at the linear sequencing in Figure 1.2, it is easy to get the impression that design is a linear process—similar to a checklist or a mathematical equation—and that when one step is completed the next one begins in sequential fashion until the correct answer is found. There is some truth to this. For example, a space cannot be built in the contract administration phase unless there are contract documents to refer to in the building process. But it can also be said that the most successful design solutions go through a much more complex process that could be described as more circular than linear.

As you will see throughout this book, the circular nature of the design process involves continual evaluation and testing of one's design decisions through various methods, followed by revision and reevaluation until the "right" solution is found. The interior designer might revisit each of the steps mapped out in Figure 1.2 multiple times, until the process is refined into the most successful approach.

Translating Research into a Design Solution

The intrigue of approaching interior design with a balance between creativity and research is that the process of finding a solution to the design problem can lead you to an infinite number of possible outcomes. When you begin the Interior Design Process with a well-thought-out research methodology that carefully identifies the relevant interior design problem or problems, every one of an infinite number of potential creative solutions to the problem passes through a complex web or filter until the strongest design solution emerges at the end of the journey.

Figure 1.2 Thorough research builds a strong foundation in the programming phase of the Interior Design Process, but research should play a role in *all* phases of the interior design project.

| 1 | 2 | 3 | 4 | 5 |
| PROGRAMMING | SCHEMATICS | DESIGN DEVELOPMENT | CONTRACT DOCUMENTS | CONTRACT ADMINISTRATION |

Research

This potential for infinite design solutions is due, in part, to the impact of the conclusions reached during the research process. It is also due to the unique influence of the individual interior designer who carries personal knowledge and experiences that act like an interpretive filter between the designer and the outside world. This allows each designer to process information differently, and often the same experience will be interpreted differently by different people. The same is true for collecting and interpreting data. The same **research question** asked by twenty design students will yield twenty different conclusions and produce twenty different projects.

If we dissect the "bird's-eye view" in Figure 1.3, at its heart we always find a body of research and information. Once a designer builds this body of research, the conclusions drawn can lead the designer to identify multiple interior design problems to be addressed. The logical next step is the identification of multiple interior design programs and **programmatic concepts** or strategies for solving the problem.

For example, a research study might focus on the impact that space planning in a hospital intensive care unit (ICU) can have on the interactions among families, patients, and health care providers. Depending on the research conclusions, Program 1 might call for an ICU with rows of open bed

Figure 1.3 This "bird's-eye view" shows how a body of design research or a research study can lead to various conclusions, each conclusion leading to one of an infinite number of design solutions.

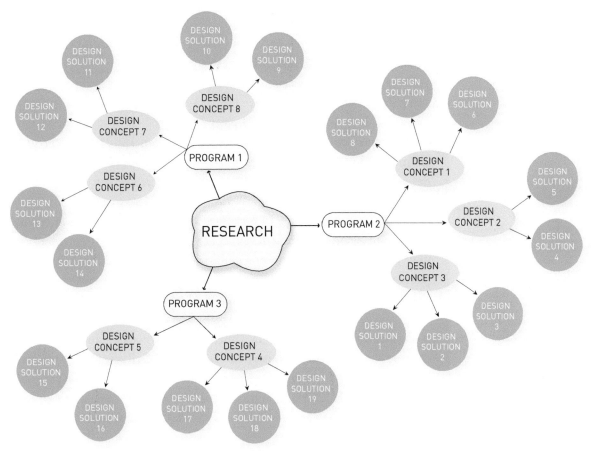

bays for patients and families and one centralized nurse's station, while Program 2 might call for an ICU with private single-patient rooms and various decentralized nurse's stations. Each program would have a different set of requirements and would lead to very different **interior design concepts** and solutions.

An interior design concept is not a three-dimensional design solution. Rather, it's a well-developed, concise, and often poetic explanation of the goals or inspiration for the eventual design solution. In the ICU example above, if we chose the program proposing private single-patient rooms, we could run that program through multiple concepts that would lead to different design solutions. Consider just two possibilities:

- A concept expressing a sense of intimacy and a family-centered environment might lead to a design solution where patient rooms are arranged in pods of three or four rooms with a decentralized nurse's station immediately adjacent. In this design solution, privacy and familiarity are maximized.
- A concept expressing a sense of family and social support might lead to a design solution where a collection of many private rooms are arranged around one larger centralized nurse's station. In this design solution, a sense of community is maximized.

Each of these concepts has meaning and expresses goals for the project, and each one leads to a very different design solution.

Once a designer or a design team has accepted a design concept, all ensuing design decisions should be informed by this design concept. This is an especially great tool when a project is undertaken by a group, because each designer can play a part in developing the concept. If the whole team commits to the concept and uses it properly, the team can create a unified design across what is often a diverse group of personalities, design styles, and philosophies.

For example, the design of an office for a doctor of Chinese medicine could be based on the strong design concept of the "Five Elements" philosophy, which describes the interactions and relationships between various phenomena, such as the organs of the body, with a goal of establishing a balance among these relationships. Using the five elements of metal, wood, fire, water, and earth to metaphorically describe these relationships, the designer could make all design decisions while taking into consideration the nature of these elements: How can they be used to create balance within the built environment and how might they impact the human experience in the space physiologically, emotionally, and spiritually? The five elements design concept would become the "glue" that creates cohesiveness across all design solutions, with the solutions possibly developed by multiple designers. Figure 1.4 presents another example of an interior design concept.

Figure 1.4 The Scripps Center for Integrative Medicine, designed by Jain Malkin, Inc., brings together traditional medicine and evidence-based alternative health care practices. The design concept utilizes the golden spiral, a sacred geometry found in the chambered nautilus shell, as a physical expression of the mind–body–spirit harmony that is the goal of integrative medicine.

There are multiple ways to approach forming a design concept. In fact, there are two main categories: art-based design concepts and research-based design concepts.

In an **art-based design concept**, the designer would apply an outside theme or concept to the space. For example, a designer interested in Picasso's *Man with Guitar* could use that painting to form an underlying concept for, say, a local coffee shop. In this example, the creative idea for the ultimate design solution of the coffee shop was inspired by a source outside of the coffee shop. Figure 1.5 offers another art-based concept.

Figure 1.5 An art-based concept for a pediatric clinic inspired by the magical experience of a child at the circus (contributed by students Darina Barry, Iris Lopez Delgado, and Jesus Urias).

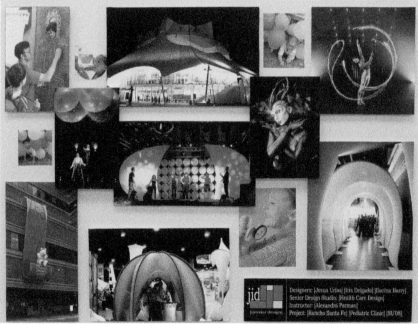

In a **research-based design concept**, the designer uses research to yield a design concept derived from analyzing the information the designer has gathered about the project or the design problem to be solved. Say, for example, that while collecting information about the appropriate location for the aforementioned coffee shop, the designer determined through interviews and casual observation that the artists in the area need a place to show their art work. The result was an "Art Gallery" design concept for the coffee shop, based on displaying local artists' work.

Sometimes it is easier to defend a design concept that has been derived from research and a thorough analysis of the needs of the project than it is to defend a design concept originating from an outside source of inspiration. However, regardless of whether the source of the design concept is derived from the project or is applied to it, the concept is to be the basis for all subsequent design decisions—from space planning to color selection. Thus, in your own work, the fundamental research needed to form your design concept is critical in the ultimate acceptance of your project solution, whether by professors, peers, or the client and/or end user of the space.

As we dissect this process, it is easy to see how all design solutions can emerge out of what was at one point an infinite number of possibilities. Over time and through the design process, the interior designer makes design decisions that lead to the ultimate conclusion that the final design solution was the right one for the identified problem. The complex network that was illustrated in Figure 1.3 served as a filter that helped the designer sort out and discard the solutions that did not appropriately address the identified problem. At the heart of this network is the interior designer's research. Through every decision-making step, the interior designer can use research-based decisions that result in a design that appropriately responds to the problems, needs, and wants identified in the programming document.

Subjectivity Versus Objectivity

As a student, you may initially find the subjective nature of interior design to be very disorienting, because it is human nature to seek out the "right" answer to a problem. The subjective nature of creativity, art, and design can cause students to feel as though they are always responding to someone else's opinion.

Subjectivity refers to conclusions drawn from the perspective of the subject's point of view, while **objectivity** refers to conclusions drawn using a methodology of evaluation that leaves out the influences of bias, agenda, and personal opinion.

With regard to the idea of subjectivity, the saying "Beauty is in the eye of the beholder" comes to mind. Subjectivity involves someone analyzing another's work from their own perspective, and it carries with it all of the experiences, filters, judgments, theories, and opinions also held by that person. Someone else's critique of your creative work, especially while you are in school, often feels subjective because much of art, by nature, finds its meaning in the interpretation of the observer.

This kind of critique can feel less comfortable to receive because it may seem to lack rhyme or reason. Often it includes phrases like "I feel . . ." or

It can be a challenge to see that the decision-making process on the artistic side of the design field actually is not devoid of rhyme or reason. The same thoughtful principles of analysis that you find in the research process can be applied to the creative side of design. Although many design decisions—such as color selection or space planning—do come from an intuitive sense or understanding that develops over time, there is a foundational study of these creative expressions. It is known as the study of **aesthetics,** from which principles and order can be extricated, revealing a rational process of design analysis. Look at the images below and decide which fence you believe is the "right" fence. Ask yourself: Which spacing between pickets appeals to you the most? Do some fences look too heavy while others look too light? What is the appropriate width of the pickets, and is this based on the spacing? Should the horizontal rails be closer together or farther apart?

Figure 1.6 Which is the "right" fence? Even a simple picket fence can be an intriguing study when approached from the philosophical standpoint of aesthetics.

How do you decide which design decisions are right for your fence? Is it a conscious decision based on specific guidelines, or is it something you feel?

Aesthetics involves the study of beauty as defined through principles such as composition, proportion, scale, balance, and harmony. For people who possess a trained eye in the understanding of these principles, even design derived from a creative source can be passed through an insightful and analytical web and be interpreted as the "right" or "wrong" solution. If you are interested in the field of aesthetics, Soetsu Yanagi's book *The Unknown Craftsman* (1990) provides a very helpful exploration of aesthetics and beauty. We encourage you to further explore the philosophy of aesthetics as a means of expanding your ability to analyze your own designs as well as the designs of others.

It is important that as a designer you allow yourself to become very comfortable with any kind of feedback, subjective or objective. The design field is an open forum, and even the most famous and successful designers have to respond to the opinions of professional peers, project consultants, the client, the user, and the general public. In the academic setting, it is the projects about which the viewers compete with one another to ask questions and express their opinions on the project, whether "good" or "bad," that tell us imaginations have been stimulated, ideas have been exchanged, intellects have been challenged, and something meaningful has happened. What would be the audience's choice in Figure 1.6?

"I think . . . ," and these expressions leave you wanting more specific answers to your question of "Why?" This is because much of the design field originates from an instinctual sense of and understanding of the elements of design—color harmony, composition, balance, and understanding of human nature, to name just a few. There is also a personal aspect to subjective criticism, which can evoke an emotional response. Thus, you will also want to seek out more objective critiques of your work, so that you can follow the rules of good design to create a successful project.

Design as Creative Problem-Solving

The first part of this chapter established the importance of research in the academic and professional Interior Design Process. The next principle to be understood as you move forward is the role of problem-solving in this Process.

The Interior Design Process evolves entirely from creative problem-solving. If you break down the complex field into its basic and essential parts, you'll find that interior design (in fact, all areas of design) is fundamentally a path of creative problem-solving and decision-making.

Everyone Should Have a Design Degree!

It has been said that everyone in any profession should get a design degree. This is because your education in design gives you a foundation as a creative problem-solver. As designers, that is what we do all day: We make decisions that solve problems. What person or professional couldn't benefit from this skill? In one way or another, problem-solving is an essential part of most careers, whether the problem-solver is the corporate manager who needs to improve employee morale or the marketing director who needs to turn an obscure product, service, or person into a household name. In the end, problem-solving is a skill that can personally and professionally benefit anyone and everyone.

If design is by definition the solving of a problem, we cannot know what to design until we first identify a problem to be solved. Thus, before the Interior Design Process has a reason to exist, a problem must be identified.

Identifying a Problem Is Your Primary Goal!

The first step in identifying a problem you'd like to try solving is to narrow your research into a focused arena that is of a manageable scope for your available time and depth of inquiry. Let's say you're interested in "green design." It's a great topic, but it's very broad. Start by reading on the topic to help you narrow your ideas. For example, you could begin researching green design in general and eventually find that you are more interested in green design practices in the manufacturing of interior design products, or that you want to know the challenges for mainstream restaurant chains adopting environmentally friendly building and business practices. In both instances, through research you have narrowed the broad topic of green design into something specific that you can connect to and begin tailoring your research to.

Examples of Interior Design Problems

An example of the relationship between the body of research and the identification of a socially current research problem could involve the growing "baby boomer" population, which is approaching the age of sixty and above. If you were to enter "baby boomers" into a basic Internet search engine such as Google.com, you would end up with millions of entries to pursue. If you entered the slightly more focused topic of "Residential Design, Baby Boomers" into a basic Internet search engine, you would still get about 43,000 possible links. If you entered "Residential Design, Baby Boomers" into an online research database that provides access to a wide variety of periodical articles, you would get hundreds, even thousands, of entries. This level of available material makes clear how important it is to focus your research as much as possible in order to isolate the most relevant sources of information.

As you find what intrigues you about the issues that baby boomers face in the design of their residences, you might notice information about the pro-

An interior design student, Jane, was interested in green design practices but did not know how to focus her ideas. Her instructor recommended that she begin reading about the broad topic of green design until something specific piqued her interest. By the next week, Jane had narrowed her focus into green residential design.

After focusing her research, she had come across an article about a new study investigating ways that a high rate of divorce and the dividing of a family might be bad for the environment. Jane explained, "Before a divorce, two people are living in the same house and sharing the same resources. For example, they both wash clothing and dishes, heat and cool the same rooms, and share dishes and other purchased items. Once the couple splits, they begin drawing from available resources independent of each other. They're still washing clothing and dishes, but they're using twice as much water as before to do it. They're heating and cooling two homes instead of one. And one of them must purchase more dishes and other items that take resources and energy to manufacture and that likely will eventually end up in a landfill somewhere."

This article and the search to identify a design problem became a new jumping-off point for Jane's research, and the next week she returned to class with an open-ended research question she could investigate further: "With the changing nature of the modern family and the potential impact of this upon the built environment, do we need to revisit the organization and design of the contemporary home in order to allow it to catch up with this situation in efficiency and functionality?"

Jane doesn't yet know if this problem is worth addressing or what the solution will be. However, her goal of seeking out a problem to solve allowed her to focus her research. Now she has an idea to pursue and the foundation for what will be a fascinating and innovative residential design project. In it she will be able to approach issues of sustainability and responsible design in a very focused and goal-oriented manner.

cess of aging in the home, also referred to as "Aging in Place." You may identify the problem that the majority of baby boomers have very active lifestyles and want to remain in their homes as they grow older, but that the typical residential space is very inflexible and not built with accessibility in mind.

In yet another interior design problem, a student began her design research by investigating how we travel and how that travel is impacted by design. Eventually she focused her research specifically on airline travel and quickly identified that there is great dissatisfaction with airline travel today. Issues included fear of flying, the expense and inconvenience of traveling with a pet, and the more common issues of excess luggage, tense environments, and the cramped and uncomfortable nature of the airplane layout.

The student's research showed her that the layout and design of our modern airplanes are similar to the layout and design of the original commercial airliners of fifty years ago, and that while our society has changed drastically since that time, our commercial airplanes have not.

Once you have identified a clear, concise, and socially relevant problem, you can take your research to a whole new level as it shifts from aiding you in *identifying* the interior design problem to aiding you in *solving* the interior design problem. Note that when you take on the challenges both of identifying a problem and of finding an interior design solution, it is critical that you draw upon valid, relevant, and in-depth sources of information.

How to Identify an Interior Design Problem

Sometimes the interior design problem is obvious to everyone involved. Often, however, it takes some investigation on the part of the interior designer to sift out the actual problem and separate it from the symptoms of the problem. There are many ways a designer might do this. As mentioned in the examples above, you might read books and articles to identify a problem that is being brought to light by another researcher or professional. This leads you to then do your own investigation into the topic to find your own solutions.

You could also talk to people around you in order to identify a design problem. Sometimes, speaking with a client is an extensive process, requiring you to search through the client's list of design "wants" in order to root out the true problem to be solved. You might also think of the problem as the client's "needs." In other words, you are identifying the problem that needs to be solved in order to make the space work for the client or any other user.

For example, a client might come to you with a design request like "We need a larger kitchen!"—and then offer you a long list of items she believes should be included in the kitchen. In order for you, as the designer, to understand the true nature of the problem, however, you could begin the conversation with the client by saying, "Please explain what is wrong with the existing kitchen." The client might respond that she cannot fit more than one cook in the kitchen at a time or that her kitchen is very disorganized. From this you could conclude that, in fact, these are simply symptoms of the real problem—that it is not necessarily the size of the kitchen that is the problem, but the poor space planning with the classic one-cook work triangle and a lack of customization for how this family stores, prepares, and cooks food. Your conversation with the client allows you to successfully separate the problems to be solved (the client's needs) both from the symptoms of the problem and from the client's list of wants, thus allowing you to design a kitchen that solves the problem rather than simply creating more space.

In Figure 1.7 you can see how the peninsula divides the spacious room into poorly proportioned spaces, allocating too much space to the dining

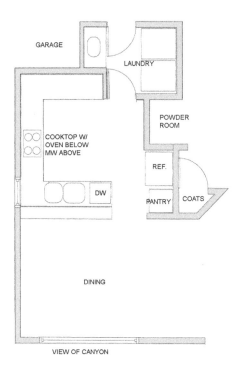

GARAGE

LAUNDRY

POWDER ROOM

COOKTOP W/ OVEN BELOW MW ABOVE

REF.

DW

PANTRY   COATS

DINING

VIEW OF CANYON

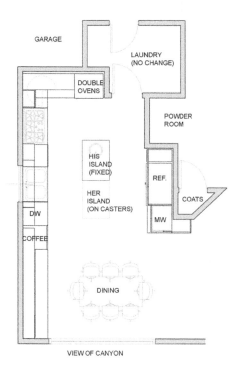

GARAGE

LAUNDRY (NO CHANGE)

DOUBLE OVENS

POWDER ROOM

HIS ISLAND (FIXED)

REF.

HER ISLAND (ON CASTERS)

DW

COATS

MW

COFFEE

DINING

VIEW OF CANYON

Figure 1.7 (above left) The problem identified by the designer was that the space in this kitchen was poorly planned. Too much space was allocated to the dining area and not enough space was given to areas for food preparation and cooking.

Figure 1.8 (above right) The solution for the space-starved kitchen was to eliminate the peninsula, opening up the room and providing more storage and greater flexibility for people and activities.

area and not enough space to the food preparation area, thus limiting the number of cooks able to use the kitchen at one time.

Figure 1.8 shows that the solution to the problem was to eliminate the peninsula, uniting the two spaces and providing room for storage and flexibility for people and activities within the space. The multi-height fixed and mobile islands replace any work surface lost by the removal of the peninsula; they provide a creative and adaptable solution.

The client also identified clutter as a problem, as is evident in Figure 1.9. While the client assumed this meant she needed a larger kitchen, further investigation by the designer revealed that the clutter was only a symptom of another problem: There was not enough flexible and custom storage in the kitchen to meet the client's needs.

The designer responded to the problem by providing the client with two solutions, shown in Figure 1.10: (1) expanded storage space, including full-height casework continuing along the wall far past the original boundary of the kitchen space; and (2) flexible storage, such as the baskets located in the movable kitchen island.

Another way a designer might identify a problem is through both indirect and direct observation of a space or behavior.

Indirect observation involves the trace evidence left behind as people interact with a space or environment. This evidence usually enables us to recognize that an adaptation of a space has occurred. This adaptation forces the space to better serve the needs of the user or users. For example, you may

Figure 1.9 (above left) The client stated that the design problem was too much clutter in the kitchen. Her conclusion was that she needed a bigger kitchen.

Figure 1.10 (above right) The cluttered kitchen was merely a symptom of the problem: inadequate storage for the client's needs. The designer solved the problem by expanding the case-work to the ceiling and along the wall, as well as providing flexible and customized storage options to help the client organize the kitchen.

walk into your classroom one day and notice that all of the drafting tables or desks have been pushed up against the perimeter walls. These tables or desks are the trace evidence of the class that met here before, and they indicate that an adaptation of the space has taken place. You, the designer, could make some assumptions about why the desks were moved. Perhaps the earlier class needed to have a round-table discussion, so they created a space in the middle of the room in order to form a circle. Perhaps the instructor gave an exam and felt that this seating arrangement was the best way to prevent students from looking over one another's shoulder. Of course, until you investigate further by directly observing the class at a later date or by interviewing one of the students or the instructor, you will not know the specific answer. But what you can definitely conclude is that the room in its current configuration did not suit the needs of the class, and so it was adapted to solve this problem.

You can also conduct **direct observation** to identify a problem. A company executive might contact you and say that employee productivity is down and that she thinks it is because employees are never at their desks. The client would like you to investigate this problem and find a design solution. You might go to the company's offices and interview the employees to find out how they work and what might be hindering their productivity, but the more effective way of gathering information could be simply to spend a couple of days directly observing the employees as they work. If you talk to them, they might tell you that they spend most of their day working at their desks. However, if you sit and watch, you might find that the client was right and this is actually not the case. In fact, the employees spend about 25 percent or more of the day away from their desks.

Perhaps the employees are not physically comfortable at their desks and are in perpetual need of a stretch break, or perhaps they have to walk to a remote break room just to get a cup of coffee, or perhaps the nature of their work demands they work collaboratively and so they must all leave their desks in order to find a table to work around. There are many reasons why the behavior might occur. To propose the right solution to the client, you must first identify the real problem to be solved.

⊛ ACTIVITY 1.1 Adapting a Space

Purpose: **To begin thinking about identifying a design problem and creating a design solution.**

Go out into your community and observe an individual or a group of people altering a space in order to adapt it to their needs. Ask yourself the following questions:

- Where is the space and what type of space is it?
- Who is using the space?
- What activities are occurring within the space?
- Can you identify how the users altered the space?
- Have they added something to the space or taken something away from the space?
- Why do you think they chose to do this?
- Can you identify why the space was not fitting their needs?
- Is the alteration a successful solution to the problem?
- If not, what design solution could you offer to solve this problem for the users of the space?

In recognizing that a space has been altered or adapted to fit the needs of a user, you have already begun the fundamental process of developing an interior design project: the identification of a problem and the proposal of a solution.

Conclusion

As mentioned above, a design project has no reason to exist until a problem has been identified. As we look at the big picture of the five-step Interior Design Process and the interior design project you might undertake in school, keep this in mind: It is your research that allows you to clearly identify the correct problem to be solved. You can then use your interior design project as a means of testing your proposed solution to that problem in the environment in which the problem occurs. Each problem you identify could lead to one of an infinite number of solutions and types of design projects. Thus, it is important to understand that the methods of investigation and information-gathering are also widely varied, allowing you to tailor your research to the unique solutions and projects you are proposing. The following chapter presents a review of some of the factors that influence how an interior designer gathers information and how the designer interprets this information.

References

Cherry, E. (1999). *Programming for design.* New York: John Wiley.

Guerin, D., & Dohr, J. (2007). *Research 101 tutorial.* InformeDesign, University of Minnesota. Retrieved December 25, 2007, from http://www.informedesign.umn.edu/

Library at University of Ontario, Institute of Technology (UOIT). (2008). *Getting started.* University of Ontario, Institute of Technology. Retrieved December 8, 2008, from http://www.uoit.ca/EN/library/main/17195/67197/step_one.html

Yanagi, S. (1990). *The unknown craftsman* (rev. ed.). Tokyo: Kodansha International.

2 Systems of Inquiry

CHAPTER OBJECTIVES

When you complete this chapter you should be able to do the following:

- Explain the roles of value systems, assumptions, and points of view in research and information-gathering.
- Understand how your point of view influences your interpretation of information.
- Define *systems of inquiry* and *systems of evaluation*.
- Explain the roles of objectivity and subjectivity in interior design research.
- Understand interior design as a blending of both the creative and subjective nature of art as well as the logical or objective nature of science.
- Distinguish between qualitative and quantitative information and data.

KEY TERMS

Assumptions

Bias

Cultural capital

Hawthorne effect

Objective

Observer effect

Point of view

Qualitative

Quantitative

Scientific method

Subjective

System of evaluation

System of inquiry

Value system

In Chapter 1 we discussed creative problem-solving as the heart of interior design. Have you ever thought about your own methods for problem-solving? How do you solve problems? Did you know that your method of problem-solving will be influenced by all of the experiences you have had that make up the person you are? These experiences shape your perspective, and your perspective is the one thing you bring to a problem that no else can.

Beginning Your Research Journey

Before you start problem-solving, spend some time looking inward—to understand your unique perspective. How you approach solving a design problem is referred to as your **system of inquiry**. Your system of inquiry will likely place interior design somewhere between art and science, combining innovative creativity with systematic research methods very similar to those used in a scientific experiment.

Cultural Capital and the Value of Personal Exploration

In their book *Reproduction in Education, Society and Culture* (1990), Pierre Bourdieu and Jean-Claude Passeron use the term *cultural capital* to refer to the knowledge, experience, and connections that have enabled a person to succeed through the course of his or her life. *Culture* could be summarized roughly as the customary beliefs, social forms, values, attitudes, and material traits characterizing the people and experiences a person grows up with, and *capital* could be described as "something of great value" (Merriam-Webster Online, 2008).

Applying that concept to your academic and professional experience, you could think of your cultural capital, or cultural value, as resulting from all of the life experiences you are gathering to make you uniquely you. Such experiences shape and form your fundamental perspectives, the assumptions you make about the world, your opinions, and what can be called your **value system** (this concept will be explored further in this chapter).

Because the design process is to some degree an artistic process, it is very personal. Take some time to explore your unique perspective so that you understand how it shapes your design process. Just as this book shares information-gathering techniques for researching a design problem to find a successful solution, it also offers information-gathering techniques to help you clarify some information about yourself.

Understanding Your Point of View

Your **point of view** is a position or perspective from which you consider or evaluate experiences, ideas, or people or objects. It can also be referred to as your *perspective*. Everyone who experiences a certain person, place, or thing will come at it from a different point of view and will have a personal interpretation of the experience (Groat & Wang, 2002). Your point of view will also influence how you approach a problem.

Your point of view is invisible, but it is always present. As an example, think about a photograph. You cannot take a photograph without a point of view. And when you look at a photograph, the point of view is not in the photo but, rather, it is the combination of the camera lens, what the photographer perceived as important, and where the photographer was standing when he took the picture. When you look at the photograph, you are indirectly seeing the photographer's point of view about the subject in the image. Think how this could vary if a child and an adult each took a photograph of the same subject. Not only would the location of the lens be different due to height differences, but what the child perceived as important about the subject could be very different from what the adult perceived as important.

Obviously, each individual's experience is greatly influenced by the point of view or position from which that person approaches the subject. You have the greatest chance of seeing a thing, place, or experience clearly if you can gain an overall objective view of the situation. Recall the "bird's-eye view" presented in Chapter 1: In any situation, there is always a bigger picture or a surrounding context to be considered.

The same principle applies to buildings, interiors, and the experiences that people have within these places. A great example, shown in Figure 2.1, is Seattle's Experience Music Project, designed by Frank Gehry. The exterior and interior of the building is a complex arrangement of geometries, colors, and materials, making each view of the exterior a unique one. Depending on where people are standing, each person might describe the experience of the building in a different way. From one vantage point the viewer might see the building as cold, gray, and metallic. From another vantage point the viewer might see the building as warm, red, and shiny, with undulating

Figure 2.1 A powerful aspect of the Experience Music Project in Seattle, Washington, is the ever-changing nature of the building's architectural character. Depending upon your point of view, as you navigate the building from exterior to interior you might describe several very different experiences.

shapes and forms. The interior of the building is designed similarly, as each new space and point of view within the space provides the visitor with a new experience.

Add to this scenario the subjective opinion of the individual, often influenced by that person's previous exposure to architecture, interior design, art, and even music. In addition, we may have emotions tied to certain experiences. For example, what is "visually stimulating" to one person may be "chaotic" and "confusing" to another.

The Role of Value Systems

Your point of view or perspective is based on your *value system* (a situation or condition you strive to maintain and will dedicate energy, time, and even money to maintaining). Your value system affects not only the decisions you make, but the sources you seek in informing your decisions (Cherry, 1999). If this concept is new to you, seek an understanding of your own value system simply by asking yourself, "What is important to me?" or "What will I exert energy to gain or maintain?" In your journal or notebook, jot down your thoughts about these questions.

You may agree with some of the following statements, in which case they are part of your personal value system. You may disagree with others, and thus you would not consider them to be part of your value system.

1. Responsible interior designers make environmentally friendly design decisions.
2. Americans should take personal responsibility for their health and well-being.
3. A strong military preserves a country's rights and personal freedoms.
4. An interior designer's deep and meaningful understanding of the end user allows the designer to design spaces that respond to the user's needs successfully.
5. Children should be in environments that stimulate their intellectual, social, and emotional growth.
6. Children have a right to play.
7. Family first.
8. In medical spaces, it is the right of the patient to maintain a sense of peace, control, and dignity.
9. Investing in our local communities preserves the hearts of our cities.
10. Design helps people.
11. You can never truly trust another human being.
12. Employees have to be watched or they will try to take advantage of the system.
13. A strong hand makes an obedient child.
14. Make peace, not war.

Did any of these statements ring true to you? Did any of them make you sad or angry? While value systems can be the result of lifelong experiences, often they are embedded in us from a very early age, perhaps by our parents or other authority figures. Or we may develop them later in life as a reaction to values that we first saw when we were children. Because of this, we tend to hold them tightly to us, and they can be hard to let go of or change.

You can tell a lot about your own value system by looking at the people you surround yourself with, the books you read, the activities you participate in, and the organizations you choose to join, just to name a few (Adams, 2001). Learn to recognize and identify the experiences that shape who you are and the point of view from which you approach the world, so that you are aware of the assumptions you carry and how they influence the decisions you make. Often your value system can be your greatest creative resource. Creative design solutions could come from considering your value system from a new perspective or from adopting and extending the perspectives and value systems of others with whom you are in contact (Adams, 2001).

The challenge for each of us as an interior designer is that our individual value systems have such a strong influence on the way we think that they can prevent us from seeking information or posing solutions that relate to a value system different from our own. This challenge becomes especially apparent in the information-gathering practices of interviewing or observation, as our value system determines the questions we ask and the questions we don't ask (Cherry, 1999), or the things we notice and those we don't, often referred to as "inattentional blindness" (Mack & Rock, 1998).

Value Systems and Assumptions: *Should It Be?* Versus *Could It Be?*

Your personal value system might have a far-reaching impact on your design process. Your value system influences the point of view from which you approach a design problem. Subsequently, your point of view influences the **assumptions** you make about the client, the user, the problem, the site, and so on. Often we let our idea of what things *should be* influence how open we are to what things *could be* and how we could make conditions better than they currently are. Your assumptions influence the kinds of questions you will ask and the information you will seek. In the book *Programming for Design*, Edith Cherry uses a great example. A designer asks a corporate client, "How much growth do you want to plan for?" This question makes the assumption that all firms want to grow, possibly based on a value system that believes company growth is good and all companies *should* want to grow. A better opening question might be "Do you want to plan for growth?"—thus taking a more neutral position and allowing the client to give more thoughtful and open answers (Cherry, 1999).

Assumptions are like small springboards along the path of information-gathering, where the ultimate goal is to find the truth or the right solution. Once you make an assumption about a situation, all other conclusions are built upon that assumption. If the assumption is inaccurate or misguided, your subsequent conclusions will likely be wrong as well (Weisberg, 2006). This concept is illustrated in Figure 2.2.

As seen in the previous example, if you ask your corporate client, "How much growth do you want to plan for?" you are assuming that all firms value growth as an asset. If you come to all of your client meetings with that assumption in mind, you might misinterpret information the client shares with you. The client might say, "We would like you to help us find a new office space to better fit our needs." If you are assuming growth is inevitable, you might spend time seeking office spaces that in the end are completely unsuitable for the client's needs. You might seek a workspace in a high-rise office building with an open floor plan and plenty of open tenant space to grow, when what the client really needs is a smaller, more intimate-feeling space in a suburban office park.

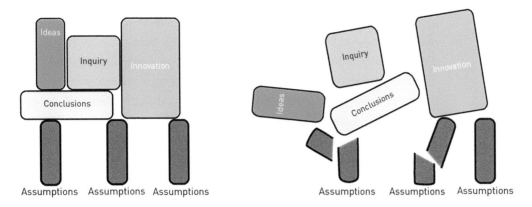

Assumptions Assumptions Assumptions   Assumptions Assumptions Assumptions

As illustrated in Figure 2.3, your interpretation of the information you gather will ultimately influence the design solutions you propose to the client. To maximize the potential solutions and outcomes for an interior design project, it is essential that you understand yourself and your own value system, that you are open to the value systems of others, and that you are able to maintain an open and neutral mind.

Systems of Inquiry

This discussion of value systems and assumptions applies to the interior design process at many levels (Groat & Wang, 2002). Just as your value system influences how you approach design, it also influences how you approach research, information-gathering, and programming. Believe it or not, it could influence other researchers and designers as well. If other researchers and designers apply your research-based conclusions to their own research process, you will indirectly influence their conclusions and solutions and even their design decisions (Groat & Wang).

The standards for evaluating the quality of the research and the accuracy of the findings depend substantially on the *system of inquiry* a researcher employs. A system of inquiry describes the researcher's assumptions about the

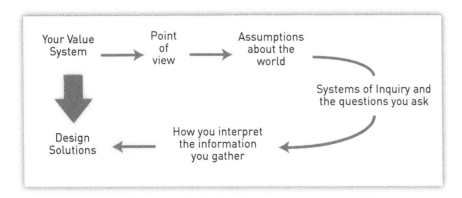

Figure 2.3 Your value system will ultimately influence the design solutions you propose.

nature of the reality—and subsequently the methods by which the researcher seeks out answers to his or her questions (Groat & Wang, 2002). In a sense, the system of inquiry is the context in which the research is conducted.

It is crucial that the assumptions influencing your system of inquiry not be flawed in any way, or else your conclusions cannot be accepted. As you analyze a researcher's system of inquiry, ask the following questions: Was it a **subjective** process or an **objective** one? Was it a **qualitative** process or a **quantitative** one? Was the research **biased** by external influences in any way? Was the research method employed appropriate for the nature of the information that was gathered? Each time you obtain information and evaluate its validity, you must evaluate the researcher's system of inquiry, as well as the researcher's value system and the assumptions the researcher made (Groat & Wang, 2002).

As you conduct research for a project, your system of inquiry is likely to frame the way your interior design research question is posed, the techniques of information-gathering and analysis, and even the practices you employ (Groat & Wang, 2002, p. 41).

As an example, let's say you are designing a dining space in the home of a family that has recently moved from a country in North Africa to a small town on the east coast of the United States. As you can imagine, the *paradigms* adopted by a family that has been living in North Africa might be very different from those of a designer from the east coast of the United States.

Take a few moments to write down in your journal or notebook some interview questions you might ask this family in a client meeting. (Chapter 6 will explore interviewing more fully.) Then review those questions and list the assumptions you made as you wrote them.

Table 2.1 presents a list of typical questions generated by students in a design studio. Notice how the wording of the questions indicates a Western

Table 2.1 Typical Interview Questions and the Underlying Assumptions They Contain

Question #	Question	Underlying Assumption
1	How many people will typically be eating in the space at one time?	Your client will only be *eating* in the space.
2	Would you prefer a rectangular, square, or round dining table?	Your client will want a table—and only one table; also, a limited number of guests will be seated.
3	Would you like to include a buffet to serve from or to provide storage space for china, silverware, and linens within the space?	Your client follows the Western practice of serving meals using table linens, individual dishes, and Western-style eating utensils.

cultural orientation and paradigm of how dining spaces are used in the home. Assumptions can limit the potential commentary you might receive from your client, and thus limit the potential design solutions.

While these questions may be valid, they are heavy with underlying assumptions. They are influenced by a preconceived and customary notion of what a dining room in the United States commonly looks like, based on typical American values and experience. Answers to these questions lead to what we know as a very familiar solution. You can see in Figure 2.4 how the number of design solutions is limited by both the questions and the options for potential answers.

Now let us broaden our perspective a little. The same questions can be reworded so that they do not project assumptions or preconceived notions on the client or end user, but instead allow for the most open-ended answers and possible solutions. Table 2.2 contains questions you might ask your client.

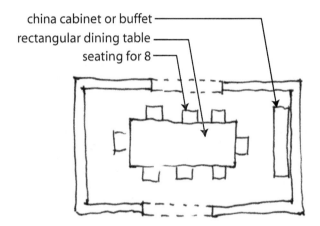

china cabinet or buffet
rectangular dining table
seating for 8

Figure 2.4 A familiar sight: a typical Western-style dining room floor plan with a dining table, eight chairs, and a buffet.

Table 2.2 Interview Questions Developed with a Broadened Perspective		
Question #	Question	Broadened Perspective
1	What are all of the activities that will take place in this space?	The activities within a space could determine the identity of the space.
2	How many people do you plan to entertain at one time?	The number of people gathering could determine the form and size of the space.
3	What kinds of meals will you serve to your guests?	The type of meal could determine the form and size of the surface used to serve the food.
4	How do you plan on serving food? Will you need a serving surface in the space?	Not everyone uses individual plates or eating utensils.

When the client was asked these broader questions, an interesting story began to emerge as to how the client would ideally use the space: "We would like the dining room to be more of an entertaining space. Traditionally in our culture guests tend to sit in a circle on the floor or on pillows, so we would like to emulate that experience in a creative way. We have also been known to have dancers and other entertainers join us, so to have an open space that could be used for this purpose and for mingling and cocktails when we host a party would be ideal. Sometimes we have a couple of friends join us, but sometimes we might invite over twenty people or more, so flexibility is key."

To get an idea of the meals the client family served and how they served them, the designer performed a participant observation. She joined the family for a dinner party and was able to watch and take notes. All of the guests were seated in a circle on the floor. The meal consisted of a whole lamb served on a large platter, along with another similarly sized platter of couscous and roasted vegetables. Both dishes were set out in the center of the circle of guests. However, there was a "guest of honor," and the lamb dish was carefully positioned so that the lamb was facing this guest. The guests did not use silverware or individual plates, but instead ate directly from the main serving dishes and used various techniques with their fingers and pieces of bread to serve themselves.

Figure 2.5 shows how this interview with its unassuming questions, as well as participant observation of the client's dining experience, led to a unique solution. The designer learned that a traditional Western dining space was not the most appropriate solution. Instead, the answer was to create an entertaining space that combined the ritual of the client family's traditional dining practices within the context of a Western-style or American home.

Figure 2.5 Asking your client the right questions can open up an endless list of potential creative design solutions. The dining room created here supports the cultural experiences of the particular client.

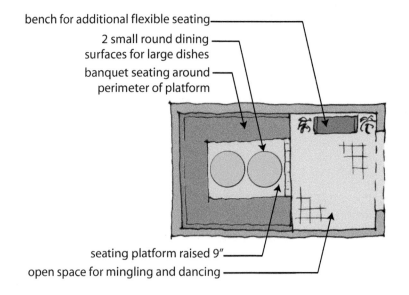

bench for additional flexible seating
2 small round dining surfaces for large dishes
banquet seating around perimeter of platform
seating platform raised 9"
open space for mingling and dancing

The solution includes both a space for dining situated upon an elevated platform with banquet seating surrounding two small, round dining surfaces, as well as an open space for mingling and entertaining. In this alternative dining room, the concept of the experience is about flexibility and socializing around dining and entertainment, while in the previous floor plan the concept was more about formality and socializing around dining alone. Neither is right or wrong. Showing them both is meant to illustrate how your system of inquiry is influenced by your assumptions and how it shapes your interviewing questions and the eventual design solutions. It also illustrates the importance of following up an interview with participation and observation in order to clarify the information you might gather during the interview.

Can you use this example to explore how value systems, assumptions, or expectations might shape your systems of inquiry and the context in which you gather information for your design process? What about how you evaluate or value the information you have gathered?

Systems of Evaluation

While a *system of inquiry* is how you pose a question and the methods you use to answer this question, a *system of evaluation* is how you personally interpret the information gathered from your system of inquiry in order to draw new conclusions. In other words, a system of inquiry influences your method for gathering information, and a system of evaluation influences your interpretation and use of the information you gathered.

Thus, depending upon your role in the field, in addition to systems of inquiry, you will also employ one or more **systems of evaluation**, which will cause you to interpret information differently than other people working in the field.

For example, a system of evaluation used by a professional expert might include issues such as functional code compliance, relevance to the design profession, viability of ideas, and formal elements and principles. An "environmental psychology" system of evaluation might interpret information as it holds meaning for the interactions between humans and their environment. A "business model" system of evaluation might relate to real estate value, investors, value of a property, the viability of a proposal with respect to making money, and the relevance that an existing business model has for a company. A "user model" system of evaluation would involve active human participation in an art or design project as community inspiration or educational experience; an example of this would be Christo's *The Gates*, a large-scale interactive art installation in New York's Central Park, shown in Figure 2.6 on the following page. In each of these instances, a person would interpret and apply information differently, depending on the context of the paradigm.

Figure 2.6 An inspirational art installation by Christo, *The Gates* was a large-scale installation in Central Park that included the nature of the surrounding context and visitors who could only interpret the art by experiencing it.

As you conduct research for your project, strive to understand how your information informs and influences your project in particular, as well as how it informs and influences the interior design field as a whole from many perspectives beyond your own. For example, you might propose a design solution, and immediately your engineer will be concerned with constructability, your client will be concerned with cost, your contractor will be concerned with available resources, neighbors might be concerned with the impact upon their ocean view, and so on. As a designer, you'll want to look at problems and information from many viewpoints in order to see the big picture and find the answer that creates a balance for all parties involved.

Subjective Reality Versus Objective Reality

Recall from Chapter 1 the discussion about the relationship that subjectivity and objectivity have to your experience of interior design as an artistic or creative field. This section of Chapter 2 expands upon that discussion and explores the two ideas as they relate to interior design research.

The most commonly questioned aspect of your research approach is whether your system of inquiry is considered subjective or objective (Groat & Wang, 2002). According to Merriam-Webster Online, *objectivity* refers to research methods that express or deal with facts or conditions as perceived without any distortion caused by personal feelings, bias, or interpretations, while *subjectivity* refers to research that might be modified or affected by personal views, experience, or background.

Although this definition presents the distinction as cut-and-dried, the reality is more complex. There is a very common debate that there is no true objective reality—that, instead, there are many subjective realities based on the life experiences of the subject, creating the point of view from which the subject interprets the world. This is the impact of having a point of view.

Have you heard the expression "He looks at the world through rose-colored glasses"? That expression refers to how that individual's life experiences influence his interpretation of the world around him, in this case reflecting an exceedingly optimistic view. We all look at a problem, question, and solution through "glasses" that reflect our life experiences—our lens of experience, so to speak. This lens affects what we see and how we see it. Unfortunately, this could mean that as we focus on one thing, we miss something else. In scientific research, where true objectivity is valued as the key to finding truth, this influence could be considered unacceptable.

According to a phenomenon in the research world known as the **observer effect**, the observer always affects the observed, and may even contribute to the observed performance or inspired expectation; that is, you cannot separate yourself, the observer, from what is being observed. (This is closely related to the Heisenberg uncertainty principle in quantum physics, where the observer, or measurer, disturbs that which is being measured, in the act of measuring it. For example, if we are trying to grasp or measure something submerged in water, the water surface is unavoidably disturbed, moving the object we are trying to grasp or measure and thus changing its true nature.)

The **Hawthorne effect**, a term coined in 1955 by Henry A. Landsberger, holds that performance or behavior will temporarily change as environmental conditions change, with this response typically being an improvement. Recall the earlier example in which a designer is hired to observe employees in a corporate office to determine the choreography of their workday and offer suggestions for how to improve employee productivity and satisfaction in the workplace. There is a good chance that because an employee knows she is receiving increased attention, she might temporarily "be on her best behavior," thus influencing and possibly skewing the results of the study.

All of these influences can impart a *bias* on whatever is being researched or studied. A *bias* is anything that produces a consistent error in the interpretation or presentation of data (Fraenkel, Wallen, & Sawin, 1999). Bias can affect both objective and subjective information-gathering. However, subjective information-gathering is influenced more by bias as it is often dependent on the researcher's point of view. For example, in conducting a feasibility study to assist a client company in locating a new rental space (discussed in Chapter 1), you might spend your lunch break driving around a prospective neighborhood to get a feeling for the area. You might conclude that the neighborhood is busy with pedestrian and automobile traffic and that it seems safe and inviting. If you were to revisit the area around 9 P.M., however, you might find that, in fact, there is significantly less pedestrian and automobile traffic at that hour and there is actually an unsafe or unwelcoming nature to the community, increasing the likelihood that security would be an issue for the client's business. In this example, your conclusions were biased by your lack of familiarity with the community, limited to only midday hours.

Objective information-gathering is not immune to the influences of bias. For example, when evaluating rental space for the client company mentioned above, to determine if a neighborhood is safe you might consult police reports to count the number of crimes reported by victims. While this data should be objective, it could be biased and inaccurate if victims in the area are reluctant to file a police report out of fear or negligence. You would want to consult multiple sources in order to verify the conclusions drawn from your information-gathering processes, whether subjective or objective.

Systemization of Research

There is an assumption in research practices that a systemization of research, or a very regimented and procedural approach, where the process and results can be easily reproduced, indicates there is always a "right" answer (Groat & Wang, 2002).

The **scientific method** is a research method that uses principles and procedures for a systematic pursuit of knowledge involving the recognition and formulation of a problem, the collection of data through observation and experiment, and the formulation and testing of hypotheses (Merriam-Webster Online, 2008). As you will see in Chapter 3, this is very similar to the basic steps used in research methods and information-gathering for the interior design process, which also includes recognizing a problem, collecting data and information, and forming a hypothesis that serves as a proposed solution to the problem. The scientific method in its purest form is considered to be both objective and systematic and thus, if used properly, should provide accurate results (Groat & Wang, 2002).

At the heart of the scientific method is a need to maintain control over the process in order to maintain this complete objectivity (Groat & Wang, 2002). For example, if a neuroscientist were conducting a controlled experiment to study aspects of *way-finding* in architecture and interior design, she might focus on how the human brain processes visual cues in the environment being navigated, such as color or images. This would be a useful study for hospitals, where visitors are likely to be under physical and emotional stress and need to find their way to a patient's room easily and quickly, especially in the case of an emergency. The neuroscientist must maintain control over the experimental process so that the results gathered from many different subjects can be measured and analyzed to produce accurate and reliable conclusions to the medical, interior design, and architecture fields.

So, you might ask, what does this have to do with my designs? You've just read about the connection between the scientific method and the interior design process, but you might still be asking, "Isn't interior design an artistic field, and by nature isn't artistic expression subjective?" Weisberg seems to agree: "Artistic creativity is an inherently subjective process since the artist brings objects into existence as he or she carries out the artistic process, while scientific discovery is an objective process that deals with objects that exist 'out there' independent of the scientist" (2006, p. 54). So, yes, interior design tends toward artistic creativity, and artistic creativity seems to be an inherently subjective process. However, interior design is not purely art—nor should it be—for design is problem-solving, while art is usually an expression or communication of meaning.

If creativity is considered subjective, scientific discovery, in contrast, could be seen as objective. Objects, events, and facts available to all of us are what scientists discover (Weisberg, 2006, p. 6), as suggested in Figure 2.7. For example, if there had been no James Watson and Francis Crick, the two men credited with discovering the double helical shape of DNA, the DNA would still have been there, waiting for its nature to eventually be uncovered. Watson and Crick had the foundation of knowledge and comprehension that put them on a path to uncovering the truth. As scientists, they did not create or invent the DNA molecule; rather, they discovered and uncovered its true shape and composition (Weisberg).

Creativity

Subjectivity

Discovery

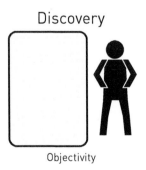

Objectivity

Figure 2.7 In the concept of *subjectivity*, the observer or creator is not separate from what is being observed or created. In the concept of *objectivity*, the observer or discoverer is or should be separate from what is being observed or discovered. Subjectivity is often associated with *creativity*, while objectivity is often associated with *discovery*.

In reality, interior design blends the creative and subjective nature of art with the logical or objective nature of science. Among the many interior design programs in U.S. colleges and universities, some provide an art-based interior design education while others provide a science- or technology-based interior design education. What kind of degree does your school offer? Understanding your school's education philosophy will enable you to better understand the goals and expectations of your program. You might ask, "Can you really completely separate these two approaches?" That is a great question, and we would respond that rather than completely separating the two, as a designer you can often locate yourself somewhere on a continuum between the fields of art and science. See Figure 2.8.

In interior design, from the perspective of art-based design, we create something new with our minds where nothing existed before. Yet we are always building upon the work of the designers who came before us, and this process alone adds a level of objectivity (or science) to our creative process. (Weisberg, 2006). Furthermore, what informs the interior design process does not have to be completely subjective or completely objective, and, ideally, it should not be. While you are gathering information for interior design, it is not necessary to control subjectivity and objectivity with the goal of accepting one and rejecting the other, but instead to recognize them so you can draw appropriate conclusions.

Your information-gathering techniques may be more objective, such as collecting census data about the demographics of a community, or they may be more subjective, such as observing the people in a community and evaluating their behavior. If you are gathering information in a way that tends toward the subjective end of the spectrum, you need to identify your assumptions or potential biases so that you understand how they might impact your analysis of information and subsequent conclusions.

Figure 2.8 On the creativity continuum—with one side being pure art and pure subjectivity and the other side being the hard sciences and pure objectivity— interior design falls somewhere in the middle as it blends your artistic vision with the research that informs your design process. Inspired by Weisberg (2006, p. 57).

INTERIOR DESIGN AND THE CREATIVITY CONTINUUM

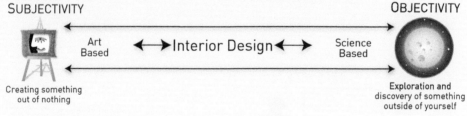

SUBJECTIVITY

OBJECTIVITY

Art Based ←→ Interior Design ←→ Science Based

Creating something out of nothing

Exploration and discovery of something outside of yourself

Sizing Up Our World: Objectivity and Relativity

Is there such a thing as truly objective research? There is, of course, the observable physical reality of the world and objects, which can be accurately defined and described through science (Groat & Wang, 2002). For example, look at a tree outside your window and describe the tree. Common responses about the tree's basic characteristics might be that it has a trunk, branches, and leaves and that the trunk and branches are covered in a material called bark.

It will not be long, however, before what seem to be simple objective observations become influenced by your subjective experiences, assumptions, and perspective. You might refer to the leaves of the tree as green, while another individual might notice a sprinkling of brown and yellow. And still another individual, possibly color-blind, might say the leaves are gray. One person might say the tree is tall, but a person from northern California, who has grown up among the great redwoods, might scoff and say the tree is rather short or small.

All of these distinctions exist because many of our methods of description are actually relative measurements, meaning that the characteristics of an object, a person, or an experience are measured or described through their relationship to something else. For example, we measure a couch relative to the dimensions on a measuring tape. In the example above, the tree might be tall relative to a bush, but it would be short relative to a redwood tree. The same relative measurements influence the process of information-gathering and research; thus, you must understand the relativity of your conclusions as they relate to something else.

The world can also be measured not only in absolutes, but in degrees. So the tree discussed above could be described as kind of tall or very tall, depending on what it is being measured against. Or a person could kind of agree or strongly disagree, as might be the case when the person is filling out a survey. When you're conducting research, be aware not only of the information that provides an absolute measurement, but the degrees to which a measurement might fall upon a continuum of possibilities. For an example, see Figure 2.9.

Figure 2.9 Opinions can be measured by degrees of agreement or disagreement—as seen in this excerpt from a survey submitted to office employees, asking them to rate their priorities on a scale of 1 to 5.

lobbies and reception areas

Your lobby and reception area make a lasting impression on every visitor. Their look and feel condition the response to everything that comes later. These areas should communicate clearly and powerfully key aspects of who you are.
Please rank each of the following phrases on a scale of 1 to 5. A "5" means the phrase strongly applies to your organization. A "1" means the phrase does not apply.

___ Bold	___ Sophisticated	___ Strong track record	___ No-nonsense
___ New kid on the block	___ Competitive	___ Award-winning	___ Wise
___ Innovative	___ Dependable/solid	___ Traditional	___ Friendly
___ Exuberant, upbeat	___ Unpredictable	___ Conservative	___ Customer-centered
___ Ahead of the curve	___ Predictable	___ Formal	___ Employee-focused
___ Insightful	___ Cost-conscious	___ Serious	___ Interesting place
___ Change leader	___ Successful	___ Irreverent	___ Challenging place
___ Trend-setting	___ Great at what we do	___ Informal	___ Supportive place
___ Unique	___ Seasoned, savvy	___ High-powered	___ Fun place

Now, revisit the phrases you marked with a 4 or 5. Draw a circle around the values you would like to see most clearly conveyed to clients, prospective employees and other visitors.

What other words or values describe your organization? _____

⊛ ACTIVITY 2.1 Understanding Relationships and Relativity

Purpose: **To work as a group to gain an understanding of the true nature of an observed object or person.**

1. As a group, select a complex yet common object, such as an upholstered chair, a sculpture, or a car. (This exercise could also work with an iconic or archetypal person, such as an image of a police officer, a firefighter, or a doctor.)

2. Each of you use your own pen and blank piece of unlined paper on which to describe the object or person as each of you sees or experiences it.

3. Share your own observations and descriptions with the group. How did group members make their descriptions? Through words, images, shapes, feelings, adjectives? Which descriptive terms were commonly used? Where did individual descriptions vary slightly or extremely? When descriptions varied, what was the object being compared against or how might the description be relative to something else? Sharing this information may take a few moments, as individuals may not be able to immediately pinpoint the experiences or assumptions that drive their conclusions.

4. As you explore the object as a group, strive to gain a better understanding of the perspectives of the other group members in order to better understand all the descriptions.

Quantitative Information Versus Qualitative Information

According to Groat and Wang in their book *Architectural Research Methods*, "At its most basic level, quantitative research depends on the manipulation of phenomena that can be measured by numbers; whereas qualitative research depends on non-numerical evidence, whether verbal (oral or written), experiential (film or notes about people in action), or artifactual (objects, buildings, or urban areas)" (Groat & Wang, 2002, p. 25). If you related Groat and Wang's statement about quantitative research back to the chapter's earlier definitions of *objectivity* and *subjectivity*, you could make a correlation between quantitative research as objective and qualitative research as subjective (Groat & Wang, p. 26).

An easy way to distinguish between the two is to identify the word *quantity* within the word *quantitative*. *Quantity* is often used to refer to a measurement of something—or "How much?"—connecting quantitative information to a measurable and often numerical result. Similarly, you can derive the word *quality* from *qualitative*, from which you might ask, "What kind?" Qualitative information discusses the character or attributes of a situation, a place, or an experience. For example, subjective, qualitative information might include a description of the peaceful quality of natural light flooding a sacred space or the dynamic quality of the sound in a concert theater.

Although *quantity* and *quality* are clearly delineated in the explanations above, the reality is that you will often use a combination of the two within any description or body of research (Groat & Wang, 2002). For example, you could calculate lighting levels to *quantitatively* describe the amount of light within a space, or you could note the bright and cheery feeling within the same space to *qualitatively* describe the nature of the light within the same space.

Case Study
A Qualitative and Quantitative Understanding of a Hotel Lobby

At times it is challenging to differentiate between *quality* and *quantity*, because the distinction is not only about your selected research method but also about your information-gathering technique and how you analyze your data. A

Figure 2.10 (below left) This sketch, created by the designer during a site visit, illustrates the general relationships of the various hotel functions to the lobby space.

Figure 2.11 (below right) The designer found that during the course of the day, patrons tended to gather around the reception desk or perch on the ends of the benches near the valet entrance. Surprisingly, the largest numbers of people tended to congregate outside of the lobby in front of the valet entrance.

high-end boutique hotel has hired you to redesign their lobby because guests at the hotel seem to make little use of it. In fact, guests have often complained that the hotel lobby and reception space seem cold and uninviting, a qualitative description.

Begin your information-gathering with a site visit to view the existing conditions. You will likely perform an informal observation in the existing lobby, watching guests and noting their behavior within the space. This would usually be considered a qualitative research method. You might take notes or make sketches like the ones in Figures 2.10, 2.11, and 2.12, depicting exactly how you see people using the space.

After this initial observation and based on your analysis of the plan, you might hypothesize that the layout of the lobby in relation to the main entrance, hotel access, parking garage, and restaurant makes it a circulation

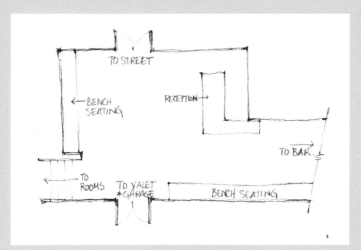

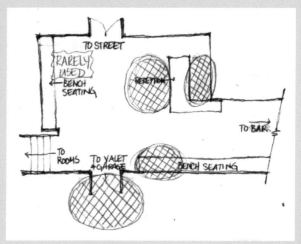

Figure 2.12 The designer made a preliminary hypothesis that because of the relationship of the hotel functions around the periphery of the lobby, the lobby had turned from being a gathering space to being more of a circulation space.

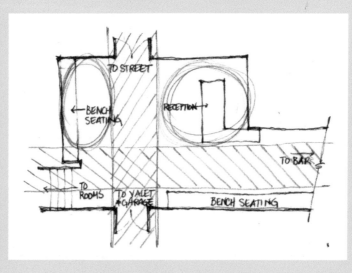

route rather than a gathering space, and thus to the guests it feels empty and impersonal. You might also conclude that the linear seating arrangements do not foster conversation; rather, they cause guests to seek other locations in which to interact.

To prove or disprove your initial conclusion, you could perform another experiment, this time quantitative. You might return to the hotel lobby and gather data for a chart that lists how many people occupy the space at various times during the day (see Table 2.3). If your initial hypothesis is true, chances

Table 2.3 Number of People in Hotel Lobby Over Time in One Day

Instructions: Record number of people in each area at each time slot.

Date of Observation: Day of Week:

Time of Day	Valet Entrance	Street Entrance	Reception	South Seating	West Seating	Center of Space
7:00 A.M.						
8:00 A.M.						
9:00 A.M.						
10:00 A.M.						
11:00 A.M.						
12:00 P.M.						
1:00 P.M.						
2:00 P.M.						
3:00 P.M.						
4:00 P.M.						
5:00 P.M.						
6:00 P.M.						
7:00 P.M.						
8:00 P.M.						
9:00 P.M.						

are that your chart will show an increase in usage during the typical lunchtime and dinnertime hours, as guests are using the lobby to access the bar and restaurant. You could use a chart such as the one below to quantitatively record your observations.

When completed, your chart indicates an increased usage of some lobby areas during the typical lunchtime and dinnertime hours. Perhaps there was also an increase in usage around 3 P.M., which correlates to the hotel's guest check-in time. These results support your hypothesis that the lobby is a circulation route used primarily to access the restaurant and bar. Notice that on both visits to the hotel, your research method was an observation. However, the conclusions from the initial qualitative note-taking and sketching were further supported by your quantitative method of data collection and charting. This broad and thorough understanding of the current use of the lobby will help you redesign it to fit the hotel management's goals and intentions to redesign the space to create a warm and inviting atmosphere for hotel guests.

Table 2.4 provides examples to help you further understand the differences between qualitative and quantitative information-gathering techniques.

Conclusion

The challenge in distinguishing between quantitative and qualitative systems of inquiry is that the same information can be gathered quantitatively as well as qualitatively. For instance, to study how patients in hospital rooms respond to artwork, you could (1) interview various patients and nurses to get their personal opinions (qualitative) or (2) develop a survey that offers a carefully selected list of art pieces supplemented with a ranking system for patients to choose from, thus producing results capable of being measured (quantitative).

In most cases, you will find your system of inquiry is most successful when it gives you a "bird's-eye view," including a balance between subjectivity and objectivity as well as qualitative and quantitative information-gathering processes.

Being an objective researcher is a challenge. So before you begin any research process, evaluate what value system, assumptions, and biases you carry with you. This evaluation will allow you to better interpret the data you gather and arrive at more accurate conclusions when determining how to successfully solve a design problem.

Table 2.4 Quantitative Versus Qualitative Information-Gathering Techniques

Research Technique	Chapter Covering This Technique	Quantitative	Qualitative
Gathering census data about a community from http://www.census.gov	5	X	
Walking around a neighborhood to get a feel for its culture	8		X
Sitting in the lobby of a hotel and charting how many people use the lobby in a three-hour time period	8	X	
Sitting in the lobby of a hotel and casually observing how people use the space over the course of a given day	8		X
Inventorying equipment for a corporate space	8	X	
Interviewing a corporate employee about his or her daily routine at the office	6		X
Photographing the existing conditions of a site	11		X
Marking a site plan with the location of utilities, such as the stand pipe and electrical meters	11	X	
Marking a map with the location of all schools within a five-mile radius of your project site	11	X	
Publishing a survey that asks people to list the number of times per week they perform a certain activity	7	X	
Interviewing potential end users of a new VA hospital about their wants and needs	6		X
Reviewing code regulations to determine the required number of exits from a building	13	X	
Interviewing an ADA consultant about accessibility requirements and opportunities (involves numerical requirements such as clearance dimensions in corridors, but also impacts how welcome all visitors feel in a highly accessible building)	13	X	X

References

Adams, J. L. (2001). *Conceptual blockbusting: A guide to better ideas.* Cambridge, MA: Basic Books.

Bourdieu, P., & Passeron, J. C. (1990). *Reproduction in education, society and culture* (2nd ed.). London: Sage.

Cherry, E. (1999). *Programming for design.* New York: John Wiley.

Fraenkel, J., Wallen, N., & Sawin, E. I. (1999). *Visual statistics: A conceptual primer.* Needham Heights, MA: Allyn & Bacon.

Groat, L., & Wang, D. (2002). *Architectural research methods.* New York: John Wiley.

Landsberger. H. A. (1958). *Hawthorne revisited.* Ithaca, NY: Cornell University Press.

Mack, A., & Rock, I. (1998). *Inattentional blindness.* Cambridge: MIT Press.

Merriam-Webster Online. (2008). Retrieved from http://www.merriam-webster.com/dictionary/

Weisberg, R. (2006). *Creativity: Understanding innovation in problem-solving, science, invention and the arts.* New York: John Wiley.

3 Meaningful Influences

When you complete this chapter you should be able to do the following:

- Understand the constructs or components of interior design research.
- Understand the relationships among design philosophy, theory, and hypotheses in interior design research.
- Share existing theories and explore how they influence the field of design.
- Uncover a personal design philosophy that influences all your design projects.
- Understand the role of existing paradigms in explaining current models of design, and understand how changing paradigms move the field forward.

KEY TERMS

Assumptions	Control variables
Constructs	Dependent variable

Independent variable

Paradigm

Paradigmatic shift

Philosophy

Propositions

Testable hypothesis

Theory

Variables

Every great work of art has two faces, one toward its own time and one toward the future, toward eternity (Daniel Barenboim).

Design Context

Interior design involves a series of complex relationships and connections. As quoted by Roberto Rengel (2008), the architect Cesar Pelli identifies at least eight:

- Connections with the times
- Construction techniques and practices
- Place
- Purpose
- Culture
- Design process
- A project's constituents
- Oneself

Also to be considered within the context of your projects are the relationships among aesthetics, the study of beauty, and the technical and human concerns (Hodge & Pollak, 1996).

An important part of the professional knowledge you develop comes from experience and personal insight. When you design a space, you draw upon your knowledge of the profession and your research to help you narrow your options. But you must also draw from your personal experience to identify the many possibilities, and from there to differentiate the good from the better from the best (Rengel, 2008). Experience and personal insight involve yet another series of relationships and connections: those among philosophy, theory, and your research. Your understanding of these concepts and how they direct your research can bring a higher level of insight to your exploration of a design problem.

What Is Design Philosophy?

According to the ancient Greeks, **philosophy** is the "love of wisdom." Often, philosophy is a tough concept to grasp because its abstract nature removes it from the concrete elements of the design field. Before explaining it, we would first like to show how it relates to the other topics to be discussed in Chapter 3: theory, paradigm, and testable hypothesis.

As you move from philosophy to theory to a testable hypothesis, you move from the general to the specific. In other words, philosophy provides general overlying concepts that you can apply to direct your ideas into one or more theories. Theories, extracted from philosophies, summarize past experiences regarding beliefs, policies, or procedures and are proposed or followed as the basis of action. A hypothesis then tests a theory and either further supports it or potentially disproves it.

For example, you might adopt the philosophy that all interior design has the power to influence humans physiologically, emotionally, and even spiritually. From there, many theories emerge about the impact of interior design on human behavior and brain function. For example, one of these theories suggests that contact with nature has a positive healing effect on humans. To test this theory, you might develop a testable hypothesis that hospital patients in rooms with a view of nature will heal faster than hospital patients in rooms that have no visual connection to nature. This is illustrated in Figure 3.1.

This hypothesis could be tested through experimentation, and in fact in the early 1980s the Planetree Model Hospital project did just that. It placed a group of patients in rooms with a view of nature and another group of patients in rooms with a view of a brick wall obstructing any connection to nature. Through the study, researchers found that patients in rooms with

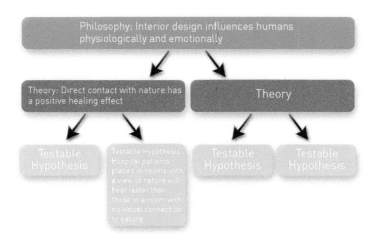

Figure 3.1 The philosophy that interior design influences humans physically and emotionally is applied by health care designers and leads to various hypotheses that can be tested within a health care environment.

views of nature healed from their wounds faster than patients with no connection to nature. The results of the Planetree project forever changed the status quo for the delivery of care in hospitals, and it further supported the theory that a connection to nature has a positive healing effect on humans.

Looking at the relationships among philosophy, theory, hypothesis, and research as a continuum, you can see in Figure 3.2 that philosophy interacts directly with theory and less directly with any testable hypothesis. The research interacts directly with the testable hypothesis and less directly with theory. Philosophy and research interact only indirectly, through the relationship between theory and a testable hypothesis.

A very clear definition of *philosophy* is "the love, study or pursuit of wisdom in understanding the nature of the universe, man, ethics, art, love, purpose, etc." (Lister, 2008). In other words, *philosophy* is a methodical and systematic exploration of what we know, how we know it, and why it is important that we know it. The significant point is that philosophy is not a thing but a process. It directs us to develop theories—and in fact there can be competing philosophies about the same topic, with various theories within each one.

The traditional categories of Western philosophic inquiry (*inquiry* again being an action word) for you to familiarize yourself with are logic, epistemology, ontology, empirical thought, aesthetics, ethical forensics, and metaphysics. Based on the areas of philosophy inquiry selected by Wheeler (2008) and his explanations of those areas, Table 3.1 provides examples of the different categories in relation to interior design.

An understanding of philosophy is important for designers from two standpoints. First, for a design researcher "philosophy creates concepts that researchers can use to direct their testing of ideas. It helps to direct research from general concepts to very specific testable hypotheses" (M. A. Pitts, personal communication, December 2008). Second, the philosophies you buy into (similar to assumptions, discussed in Chapter 2) are often influenced

Figure 3.2 Philosophy and research interact only indirectly, through the relationship between theory and a testable hypothesis.

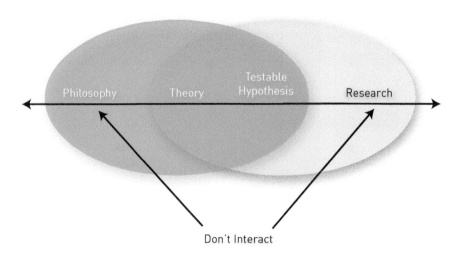

⊛ Table 3.1 Categories of Philosophical Inquiry

Area of Philosophical Inquiry	Explanation	Example of a Design Application Within This Area of Philosophical Inquiry
Logic	The use of critical thinking—particularly binary Yes/No thinking and inductive/deductive reasoning—as a means of testing ideas and debate.	Active storage versus dead storage—placing frequently used items in easily accessed storage and infrequently used items in remote storage, such as in a kitchen or home office.
Epistemology	The study of how we know things with any certainty, and what limitations there may be to our ability to think, perceive, and understand.	What are "designerly ways of knowing"? How does a designer think and how does this influence his or her problem-solving? (Cross, 2007).
Ontology	The study of being, what constitutes objective and subjective existence, and what it means to exist.	Using ethnography studies to develop a deep understanding of how your end users will experience a space.
Ethical Forensics	The study of what is right and wrong, why it is right or wrong, and whether a common basis for absolute morality can be found outside the individual mind in the laws of nature or the community.	The level of responsibility for interior designers to make environmentally conscientious design decisions.
Aesthetics	The study of what makes some things seem beautiful that have no practical benefit, and whether these things are necessary in some way.	The turn-of-the-century "Machine Aesthetic," exploring architecture and design as a reflection of the newly available technology of the era—for example, "buildings as machines to live in."
Empirical Thought	The practice of controlling observable phenomena to test hypotheses with repeatable experiments (an idea that has become profoundly important for scientific proof, though it is not, as many people mistakenly argue, the *only* basis for scientific proof).	The Planetree Model Hospital or other experiments contributing to evidence-based design in health care.
Metaphysics	Speculative thought about matters outside the perceivable physical world.	What defines "Sacred Space"?

by the value systems you have identified with, so your philosophy will also influence your system of inquiry and the direction of your research.

Frequently, the term *philosophy* is used somewhat nebulously. Speakers often mistakenly say, "My philosophy about X is . . ." when they really mean, "My opinion about X is . . ." or "My attitude toward X is . . ." (Wheeler, 2008). Your understanding and adoption of a design philosophy is a guide for your designs and how you make your mark on the design field. The next section of this chapter explores how you can use your understanding of existing architecture and design philosophy to develop your own personal design philosophy.

> Philosophy studies the *fundamental* nature of existence, of man, and of man's relationship to existence. . . . In the realm of cognition, the special sciences are the trees, but philosophy is the soil which makes the forest possible (Rand, 1974).

Developing Your Personal Design Philosophy

A personal design philosophy is a critical element in guiding your approach to the design process. Design philosophy comprises the general concepts that form the foundation of interior design. Because your philosophy is reflected in what you do, the way you design will express your personal design philosophy.

Three Case Studies
Designers and Their Philosophies

Richard Meier

Architect Richard Meier's signature style is the crisp elegance of the white used in all of his buildings. In the book *Richard Meier Architect*, he expresses his philosophy about the use of white in architecture: "White is light. The medium of understanding and transformative power" (Frampton & Rykwert, 1991, p. 6). In the film *Concert of Wills: Building the Getty* (Maysles, Froemke, & Eisenhardt, 1997), which covers the experience of Richard Meier and his client, the Getty Foundation, in designing and building the Getty Center in Los Angeles, Meier states that *white* is "the abundance of color" as it reflects the light and all colors of the surrounding landscape. In the film, during the museum's construction one of the contractors on-site can be heard saying, "Richard Meier's design philosophy requires an exactness of detail. It's how he's gotten his reputation; it's how he's earned it."

Richard Meier's philosophy is expressed not only in what he designs, but in the way he designs it; in the way the implied line from a seam between two pieces of stone on the building façade will carry through and be expressed on the opposite side of the building; or in the way he plans the spacing and orientation of each table in the café spaces. This can be seen in Figure 3.3. Meier's design philosophy means that he misses nothing and that no element of the design goes untouched by his hand or influence.

Figure 3.3 At the Getty Center, attention to detail creates precise relationships among all design elements.

Louis Kahn

Architect Louis Kahn's personal design philosophy was that architecture should elevate the human condition and reveal the true nature of reality. This philosophy—this belief that architecture could lift the human spirit—guided the design of all his buildings. Consider the examples in Figure 3.4.

When designing the Salk Institute for Jonas Salk, Kahn applied a specific philosophy that related to creating a monastic environment for the scientists living, working, and meeting for a higher purpose. Both Dr. Salk and Louis

Figure 3.4 The design philosophies of Louis Kahn have been highly influential in modern and contemporary architecture.

Kahn had visited the Monastery of St. Francis of Assisi in Italy (shown in Figure 3.5) at different times and were impressed by it for different reasons. They agreed that the life of a scientist was similar to that of a monk, with both scientists and monks dedicating their lives to benefiting humankind. The architecture and design of the facility would be a source of inspiration, elevating the mental capacity of all who worked there, while also providing the functional requirements of a typical lab. Much like they were undertaking an artistic or spiritual endeavor, scientists would benefit from being in such a place.

Figure 3.5 The design philosophy of the Salk Institute in La Jolla, California, was inspired by the Monastery of St. Francis of Assisi.

Ray Eames

Designer and filmmaker Ray Eames founded her design philosophy on the study of the abstract qualities of ordinary objects and on presenting everyday things in new ways and relationships. She celebrated the "everyday" by elevating mundane, or commonplace, elements to a higher plane. At a time of factories and mass production, she expressed that when an object is being designed for mass production, not only must the object itself make sense, but also the mass repetition of the object must make sense. For example, a single chair has an impact, but when the chair is mass-produced its impact changes; now it has an impact on the environment, an impact of color, and

Figure 3.6 Ray Eames' personal design philosophy is expressed through this study of the impact of mass-produced chairs.

Figure 3.7 The impact of Ray Eames' design philosophy is expressed in the lobby of the Johnson & Johnson offices in New York City, designed by Lalire March Architects. Vintage product boxes are mounted to the wall in a sunburst pattern that reflects the corporate brand and company history (Renzi, 2008, May).

an impact of pattern, to name just a few. Eames studied the mass reproduction of objects and concepts, treating the collection of objects as a whole, rather than treating simply the object itself (Eames Office Resources, 2006). In Figure 3.6 you can see Eames' expression of this philosophy.

Other designers put Ray Eames' philosophy into practice—for example, the mundane and usually unappealing pharmaceutical product boxes used to make an art statement in the offices of Johnson & Johnson in New York. See Figure 3.7. Through excessive and purposeful repetition, the vintage boxes are elevated to a higher meaning and purpose, reflecting a sense of nostalgia and the long significance and history of the company, which is over one hundred years old.

Another example that could be said to draw on Eames' philosophy of finding a design purpose for a mass-produced object is shown in Figure 3.8.

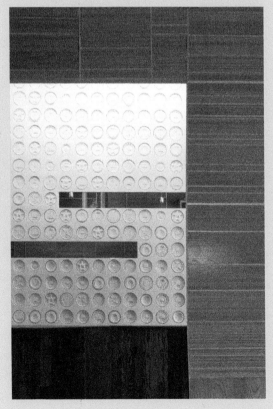

Figure 3.8 In the INI ANI coffee shop in New York City, LTL Architects elevated a mundane object familiar to many by casting coffee cup lids in plaster to create a powerful wall feature.

Just as any philosophy consists of many questions and concepts to be explored, there is not just one design philosophy but many, and you as a designer will benefit from knowing which design philosophy or philosophies you identify with or believe. The activities below are a good place to start the process. (In Chapter 4, you will have a chance to explore your philosophy even further—using a graphical format to create a "personal collage.")

Another way to identify your personal design philosophy is to spend time studying philosophies being discussed in the forums of other interior designers and philosophers. Your personal design philosophy does not have to be completely unique. As discussed previously, philosophies are general and broad, so it is common for a designer to adopt a philosophy that has been adopted by many others. Once you adopt a philosophy, you can focus on how that philosophy applies specifically to you.

For example, you might adopt the philosophy discussed previously: that all interior design influences humans physiologically and emotionally. You may further believe that interior design can affect us spiritually. From here, you could develop a new theory, perhaps related to the spiritual influence of space. Or you might adopt the theory that the use of contemporary architecture and design for sacred spaces is a denial of the transcendent and that contemporary architecture and design are too secular for a sacred space. On the other hand, you might adopt the theory that, through form, light, and color, using contemporary architecture and design for sacred spaces provides the freedom of expression required of a space dedicated to a spiritual pursuit. Either way, you are making a choice about what you believe in and you are designing according to that belief.

ACTIVITY 3.1 Researching the Design Philosophies of Three Famous Interior Designers

Purpose: **To study how an interior designer's philosophy is reflected in his or her work.**

1. Identify three well-known interior designers (or architects), and use literature and research to identify their personal design philosophies.
2. Collect multiple examples and images of their work. Study the projects, searching for common threads in expression of form, design applications, aesthetics, etc. See if you can identify how each designer or architect has applied and expressed that philosophy in his or her proj-

ects. How do the designer's beliefs about design come through in his or her work? Do you see what the designer or other critics see?

3. Share your findings about the designers, their philosophies, and their work with the class. Get a new perspective by seeing if any of your classmates see things differently than you.

Your personal design philosophy can and should change over time. You will not be the same person in five years that you are today, so why should your philosophy not grow with you? Let the evolution of your philosophy be a reflection of your evolution as a designer.

ACTIVITY 3.2 Searching for Your Personal Design Philosophy

Purpose: **To develop a philosophy by asking questions and contemplating the answers.**

This Activity is divided into four parts that you can expand upon by using the questions as cues. Jot down your thoughts and ideas in your journal or sketchbook.

These questions require some thought, and you will probably benefit from discussing them with your teacher or classmates. Most of us become more thoughtful about the "big" questions when we share them with our peers or mentors, consider their responses, reevaluate our positions, revise our thoughts, and then talk some more.

Note: This Activity cannot be completed in a distracting atmosphere. Take yourself to an inspirational place, perhaps somewhere as simple as a park bench, a local coffee shop, or the beach. First jot down whatever thoughts come to mind in response to the questions in the following four parts. Later you can refine your words into a concise statement that extracts the essence of your thoughts.

PART 1: To What End? What are my objectives as a designer?

Start by describing where you want to end up. In other words, what are your objectives or goals as a designer? The rest of your philosophy statement should support these objectives or goals. (Note: These objectives or goals should be achievable and relevant to issues of design today, so avoid vague or overly grandiose statements. On the other hand, you will want to demonstrate that you strive for more than mediocrity or more than just nuts-and-bolts solutions to design problems.) What is your problem-solving strategy? What do you believe are your responsibilities as a designer: to the client, to the user, to society as a whole? Have you read philosophical discussions in journals, articles, or books that speak to you about the shortcomings or needs of the built world that you would like to address?

PART 2: By What Means? How do I accomplish these objectives?

When you have a clear idea about your objectives or goals as a designer, you can discuss the methods that you want to use to achieve those objectives. Here is where you display your knowledge of design theory. You will want to explain specific strategies and techniques, tying them directly to your design objectives and explaining how each approach accomplishes that purpose.

Discuss here how you make decisions about design principles such as form, balance, contrast, hierarchy, harmony, or unity. Furthermore, explore which principles of design are most important to you and your design objectives.

Articulate your ideas by relating them to precedents and examples where you have found the same methods applied to architectural forms or interior spaces. You could even include images of other designers' work at this point, further supporting your ideas. Don't limit yourself to a local perspective here, but think nationally or even internationally as you search to identify how you will accomplish your design objectives.

PART 3: To What Degree? How do I measure my success?

Discuss how you intend to measure your success. If you have successfully applied the methods you outlined, how do you know when you have accomplished your design objectives? What is your scale of measurement? Is it the grade you get in class? Is it the opinion of others? Is it the response of the client or the end users? Is it the aesthetic appeal to a certain group, such as your client, users, teachers, professional critics, or your peers? Who decides whether you have identified the correct design problem and solved the problem successfully? Exposing our designs to the subjective opinions of others can be a touchy subject, so it is important to establish your own criteria for success and achievement of objectives. What are your assessment methods?

PART 4: Why? Why do I do what I do?

Here is where you can be, if not grandiose, at least a bit grand. What, to you, are the great and wonderful rewards of interior design? Why is design important? How do you want to use design to make the world a better place? When you are overworked and feel undervalued, to what ideals do you return in order to rejuvenate and inspire yourself? How do you want your designs to make a difference in the lives of others? (This Activity was inspired by the format of Haugen, 1998.)

⊛ ACTIVITY 3.3 Identifying Your Personal Design Philosophy

Purpose: **To extract the essence of your philosophical process.**

1. From all of your notes and writings from the previous Activity, select the ten isolated phrases or sentences that you find to hold the most truth. Write these ten phrases or sentences on ten separate note cards.

2. Begin arranging and rearranging the note cards to create meaningful relationships. For example, some sentences might make similar points, or you might prioritize or rank the statements in some way, or perhaps you can create categories. As you categorize and organize, some of the statements will seem like tag-alongs that do not belong in the group. Discard those note cards.

3. From the remaining cards, see if you can extract a meaningful and concise message about design that you can relate to or that feels inspiring and truthful to you.

4. Practice simplifying your ideas into one or two statements that you can say out loud to yourself and then to a peer. When we hear ourselves say something out loud, we become very aware of the content of what we are saying and become better critics of our own ideas.

5. Finally, on another note card write your complete statement. This is your personal design philosophy. Post it where you can see it while you are working, so you can use it as a guide for instilling meaning and cohesiveness in your projects.

Understanding Theory

Design and Architectural Theory look for alternatives to what we have, are forward looking, the ultimate ambition of theory is that it would not be needed (Hodge & Pollak, 1996).

Because what we do is not governed by biology alone—one could say that architecture is not governed by just keeping warm and dry—we need theory to organize the . . . systems we use (K. M. Hays, quoted in Hodge & Pollak, 1996, p. 40).

Let's take a step away from the general toward the specific—to discuss theory and how it relates to interior design. At times the terms *theory* and *philosophy* are used interchangeably, but this should not be the case. Granted, it can be difficult to see the fine line separating the two. The main difference between philosophy and theory is that while philosophy is a process, or something you do, theory can be considered a thing—an idea. While philosophy asks questions and pursues answers, theory offers an explanation: a currently accepted conclusion developed through either philosophy or experimentation. The word *conclusion* is used loosely here, for theories are often modified or challenged by both philosophy and experimentation. A *theory* is a currently accepted conclusion about a topic. Further testing can support and uphold the theory as true, or it can prove the theory wrong, in which case the theory is discarded, a new theory takes its place, and the process continues.

As theory applies to your design research, keep in mind that "when researchers are about to begin working on a research problem, they look for a theory to guide their work. It is important, however, to make a distinction in the difference between research methods and theories in the study of interior design. On the one hand, with research methods, we have the information or data that you will collect and the method or technique you use to collect that data, and on the other hand we have the theoretical interpretation that you apply to that data" (Weisberg, 2006).

Theory helps address difficult concepts, such as "the public." What is the "public"? You reframe it with a theoretical discussion in the studio before you even design a public space (R. Vaccarino, quoted in Hodge & Pollak, 1996, p. 46).

Theory "is a set of interrelated ideas or a set of relationships, and it provides a system or a filter for planning and conducting research and then for making sense of its findings" (Guerin & Dohr, 2007, part II, p. 1). Theory can be very general about design as a practice, or very specific, applying design principles, such as balance, symmetry, hierarchy, and unity, to design elements, such as color, texture, and shape (Guerin & Dohr). The layers of theory interact and influence both one another and the ensuing design solutions.

Just as the overall field of philosophy is made up of categories, **theory** comprises the following:

1. **Constructs**, or the components of a theory
2. **Propositions**, or the facts or established rules
3. **Assumptions**, or positions that cannot be proved or disproved but are assumed and must be met in order for the theory to be explored and used

Design researchers use these components of theory to guide their system of inquiry, and designers can use them to guide their design decisions (Guerin & Dohr, 2007).

In their article "Research 101" (2007), Guerin and Dohr dissect the example of color theory to illustrate the components of the theory. Table 3.2 provides explanations and examples for each of these components as it relates to color theory.

Table 3.3 on page 64 explains a number of helpful, frequently used theories identified by Guerin and Dohr in their "Research 101" tutorial (2007, part II, p. 2). Notice that not all theories included are specific to interior design, but are specific to issues related to interior design, illustrating why it is important to take a cross-disciplinary approach to design. Keep in mind that

Table 3.2 The Components of Design Theory

Components of Design Theory	Explanation	Example: Color Theory
Constructs	The components or individual parts that make up a theory.	Color theory constructs include hue, value, and chroma.
Propositions	The facts or established rules related to the theory.	Color theory propositions are that warm, dark, and bright colors advance and cool, light, and dull colors retreat. This proposition has been established through research.
Assumptions	Positions that cannot be proved or disproved, but are assumed and must be met in order for the designer to explore and use the theory.	One color theory assumption, which no one disputes, is that color is a mixture of light.

Figure 3.9 At the Salk Institute, Louis Kahn designed a building expressing monumentality and democracy. Monumentality is seen in the powerful symmetry and rhythm, while democracy is seen through the application of visible hierarchy and functional flexibility, making it possible to accommodate a wide variety of people, activities, and changing technology.

The application of various layers of design theory can be seen in La Jolla, California, at the Salk Institute designed by Louis Kahn. There, Kahn applied his theories about *monumentality*, which he defined as "a spiritual quality inherent in a structure which conveys the feeling of its eternity," to create a comparison to the timeless and whole nature of the Parthenon, as architectural symbol of Greek civilization (Kahn, 1944, as quoted by Latour, 1991). He also applied his theories about *democracy*, making the statement that "anyone with a mind for the arts or humanity can contribute to the evolution of science." Kahn's expression of his theories of monumentality and democracy can be seen in Figure 3.9.

Kahn's theory was that a building designed to express monumentality and democracy would support a model for his philosophy (which we previously discussed—that of creating a timeless and monastic environment suitable to the higher activities of study and discovery happening at the Salk Institute. Monumentality influenced his application of the design principles of proportion and balance and of symmetry and rhythm. Democracy influenced his approach to the principles of hierarchy and flexibility.

For example, Kahn used hierarchy to separate the "served" and "servant" spaces. The laboratories, which contain the primary function of experimentation, are served by the service towers, which house support services such as restrooms, vertical circulation (stairs, elevators), and fire extinguishers.

Flexibility was important because the client, Jonas Salk, did not know who would be coming to the facility. Kahn had to create spaces that would accommodate all kinds of people, equipment, and research methods. Flexibility also allowed for changes in technology in the future. As can be seen in Figure 3.10, the resulting labs are large open spaces,

each of them approximately the size of a football field, with no interior columns. All services are located in "interstitial pipe spaces" above the labs; these spaces constitute an expanded plenum—an entire floor above each lab floor to allow for ease of access during repairs or change in services that would not affect the work in the labs.

Kahn's approach to these design principles, influenced by his theories about monumentality and democracy in architecture, led to a "truth in materials," resulting in the use of a simple palette of concrete, glass, wood, roman travertine, and stainless steel, as shown in Figure 3.11. All materials reveal how they were assembled and installed, celebrating their contribution to the structure of the buildings. There is no applied color. Nothing is painted or stained. Instead, the concrete and travertine are neutral, and they change color—from pale gold to deep crimson—as the sun rises and sets. This is accented only by the blue of the ocean, the blue of the sky, and the white of the clouds.

At this scale, the simplicity and honesty in the materials palette supports the original philosophy of the purity of a monastery and the uninterrupted timelessness of the institute's connection to the earth, ocean, and sky.

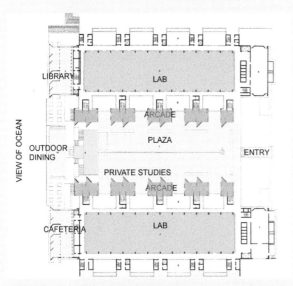

Figure 3.10 At the Salk Institute, the open plaza creates a strong line of axis heading straight to the sea. Placed symmetrically on either side of the plaza are private offices with views of the ocean, and layered behind the offices are large open laboratories designed for maximum flexibility.

Figure 3.11 The Salk Institute expresses "Truth in Materials," with no applied decoration inside or outside—only concrete, glass, wood, Roman travertine, and stainless steel are used.

Table 3.3 Common Design Theories Described and Applied

Theory	Description	Design Application
Diffusion of Innovation	The process by which new ideas are gradually communicated over time through a social system (Rogers, 1995).	Used to identify early adopters or innovators of new technologies or ideas in design practice (CAD or sustainable design). Characteristics of adopters/innovators can be determined and educational experiences can be developed to increase the use of the innovation and to educate those who are not adopters. Clients could be identified who would accept innovative design solutions.
Environmental Preference Theory	People process environmental information to increase their chances of "survival" and to improve their welfare. People need to make sense of, and acquire additional information about, their environment in order to better predict what might occur and to plan their actions accordingly (Kaplan & Kaplan, 1982).	Certain interior design attributes add to people's preference for an environment. For example, certain amounts of complexity, mystery, coherence, or legibility are necessary for comfort, function, and stimulation. However, too much complexity can overstimulate and confuse people, causing decreased preference.
Human Ecosystem Theory	People interact with one another and with their environments, specifically the social, designed, and natural environments. People affect their environments, and environments influence how people behave (Guerin, 1992).	Useful in identifying all of the components that affect how a designed environment will be used. Can help determine how environments (social, designed, or natural) influence human behavior.
Maslow's Hierarchy of Human Needs	Humans have a hierarchy of needs ranging from lower-level needs for survival and safety to higher-level needs for intellectual achievement and self-fulfillment. Lower-level needs (survival, safety, belonging, and self-esteem) must be met before the higher-level needs (intellectual achievement, aesthetic appreciation, and self-actualization) can be addressed. People's behavior at a particular moment is usually determined by their strongest need (Thompson, 2002; Woolfolk, 2004).	Prompts designers to look at the whole person and the interrelation of physical, emotional, and spiritual needs. For example, a child who is not fed before going to school may not respond to a beautiful interior designed with an emphasis toward the promotion of learning. If an office is in a "bad" part of town and employees fear for their safety, they may be more concerned with their security and less with their productivity, no matter how supportive their work environment.

Theory	Description	Design Application
Narrative Theory	A process used to identify meaning for people within an interior design (Ganoe, 1999). Personal meaning is expressed through written narratives, providing an avenue for discussion. Narratives help determine the relationship between a space and people, as well as what spaces mean to people.	Used to demonstrate how people's experiences are connected to the interior environment. Development and use of design criteria are determined through a verbal or written narrative. Clients can relate their understanding and feeling about an interior space, which the designer can use to develop meaning for them through the design solution. Provides a way of identifying "meanings of places" for clients. Can be used with people from diverse backgrounds to uncover how meaning varies across different populations and how meaning may change over time.
Place Attachment Theory	Affective experiences, personal feelings, and emotions associated with a place are central to people's ability to attach meaning to environments and are based on subjective personal preference (Altman, 1992).	Can be used to identify design features that are meaningful. These features can be incorporated into a design solution, providing a more functional and emotionally fulfilling environment for the user.

References

Altman, I. (1992, July). *Place attachment and international relationships*. Paper presented at the International Association for People-Environment Studies, Marmaras, Greece.

Ganoe, C. (1999). Design as narrative: a theory of inhabiting interior space. *Journal of Interior Design Education and Research, 25*(2), 1–15.

Guerin, D. (1992). Framework for interior design research: A human ecosystem model. *Home Economics Research Journal, 20*(4), 254–63.

Kaplan, S., & Kaplan, R. (1982). *Cognition and environment: Functioning in an uncertain world*. New York: Praeger.

Rogers, E. (1995). *Diffusion of innovation* (4th ed.). New York: Free Press.

Thompson, P. (2002). *The accidental theorist: The double helix of everyday life*. New York: Peter Lang.

Woolfolk, A. (2004). *Educational psychology* (9th ed.). Boston: Pearson Education.

Source: Figure 1. Theories Useful for Design and Human Behavior Research. In "Part II, Research Vocabulary," of *Research 101 tutorial*, by D. Guerin, J. Dohr, & K. Bukoski, InformeDesign, University of Minnesota. Retrieved December 25, 2007, from http://www.informedesign.umn.edu/_doc/Research_101_Part_II.pdf, page 2. Reprinted by permission.

this list is by no means complete. Rather, it is a reference to get you started on your understanding of theory and its application to design research.

As you conduct research for your interior design project, you will determine if your research findings agree or conflict with the propositions put forth by the theory that is guiding your research. This is how you then add to or develop a theory. It's also one of the ways you are contributing to the body of knowledge in interior design and providing other researchers with more information about how people may behave in a built environment (Guerin & Dohr, 2007).

Understanding Paradigms

A basic explanation of the term **paradigm** is that it sets an example for others to follow. Although that explanation sounds simple, the concept of paradigms can be difficult to grasp. Frequently, the word *paradigm* is used synonymously with the word *theory*, but although they are closely related, there is a distinct difference between paradigm and theory.

The easiest way to define *paradigm* is to explain that it is a means of communicating ideas or theories among large groups of people, which leads to a universal acceptance of "This is how it is done." Once accepted and upheld, a paradigm then serves as a model or reference for "This is how it *should* be done," and patterns of behavior that fall into that paradigm then follow. Similar to the way an architect creates a building model to communicate ideas to the client, a paradigm is the model that communicates the accepted application of a theory, highlighting its key characteristics. But the paradigm is not the theory itself.

An interior design paradigm is an accepted and upheld example or prototype for how a theory "should" be expressed through its application to the built world. For example, one paradigm in the interior design field is that of the traditional single-family dwelling in the United States, which includes a kitchen, a dining room, a formal living room, a family room or den, a master bedroom and bath, and a number of smaller bedrooms and baths in various configurations. That is the paradigmatic model for a typical U.S. home. It was perhaps influenced by historical theories about public spaces versus private spaces or by theories about cultural identity and an expression of prosperity.

As seen in Figure 3.12, what's exciting about paradigms is that simply through their existence they give us an opportunity to break free from them. Over time and as the world changes, we often outgrow paradigms; as we hold on to the idea of what "should be," the paradigm begins to hold us back. It is at this point that we use the development of new theories to guide us in how we can break out of an existing paradigm and begin a new one—this change is called a **paradigmatic shift**.

A scientific revolution according to Kuhn is marked by a radically new and more successful organization of the world. There is a paradigm shift and the old way of seeing things is replaced by a new vision. Kuhn noted that his book "portrays scientific development as a succession of tradition bound periods punctuated by non-cumulative breaks" (Kuhn, 1970, p. 208, quoted in Viney & King, 2003). Following a revolution the

Figure 3.12 A *paradigm* is an upheld model of the nature or condition of behavior, form, function, or meaning. As conditions change and new theories emerge, a paradigm will no longer be upheld as a prototypical model. At this point, we see a paradigmatic shift.

old paradigm is displaced and there is a move back to normal science that works within the broad outlines provided by the new paradigm (Viney & King, p. 22).

For example, the paradigm of the traditional single-family dwelling is beginning to shift to a paradigm that dismisses rigid and compartmentalized rooms in exchange for spaces of flexibility and freedom that respond to the very diverse lifestyles of the new millennium. Some precedents of this paradigmatic shift came with the early-twentieth-century residences of Frank Lloyd Wright, breaking down traditional spatial compositions within the residence and creating open floor plans that escaped the compartmentalized nature of traditional homes.

At the Salk Institute, Louis Kahn broke free of an existing paradigm for research laboratories by separating the functions of the traditional laboratory into spaces that would move knowledge forward. Kahn dismissed the standard laboratory scheme, a one-story box with a long corridor down the middle (Wiseman, 2007, p. 94). He envisioned the laboratory as a combination of three kinds of spaces: (1) space for experimentation, (2) space for private contemplation, and (3) space for social interaction. "The simple beginning requirement of the labs and their services expanded to cloistered gardens, studies over arcades and spaces for meeting and relaxation interwoven with unnamed spaces for the glory of the fuller environment" (Ronner & Jhaveri, 1987, p. 131).

Paradigms are essential to the development of your thesis, as they are the jumping-off point. You must understand current models before you can decide whether to support them with your design or to make a deliberate and meaningful break from them to construct a new model.

Understanding a Testable Hypothesis

A **testable hypothesis** is a statement or an "educated guess" that suggests a specific relationship(s) among a theory's constructs or components. Researchers test hypotheses to form new knowledge about an existing theory (Guerin & Dohr, 2007, part II, p. 3). Based on whether the hypothesis is

Table 3.4 Problems, Hypotheses, and Solutions

Step 1. Identify a problem or pose a research question.	Step 2. Propose hypotheses that could answer the problem or question.	Step 3. Select one of the proposed hypotheses and test it.
Why do our office employees seem less productive?	1. There are not efficient spaces for productive teamwork.	1. Provide teaming areas for collaborative work.
	2. The temperature in the office is too cold to concentrate.	2. Suggest window treatments that prevent the transfer of cold outside temperatures into the office space.
	3. Unsafe working conditions and poor office ergonomics have led to increased injuries and more time out of the office.	3. Specify ergonomically correct task chairs and desk arrangements.
	4. The sterile office environment is not stimulating enough.	4. Select a palette of dynamic paint colors for employee workstations.
	5. The poor acoustics in the office are causing poor concentration and concerns about employee and client privacy.	5. Specify a noise-masking system for the open office spaces.

correct or incorrect, it serves as a starting point for further research and investigation (Zeisel & Eberhard, 2006, p. 80).

Referring back to the color theory example in Table 3.2 on page 61, a testable hypothesis related to color theory explains a specific relationship among the constructs of hue, value, and chroma. For example, you could form the hypothesis that colors applied to create a high level of contrast (a relationship between hue and value) between horizontal and vertical surfaces in an assisted-living facility will result in a reduction of accidents and injuries among elderly residents. You could test this hypothesis by recording the current rate of injuries in an existing assisted-living facility, applying the suggested change to the space, and making a record of subsequent injuries. Assuming all other variables, such as the age of the subjects or the number of residents, remained the same, you would compare the two sets of data and determine if your hypothesis is correct or incorrect.

A hypothesis tests a theory by defining the **variables** in the related experiment. The variables in an experiment are the properties or characteristics in the research question that can take on different values. There is usually an

What's a variable?

A variable is an object, event, idea, feeling, time period, or any other type of category you are trying to measure. There are two types of variables: independent and dependent.

What's an independent variable?

An independent variable is a variable that stands alone and is not changed by the other variables you are trying to measure. For example, a person's age may be an independent variable. Other factors, such as his favorite food, the school he attends, or his grade point average, are not going to change the person's age. Age is a constant. In fact, when you are looking for a relationship between variables, you are looking to see if the independent variable causes a change in some other, dependent variable.

What's a dependent variable?

A dependent variable is something that depends on other factors. For example, a test score could be a dependent variable because it could change. Various factors could affect it—for example, how much you studied, how much sleep you got the night before you took the test, or even the noise level in the classroom where you took the test. Usually, when you are looking for a relationship between two things, you are trying to figure out what makes the dependent variable change the way it does.

Many people have trouble remembering which variable is the independent variable and which is the dependent variable. An easy way to remember this is to insert the names of the two variables you are using in the following sentence:

(Independent variable) causes a change in (Dependent variable), and it isn't possible that (Dependent variable) could cause a change in (Independent variable).

For example:

(Time spent studying) causes a change in (Test score), and it isn't possible that (Test score) could cause a change in (Time spent studying).

We see that time spent studying must be the independent variable and the test score must be the dependent variable, because the sentence wouldn't make sense the other way around (NCES, 2008).

independent variable, the property that is changed or manipulated to determine the effects on the **dependent variable**, which is the property that is affected by the change of the independent variable. In the example of the assisted-living facility, the independent variable would be the application of high-contrast treatments to the horizontal and vertical surfaces and the dependent variable would be rate of injury among residents (Guerin & Dohr, 2007, part II, p. 4).

An example of variables would be a study to determine the effect of class size on student learning in schools. The class size could be the independent variable, which affects student learning, the dependent variable. The study could be conducted with a class size of 20 and a class size of 100 to determine if class size (independent variable) affects student learning (dependent variable, which is dependent on class size) (Guerin & Dohr, 2007, part II, p. 4).

In both of the above examples, there are also **control variables**, which must remain constant in order to determine the relationship between the other variables. Examples might be maintaining the same age range among residents in the assisted-living facility or having the same teacher and/or assignments for both class sizes (Guerin & Dohr, 2007, part II, p. 4). Outside of the independent and dependent variables, all other variables should be constant in order to eliminate their having an impact on the results.

To paraphrase and simplify this process, forming a testable hypothesis is like saying, "If I do this, this will happen." It is your best "guess" about the outcome of research based on existing literature, research, or theory about the topic. It can be said that every design solution is a hypothesis or a prediction by the designer that the design solution will work. The more "guessing" you can take out of the hypothesis, by applying research to the problem being solved, the more likely it is that the design solution will be functional, meaningful, long-lasting, and aesthetically pleasing.

Another hypothesis applied directly to interior design could involve an executive who believes that soundproofing the office walls will result in higher productivity and morale among employees. She and her interior designer persuade the board of directors to install soundproofing in three employee offices. The executive's hypothesis is that the effect of soundproofing the offices will be higher output, on average, than for employees in offices that are not soundproofed (Fraenkel, Wallen, & Sawin, 1999, p. 280). In this case, the independent variable is that some rooms have soundproofing while others do not; the dependent variables would be employee productivity and morale. If the executive's hypothesis is correct, the experiment will reveal (1) that acoustics influence the productivity and morale of her employees and (2) that investing the money to install soundproofing will pay off in the long run. Having this research to back up her proposal will make it easier for the executive to sell her idea to the board of directors.

Conclusion

As an interior designer, you're not expected to also be a scientist. So it is important to clarify how the formulation of a hypothesis should be applied within the context of interior design.

In Chapter 2 we discussed the scientific method, which includes variations involving the following steps (Cherry, 1999, p. 37), one of which is the formulation of a hypothesis:

1. Pose a question.
2. Collect pertinent evidence.
3. Form a hypothesis.
4. Deduce the implications of the hypothesis.
5. Test the implications.
6. Accept, reject, or modify the hypothesis.

Although it is necessary to understand the principles of the scientific method and hypothesis-testing in the gathering of information, research for interior design uses this knowledge as a springboard to inspiration. While the paradigm of scientific research can serve as a foundation and guideline for how to conduct research, it can also help you recognize that in design the variables are always changing—each project is different, whether the variable is the client, the user, the site, or other conditions. You must understand and respond to these changing variables in order to be able to make accommodations as circumstances change. Research-inspired design can expand the potential of the Interior Design Process. This research is not a rigid set of rules; instead, it's a way of opening your eyes to the realm of possible innovations, solutions, and creations you might never have imagined otherwise.

References

Cherry, E. (1999). *Programming by design*. New York: John Wiley.

Cross, N. (2007). *Designerly ways of knowing*. Boston: Birkhäuser Basel.

Eames Office Resources. (2006). Charles and Ray Eames: A legacy of invention. Retrieved May 9, 2009, from http://www.eamesoffice.com/index2.php

Fraenkel, J., Wallen, N., & Sawin, E. I. (1999). *Visual statistics: A conceptual primer*. Needham Heights, MA: Allyn & Bacon.

Frampton, K., & Rykwert, J. (1991). *Richard Meier architect* (vol. 2). New York: Rizzoli.

Guerin, D., & Dohr, J. (2007). *Research 101 tutorial*. InformeDesign, University of Minnesota. Retrieved December 25, 2007, from http://www.informedesign.umn.edu/

Haugen, L. (1998). *Writing a teaching philosophy statement*. Center for Teaching Excellence, Iowa State University. Retrieved May 9, 2009, from http://www.celt.iastate.edu/teaching/philosophy.html

Hodge, B., & Pollak, L. (eds.). (1996). *Studio works 4: Harvard University Graduate School of Design (No. 4)*. New York: Princeton Architectural Press.

Latour, A. (1991). *Louis Kahn: Writings, lectures, interviews*. New York: Rizzoli.

Lister, E. M. (2008). *Glossary*. Miriam's Well. Retrieved June 18, 2008, from http://miriams-well. org/Glossary/

Maysles, A. (Director), Froemke, S. (Producer), & Eisenhardt, R. (editor) (1997). *Concert of Wills: Making the Getty Center*. Maysles Films, Inc.

National Center for Education Statistics (NCES). Kids' zone: Create a graph. Retrieved May 9, 2009, from http://nces.ed.gov/nceskids/createagraph

Rand, A. (1974, March 6). *Philosophy: Who needs it?* Address presented to the graduating class of the U.S. Military Academy, West Point, NY.

Rengel, R. (2008). *Thinking as designers: Heuristics and patterns as vehicles to insight*. Speech presented at the University of Wisconsin, Madison.

Ronner, H., & Jhaveri, S. (1987). *Louis I. Kahn: Complete work 1935–1974*. Boston: Birkhäuser Basel.

Viney, W., & King, D. B. (2003). *A history of psychology, ideas and context*. Boston: Allyn & Bacon.

Weisberg, R. (2006). *Creativity: Understanding innovation in problem solving, science, invention and the arts*. New York: John Wiley.

Wheeler, K. (2008). *Literary vocabulary*. Dr. Wheeler's Web site. Retrieved May 9, 2009, from http://web.cn.edu/kwheeler/lit_terms.html

Wiseman, C. (2007). *Louis I. Kahn: Beyond time and style: A life in architecture*. New York: W. W. Norton.

Zeisel, J., & Eberhard, J. P. (2006). *Inquiry by design*. New York: W. W. Norton.

4 Brainstorming

CHAPTER OBJECTIVES

When you complete this chapter you should be able to do the following:

- Explore personal interests and motivations in the design field.
- Develop brainstorming techniques to rapidly generate and analyze many ideas about and solutions to a design problem.
- Identify a research question that you will answer through your research process.
- Provide sources of inspiration for the creative design process.

KEY TERMS

Brainstorming
Broad topic
Capstone project
Concept mapping
Conceptual blockbusting
Creativity
Innovation

Lateral thinking
Narrowed topic
Professional portfolio
Research question
Restricted topic
Thesis
Vertical thinking

As Julia Cameron expresses in her book *The Artist's Way* (1992), art is not something you do; it is a way of life. Creative fields such as interior design do not begin and end at the doors of your school or place of work, but instead seep into your daily life. By the same token, what you experience in the choreography of your daily life tends to seep into your designs. It is essential that you approach your interior design profession in a way that is harmonious with your personal value systems and philosophical approach to design. This helps to create clarity and consistency in your professional decisions and business practices that will reinforce your identity and success as a designer.

Your Professional Identity

Your value systems and how they influence your identity as a designer will direct your professional path, beginning in school. Your approach to your studio projects will influence your design decisions, and it will be expressed as you develop the body of work that will eventually become your professional portfolio. Your **professional portfolio**, used as a tool in obtaining employment throughout your career, is a collection of your body of work that marks your experience, growth, and progress over time. As Figure 4.1 shows, your portfolio expresses who you are as a designer, and the message you communicate with your portfolio often influences which types of job you will be offered.

Usually the most developed piece in your portfolio will be your **capstone project**, also known as your *thesis project, senior project,* or *graduate project*. This project can last from six months to a year and is intended to be a synopsis of the professional skills you gain during your interior design education. Because of its importance in your portfolio, your capstone project is usually highly influential to guiding you to the type of job you obtain after graduation. This means that before you select a capstone project, you should

Figure 4.1 Your personal value system often has both an indirect influence and a direct influence on the jobs you will seek and accept in your career.

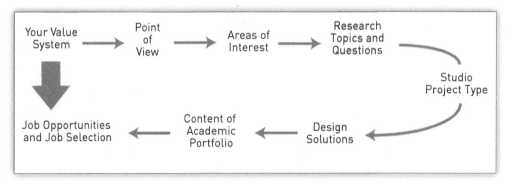

have a clear understanding of your identity as a designer and what you want both from the capstone process and as a professional. We will cover the many potential options for your project type later in the chapter.

The thoughts and exercises in this chapter are intended to provide you with opportunities to explore your personal interests, visions, and priorities, as they may eventually relate to your professional path. This should be a fun process, so take your time and remain open-minded. Try not to let your existing value systems or the beliefs you hold at this time influence the conclusions you draw from the activities and questionnaires in this chapter. Instead, try to maintain a fresh outlook and be open to the potential for something new and exciting to emerge.

Nurture Your Delicate Ideas

Allow your ideas to flow honestly and openly without judgment or fear. A great challenge for a creative person (or anyone, for that matter) is to eliminate any filters or conceptual, cultural, or perceptual blocks that may prevent the person from maximizing all of the potential creative ideas and options.

As you face the opportunities presented by a design problem and seek a creative solution, you might spend more time rejecting young ideas than you spend exploring and nurturing them. As James Adams says in his book *Conceptual Blockbusting* (2001, p. 49), "If you analyze or judge too early in the problem-solving process, you will reject many ideas." This is detrimental for two reasons. First, newly formed ideas are fragile and imperfect; they need time to mature and acquire the detail needed to make them believable. Second, ideas often lead to other ideas, laying out a path that can lead to something great (Adams).

Metaphorically, you could say that ideas are a lot like delicate seedlings, needing the chance to grow naturally and develop to their full potential. If you plant a tree, you have to wait for it to grow. If you judge it as a tiny seedling for not looking like the grand tree you had envisioned, you might prematurely squash it, never giving it a chance to evolve into what it could be.

The following Activity was inspired by Julia Cameron. In *The Artist's Way* (1992), Cameron speaks of identifying the enemies of your creativity so that you can nurture your young ideas within an environment of empowerment and safety. Once you let an idea incubate for a while, developing and growing, you will find you have more confidence in its value, as it has been shaped and perfected. This nurturing process does not mean that every idea you have will be a booming success; it means that through a refining process you learn to discern when to continue to push an idea through and when to let it go—not out of emotional judgment, but out of an understanding of its strengths, weaknesses, and real potential.

Purpose: **To record your stream of consciousness, without stopping, for ten minutes—to explore questions about yourself and your value systems.**

For this Activity you will need a personal journal. It should feel good in your hands and be easy to carry anywhere.

When we are being creative, we see ideas popping up all over in our minds. However, only a very few of those ideas do we ever develop enough to put down on paper, much less turn into a realized design. This is because we constantly judge our ideas, and we often decide prematurely whether they are worth expressing. This means that some potentially brilliant ideas could be eliminated before they ever see the light of day.

Normally when we write, we pause occasionally to process our thoughts before we continue writing. This is the filter of judgment referred to above, and in free-writing this is what you want to avoid. Within the ten minutes of free-writing, just as the stream of consciousness never stops, the writing should never stop and the pen should never leave the paper. Cameron advises that if you don't know what to write, then simply write, "I don't know what to write" until the next thought comes into your head and you write it on the page. Pay no attention to proper grammar and give no thought to who will read the work. The writing should simply be words passing through your mind, along your arm, down to your fingers, out to the pen, and onto the paper below.

This Activity could be something you introduce into your daily life to help free your mind and release your ideas. It could also be an activity you do before or at the beginning of your studio class to help you prepare for the day's class. Either way, it is your own process and it could be a tool you carry with you far beyond your time in school.

Reflection Questions

The following questions can help you begin the free-writing process.

- Why did you choose this professional path? Consider this question from the standpoint of the journey that led you here rather than the actual cerebral decision-making process. Trace that journey for yourself.
- Do you see yourself as an artist? What message do you want to give to the world? What kind of a mark do you want to make? What answers do you seek? Can this studio become an opportunity to further explore your own personal questions? How do you want to grow over the next year?

- What inspires you? What makes you angry? What makes you laugh uproariously? Have you ever wanted to hit something? If yes, why?
- How can you create a fusion of your personal life, the elements of this world that move you, and the art that you create every day in your designs and drawings?

For people who are more visually oriented, the process of writing can be cumbersome in the beginning. If this is the case for you, we encourage you to use the free-writing as a tool to help you practice expressing yourself with words, and with freedom from judgment let this skill evolve for you. In the meantime, however, the following Activity is a way for you to use a more visual method to explore the same questions about yourself and your value systems.

⊛ ACTIVITY 4.2 Personal Collage

Purpose: **To use a visual method to explore questions about yourself and your value systems.**

For this Activity you will need the following:

- A source of images, such as magazines, the Internet, and personal photos
- An 11" × 17" piece of black foam core or other 11" × 17" black mountable surface
- Double-stick tape, glue, or other means of mounting images to the board

1. From magazines or any other graphic source, collect thirty or more images that reflect your thoughts and feelings about design and your experiences as a design student. For every image you choose, go with your gut instinct even if you do not understand or are challenged to explain why you are selecting the image.
2. Lay all of the images out in front of you on a large table or the floor. Sort through them, ponder them, and then select ten of the images that speak to you the loudest.
3. On your black foam core, create a collage of the images, sticking them to the surface using glue or double-stick tape.
   - Think about how you are arranging the images. Which images are next to one another? Do some images overlap? Are some

touching while others are separate? Do you want to make some of the pictures bigger and brighter and some smaller or show them in black and white?

4. Look at the collage you have created—the images and the relationships between them. What does the collage tell you about yourself and your identity as a designer? Are any messages being communicated that are worth listening to? Are there any patterns to follow? Do you see any references that could be attached to a specialty within the design field, such as hospitality, healing environments, or an innovative new residential design? Can you see your personal style emerging from the images? Do you see anything that surprises you? See if you can translate what you see in the collage into a verbal expression of your interior design philosophy.

5. Consider photographing or scanning your collage to reproduce and include as an 8½" × 11" image at the front of your project binder or journal. This way the message is not lost after the Activity, but instead is carried with you, shaping your direction as you grow as a designer.

Now that you have spent some time asking yourself who you are as a designer, the next questions to explore are these: Where do you want to be? What type of design do you love, and for what type of design firm do you want to work? How do you want your office to feel? With what kind of people do you want to work? Where do you want to live? It is important to know where you want to be so that you can map your plan for getting there.

Even within two firms that provide basically the same services, the people and daily cultures could vary greatly. Ideally, your thesis project should be aimed at the type of work you want to do after graduation. Thus it is important to have in your mind a clear idea of where you are going.

Dive into Your Strengths!

Have you ever heard the expression "Know your weaknesses"? We believe your greatest success in life will come not only from knowing your weaknesses, but also from focusing your energy into your strengths, allowing them to carry you into a professional niche where you can succeed to a point of excellence. Nurturing your strengths will open the door to the greatest job satisfaction, as we all tend to enjoy doing the things we're especially good at. In school, you can better ensure an enjoyable and successful capstone or thesis process if you can focus it around an area that you already know interests you and that uses skills at which you excel.

Do you know what excites you about interior design? Take a few moments to jot down some thoughts about this question. As you answer it, think not only about your personal interests, but also about how you want your designs to reach beyond yourself to impact others. Think about the types of places and people that inspire you, concern you, or draw an emotional response from you. Where do you find meaning in this field? The following is a list of ideas developed by students seeking their own inspiration for opportunities to better the world through design:

1. How can fresh produce and healthy food be brought to low-income neighborhoods that often lack these resources?
2. How can color affect the human experience psychologically and physiologically?
3. How can we bring playtime back into educational spaces for children?
4. How can we help patients in hospitals maintain their sense of dignity and control?
5. What is the quality of life in nursing homes?
6. How can I redefine the spaces we live in?
7. How can we reduce waste and increase sustainability and efficiency in retail spaces?
8. How can I revitalize the cultural identity of a community?
9. How can I empower people with limited mobility through the application of Universal Design?
10. Can ADA regulations be treated as an opportunity for artistic expression in a public space?
11. What would make a truly unique vacation experience?
12. How can design protect public safety?
13. How can art stimulate creativity for scientists?
14. Can imagery and metaphors be used to extract the deep-seated needs of a user population?
15. What does it mean to be a war veteran and what is the best way to heal a wounded soldier?
16. How can design instill a deeper and richer life experience within a space?

The design firm fathom (spelled with a lowercase "f") posed the following inspirational question for a recent project: How can a Vietnam veteran change the face of the Veteran's Administration? This question created an exciting challenge that drove them to change the nature of what the VA "should be" into what it "could be." With fathom's inspiring approach, the new VA became less of an institutional organization, but one that promoted the experience of healing—physically, mentally, and spiritually. (See Figure 4.2.)

Figure 4.2 An inspiring research question, such as "How could a Vietnam veteran change the face of the VA?," can translate into an inspiring design project.

translation into design

Create a **less institutional** environment that **promotes healing;** physical, mental and spiritual.

SELECT DESIGN OBJECTIVES:
Provide both social and activity space for all generations of veterans.
Front porches and balconies feel more homey, less institutional.

SELECT HUMAN OBJECTIVES:
Occupational and recreational activities should be available during convenient hours.
Photographs in doctors' offices encourage a human connection with the patient.

The Activities within this chapter are meant to help you identify your strengths in order to choose what topics you might pursue for your capstone design project. Interior design is a complex field that involves many different types of projects and people, so this is an opportunity to select which ones interest you most. Once you have identified your personal interior design interests, this information will be circulating in the back of your mind as you conduct your research, develop research questions, identify design problems, and eventually pose a thesis statement that will propose a solution to the design problem you have identified.

Identify a Problem to Solve

As you look at the lists of interior design–related issues, spaces, and end users on the following pages, think about where you could make a change for the better. It is okay if you don't yet know "how" you will make a change for the better. What matters is that you can identify a problem connected to one of the topics listed below and feel compelled or motivated to use your talent and professional skills to solve it.

In his book *Creativity* (2006), Robert Weisberg references a "Model of Creativity" developed by Teresa M. Amabile. The essential element in this model of creativity is the role of motivation. In her 1983 study, Amabile found that "a person's attitude toward a task is critical in determining whether he or she will respond creatively to it. If the person finds the task intrinsically motivating—that is, if he or she is interested in the task for its own sake and not because of some extrinsic reward that might come about as a result of a successful performance—the chances of the person's producing an innovative response will be maximized. One hears individuals who work in creative fields—writers, artists, scientists—say again and again that they do what they do because they love it, and the fact that they make a living doing it is only a bonus" (Weisberg, p. 99).

In *Conceptual Blockbusting* Adams says, "Motivation is essential to creativity" (2001, p. 69). The reality is that no matter how talented you are, problem-solving and the design process involve tedium, frustration, and challenges. Adams goes on to say that "unless you truly want to solve a problem you will probably not do a very good job" (p. 69). That means that unless you are convinced that a change needs to happen in a certain area within the realm of interior design, you are not likely to question or hypothesize and propose a solution for how that change can and will happen (Adams, 2001).

If you do not carefully select a design problem that you are motivated to solve, your capstone project could be a tedious and arduous process to be endured for almost a year. So choose an area that will maintain your interest throughout the capstone process. The greatest satisfaction comes when you are presenting your project to your jury of critics and you see an audience of academic and professional peers who are there because the problem you have chosen to solve and the topics you have explored and incorporated in this process matter to people. You have embarked on a design journey that is meaningful not only to you but to others as well, and the conclusions you draw will be added to the body of knowledge that makes up the foundation of the interior design field (Adams, 2001).

ACTIVITY 4.3 Personal Interest Questionnaire

Purpose: **To help you extract your personal interests, strengths, and motivations, so that you can recombine them in new ways to find a project idea that inspires you.**

Answer the following questions:

1. What three classes or studio projects in school have inspired you? Explain why.
2. What five things interest you outside of school?

3. What three architects, designers, designs, or styles inspire you?

4. What three places or spaces anywhere in the world do you find interesting or inspiring?
   - Choose one of these spaces and expand on why you find it to be interesting.

5. Are there any social, political, economic, health-related, or design issues that you have been thinking about lately? Have any problems come to your attention recently that you wish you could solve?

6. Outside of interior design, what fields do you find interesting or exciting?

7. In interior design or other fields, what topics do you tend to read about in books and magazines or on the Internet?

8. What five design issues, types of interior spaces, or people would you most like to study?

9. List five changes you would like to make to the world if you could:
   I would like to _____.
   I would like to _____.
   I would like to _____.
   I would like to _____.
   I would like to _____.

Within every project type you encounter, whether in school or in the professional world, there are areas of focus and design issues you will be faced with and will have to learn more about. Some of the time, the area of focus or issue will be of great interest to you and you will enjoy learning about it and adding it to your list of skills. Other times, you will be trying just to resolve issues and move on.

ACTIVITY 4.4 Selecting Your Design Issue (Inspired by InformeDesign.com)

Purpose: **To help you identify design issues you are motivated to study further.**

As a student creating your own project, you have the opportunity to select the design topics and issues you want to expose yourself to, learn about, and perhaps even become an expert in. In fact, it is often within the following list that students find inspirations for their thesis topic and thesis statement.

Take a few moments to look over the list below. As you think about the type of design project you want to explore, which one of these design topics or issues interests you? Place a checkmark next to each of the topics or issues that are of interest or importance to you, or that you foresee will be important to your thesis or your project. Don't worry about checking too many or too few. This exercise is simply meant to help you explore your interior design interests.

This is by no means a detailed or complete list of how many day-to-day issues we deal with as interior designers. And of course, as you begin to specialize in the field, you will encounter some issues more than others. This Activity is simply a way to get you brainstorming about what you will explore in your capstone project. Are there any areas not touched upon that you would like to add to the list? If yes, simply write them in at the end and place a checkmark next to them.

Selecting Your Design Issue: What Do You Want to Become an Expert In?

Building Materials, Finishes, and Systems

__Audio/Visual, Videoconferencing
__Carpentry/Fabrication/Manufacturing
__Cleaning and Maintenance
__Daylighting, Skylight, Glazing
__Identification Devices/Signage
__Mechanical Systems

__Security and Life Safety Systems
__Site Issues/Building Orientation
__Storage Specialties
__Structure/Building Envelope
__Visual Display/Presentation

Design and Aesthetics

__Acoustics
__Aesthetics
__Color
__Conceptualization and Visualization
__Design Theory
__Elements of Design
__Energy Efficiency
__Gender Influence/Preferences
__Historical Context
__Historical Renovation/Restoration

__Influence of Culture/Ethnicity
__Influence of Time
__Lighting Design
__Narrative/Meaning in Design
__Principles of Design
__Problem Identification/Solving
__Spatial Composition and Articulation
__Sustainable/Green Design
__Universal Design

Furnishings, Fixtures, and Equipment (FF&E)

__Custom Fixtures/Furniture Design
__Decorative Elements/Accessories/Art
__Equipment Selection, Specifications
__Fixtures Selection, Specifications

__Furnishings Selection, Specifications
__Textile Selection, Specifications
__Window Treatments

Codes and Safety

__Americans with Disabilities Act (ADA)

__Disaster/Recovery Planning

__Environmental Health

__Fire Codes/Life Safety Principles

__Planning and Policy

__Toxic Waste Management

Personal/Individual Needs and Factors

__Cognition/Perception

__Development and Learning

__Environmental Control

__Ergonomics

__Health Effects

__Identity and Status

__Meaning and Symbolism

__Orientation, Way-finding

__Personalization of Space

__Physical/Anthropometrics/Functional Requirements/Accessibility

__Preference/Attitude

__Privacy/Social Interaction

__Productivity and Performance

__Psychological/Social

__Quality of Life and Well-Being

__Safety and Security

__Sensory Responses

__Stress

__Territoriality/Defensible Space

__Transitions: Birth, Death, Marriage

Design Business and Process

__Adaptive Reuse

__Budgeting

__Business Practices and Technology

__Client Contact/Interaction

__Codes

__Community and Public Service

__Ethics

__Facility Operations, Maintenance

__Integration of Technology

__Renovation and Expansion

__Research/Research Methods

__Space Allocation and Office Standards

__Space Planning

__Strategic Planning

__Tenant Improvement

Is there anything we have left out?

__ _____

__ _____

__ _____

__ _____

Interior design topics and issues can have a great impact when you are applying for jobs. They present you with a chance to set yourself apart from other applicants as being an expert in the design topic or issue you explored extensively in school. Sometimes a firm is looking for a designer who has a particular interest or field of experience or study that will help them fill a gap within their current design team.

Purpose: (1) To reveal the diversity of project types available to you, and (2) to help you focus your project on a type of space that interests you.

Take a few moments to look over the list below. As you think about the type of design project you want to explore, which one of these spaces stands out to you? Place a checkmark next to each of the space types that are of interest to you. Don't worry about checking too many or too few. This exercise is simply meant to help you explore your interior design interests. Are there any areas not touched upon that you would like to add to the list? If yes, simply write them in at the end and place a checkmark next to them.

The Spaces: What Type of Space Are You Interested in Designing?

Corporate

__Bank/Financial Institution
__Communications/Conference Center

__Industrial/Production/Distribution
__Office/Headquarters/Satellite

Entertainment

__Amusement/Theme Park
__Auditorium/Amphitheater
__Concert/Lecture Hall

__Movie Theater
__Nightclub/Special Events
__Performing Arts Theater

Government/Institutional

__Correctional Facility
__Court
__Day Care Center
__Embassy
__Federal Building
__Fire Station
__Governmental Agency
__Library
__Military Base

__Mortuary
__Museum/Gallery/Zoo/Historical Site
__Police Station
__Public/Recreation/Community Center
__Religious Facility/Sacred Space
__School/Educational Facility
__Transportation Facility
__University/College/Institute
__Waste Management Facility

Health Care

__Ambulatory Care/Outpatient Treatment
__Assisted Living/Nursing Home

__Clinic
__Emergency Room

__Hospice Care   __Rehabilitation
__Hospital/Operating Rooms/Suites   __Satellite Facility/Mobile Unit
__Intensive Care/Acute Care   __Wellness Center
__Laboratory

Hospitality/Restaurant

__Auditorium   __Cruise Ship
__Bar/Lounge   __Fast Food
__Catering/Weddings   __Hotel/Motel/Lodging Facility
__Casino   __Restaurant/Café/Theme Restaurant
__Conference/Convention Center   __Visitor Center
__Country Club/Resort   __Winery

Outdoor Space

__Beach/Waterfront   __National Park/Visitor Center
__Camp   __Park and Green Space/Landscape
__Farm   __Pedestrian Environment
__Garden   __Urban Landscape/Playground

Residential

__Assisted Living   __Neighborhood/Planned Community
__Community Shelter   __Public/Subsidized/Affordable Housing
__Mobile Home   __Second/Vacation Home/Time Share
__Model Home   __Senior Housing
__Multi-Family Residence   __Single Family Home

Retail/Store Planning

__Boutique/Specialty/Salon   __Home Improvement
__Department   __Hypermarket/Kiosk
__Discount/Outlet/Value-Oriented   __Shopping Center/Mall
__Food Retail   __Showroom/Wholesale

Sports and Fitness

__Aquatic Center   __Health Club/Spa
__Arena/Stadium/Olympic Gym   __Sports Facility/Golf/Tennis

Is there anything we have left out?

__ _____   __ _____

__ _____   __ _____

No project exists without an end user or users who will be experiencing your design day in and day out. To help ensure that their experience will be what you envision for them, you must develop a deep understanding of your end users. Their wants and needs, the rituals of how they will use the space, and their physical, mental, and emotional state: all must be considered in your design process. It's understood that it is your responsibility to always be conscientious of your end user's safety and well-being.

ACTIVITY 4.6 Selecting Your End User (Inspired by InformeDesign.com)

Purpose: **To consider the type of user you are interested in designing for, or the type of user who will most likely be using your space.**

Take a few moments to look over the list below. As you think about the type of design project you want to explore, which one of these user groups would you most likely find in your space? Place a checkmark next to each of the end users that is relevant to your project or for whom you are interested in designing. Are there any groups not touched upon that you would like to add to the list? If yes, simply write them in at the end and place a checkmark next to them.

Selecting Your End User: Who Do You Want to Design For?

Ability/Disability/Characteristic

__Challenged: Physical/Neurological
__Cognitive/Learning
__Education Level
__Gender/Identity
__Genetic Disorder
__Gifted/Genius
__Hearing Impaired
__Language/Culture/Heritage

__Psychological/Emotional
__Race/Ethnicity
__Socioeconomic Standing
__Special Talent or Skill
__Vegetarian/Vegan
__Vision Impaired
__Weight/Obesity/Anorexia

Age

___Adolescent/Teenager
___Infant
___Senior and Elderly/Aged Adult

___Toddler/Preschool
___Young and Middle-aged Adult
___Youngster/Youth

Worker/Occupant Type

___Activist
___Actor/Performer
___Administrator or Manager
___Animal/Pets/Livestock
___Apprentice/Intern/Trainee
___Athlete
___Audience/Spectator
___Business Traveler
___Captain/Commander
___Caregiver
___Child
___Citizen/Neighbor
___Client
___Crew
___Employee
___Executive
___Families
___Foster Child
___Groups
___Guest
___Homeless/Displaced
___Homeowner
___Interviewer
___Laborer
___Leader
___Manager
___Member

___Men
___Mentor/Disciple
___Owner
___Parent/Step-parent
___Passenger
___Patient
___Patron/Shopper
___Politician
___Principal/President
___Professional
___Refugee
___Religious/Spiritual Leader
___Renter
___Researcher/Scientist
___Resident/Occupant
___Security/Officer
___Soldier
___Staff
___Student
___Teacher/Educator/Instructor
___Technician
___Trainer/Trainee
___Traveler
___Victim
___Visitor/Spectator
___Women
___Worshipper

Is there anything we have left out?

___ _____

___ _____

___ _____

___ _____

Brainstorming and Creativity

> Brainstorming is a process that can be used individually or in groups to come up with a quantity of alternatives by spontaneously generating ideas and by deferring judgment on them (Sanoff, 1991, p. 8).

The Activities in this chapter are intended to get you to start brainstorming. **Brainstorming** is a nonjudgmental free flow of ideas, and it is your most valuable tool as an interior designer and problem-solver. Consider Figure 4.3. Brainstorming allows you to get ideas out on the table before your brain has a chance to edit them. It also allows you to avoid the common trap of settling on the first workable idea that comes along and consequently eliminating the chance that an even better solution might have been just around the corner (Adams, 2001).

> The natural response to a problem seems to be to try to get rid of it by finding an answer—often taking the first answer that occurs and pursuing it because of one's reluctance to spend the time and mental effort needed to conjure up a richer storehouse of alternatives from which to choose (Adams, 2001).

The "habits" that human beings form allow us to solve the infinite list of intellectual problems that come our way, through rapid and efficient methods. Habits have been essential to our survival as a species, because we'd never get anything accomplished if we had to formally process all of the stimuli that come into our perception. Habits of thought and behavior ensure our

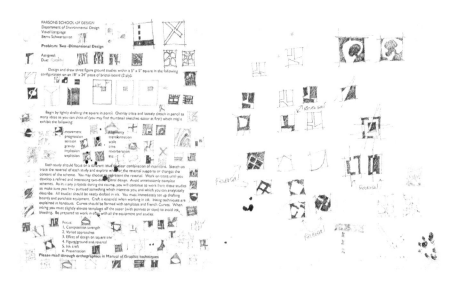

Figure 4.3 This example of a "cube project" beautifully illustrates the process of brainstorming—an abundant flow of ideas, resulting in many potential solutions to a design problem, each one explored without judgment and given the chance to become something more.

survival by allowing us to focus our attention on only what is needed in order to accomplish the task or goal of the moment (Adams, 2001).

This tendency toward habit is the functional reason why we adopt the assumptions mentioned previously—which can include stereotypes, labels, categories, and associations—as well as adopting systems of organization and operation. Habit is like an automatic filing system (Adams, 2001). From a professional standpoint, this forming of habit can result in a designer always drawing upon an existing list of "solutions" that come from preconceived notions, assumptions, and categorizations of what a design solution *should* be, rather than contemplating and exploring the infinite possibilities for what a design solution *could* be.

There is value in building an interior design project and design solutions based on improving upon what you already have. But do not overlook the potential for imagining a new definition of what it could be (Adams, 2001, p. 61).

In *Conceptual Blockbusting* (2001), Adams says, "To the extent that more concepts are generated, decision making becomes more complicated. However, more alternates result in a greater probability of a better solution. Certainly more alternates are likely to permit a more creative solution, since initial concepts tend to be closely related to tradition" (p. 121). Use your brainstorming capacity to create as many alternative questions, answers, or solutions as possible.

Creativity asks you to go beyond what is considered the norm or the accepted "right" answer. While habits are safe, creativity is daring. Sometimes it is our habits of thinking and doing that make up the filter of judgment that blocks young ideas that could have been great. This is why uninhibited free-writing and brainstorming are essential parts of the creative process. They provide a safe environment in which you can practice breaking your habits, allowing you to conjure creative options in response to any question or problem (Adams, 2001).

This point is essential when you're selecting design topics to pursue and making your choices for a capstone project, which will be discussed later in this chapter.

Concept Mapping

Using the previous exercises and drawing upon your list of potential topics for your capstone or thesis project, a tool called **concept mapping** will help you combine words with visual imagery. This tool is inspired by Burkhardt, MacDonald, and Rathemacher's book *Teaching Information Literacy* (2003).

In simple terms, concept maps are a sort of "family tree" for your thoughts and ideas. Creating this family tree for your ideas allows you to track and organize your thoughts throughout the research and design process.

Concept mapping is being introduced here to help you begin narrowing the field of potential research available to you as you begin the capstone process. But keep in mind that concept mapping can be used through any phase of the Interior Design Process, from programming to contract administration.

Designers usually do not form ideas in a sort of vacuum where they sit down, scrunch up their eyes, and wait for the genius idea to pop out onto the paper. As IDEO's Peter Skilman puts it: "Enlightened trial and error succeeds over the planning of the lone genius" (Koppel, 1999). Usually, design occurs as a "creative back and forth" relationship among the information gathered, literature, inspiration, and the formation of an idea in the designer's mind. Furthermore, ideas are often inspired from other ideas. As the depth of your research grows, the intricacies and complexity of your concept maps will grow, with additional ideas, information, and concepts. All these ideas growing and building upon one another can be overwhelming. Concept mapping helps you to keep track of where your ideas have been so you can more clearly see the direction they are heading. (See Figure 4.4.)

There are two layers of concept mapping:

- When you use it simply for brainstorming, putting thoughts and phrases on paper in an uninhibited but organized way—similar to free-writing, but with an added layer of organization and order.

Figure 4.4 Placing your initial idea at the center—in this case adaptive reuse—you can use a concept map to explore many facets of the original idea in an uninhibited yet organized way. Color, graphic annotations, and symbols create connection and meanings among ideas. Figure courtesy of student Rain Perry.

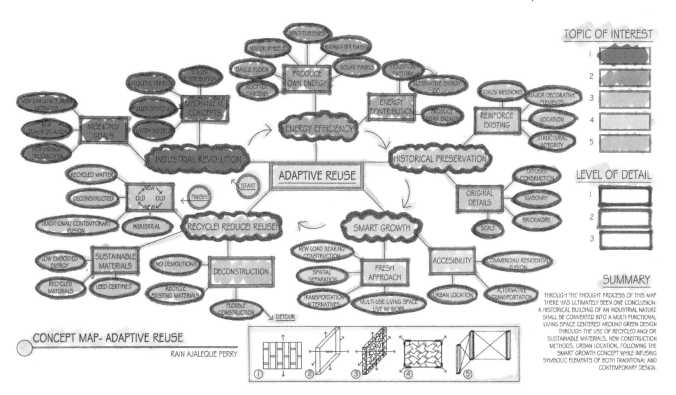

- When you use it to create a record of your chain of ideas and research from their origins to their conclusions—marking and recording every relationship and connection linking them all together.

The uses for this tool are many and flexible. Just like a road map provides directional information for moving from one point to another, a concept map provides directional information about your thought process and helps you make connections between often remote ideas in your mind—except that on this occasion the map is not provided for you. Rather, you are creating the map yourself, as you go, tracking each step so you don't forget where you have been and can see where you will be going. Concept mapping lets you explore many ideas, without getting lost or overwhelmed in the process. Concept mapping also helps you retrace your way back through earlier ideas, often finding exciting new paths as you navigate from one idea to the next. This can be especially helpful when you are experiencing a creative block and you need that little push of inspiration to move you forward.

A concept map can look very similar to the relationship diagrams you might draw up in the schematic stages of a design project, but it has the potential to become much larger. Consider doing your concept mapping (Activity 4.6) on large pieces of newsprint or butcher paper, so there are no edges of the paper to inhibit or stop the potentially explosive process. This could even be a group activity when done on a blackboard or whiteboard.

The goal of the concept map is to brainstorm ideas and then mark the meaningful relationships among them. Figure 4.5 is an example of a concept map created by a group of students in a studio class. You can see that some ideas or concepts—such as "marriage" and "honeymoon" or "marriage" and

Figure 4.5 Some ideas, such as the traditional Western concept of a wedding and a church, are easily connected with or without a concept map. Concept mapping can help you make more creative connections, such as the connection between marriage and cross-cultural weddings or commitment ceremonies. This connection alone could lead you in many exciting and innovative directions.

"church"—were directly related, while other ideas—such as "church" and "nontraditional wedding ceremonies," or "cross-cultural ceremonies" and "sacred spaces"—were more remotely connected. When you see these concepts on paper, the ideas that once seemed only remotely related might hold more meaning than those ideas that are directly adjacent on the concept map.

Concept mapping translates easily from academics to the interior design profession. It would be used in much the same way at work as it would in your academic process. It can help you sort out challenging and complex concepts and ideas. Also, creative blocks don't stop with school, and concept mapping can help you get over those creative blocks, from information-gathering to programming to contract administration. Most frequently, its value is found when you're working in a group around a conferencing or teaming table, trying to keep track of many different concepts and ideas coming from many different people. For now, use it to help you find connections between ideas that might eventually lead to your asking questions that could become the foundation for your interior design capstone project.

ACTIVITY 4.7 Build Your Own Concept Map

Purpose: **To help you further explore the interests you checked in the previous Activities. This brainstorming Activity may also help you see ways to combine those interests with your own personal and social interests.**

For this Activity you will need a large, blank piece of paper and an open mind. Note: You could use your journal for this Activity, although you'll likely find that a journal or notebook doesn't give you room to explore as freely as you would like.

Select a topic, design or otherwise, that you are personally interested in, and write it large in the center of the page. From there, use free association to connect this topic with any other thoughts that come into your mind. Each time you relate one topic to something else, write it down and connect the items with a line or other meaningful graphic. Sometimes you'll see that a new idea can be connected to an idea you have already written down.

Use circles, arrows, stars, or other graphics to make meaning out of the connections you are making. You are brainstorming to help you find a focus for your interior design project, so always be thinking about how interior design can influence your ideas or be influenced by them. This tool can be used well beyond the initial planning phase of your project. As you get further into your research, concept mapping can help you overcome any blocks in creativity, resources, or direction you may experience.

Identifying Your Research Topic

At this point you should have a pile of ideas on your hands, and concept mapping likely has helped you to create some meaningful connections that you hope to explore further.

The next step is to turn these ideas and connections into an interesting and open-ended research question or questions that reflect your personal value systems and your professional interior design interests. Once you identify your research questions, they will drive your research process as you seek all the possible answers to these questions. Eventually this will lead to the identification of a problem and a proposal, called a **thesis**, asserting how you will use design to solve the problem. Thesis will be discussed further in Chapter 9.

There are various ways you can research a topic. Some of them (adapted from Groat & Wang, 2002) are listed below to help you begin developing your own research topic.

1. Analyze, critique, and suggest improvements to an existing body of work or theory.
2. Compare multiple approaches to an existing body of work or theory.
3. Examine another person's existing theory to test a related idea or theory of your own.
4. Question or test an existing theory.
5. Expand upon an existing concept or theory.
6. Offer solutions to a problem that has not yet been solved.
7. Relate two previously unrelated concepts or theories to create a new one.

From this list, can you see how a previously explored *theory* (a belief, policy, or procedure followed by practitioners in the interior design field) can inspire you by giving you a place to start your research? You can then use your imagination or even concept mapping to build upon an existing idea and create new ideas and connections.

Narrowing Your Research Topic

The amount and variety of literature available to interior design professionals can be overwhelming. You will need to whittle your broad research topic down to a narrowed topic that will bring you closer to your project goals and help you to manage your research process.

There are three layers of narrowing that can help you to appropriately focus a topic:

Let's say you found yourself inspired by the Jewish Museum in Berlin, designed by Daniel Liebskind. The architecture of his museum was designed to reflect the nature of the Jewish experience in German history. A goal of the museum architecture was for the spaces themselves to communicate a message about the experience, through principles like form and light, rather than relying solely on the museum exhibit to tell the story. The result is powerful and emotionally charged spaces that allow the visitor to walk in the shoes of the Jewish experience in Germany, if only metaphorically.

As a student you could take Liebskind's concept about the museum experience and expand upon it to create a new concept. Perhaps the Jewish Museum becomes an inspiration for a Museum of Religion and Spirituality, where the concept is expanded from the experience of one culture to using design to communicate the experience and identity of many cultures, religions, or practices—like a "universal language" that can communicate messages and meaning among many people with vastly different backgrounds. This new concept allows you to build upon Liebskind's valuable contribution to the field, adding a new layer of complexity, problems, exploration, and innovative solutions.

The goal here is not to reinvent the wheel, but to let your capstone research and design evolve out of an existing familiarity and interest in an existing theory, project, project type, design topic, or end user type (Groat & Wang, 2002).

1. The first layer is your **broad topic**. The broad topic is often the area of interest you begin with. It could be a key word, a subject, an author's name, or a title, which you enter into a search engine or database. It is also the idea that tends to be found at or near the center of your concept map.

2. After you begin researching your broad topic, your **restricted topic** focuses your broad topic in the direction you feel you want to take. For example, your broad topic might be "Health Care Design." Once you begin to research that topic, your restricted topic might be "Evidence-Based Design for Assisted Living Facilities."

3. It's likely that you will need to focus down even further, to a **narrowed topic** that allows you to identify information specific to a geographical region; type of space; type of user, issue, or problem; or other narrowed category. For example, you could narrow the restricted topic "Evidence-Based Design for Assisted Living Facilities" one more time: to designing specifically for the medical staff to create nurturing spaces for the healers in Assisted Living Facilities. In this case, you have narrowed

your broad topic down to an issue that is relevant to a specific user group within the body of health care design. Usually the ideas that are most connected to your narrowed topic can be found at the outskirts of your concept map.

While a research topic should not be too general, it also should not be too restrictive (Groat & Wang, 2002, p. 52). If you begin with topics that are too broad, the goals and potential problems to be identified are usually too vague. Further, if your topic is too broad or even too restrictive it will be difficult to easily identify a usable body of literature. If the topic is very broad, you will be consulting across an overwhelming range of literature, and if the topic is very narrow then there may not be enough literature to consult.

For example, as a research topic, "Green Design" could be too broad; there are many narrowed topics under this broad topic and you must understand them in order to incorporate "green design" into a project. In the following examples, the topic of green design has been narrowed:

1. Straw bale construction
2. PVC-free materials and products
3. Adaptive reuse
4. Bio-mimicry
5. Smart growth and new urbanism

(Note: An example of a research topic that might be too restrictive would be the use of PVC-free materials in residential design. This topic might not provide the potential for diverse and innovative exploration you would want for a year-long capstone design project.)

In their book *Architectural Research Methods*, Groat and Wang offer an example of a research question that is just right: "What is the length of stay of nursing home occupants in 'homey' interior environments versus the length of stay in facilities with more 'institutionalized' decor?" (2002, p. 54).

Other provocative examples of research topics and questions are:

1. What is the adoption rate for animals in shelters with a social and interactive environment for the animals, versus a shelter that isolates the animals?
2. How quiet should a library be? Is the traditional model of silent behavior within libraries still appropriate for today's cultures of learning and information-sharing?
3. What is the best way to group patients in children's hospitals: by age or by medical condition?
4. In hospital patient rooms, is the type of art preferred by interior designers different from the art preferred by the patients?

Turning Your Research Topic into a Research Question

The questions you begin to naturally develop as you narrow your research topic are called your **research questions**. Your research question (or questions, as is often the case) will be open-ended, leaving room for many answers to surface. It is these emerging questions that inspire and motivate the research process.

These are the elements of a good research question for interior design:

1. It is a valuable idea worth pursuing.
2. It is simple and concise.
3. It takes on only one issue at a time.
4. It has a connection to the built environment.
5. Information on the topic is readily available.
6. It is current and relevant.
7. It is open-ended and could generate many answers.
8. It always keeps in mind that in the end you are going to be solving a problem through design, and it evolves accordingly.
9. It is specific to the domain of interior design.

Table 4.1 is full of examples of how students have taken a broad topic, narrowed it, and then developed it into a thoughtful and provocative research question that they could begin exploring and seeking answers for.

When you select your research topic and develop research questions, inspiration could come from anywhere and simplicity is often the key. To show

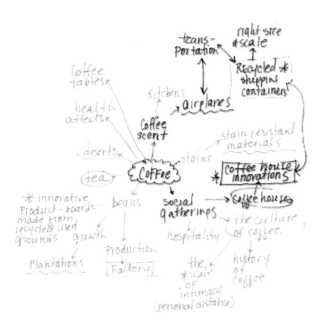

Figure 4.6 In this concept map, the broad topic of coffee led to an intriguing exploration of ideas and thoughts, including social gatherings and even the relationship between coffee and transportation.

Table 4.1 Focusing a Broad Research Topic into a Specific Research Question About the Topic

Broad Topic	Transportation	Spatial Composition	Universal Design	Gyms	Hotels
Restricted Topic—*chooses a direction*	Airline travel	Efficient use of space	Wheelchairs / Mobility tools	Specialty gyms	Integrating green design into hotels
Narrowed Topic	Traveler experiences in airports including check-in, security, and boarding	Flexibility and adaptability in multi-family residences	Resistance to aesthetics of federal accessibility regulations	Children as "users" of a gym	Promoting and designing for "green behavior" among hotel guests
Category—*related to your restricted topic*	Airline travelers—*a type of user*	Multi-family residences—*a type of space*	Aesthetics related to ADA—*a type of issue or problem*	Children who use gyms—*a type of user*	"Green behavior"—*a type of issue or problem*
Research Question	As travelers must be at the airport two hours before a departure, they have a harder time putting their work and personal lives on hold. Are airports adapting to the changing needs of passengers?	As the value of space and land increases beyond what many can afford, how can the principles of flexibility and adaptability help us to address this problem?	Is universal design really aesthetically limiting, or have we let our preconceptions limit our universal design solutions?	In a society with increasing health-related problems, is there an effective way to promote health and fitness for children?	Green design in hotels can accomplish only so much if the guests are not active participants. How do we design a hotel to create "green behavior" among guests and hotel staff?

how a very simple broad topic can turn into an interesting research question and eventual capstone project, consider the example of "Coffee." Because coffee is something we are all familiar with, you might assume that it is too simple to be a research topic. But in fact this simple word could lead you to ask questions about coffee houses, coffee factories, coffee plantations, innovations in coffee preparation equipment, etc. See Figure 4.6.

Table 4.2 shows how the process of narrowing the topic of coffee could take multiple paths, leading to some intriguing and interrelated questions

Table 4.2 A Simple Topic Can Lead to Intriguing Research Questions

Broad Topic	Coffee	Coffee	Coffee
Restricted Topic	Coffee houses and social gatherings	Coffee scent	Coffee house innovations
Narrowed Topic	Appropriate scale and proportion for intimate social interaction in U.S. culture	Coffee as used on airplanes and other forms of transportation	Innovations in travel and coffee service/coffee on the go in Western Europe
Research Question	Could the size and scale of recycled shipping containers be an innovative solution to coffee house design?	Could recycled shipping containers bring an element of green design to coffee houses?	Can the coffee house come to the customer rather than the customer having to go to the coffee house?
Proposed Answer			

Figure 4.7 Perhaps when the company Illy developed its innovative idea for a "push button coffee house"—a mobile all-in-one coffee house, constructed out of recycled shipping containers and complete with seating, kitchen, and even Internet access for patrons— they went through an exciting brain- storming process to explore many potential ideas.

to be investigated through research and eventually design. (See Figure 4.7.)

Now, using your own topics of interest, complete the following Activity. This will help you narrow your own research topic or topics into a series of potential research questions to pursue for your capstone project. Remember that there are no right questions or wrong questions to ask. They should be honest expressions of your own thoughts and interests. If it isn't a question you really have, do not include it here.

⊛ ACTIVITY 4.8 Transforming Your Area of Interest into a Research Question

Purpose: **To help you narrow your chosen research topic into a more focused research question to answer with your research.**

For this Activity you will need a pencil and the charts provided below. Feel free to sketch up your own chart if you need more columns or rows.

Select any words or ideas from your concept map and insert them into the space next to "Broad Topic" on the chart. You can either begin in the center of your concept map, working outward, simultaneously developing your concept map and your chart, or you can spend some time with the concept map until you come across an idea that intrigues you. Then switch to focusing your ideas, using the chart to navigate and record your process.

This Activity should help you take a broad and often overwhelming topic and focus it in a way that is both interesting and meaningful to you. The goal is to discover a question you are interested in using to help you begin your research process. Seeking the answer to this research question is the catalyst to your design project.

Table 4.3 includes two examples to help you get started, including how one might apply the previous example of "Marriage" and "Nontraditional Weddings." You can see in the example of "Marriage" how the concept map and the narrowing grid in Table 4.3 can be used together. You can also see that sometimes there is more than one question to pursue—and that is perfectly acceptable.

Spend some time contemplating the questions you have developed. Ask yourself the following questions:

- Are the questions truly related to a personal interest that you feel motivated to pursue?

Table 4.3 Identifying a Focused Research Question

Broad Topic	(Example) Dining Practices	(Example) Marriage	Your Broad Topic Here . . .	Your Broad Topic Here . . .	Your Broad Topic Here . . .
Restricted Topic	Dining Practices in Japan	Non-Traditional Wedding Ceremonies			
Narrowed Topic	Japanese Tea Ceremony and Tea Houses	Churches/ Sacred Spaces			
Research Question	Has the traditional Japanese tea house changed over time to reflect modern culture?	Is the traditional church an appropriate setting for today's non-traditional wedding ceremonies? What type of space would best suit this activity?			
Proposed Answer					

- How many different broad topics did you explore?
- Were your broad topics all very different, or did you find a pattern of similarity emerging?
- Are there one or two questions you can envision exploring through an exciting design process?
- Do these questions pertain to relevant and current topics of discussion in the interior design field that will entice others to become interested in your project?

Seeking Innovation

> The critical element in calling some product creative is that it be new; if a person produces something that he or she has produced before, then that product is not creative (Weisberg, 2006, p. 60).

The "creative product" that Weisberg is referring to can also be called an **innovation**. The heart of the capstone project is the search for innovation. In this project, as in all your design endeavors, you ask questions in order to identify where improvements or breakthroughs need to be made and where answers need to be found. Now that you have identified a research question or questions to investigate, remember to seek an innovative solution. Step beyond your preconceived notions and find answers that take your knowledge of the field to a new place. Take the initiative to "think outside the box," and use this opportunity to teach yourself and others something new and exciting about interior design. (See Figure 4.8.)

The goal of your capstone project, or of any research into your field of study, is to "make a novel contribution" (Weisberg, 2006, p. 62). Focus upon innovation and adding to the body of knowledge within your field: interior design. You are building upon all of the knowledge that exists within your professional domain. You're making your mark upon it (Weisberg).

Because each professional field and its body of available knowledge are always moving, a novel contribution to the field "can change the direction of the field, or propel the field in any number of directions" (Weisberg, 2006, pp. 70–71, referencing studies by Sternberg, 1999, develops one of those ideas; Sternberg, Kaufman, & Pretz, 2002). Your ideas might support the

Figure 4.8 Exploring ideas "outside the box" often leads to interior design solutions that respond to design problems and issues in a new and exciting way.

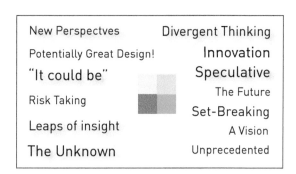

direction in which interior design is already headed, or they might propel it in a direction that is entirely different. This is another way in which your conclusions and work have the power to affect other members within interior design (Weisberg).

Innovation can happen at any level in the interior design project. It could happen in your selection of research topic, or perhaps in how you program the spaces in your building, or in how your project explores some specific subcategory of design with a new approach. If innovation is there in the beginning, in the end it will infuse your design solutions. Innovation could even be how your project combines and cross-pollinates issues of interior design with other academic fields of study, such as proxemics, human factors, anthropology, psychology, or even the neurosciences.

If you can master the idea of **conceptual blockbusting**, or breaking through the "mental walls that block the problem-solver from correctly perceiving a problem or conceiving its solution" (Adams, 2001, p. 13), then you have mastered the secret to innovation: breaking down your preconceived notions and letting your mind go beyond what it already knows and understands. The following are some of the fundamental elements of conceptual blockbusting:

- Avoiding analyzing or judging too early in the problem-solving process
- Avoiding taking only the first answer that occurs
- Using your brainstorming capacity to create as many alternative questions, answers, or solutions as possible
- Developing confidence in your work and ideas

In his book *New Think*, Edward De Bono speaks of the difference between **vertical thinking** and **lateral thinking**. "Vertical thinkers take the most reasonable view of a situation and then proceed logically and carefully to work it out. Lateral thinkers tend to explore all the different ways of looking at something, rather than accepting the most promising and proceeding from that. . . . The great thing about vertical and lateral thinking is that you don't have to accept one over the other; you can use them both to reach the best outcome. You can use lateral thinking to generate your ideas and use vertical thinking once you are focused and ready to develop one of those ideas" (1968, p. 23).

Once you have these two concepts in your mind, consider this further observation from De Bono:

It is possible to deal with a subject by carefully proceeding from one point to another. It is possible to describe a building by studying the architect's plans, starting first with one elevation and then going on to another, working one's way methodically over the details. But there is another way of getting to know a building, and that is to walk around it, looking at it from all sorts of different angles. Some of the views will overlap, but in the end a good

- What if you tend to rely on repeatedly using the solutions that have worked for you time and time again: using the same ideas or walking the same path? This is similar to the way that trails are made in a forest. As you walk the same path over and over, the ground becomes packed harder and a rut begins to emerge. You can probably see where this image is going. As you pack that rut harder, and you apply more pressure in the same places as you walk the same path again and again, everything that lies in the strata below will begin to crystallize. This crystallization makes it harder and harder to unearth those untapped innovative ideas that could be lying beneath. Do your best to try out new ideas, and never be afraid to forge a new path.

- Coming from another angle, in *New Think* (1968) De Bono warns against a problem that students frequently experience. In an effort to unearth a new solution to a problem, you eagerly begin "digging a hole" to find that new and innovative idea, often digging and digging where in fact there is no innovative idea to be found. It is important to know when to abandon the search and start digging somewhere else. Sometimes you simply cannot get to a solution from a certain point. Perhaps the resources are not there, or there isn't enough time to work it out, or the proposed solution may just not work. That's okay. Just step back, reevaluate the situation, and take a new approach.

- When you try to uproot as many options as possible in your design process, sometimes your efforts at lateral thinking bombard you with developing ideas and with the fear of picking one to pursue. You could call this fear of confronting the pile of ideas "paralysis by analysis." You become afraid that you might select the wrong idea to pursue and that then you'll have wasted all this time and will have to start all over again.

  This is the conundrum of thinking vertically in a lateral process. There is no such thing as having to start all over. Every move you make in the design process moves you toward an end point. The path will never be direct. You might change direction, but you could not have gotten to the point of knowing to change direction if you had not taken the steps to that point. See Figure 4.9.

- In the design process, as with everything in life, you have no way of knowing you have chosen the wrong path until you start down it. If you find that the path you chose is the wrong one, it means you have ruled out that option as a possibility and now you are one step closer to finding the right solution.

  If after two years of research a scientist has discovered that a particular drug does not cure cancer, would you consider his research a failure? No. He has ruled out this drug and has added to the body of knowledge in the field, informing other scientists that this drug does not work—making his research valid and relevant.

  For your design process this experience can be seen as satisfying, like checking off items on a to-do list, continuously shortening the list of potential solutions to your design problem.

- As Adams puts it in *Conceptual Blockbusting*, "Conceptualization is risky and new ideas are hard to evaluate" (2001, p. 39). The difficulty of evaluating your ideas leads to a lack of confidence. But let's look at the big picture. Let's say you have a young, new idea and are afraid to put it out there, but you have done your research, you have explored precedents and built upon the successes and failures of other projects, and in your heart you feel it is a good design solution. Ask this question: What is the worst that can happen? And as Cameron advises in *The Artist's Way*, "Leap and the net will appear" (1992, p. 2).

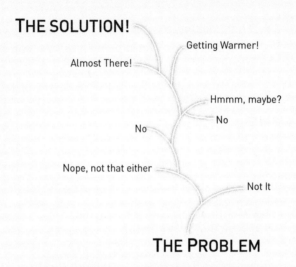

THE SOLUTION!

Getting Warmer!

Almost There!

Hmmm, maybe?

No

No

Nope, not that either

Not It

THE PROBLEM

Figure 4.9 The path from the problem to the solution may involve retracing your steps, but you never end up back where you started. Instead, you are always in a new place, one step closer to the solution.

general view of the building is obtained and it may turn out to be more real than that obtained by a detailed study of the plans (De Bono, quoted in Adams, 2001).

In the quote just above, the first approach—carefully reviewing all the details—is an example of vertical thinking, while the second approach—looking on from many angles—is considered lateral thinking. This combination of approaches could be applied to our previous discussion about how, by nature, design is a circular process rather than a linear one. Some steps might overlap or even be revisited, but in the end the overall approach is more complete, thoughtful, and responsive to the evolving needs of the project. The value of taking an exploratory approach to a creative problem, rather than following a systematic predetermined path, becomes clear.

Also consider that since the "traditional," or familiar and thus easier, solutions are often the ones to come first, placed on the surface of the process, it makes sense that you need to dig deeper to get to the fresh, as-yet-unexposed ideas that are ready to come to the surface. This process takes more effort but can uncover more influential solutions (Adams, 2001).

To sell your ideas to an instructor, a critic, or a potential client, you need to own your ideas and you must propose them with confidence. To help you develop a confidence in your work and ideas, ask yourself the following questions, inspired by *Conceptual Blockbusting* (Adams, 2001, p. 46).

The next time you are having difficulty deciding whether to push an idea, write a short Catastrophic Expectations Report (C.E.R.):

1. First, looking at your idea, write down EVERYTHING you could be criticized for or judged on with regard to it. Be specific as you get into the minds of your critics.
2. Now look at the same idea and precisely detail exactly what would happen to you if EVERYTHING went wrong with the idea. What is the worst-case scenario?
3. Now that you have dumped all of your fears onto a piece of paper outside of yourself, look at what you have written and make some evaluations of the situation. Can you separate the subjective judgments from the objective issues that can and should be addressed now in order to make your idea stronger?

Use the C.E.R. process as an opportunity to make your idea even stronger. By putting yourself in the mind-set of the critics, you give yourself an opportunity to find the answers to their questions. You will be confidently prepared to answer those questions, realizing that the worst-case scenario to your idea proposal probably is not something you can't handle if you are just willing to step out on a limb.

In the end, creativity requires the ability to form complete, well-developed thoughts. But sometimes the greatest potential comes from the ability to take our strong ideas and some of our weak ideas, and some of our silly ideas, and some of our crazy ideas, and recombine and manipulate them to invent something new and successful (Adams, 2001).

Seeking Inspiration

This book spends a lot of time guiding you along the path of academic research. However, at no time in the process should you forget that just as research should not be separated from the Interior Design Process, neither should creativity.

Table 4.4 Sources of Inspiration

Personal	Literature	Performing Arts	Media
Instructors, Mentors, Friends, Family, Peer work, Professional journals, People-watching, Personal hobbies, Historical icons	Poetry, Libraries, Bookstores, Bibliographies of books you read	Theater, Plays, Movies, Music, Performance art, Concerts	Television shows, Documentaries, Internet blogs and forums, Political commentary
Professional	**Culture**	**Technology**	**Other**
Related creative fields, such as graphic design, furniture design, or fashion design; Trade shows, Conferences, Company branding, Automobile design	Museums, Art, Religion, Philosophy, Arts & Crafts, Outsider art, Graffiti, Tattoos, Photography	Scientific breakthroughs, Inventions	Where do you find inspiration?

Never underestimate the abundance of inspiration in the world. You can get creative when it comes to where you seek out innovative ideas for your interior design project. A great place to start is by using concept mapping or other conceptual blockbusting tools. These are especially helpful when you experience creative blocks. Table 4.4 is a list of places where you may find inspiration. Add your own sources to the list.

Another, often underestimated, source of inspiration is simply seeing the reality of things as you look at them from a different perspective. Go outside and find a place where you can watch the sunset with the best view possible. As the sun is lowering in the horizon and you experience the filtering of light through the sky, you think it couldn't be any more beautiful. Now turn away from it. That's right, face the other way. Now look at the world around you. What do you see? What do you hear? What do you smell? Can you describe it? Perhaps the way the light reflects off the windows of homes or other buildings, the way your skin seems to glow with warmth, the pink of the clouds, the chirping of the birds or cicadas, the smells of dinner cooking, the sounds of kids riding their bikes home from play. Who knows what you will see, but one thing is for certain: You will see the sunset in a whole new way.

References

Adams, J. L. (2001). *Conceptual blockbusting: A guide to better ideas.* Cambridge, MA: Basic Books.

Burkhardt, J. M., MacDonald, M. C., & Rathemacher, A. J. (2003). *Teaching information literacy.* Chicago: American Library Association.

Cameron, J. (1992). *The artist's way: A spiritual path to higher creativity.* New York: Tarcher/Putnam.

De Bono, E. (1968). *New think.* New York: Basic Books.

Groat, L., & Wang, D. (2002). *Architectural research methods.* New York: John Wiley.

Koppel, T. (ed.). (July 13, 1999). Deep dive [television series episode]. In James Goldston (executive producer), *ABC News: Nightline.* New York: American Broadcasting Corporation.

Sanoff, H. (1991). *Visual research methods in design.* New York: John Wiley.

Sternberg, R. J. (1999). A propulsion model of types of creative contributions. *Review of General Psychology, 2,* 83–100.

Sternberg, R. J., Kaufman, J. C., & Pretz, J. E. (2002). *The creativity conundrum: A propulsion model of kinds of creative contributions.* New York: Psychology Press.

Weisberg, R. (2006). *Creativity: Understanding innovation in problem solving, science, invention and the arts.* New York: John Wiley.

Part Two

Information Gathering

Part Two of *Research-Inspired Design* contains chapters that delve into the data collection methods, from the basics to innovative approaches. We have included many activities that will help you explore and document the built environment as it pertains to the design problems you have chosen to solve.

5 Identifying Information Sources

When you complete this chapter you should be able to do the following:

- Understand how to conduct a literature review as the beginning of the information-gathering process.
- Determine the validity and reliability of information sources.
- Apply basic information-gathering methods and strategies.

KEY TERMS

Abstract

Acronym

Archive

Bibliography

Citation

Conservator

Keyword

Library catalog

Literature review

Online database

Peer review

Plagiarism

Primary source

Research strategy

Secondary source

Tertiary source

Working bibliography

Think of your design project as a collection of ideas you will eventually defend in front of a jury of professional peers or in front of a client. To do this successfully, it is important that you continuously seek out valid and reliable sources that provide accurate information. Information based on erroneous sources will not allow you to draw valid conclusions, nor will it give you an accurate picture of the issues. Your project is only as solid as your information. A project built on faulty information is like a house built on a poor foundation. It will not hold up! So where can you find valid information?

Identifying Information and Research Sources

The body of knowledge that is available to us all can be overwhelming; it can produce a sense of anxiety about researching a topic. This chapter is a tool to aid you, first, in identifying appropriate information sources for the interior design field and, second, in developing a research strategy for successfully solving any design problem.

To ensure that you are accessing all of the information available on a topic, you must go beyond the efficiency of the computer or the Internet, or the comfort of your own home or classroom. It is essential that you go out into the world and actively pursue information and resources from a variety of sources. This may involve talking to experts or sifting through old maps or taking a walk around a neighborhood (Burkhardt, MacDonald, & Rathemacher, 2003). In this information age, if you can apply the same commitment and resourcefulness to your information-gathering that you apply to the design phases of a project, the possibilities for exploration are endless.

Formal Research Methods Versus Informal Research Methods

As discussed in Chapter 1, a research method is a means by which a person gives order to answering questions and testing responses. Some researchers apply a very formal or systematic method that can be easily explained or replicated by another researcher, much like the scientific method used in other fields of research. Using this method, a researcher could design a system of investigation, similar to a controlled experiment, and then apply the same system in a step-by-step manner to research many different types of design problems (Guerin & Dohr, 2007).

On the other hand, there is informal research methodology, in which a researcher does not have a rigid plan for conducting research (Guerin & Dohr, 2007). Instead, the researcher most likely follows a series of information paths or routes that develop and build upon another, and the research

Museum Exhibit Planning:
One Professional's Research Methodology

Before a museum exhibit can be successfully designed, a large body of research must be collected. The research can involve an understanding of the museum visitor, the museum site, and most important, the message to be shared throughout the exhibit path.

The museum exhibit planner Alice Parman (no relation to the author of this textbook) sees her exhibit-planning process as being driven by both creativity and research. Upon being hired by a client or a museum, she does extensive background research on the museum itself as well as the exhibit topic, primarily through reading and review of historical documents. As we'll see, primary sources play an integral part in her exhibit-planning process.

When Alice was hired to plan the exhibits for the Lincoln Museum in Fort Wayne, Indiana, her budget allowed for an entire month of research and information-gathering. This commitment of time and money to research enabled Alice to gather a substantial body of contextual information and prepare appropriate and thorough questions for her first "start-up" meeting with the client.

On any new project, the start-up meeting with the client is yet another place to do extensive information-gathering. When the client is a museum, for example, this first meeting provides the perfect opportunity to study and document the museum, the site, and the surrounding context and culture. Not only does Alice interview her clients about their wants and needs, and what they see as their museum's mission, she also gathers information sources such as historical documents, maps, and artifacts. She observes the museum's employees and visitors and gathers information and documentation about the neighborhood, the local culture, and the local people. Her relationship to the site becomes very thorough and involved.

In another start-up meeting—with the client team from the Museum at Warm Springs in Oregon—Alice's research into the culture of the community supporting the museum led her to interview a group of local tribal elders. These men and women described their life experiences and shared their observations of how the community had changed over time. The historical events and anecdotes they recounted enabled Alice to build museum exhibits that presented both an accurate depiction and an intriguing story.

process and the design project unfold in a flexible manner. In this informal methodology, the researcher's information-gathering responds to the research itself rather than following a prescribed system, and thus the researcher often has more freedom to follow unexpected twists and turns. The main drawback of informal research is that it may be difficult for another person to replicate.

Each of these approaches—systematic or informal—has an appropriate application, and during the course of a project both methods can be applied. Often, in the preliminary stages of information-gathering, a design researcher will use a more informal research method until specific concepts and solutions are identified and need to be evaluated and tested before being implemented.

Primary Sources Versus Secondary Sources

"Primary sources are usually the topic that other sources comment upon" (Groat & Wang, 2002, p. 60). It is important to be able to distinguish between **primary sources** and **secondary sources**. The goal is to develop an innate understanding of the two, so that eventually the distinction is not something you are continuously evaluating, but instead is something you instinctively understand. Being able to make the distinction will give you a certain understanding about the nature of your research source and the value and appropriate application of the information you are gathering.

The fundamental difference between primary sources and secondary sources is in the number of times the information has been reprocessed and resynthesized (Burkhardt et al., 2003, p. 9). The closer you can get to the original source of the information, the study, or the work of art, the less biased your information will be.

Consider this analogy: If you take an original photograph and make a copy on a copying machine, the reproduction will often vary in its exact representation of the original, based on the quality of the equipment and the operational accuracy. If you then make a copy of the copy, you again increase the chances that the integrity of the original document might be compromised and that some of the information from the original photograph might be lost or interpreted incorrectly. Someone viewing the second copy might mistake the identity of a person in the photograph or the identity of an object or a word. You can put the original photograph next to the copy of the copy and perceive an obvious difference between the two.

The same is true when you're evaluating sources. While you don't need to assume that a secondary source, or even a **tertiary source**, is invalid, you'll need to use a critical eye to discern any underlying biases, personal agendas, inaccuracies, or omitted information.

Ideally, a primary source is an objective and thus unbiased source, while secondary sources can be subjective and may involve much opinion on the topic. One might question, however, if there is such a thing as a truly objective source. For example, with computer programs like Adobe Photoshop widely available, even photographs—which at one time were considered accurate and unbiased proof of an event or object—can be manipulated in ways that make it necessary to always question the authentic nature of the image. Furthermore, as will be discussed later in this chapter, researchers themselves can put a biased spin on their interpretation of the information they gather, regardless of the purity of the source. Thus, as mentioned before, when you are drawing upon secondary sources, or even highly biased primary sources, responsible researching demands that you seek another perspective in order to gather the most objective understanding possible.

Rather than being frustrated by this process, a good researcher embraces it. Sometimes having two or more very different perspectives on a topic can actually enrich your research process and add an interesting dynamic and depth to your problem-solving process.

Primary Sources

These are contemporary accounts of an event, written by someone who experienced or witnessed the event in question. These original documents (that is, they are not written about another document or account) are often diaries, letters, memoirs, journals, speeches, manuscripts, interviews, and other such unpublished works. They may also include published pieces such as newspaper or magazine articles (as long as they are written soon after the fact and not as historical accounts), photographs, audio or video recordings, research reports in the natural or social sciences, or original literary or theatrical works (University Library, University of California, Santa Cruz, 2007).

Generally speaking, primary sources can be highly diverse and exciting. They are considered the original piece or event, or the original account of a piece or event, upon which further studies and analyses are done. Generally, primary sources are the "materials on a topic upon which subsequent interpretations or studies are based" (Hairston & Ruszkiewicz, 1996, p. 547).

As we look more specifically into the fields of architecture, interior design, and other creative arts, there are many examples to draw from. These could be, but are not limited to, the following:

An Original Creative Piece as a Primary Source

- An original work of art, such as a painting or sculpture
- A building
- An historical site
- An interior space
- Construction documents
- A musical piece
- A novel

- A performance or event
- Data from a research study

Direct Documentation of the Original as a Primary Source

- Photographs of a building or interior space
- Personal interviews with architects, designers, or other creative professionals about their own work, or an audio or video of an interview with one of these professionals
- Audio or video about the construction of a project
- A professional peer-reviewed journal article explaining the results of a research study or the data from a research study
- A survey or questionnaire about the topic
- Personal observation about the place or topic
- Building measurements taken by a draftsperson for creating original floor plans
- Current satellite images
- Your direct observation of an environment or behavior

Statistics or Factual Information as a Primary Source

- Demographical statistics and census data
- Data from an academic or scientific study
- Building codes or regulations from a government Web site or codes book
- Specification information for a design or architectural product (for example, the Coefficient of Friction [COF] for a specified ceramic floor tile)

Secondary Sources

The function of a secondary source is to interpret primary sources, and so can be described as at least one step removed from the event or phenomenon under review. Secondary source material interprets, assigns values to, conjectures upon, and draws conclusions about the events or topics or things documented or observed in primary sources (University Library, University of California, Santa Cruz, 2007).

Secondary sources are usually found in familiar places such as published books or magazine articles, but they can also be drawn from documentaries, TV specials, or simple observation of trace evidence left behind by humans interacting with an environment.

An example of observing trace evidence as a secondary source would be observing desks in a classroom that have been moved from their usual linear arrangement and pushed up against the perimeter walls, leaving an open space in the center of the room. This residual or trace evidence allows you to analyze the situation and conclude that the usual layout of the classroom did not work for the previous class and thus an adaptation was made. You can then interpret why you think this adaptation might have been made. Trace evidence will be discussed in depth in Chapter 8.

Secondary sources can often yield contradictory information, as the "facts" are interpreted in different ways or are relayed in differing manners. Thus, in academic research, secondary sources are only as credible or as valuable as their circumstantial affiliations. Especially when drawing upon secondary sources, it is important for a researcher to include multiple points of view about the topic or issue in order to ensure that all perspectives are being explored and analyzed.

In architecture, interior design, and other allied arts, examples of secondary sources could be, but are not limited to, the following:

Analytical Review of the Original as a Secondary Source

- Reference material about the piece, such as a history book or a textbook
- A book about the piece or topic
- A discussion or debate on the topic
- A magazine or newspaper article on the piece or topic
- A TV special or documentary about the piece or topic
- Indirect observation of trace evidence associated with the environment or behavior

If you were interested in studying a cutting-edge product and how it is being applied in interior design projects, you would have a number of choices: You could consult primary sources, such as research studies done on the product; or you could interview end users of a space where the product is applied; or you could review secondary sources such as a magazine article about the product or project.

(Inspired by and adapted from Burkhardt et al., 2003, p. 11)

Purpose: To develop your skill at discerning primary sources from secondary sources.

For this exercise:

1. Read the list of research sources below.
2. Look up any names or terms that are not familiar to you.
3. Identify each source as primary, secondary, or tertiary and as objective or subjective.
4. Place your answers in the grid below.

To help get you started, the following are examples of each category:

	Objective Source	Subjective Source
Primary Source	Medical records	A personal interview with a hospital patient
Secondary Source	Doctor's recollection of medical records during a court hearing	An interview with a hospital patient's family members
Tertiary Source	Published research study done over time on patient's medical records	Documentary about patient's and family members' hospital experience

Based on your answers, what can you conclude about the nature of the different types of sources? Share your conclusions with the instructor and class, and discuss any differences in your answers.

Sources

- A walk around the gardens and galleries at the Getty Museum in Los Angeles
- A documentary film about Richard Meier, the architect of the Getty Museum in Los Angeles

- A sculpture from the Getty Collection
- A photograph, taken at sunset, of the Salk Institute, designed by Louis Kahn
- A book about the Guggenheim Museum in New York City
- Data from a lighting design research study
- From the *Journal of Interior Design*, an article explaining the practical application of a study about lighting design
- In *Interior Design* magazine, an article about a retail space
- Lecture notes from your Interior Design Studio class
- A textbook for your History of Interior Design class
- A term paper for your History of Interior Design class
- An antique Chippendale chair
- A site plan of the Getty Museum
- Construction documents for the Getty Museum
- A textbook about space planning in contemporary residential spaces
- A journal entry
- An e-mail from an instructor
- An interview with a rabbi discussing your questions about the Torah
- An interview with a Buddhist monk about meditation practices
- The Koran or Qur'an
- The Bible
- A personal interview with Richard Meier, the architect of the Getty Museum in Los Angeles

Judging the Validity of a Source

When you're evaluating any research source, your best approach is to do as Euripides advised: "Question everything." Don't automatically assume accuracy in any source of information. According to James Adams (2001), incorrect information is like a runaway train and can carry you completely in the wrong direction. The following questions can help you ascertain the nature and value of material you're considering:

- How does the source know these details? Is the information coming from firsthand experience? (University Library, University of California, Santa Cruz, 2007)
- Where was this information obtained—from personal experience or from reports written by others? (University Library, University of California, Santa Cruz, 2007)
- Are the source's conclusions based on a single piece of evidence, or have many sources been taken into account? (University Library, University of California, Santa Cruz, 2007)

- What is the age or gender of the source?
- What is the political affiliation of the source, or what are the personal interests of the source?
- What is the background of the source? With what company, academic institution, or special interest group is this source affiliated?
- Have you considered consulting multiple sources, such as an interview and casual observation, in order to get a thorough and complete perspective on the issue at hand?
- Under what conditions was the information gathered? Did the conditions provide for an honest and thorough collection of information?

Ultimately, all source materials of any type must be assessed critically, and even the most scrupulous and thorough work is viewed through the eyes of the writer/interpreter. Anywhere there is room for interpretation or translation, there is the possibility of miscommunication, mistranslation, opinion, or bias. Take this into account when attempting to arrive at the "truth" of a piece or an event, as it can be concluded that no account is truly unbiased. Always maintain healthy skepticism about information sources. This will enhance your academic and professional credibility, whether you're defending your academic project or proposing a new and exciting design idea to a client.

Making Research Work for You

Each designer, design project, and design problem is unique. There is no prescribed system for how you conduct your research. This gives you the flexibility and freedom to make the research process work for you. You do not have to use every research technique for every project. Rather, keep in mind the nature of the project; the issues, problems, and topics being evaluated; your own strengths; and your understanding of the issues, problems, and topics—all of these can help you to decide what research methodology and techniques will best serve you in creating a successful design solution and project. This textbook is intended to provide you with these tools, but you must use them in a fashion that works for you.

Before you can gather information, you must know where to find the information and you must develop your research strategy. Your **research strategy** allows you to decide, first, what information you need; second, where it might be found; and third, how you will get it. Table 5.1 provides a general overview of the types of sources an interior designer might draw upon to create a research strategy. Chapters 6 through 8 explore specific techniques for using these sources to maximize your information-gathering potential. In Table 5.1 these sources are organized into five categories: Literary, Personal Reports, Observation, Factual, and Evaluation.

Table 5.1 Sources for Creating a Research Strategy

Research Method	Research Source	Explanation	Examples
Literary	**Books** Fiction Nonfiction Topical Instructional Guidebook Textbook	A literary composition bound together in a volume	*Shaping Interior Space* by Roberto J. Rengel (2007) *Interior Design* by John F. Pile (2003)
	Periodical Articles **Magazines** Popular	Serial publications targeted at a mass audience, covering current events or personal interests for entertainment purposes and not requiring any knowledge of a specific field in order for the articles to be understood	*New Yorker, Newsweek, National Geographic, Fast Company*
	Trade or Industry	Serial publications presenting industry information, often focusing on trends, in a graphical and interesting manner in order to appeal to industry professionals as well as to laypeople who have an interest in the topic	*Interior Design, Architectural Digest, Metropolis, Dwell, Natural Home*
	Peer-Reviewed Journals	Serial publications containing articles about industry-specific research studies, usually intended for a scholarly audience. Typically, journal articles undergo a review of the content before being accepted for publication.	*Journal of Interior Design, Health Environments Research & Design Journal, Intelligent Buildings International*
	Newspapers	Serial publications, usually published daily, containing information related to national as well as local news, events, advertisements, and other information	*USA Today, New York Times, Wall Street Journal,* local newspapers

continued

Research Method	Research Source	Explanation	Examples
Personal Reports	*Interview*	Original source of information elicited from a person in order to find out what that person knows, believes, feels, wants, does, or expects	
	Formal	A predetermined list of questions given to an individual, ordinarily customized for the individual	**Client-Based Interview** Conduct a "Start-Up" meeting with your client to find out goals and needs. **User-Based Interview** Interview a mother-in-law who is moving in with her children and grandchildren, in order to design her personal space within the home. **Expert Interview** Interview a member of the clergy when designing a spiritual space. **Professional Interview** Consult a structural engineer when designing a mezzanine in a retail space.
	Informal	Very brief and often unplanned meeting or conversation with a person to ask non-invasive questions. An informal interview may lead to a formal interview.	**Impromptu Conversation** Ask a resident briefly about living in the neighborhood.
	Surveys	Using a standardized questionnaire—a predetermined list of questions given uniformly to a sample population	**End User Questionnaires** "Student Satisfaction" surveys distributed by your school to get feedback about school conditions, services, and resources. In this case, the student is the user group of the school.
		Can be used to help you identify your end user when this group is unknown	**Focus Group (or Potential End User) Questionnaires** Distribute a questionnaire in a community to determine if the residents would support a new bar or restaurant.

Research Method	Research Source	Explanation	Examples
Observation	*Anthropological* **Environment– Behavior Casual**	Observing behavior in an environment with an open-ended possibility for information-gathering. Usually this method adopts a "just looking" attitude; then, any information gathered can be used to establish a theory or conclusion about what was observed.	**Shadowing** Observe employee behavior in an office over several days to identify possible problems interfering with office productivity.
	Systematic	Observing behavior in a space or an environment with specific goals in mind for information-gathering. Often, the designer uses this observation technique to enforce or dismiss a theory or conclusion already in place.	**Place-Centered Mapping** **Person-Centered Mapping** **Experiment** Conduct an observation in a controlled environment using the scientific method. **Simulation** Construct a model or prototype to be used to determine response or behavior.
	Physical **Field Survey**	Gather information about a site or a building in a comprehensive manner.	**Existing Conditions Report/ As-Builts** Measure and record dimensions of existing building shell. **Inventory** List and photo-document client's existing equipment or furniture inventory. **Site Visit** Take photos and sketch significant features of the site and building in order to produce an Existing Conditions Report. **Case Study** (also called a **Precedent Study**) Review a study of a previously completed project with conditions relating to your own project, serving as a prototype or an example of both successful and unsuccessful design solutions.

continued

Research Method	Research Source	Explanation	Examples
	Trace Evidence	Observe objects left behind or removed after an interaction between people and a space, in order to form a conclusion or theory or prove or disprove a theory or conclusion already in place.	**Maps** Historic, street, land use, zoning, etc. **Accretion** Graffiti on a wall, a bicycle lying in a front yard, writing left on a chalkboard in a classroom **Erosion** A dirt pathway in the grass, a worn handrail, an empty trash can or dumpster
Factual	*Statistics*	Quantifiable data usually presented in numerical format	Demographic information about a city, found in a census
	Codes	A set of rules, mandated by law, governing the construction in and around buildings and usually aimed at preserving the safety of the end users	International Building Code (IBC)
	Other Governmental Regulations or Guidelines	There are various types of Web sites published by the government:	
		Local	City Planning or Building Departments that issue permits Chamber of Commerce or Business District Web sites
		Regional	Department of Planning and Land Use Department of Environmental Health
		Federal	USA.gov Americans with Disabilities Act – www.ada.gov

Research Method	Research Source	Explanation	Examples
Factual	*Trade Organizations*	Web sites promoting the common interests of an industry or a trade	International Interior Design Association (IIDA), American Society of Interior Designers (ASID), American Institute of Architects (AIA)
	Product Specifications	Information about a building product or material, often published by the distributor, usually listing the manufacturer, dimensions and weight, composition or content, strength and durability, safety ratings, and maintenance guidelines	The coefficient of friction (COF) for a ceramic floor tile specified in a bathroom
	Research Data	Systematically and objectively collected information from a controlled study	Research study into the impact of design on the health of babies in neonatal ICUs
Evaluation (occurs during design development and later phases of the Interior Design Process)	*Heuristic Evaluation*	An inexpensive testing method involving a checklist of a project's goals and requirements; used to evaluate the usability of a design and detect design issues or flaws needing to be resolved	A list of criteria used by a design team to evaluate whether the project accomplishes pre-established goals; similar to the grading rubric used by a jury panel at a student design presentation
	Usability Testing	Creating a prototype or mock-up of a space, then observing a subject interacting and performing required tasks within the simulated environment to detect design issues or flaws to be resolved	Building out one patient room in a hundred-patient-room hospital wing, and observing twenty-five nurses performing ten predetermined tasks related to expected methods of providing health care within the space
	Post-Occupancy Evaluation	A performance review of a completed project after the client has occupied it for an extended amount of time	Evaluating the energy-consumption rates of a building one year after new energy-efficient equipment was installed. If there has not been a reduction in energy use, the evaluation can include interviewing and observing the staff to determine if they have been trained to use the new equipment properly.

Conducting a Literature Review

Research begins the moment you develop an open-ended question or questions that you want to find the answer to. This open-ended question is called a research question, and it is the motivation behind your research. To find the answers to the research question, often the first task is to conduct a **literature review:** reviewing the available literature on the topic. In this context, *literature* refers to "a body of information, existing in a wide variety of stored formats that has conceptual relevance for a particular topic of inquiry" (Groat & Wang, 2002, p. 46). In other words, it is the body of knowledge that has been customized to fit the research question (Groat & Wang).

A literature review is both (1) a preparatory process and (2) a written document. It's a *preparatory process* in that it includes "the totality of activities that the researcher undertakes to use that body of information in such a way that a topic of inquiry can be competently defined and addressed." By conducting a broad review of the literature on a topic, you will see a topical focus begin to emerge that will be customized to fit your research question (Groat & Wang, 2002).

It's a *written document* in that as your literature review progresses, you should create a written document that includes the following information:

- An introductory statement of the general intent of the literature exploration. This includes suggestions for the ultimate direction of the proposed research to come.
- A summary of the lines of existing research that provide background for the proposed research; this usually involves grouping the annotated items into common larger themes.
- Observations on the state of the literature in terms of how it can be expanded by the proposed research. In other words, the reviewer needs to identify specific areas that have not been covered by the extant literature, arguments that he or she wishes to challenge, or subjects of study that can be reconfigured by a new conceptual framework (Groat & Wang, 2002, p. 47).

Your literature review is not limited to the beginning of your research study (Groat & Wang, 2002, p. 57). As your ideas emerge, you can constantly trace the history of these ideas. Similar to your concept map, your literature review is the "Family Tree" of your literary research method, helping you to see the roots and branches of your design problem as you seek its solution. Your literature review should identify and separate primary, secondary, and tertiary sources as essential to framing the logic of your research study and how this information led to the formation of a new theory of your own (Groat & Wang, p. 63).

Words Matter

As part of conducting your literature review, it is helpful to identify the "buzz words" of your realm of research to include as search topics. These buzz words are often descriptors of a reality that many people have accepted but few can actually define (Groat & Wang, 2002). An example of a buzz word in interior design is *sustainability*. Recently, a student was interviewing a well-known architect to discuss her thesis about an environmentally responsible grocery store. She began the conversation by using the term *sustainability*, at which point the architect asked if she knew what the word means. The student gave her definition of the word, and the architect immediately corrected her, stating that the word is used far too much, used synonymously with *green design* and *eco-friendly design*, while few individuals actually understand the correct definition. For the student to continue her research, it is important that she define this word and understand its various applications and nuances, as the various bodies of literature might apply the term differently.

You should also be aware of professional **acronyms**: one-word abbreviations made up of the first letters of the words of a more complex term, such as *ASID* to refer to the American Society of Interior Designers. Using acronyms is often a subtle way of separating those who belong from those who do not, and it is much easier for you to be respected by the professionals you hope to learn from if you are familiar with the acronyms that will come up in conversation.

The following steps will help you to conduct a successful literature review:

- Knowing where to find the sources
- Having a system for organizing and retrieving
- Bringing motivation and imagination to the task (Groat & Wang, 2002)

Use the following techniques to track your research:

- If you are in ownership of the work, mark up the original as the ideas emerge from what you are writing (Groat & Wang, 2002).
- Create note cards (Groat & Wang, 2002). "The writing of a note is the first step towards framing an idea" (Barzun & Graff, quoted in Groat & Wang, 2002, p. 67).
- Create an ongoing outline on the computer that is well organized, then use the information from the literature, as well as the new ideas, to "fill in the blanks" (Groat & Wang, 2002).

- Use your software's color-coding tool as an organizational quick reference to identify information from different sources.
- Develop a system to keep track of the difference between sources, information, and ideas.

You can use the following points as guides to the relevance of your literary sources:

- Who is the author? Is this person a professional in the field? What academic institution, companies, or organizations is the author affiliated with? Is there a reason to suspect that the author's work might be biased in any way?
- Is the source relevant to your topic? Do the title, subtitle, description, subject headings, and abstract help you to determine how directly the particular source addresses your topic (Axelrod & Cooper, 2008, p. 715)?
- What is the publication date? How recent is the source? For current controversies, design trends, and technological developments, you must consult current material. If it is an historical topic, you will want to look at contemporary perspectives, but eventually explore older sources that are closer to being primary sources and are thus more authoritative perspectives (Axelrod & Cooper, pp. 715–716).
- Is this a peer-reviewed source? Are there any other reviews recommending this book, or has it been compared to an author you respect or admire?
- What is the description of the book? Does the length indicate a brief treatment of the topic or an in-depth treatment? Does the included abstract indicate the focus of the work (Axelrod & Cooper, p. 716)? Different books are written for different people, so who is the book geared toward? Academics? Professionals? Students? Those with a personal interest?
- What is the content of the book? Does it include photographs of work or illustrations that may elaborate on information contained in the text? Does it include a bibliography that could be a valuable tool for leading you to other works and resources (Axelrod & Cooper, p. 716)?

The Value of a Working Bibliography

A **bibliography** is a complete list of any and all sources used by a researcher—student or professional—in pursuing an area of research. A complete and thorough bibliography includes any written works quoted or referenced, such as books, magazines, or newspapers, as well as all other materials drawn upon for information, such as interviews, audio or video recordings, statistical sources, case studies of existing buildings, and Web sites.

It is especially important to always give credit to anyone or anything that has offered an identifiable and significant contribution to the development of your research and design project, and this information must be represented within the bibliography of the project. A bibliography demonstrates your rigorous attitude toward the exploration of your project, as well as the breadth and depth of your research into finding both a real and relevant design problem and a successful solution (University of London, Postgraduate Online Research Training, 2008).

The role of academic and professional interior design research and subsequent conclusions is to add to the available body of knowledge in the interior design field. Your academic design project does not end at the walls of your school. Chances are that you are exploring a question and problem that other students and professionals have also explored. Thus your bibliography will demarcate a specific field of knowledge about interior design that could become a valuable resource for other academics, students, and professionals pursuing similar interests (University of London, Postgraduate Online Research Training, 2008). As researchers examine this available body of knowledge, your bibliography enables them to easily and quickly find the original sources you incorporated into your project, possibly helping them in their research. It also allows any interested party to check the validity and truth behind the solution or solutions you are posing for the problem you have identified.

Acknowledging Sources and Avoiding Plagiarism

Plagiarism is defined as the "unacknowledged use of another's words, ideas, or information" (Axelrod & Cooper, 2008, p. 748). Often it seems as though plagiarism does not apply to interior design, because interior designers are producing built environments and not necessarily papers or other written documents. But this is not true! The field of interior design involves written communication through proposals, project programs, and professional correspondence. It is also important to recognize that plagiarism is not just about written work. It can also apply to other works such as musical compositions, drawings, and even abstract ideas.

Some of you may remember that in 1990, the singer and performer Vanilla Ice was accused of stealing the bass line of the 1982 song "Under Pressure" by Queen and David Bowie. The ensuing legal case was publicized all over the country, showing everyone the impact that plagiarism can have on an artist's career. That is just one very high-profile example of an accusation of plagiarism originating from a source other than a written work.

Plagiarism is not always about bad intentions. It can also result from irresponsible research methods. If you do not understand the appropriate conventions for acknowledging sources, you could plagiarize unintentionally—

There is an inaccurate perception that a bibliography is always a polished and complete work, consisting only of references actually cited. This misperception often causes students to put off preparing the bibliography until the final project page is written and the last line is drawn. However, we believe that you can actually have two kinds of bibliographies: not only a final, complete list of works cited, but also a **working bibliography** that lists each and every source you considered during the research process, including sources you discarded as being irrelevant.

The working bibliography can be a great time-saving tool. Keeping a highly detailed and accurate record of all the sources you consulted in your research allows you to avoid the following frustrating situation: You are two months into an in-depth and exciting interior design project when you come across a question you need to have answered. You identify the name or title of a source that seems to promise great new data and information in response to your question; however, your library does not carry the source. You spend several hours over a couple of days locating the source through an interlibrary loan program, waiting for it to arrive, and then making a special trip to your own library to pick it up. You get there, grab the source waiting for you, and then you realize that this is a source you already looked through before and found to be completely irrelevant. You had discarded the source and completely forgotten about it. Because you never made a note of the source and its relevance or lack of relevance in your working bibliography, you wasted valuable time and now have to start your search over again.

and suffer the same consequences as a student who simply does not want to do the work and hands in another student's assignment as his or her own. You should always familiarize yourself with the plagiarism policies at your own institution.

According to The Online Writing Lab (OWL) at Purdue University (2008), the way to avoid plagiarism is to "always give credit where credit is due." The following list from their Web site includes examples of when it is necessary to cite your work:

- Words or ideas presented in a magazine, book, newspaper, song, TV program, movie, Web page, computer program, letter, advertisement, or any other medium
- Information you gain through interviewing or conversing with another person, face-to-face, over the phone, or in writing
- When you copy the exact words or a unique phrase

- When you paraphrase another person's words or ideas
- When you reprint any diagrams, illustrations, charts, pictures, or other visual materials
- When you reuse or repost any electronically available media, including images, audio, video, or other media

Information Communication and Citation Formats

It is important to consult with your instructor about the style of formatting that he or she prefers you to use for your project. While there is not one universally accepted system for acknowledging sources, a method commonly used by students for documenting bibliographical information is the Modern Language Association (MLA) format. However, based on your field of study, there are other options, such as *The Chicago Manual of Style (CMS)* and the American Psychological Association (APA). APA style is more common to professional-level interior design research, while MLA style is more often used in schools.

- MLA style and format—Consult the *MLA Handbook for Writers of Research Papers* (6th edition), by Joseph Gibaldi, or the *MLA Style Manual and Guide to Scholarly Publishing* (2nd edition), also by Joseph Gibaldi.
- CMS style and format—Consult *The Chicago Manual of Style* (15th edition), by the staff of the University of Chicago Press, or subscribe to *The Chicago Manual of Style Online* at http://www.chicagomanualofstyle.org.
- APA style and format—Consult the *Publication Manual of the American Psychological Association* (5th edition), by the staff of the American Psychological Association. For more information about APA style, the Web site is http://www.apastyle.org.

There are two levels of **citation** you should be aware of:

1. Citing within the body of the text, usually at the end of a paragraph or with footnotes or endnotes, in order to give credit for information taken directly from another source.
2. The bibliographic list of works cited, which is a summary of all sources drawn upon during the process of researching and designing your project.

Citing Within the Body of Text

The only time you would not use an in-text citation for a source in your writing is when that written information is considered common knowledge or when you are including your own original ideas. Since the definition of *common knowledge* can be a bit hazy, it's advisable to cite everything in order to be as thorough as possible.

The basic formula for citing sources with the MLA format is to include—in parentheses at the end of a paragraph or after a direct quote or paraphrasing—the author's last name and the page number of the information being referenced. Other citing formats require that you include the author and copyright date of the published work being cited. Since each format varies slightly, it is important to carefully follow the rules of the format required by your instructor.

Bibliographical List of Works Cited

As with in-text citations, it is important to consult with your instructor to ensure that you are using the appropriate format. Your bibliography should contain more than just textual sources such as books and periodicals. The following is a list of additional sources you would include in your bibliography. (Keep in mind this is not necessarily a complete list; again, consult with your instructor about his or her expectations.)

- A dictionary entry or other reference book, such as an encyclopedia
- A specific document from a Web site
- A TV show, documentary, or other film
- An entire Web site
- A portion of a Web site
- An e-mail message
- An interview
- A collection of work, such as photographs or documentaries
- Maps, site plans, building plans, or other similar records
- Census records or other statistics

Your developing bibliography is like a record of all the steps you have taken in your information-gathering, and it reflects the diverse nature of research and how you have chosen to navigate this process.

The Role of the Internet in Data Gathering

In academic and professional research, if you intend to use the Internet as a source you should view it critically. The Internet is a dumping ground for any and all information, with that information often placed on a Web site by unknown sources, each with its own agenda; thus, the accuracy of that information is always questionable. There is no system of checks and balances, no professional peer review, to establish the credibility of information, and many sites are operated by individuals with a particular bias (Ballast, 2006, p. 28). Online "blogging" is a perfect example.

When a professional submits a manuscript for publication as an article or a book, the manuscript is distributed to a variety of other professionals in the field for review. Through this **peer review** process, the accuracy of the information and its relevance to the field are verified. This helps to ensure that the published information is valid and accurate. Unfortunately, the Internet does not have the same system to verify the accuracy of information, so you must always be critical of information taken from the Web.

Despite this, the use of the Internet should not be discounted entirely. It can hold great value, especially in the preliminary stage of the research process, as a tool for planning your research. The Internet can also be used to find a source of information, and it can help you contact that source directly. For example, while "surfing the Net," you may find a blurb about a scientist who is studying the effects of lighting on retail environments. In this case, the Internet is the tool that informs you that the study exists and who performed it. Now you can track down the actual study to use as a source in your research, or you can contact the scientist to request an interview. The Internet is a great tool to help you brainstorm topics, track down sources or experts to talk to, explore online catalogs and databases, or research the background of a company or an individual. If you are seeking experts to interview for your project, the Internet can help you locate these experts, by providing professional background information as well as an e-mail address or other contact information.

There are various types of sites on the Internet, and each has its unique value to your research process:

- Local, state, and federal government agencies, with Web addresses ending in ".gov," such as the Census Bureau and Americans with Disabilities (Burkhardt et al., 2003, p. 72). These Web sites can provide authoritative information on building code requirements, laws, regulations, and permitting procedures (Ballast, 2006, p. 28).
- Educational institutions, with Web addresses ending in ".edu," such as universities, institutions, and museums like the Smithsonian Institution. These Web sites can often provide information on the latest trends in a field and how you might access more information about the topic.
- Nonprofit organizations and associations, with Web addresses ending in ".org," such as the American Society of Interior Designers and professional and trade associations like the Architectural Woodwork Institute.
- Commercial sites with Web addresses ending in ".com," the largest body of Web sites to be found on the Internet, which advertise a product or service (Burkhardt et al., 2003, p. 72). Recall the caution in the first paragraph of this section.

A further note about .com sites: Although commercial sites usually are trying to promote a product that may make them inherently biased, they can also provide current and relevant data for a product, and they are valuable when they're specifying materials, furniture, lighting, and other architectural and interior design products. However, if you need unbiased information in order to compare several manufacturers of the same product type, you should select another source (Ballast, 2006, p. 28). Trade associations, such as the Lighting Research Center, are often a good source for this type of comparison information.

Just as a compass might help a hiker find his way in a complex forest, the Internet can help point you in the right direction. Once a direction has been found, it's your responsibility as a researcher to follow that path to appropriate and credible sources from which to make informed design decisions.

The following are some useful Web sites to consult in your research process:

- American Institute of Architects (AIA)—http://www.aia.org/
- American National Standards Institute (ANSI)—http://www.ansi.org/
- American Society of Heating, Refrigerating and Air-Conditioning Engineers (ASHRAE)—http://www.ashrae.org/
- American Society of Interior Designers (ASID)—http://www.asid.org
- Americans with Disabilities Act (ADA)—http://www.ada.gov/
- Companies, such as Herman Miller, Inc.—http://www.hermanmiller.com/
- Cooper-Hewitt National Design Museum—http://www.cooperhewitt.org/
- E-Architect—http://www.e-architect.com/
- International Interior Design Association (IIDA)—http://www.iida.org
- Material Connexion—http://www.materialconnexion.com/
- National Fire Protection Standards (NFPA)—http://www.nfpa.org
- National Trust for Historic Preservation—http://www.preservationnation.org
- National Register of Historic Places—http://www.nps.gov/nr/
- Office of Statewide Health Planning Department (OSHPD)—http://www.oshpd.ca.gov/
- U.S. Census Bureau—http://www.census.gov/
- U.S. Department of Housing and Urban Development—http://www.hud.gov/ (Once at this site, look for a link to http://www.huduser.org/, which leads to publications, periodicals, ongoing research, bibliographic databases, etc.)
- U.S. Green Building Council—http://www.usgbc.org
- U.S. National Park Service—http://www.nps.gov

Online Databases

You have learned about the value of the Internet as a tool in identifying information sources, but the Internet can give you access to other tools as well, such as online databases and library catalogs. You are likely very familiar with browsing the Internet to find information, a product, or a service. But when you have access to online databases and library catalogues, the same search process can yield valuable, in-depth, credible, topic-specific information.

Online databases—accessible through the Internet, via a subscription—are collections of computer records, primarily periodicals such as magazines, newspapers, and journals that have a common format and content. These periodicals are organized in the database for rapid search and retrieval using subject headings and keywords from the research topic. **Keywords** are used to locate specific articles within these larger bodies of information (Undergraduate Library, University of Illinois, Urbana-Champaign, 2007). For example, once you enter a keyword, the database will take you to a periodical, such as *Interior Design* magazine, and then within that periodical will locate a specific article that is relevant to your keyword.

Databases can be easily accessed through school or public libraries that subscribe to the services. At the library, simply ask what databases are available; the librarian will be able to provide you with a password for access.

The organization of databases provides more relevant results through the use of subject headings and descriptors. You may also search for keywords in specific fields, such as author and title, and limit the results using various criteria (Undergraduate Library, University of Illinois, Urbana-Champaign, 2007). These search tools sift through thousands of articles within seconds, presenting you with the articles most relevant to your topic—a much more efficient method than flipping through a stack of magazines by hand.

Another benefit of using an online database is that database content has undergone a professional peer review, and the information found in an online database is more reliable than the unregulated information found on the Internet. Usually, databases provide access to full-text magazine and journal articles, whereas an article obtained through the online version of the periodical is not necessarily the full-text version of the article unless you have purchased an online subscription to the periodical (Undergraduate Library, University of Illinois, Urbana-Champaign, 2007). Using an online database can lead you straight to the article you need while still providing the at-home, at-work, or at-school convenience of the Internet.

When searching databases or catalogs, do not limit yourself to only art- and design-based sources. The interior design field is becoming increasingly cross-disciplinary as designers team up with other professionals, such as psychologists, neuroscientists, and anthropologists, to obtain a broader understanding of the human experience within the built environment.

Taking a cross-disciplinary approach can provide multiple perspectives and approaches to the same topic. For example, if you wanted to find information about the impact of lighting on customer purchasing in a retail environment, in the *Journal of Interior Design* you might find a relevant study that explores how lighting changes affect customer purchasing behavior, and what seems to be the most appropriate lighting solution. You might also find an article in the *Journal of Environmental Psychology* or *Trends in Cognitive Sciences* that examines the emotional or physiological impact that lighting has on the human experience or brain and why this might impact human behavior.

Following are some helpful online databases available to interior design students, including a description of what the database can be used to find:

- *Avery Index to Architectural Periodicals*—This index, provided by the Getty Research Institute in Los Angeles, contains more than 620,000 listings of journal articles on architecture and design, including bibliographic descriptions on subjects such as the history and practice of architecture, landscape architecture, city planning, historic preservation, and interior design and decoration. This database is attached to the Avery Architectural and Fine Arts Library at Columbia University and is operated by Research Libraries Group (http://eureka.rlg.org/).
- *Design Abstracts Retrospective (DAR)*—This retrospective of *Design and Applied Arts Index* provides broad international coverage on a wide range of subjects in the fields of design from 1903 to 1986, with some sources dating back to 1894. This database places particular emphasis on European publications, and it covers more that one hundred design and design-related journals, most of which have ceased publication but that are distinctly important to the development of design concepts in the early twentieth century (ProQuest, 2008).
- *Design and Applied Arts Index (DAAI)*—This is the leading source of abstracts and bibliographic records for articles, news items, and reviews published in design and applied arts periodicals from 1973 onward, covering both new designers and the development of design and the applied arts since the mid–nineteenth century. Disciplines surveyed include ceramics, glass, jewelry, wood, metalsmithing, graphic design, fashion and clothing, textiles, furniture, interior design, architecture, computer-aided design, Web design, computer-generated graphics, animation, product design, industrial design, garden design, and landscape architecture (ProQuest, 2008).
- *Corbis*—Corbis offers access to stock photography covering a vast range of subjects, including architecture and design.
- *eJournals and eBooks (such as those provided by ProQuest Direct, Science Direct, Ideal, and NetLibrary)*—These are the digitized versions of con-

ventionally printed journals or books. They provide convenient access to a complete publication through the Internet.

- *Hoover's*—This database provides access to information about companies, people, and industries. See their Web site at http://www.hoovers.com.
- *InformeDesign.com*—This is a "research and communication tool" for interior designers. It allows you to search by topical categories and provides access to an **abstract**, or summary, of each article. Once you identify a valuable article, you pay a per-article fee to obtain the full-text document.
- *Oxford Reference Online*—This is one of the largest collections of references in the world, providing authoritative information covering the complete subject spectrum: from General Reference and Language to Science and Medicine, and from Humanities and Social Sciences to Business and Professional (this description taken from their Web site, http://www.oxfordreference.com).
- *WilsonWeb*—WilsonWeb contains academic journals covering a broad range of topics and subjects. The company's Web site, http://www.hwwilson.com, provides guidelines for conducting effective searches.

Library Catalogs

While an online database can provide access to periodicals independent of the researcher's location, **library catalogs** provide information describing resources owned by a specific library. A library's online catalog will provide access to the collections of library materials owned by the library, and, unlike an online database, a library catalog usually includes a very diverse collection of options, such as books, journals, magazines, newspapers, video recordings, sound recordings, music scores, maps, and government documents (University of Illinois, Urbana-Champaign).

As previously discussed, an online database can provide direct access to the full-text periodical article itself through the Internet. Library catalogs differ in that they offer only the location of the source within the library system and the current availability. Once the source is located through the online library catalog, the researcher must physically retrieve the source from the library shelves.

The Library of Congress—with the biggest library catalog in the world—can be accessed at http://www.loc.gov. Because this is a library catalog, the works themselves cannot be accessed through the site, but searches on this site enable many topical directions and connections to emerge (Groat & Wang, 2002).

Archives

Archives, which provide a limited-access repository of materials, are usually connected to a particular entity, such as a government body, an organization, an institution, or even an individual. Archives are organized and maintained for long-term safekeeping and for selective review and use. In relation to design, archives might contain items such as lecture notes, maps, transcripts, recordings, and photographs, to name just a few (Groat & Wang, 2002).

To access an archive, you must make prior arrangements for accessing the material. Usually you must set an appointment time to meet with a **conservator** or other professional who will help you review the archived material and observe the process, ensuring the proper preservation of the item.

To see what might be available in one of many archives across the United States, visit the Web site of the U.S. National Archives, which can be accessed at http://www.archives.gov/ (Groat & Wang, 2002).

Selecting the Most Promising Resources

In today's "information age," it is easy to get distracted by interesting and enticing data that might sound exciting but is not likely to be useful for the focus of your specific research or thesis topic. The research process can be time-consuming, so you never want to waste time reading or pursuing a resource that is not relevant to your topic or project, regardless of its appeal. And, as mentioned earlier, you also do not want to waste time pursuing a resource that may not actually be accurate or valid.

That being said, while you want to remain focused and efficient, it is important to not limit yourself to only one perspective on your topic. For example, if two politicians write about the topic of affordable housing, one politician might conclude that it is the government's responsibility to provide affordable housing, while the other politician might conclude that the marketplace should control the cost of housing with incentives like low-interest loans that increase buyer purchasing power. In this instance, the topic of affordable housing is the same, but the ideas and solutions that the politicians have proposed are very different. Both perspectives are valuable for getting a more broad-based understanding of both the issues and the potential solutions. It is fairly typical that there are multiple authors covering any given topic, or that various opinions are readily available. This variety provides the greatest opportunity for exhausting all options, and it increases the chances of finding a successful solution to the design problem being investigated.

Conclusion

A thorough literature review can ensure that you have explored all of the possible directions for your research topic and question. It will give you an overview of the latest information and lead you to the appropriate sources for gathering further information. Conduct your literature review with a critical eye in order to identify bias and other influences on the information presented and to be open to exploring varying points of view—as they will give you a more complete story.

The following chapters will take the research methods listed in Table 5.1 and provide a detailed explanation of the techniques associated with each method and how you might apply those techniques to research your interior design problem, project, and solutions. We also provide questions to aid you in determining which techniques will be a valuable and promising means of obtaining the information you need to answer your questions about the built world and the human experience within it.

References

Adams, J. L. (2001). *Conceptual blockbusting: A guide to better ideas.* Cambridge, MA: Basic Books.

Axelrod, R., & Cooper, C. (2008). *The St. Martin's guide to writing* (8th ed.). Boston: Bedford/St. Martin's.

Ballast, D. K. (2006). *Interior design reference manual: A guide to the NCIDQ exam* (3rd ed.). Belmont, CA: Professional.

Burkhardt, J. M., MacDonald, M. C., & Rathemacher, A. J. (2003). *Teaching information literacy.* Chicago: American Library Association.

Groat, L., & Wang, D. (2002). *Architectural research methods.* New York: John Wiley.

Guerin, D., & Dohr, J. (2007). "Research 101 Tutorial." InformeDesign, University of Minnesota. Retrieved December 25, 2007, from http://www.informedesign.umn.edu/

Hairston, M., & Ruszkiewicz, J. J. (1996). *The Scott Foresman handbook for writers* (4th ed.). New York: HarperCollins.

The Owl at Purdue. (2008). "Is it plagiarism yet?" Retrieved January 11, 2008, from http://owl.english.purdue.edu/owl/resource/589/02/

ProQuest. (2008). "CSA illumina." Retrieved February 5, 2009, from http://www.csa.com/

Undergraduate Library, University of Illinois, Urbana-Champaign. (2007). "How databases and online catalogs differ." Retrieved December 26, 2007, from http://www.library.uiuc.edu/ugl/howdoi/compare2.html

University Library, University of California, Santa Cruz. (2007). "How to distinguish between primary and secondary sources." Retrieved December 30, 2007, from http://library.ucsc.edu/ref/howto/primarysecondary.html

University of London, Postgraduate Online Research Training. (2008). "Building up your bibliography." Retrieved January 25, 2008, from http://port.igrs.sas.ac.uk/bibliography.htm

6 Interviews

CHAPTER OBJECTIVES

When you complete this chapter you should be able to do the following:

- Identify interviews that need to take place.
- Select and recruit interviewees.
- Prepare a predetermined list of questions.
- Confidently conduct and record the interview.
- Evaluate the information collected in an interview and incorporate it into the body of research for your project.

KEY TERMS

Client

Closed-ended question

Compound question

End user

Final summary

Focus group

Formal interview

Funnel

Generally guided

Informal conversation

Information interview

Interview

Inverted funnel

Leading question

Loaded question

Metaphor

Neutral question	Questionnaire
Open-ended question	Reconstruction
Participant end user	Secondary question
Post-interview assessment	Self-report
Post-interview record	Standardized questionnaire
Potential end user	Tagged statement
Primary question	Transcription
Probe	Tunnel

Conducting personal reports involves taking information directly from an individual or a group of people. An **interview** is a type of personal report in which two or more people discuss personal or professional matters, in which one person asks questions of the other. For the purpose of interior design, it means to query someone to obtain information relevant to a design project.

According to Michael Patton, there are six areas of inquiry that can be asked in past, present, or future tense (1990):

1. *Behaviors*—About what a person has done or is doing or will do
2. *Opinions/Values*—About what a person thinks about a topic
3. *Feelings*—Note that respondents sometimes respond with "I think . . . ," so be careful to note that you're looking for feelings.
4. *Knowledge*—What someone knows factually about a topic
5. *Sensory*—About what people have seen, touched, heard, tasted, or smelled
6. *Background/Demographics*—Standard descriptive or background questions, such as age, education, residence, or income level

Conducting Interviews

The interview process can be uncomfortable or intimidating. You may be afraid to ask questions, especially when dealing with people you don't know. However, the interview process is *essential* to the field of interior design.

Further, interviewing is a skill, not a talent. You can become more confident and adept at this process through continued practice and experience of what works and what does not work. Watching skilled interviewers such as Diane Sawyer or Barbara Walters can help you build confidence and pick up some of the non-verbal cues that help an interview succeed. Another resource might be the interview techniques developed during the 1950s by such pioneers as Dr. Alfred Kinsey, author of *The Kinsey Reports on Human*

Sexual Behavior (1948–53), and Robert K. Merton, author of *The Focused Interview* (1951). These books served historically as groundbreaking additions to the expanding exploration of interview techniques.

Information interviews are concerned with gathering information to discover meanings and to test theories. A *theory* is a description of reality, or a proposed view that seeks to make sense of the interrelation of phenomena, events, or behaviors. As a systematic and formalized expression of all previous observations, a theory can be disproved only through further testing or future observation. Consider the theory of evolution, the theory of relativity, or the string theory. In interior design, too, we may construct theories in order to explain, predict, and master phenomena (for example: inanimate things, events). Recall the extensive discussion of theory in Chapter 3.

You might use an information interview to test a theory or to help discover a problem to solve. For example, if you have a theory that management's views about the open-office plan arrangement differ from employees' views about it, you could set up information interviews to ask questions that target how staff members on both sides feel about their sense of privacy, control, and efficiency. Through your questions, you would seek to reveal the beliefs underlying the way the office is arranged and also to reveal the feelings (intended or unintended) that result from the furniture arrangement in this particular office and from, notably, its lack of full-height walls. Your theory that management prefers easy visibility and control of the office while employees prefer more privacy may be supported or refuted by the data you collect in your interviews.

Information interviews are most often focused interviews (carried out one-on-one or in groups), but they could also be telephone interviews, videoconferencing, exit interviews, oral histories, investigational and journalistic interviews, medical case histories, professional consultation, or diagnostic interviews. Although any of these types of interviews could be part of the experience of an interior designer, this chapter focuses on information-gathering for research, giving special attention to in-depth or probing interviews, specifically for interior design during the programming and design phases. What are the different types of interviews for interior design?

Types of Interviews

As you read about the following types of interviews, consider which ones would be most appropriate for your project.

Client-Based Interviews

Interior designers interview clients to find out their goals, wants, and needs. Sometimes designers use the term **client** to mean all possible users of

The exhibit planner Alice Parman, Ph.D., introduced in Chapter 5, approaches client-based interviews using what she refers to as a "Start-Up Agenda" (personal communication, 2008). In the list below, this agenda has been adapted to suit the needs of interior designers.

1. Define and discuss the institution's mission or corporate identity.
2. Identify the decision-makers and the stakeholders. List all project members and their responsibilities. Are there current or potential partners or corporate sponsors?
3. What is the scope of the project? What is the expected timeline and what are the budgetary constraints?
4. Define project goals.
5. Describe end users: staff, visitors, patrons.
6. What are the biggest problems to be solved? What elements must be incorporated?
7. What reference materials or sources of information are available for further investigation? Who is available for interview? Discuss access for observation/surveys.

the space. However, this textbook uses *client* to refer specifically to the owner, organization, corporation, company, or decision-making agent who would be responsible for hiring the designer, making the key design decisions, and/or funding the project. Your design project has a real client or an acting client. What do you want to know from your client? Obvious question content will address budget, function, location, size, and expected number of end users. In an interview, you must also ask questions to determine the client's underlying values, belief system, and goals, and the mission of the project.

An historical example of a good client/designer relationship was the interaction of architect Louis Kahn with his client Dr. Jonas Salk in the design of the Salk Institute for Biological Studies. Through extensive interviews and discussions, Kahn was able to understand the client's values and goals. Salk told the architect that he wanted "a place where Picasso would feel welcome." Kahn translated: "He meant that anyone with a mind in the humanities, in science or in art could contribute to the mental environment of research leading to discoveries in science" (Ronner & Jhaveri, 1974). See Figure 6.1.

End User–Based Interviews

Interior designers interview people to find out the choreography of how they will use the space. There are ordinarily different kinds of **end users** in a

Figure 6.1 Interview techniques can uncover client's values. Dr. Jonas Salk (pictured right) told the architect Louis Kahn that he wanted "a place where Picasso would feel welcome." Kahn translated, "He meant that anyone with a mind in the humanities, in science or in art could contribute to the mental environment of research leading to discoveries in science" (Ronner & Jhaveri, 1974).

particular project. For example, in a daycare center there would be administrative staff, full-time and part-time care providers, volunteers, and mothers and fathers who drop off their children—as well as the children themselves. It is also necessary to consider the maintenance and security staff, who might also be interviewed for their experience and opinions.

In the case of the Salk Institute for Biological Studies, the end users were scientists engaged in groundbreaking research at the cellular or molecular level of life. Because Dr. Salk did not know who would be coming to his new facility, architect Louis Kahn interviewed scientists engaged in research at the University of Pennsylvania for a project that Kahn had already completed: The Richards Medical Laboratory at the University of Pennsylvania. There is an interesting distinction between wants and needs, almost a dichotomy in this instance, which Kahn eloquently describes. The scientists, according to Kahn, "said they are so dedicated to what they are doing that when lunchtime comes all they do is clear away the test tubes from the benches and eat their lunch on these benches. I asked them was it not a strain with all these noises? And they answered . . . everything was terrible including the noise of the air conditioning system. So I would not listen to them as to what should be done" (Ronner & Jhaveri, 1974, p. 138). In this quote, we can see that Kahn realized that the wants of the scientists did not necessarily match their needs. Kahn summarized the needs he gleaned from the interview as follows: "I realized that there should be 'a clean air and stainless steel' area, and 'a rug and oak table' area. . . . The garden became the outdoor spaces where one can talk. Now one need not spend all the time in laboratories" (p. 138).

Two subgroups of end users would be the **participant end user**, the current or future user of the space, and the **potential end user**, a person who possesses the characteristics of someone who potentially would use the space. In a museum project, identifying a potential end user may involve (1) asking questions of people who have visited a similar type of museum or (2) selecting potential end users from among people who are interested in a particular type of art or who live in the neighborhood. A **focus group** is a small group of potential users of a particular service, product, or space who have been prescreened for certain characteristics—for example, expectant mothers who plan to work (for a daycare center). Note: The focus group will be discussed in greater depth in Chapter 7, because focus groups can be used for surveys as well.

In the example of the Salk Institute, the architect Louis Kahn interviewed scientists from the Richards Medical Laboratory project to gather information to inform his next project, the Salk Institute project. The scientists were members of a target market; that is, Kahn identified them as potential users of the new laboratory, and their level of experience matched the level of experience of persons who might use the new laboratory in the future.

Consider a second example: An interior design student was charged with researching the homeless problem in San Diego, California, in order to design a facility that would meet the needs of the homeless population in that city. First, the student collected information on a variety of topics; her sources ranged from government Web sites to a tour of a local homeless shelter. Her research question: In the local services for the homeless, what gaps exist that prevent a homeless person from returning to a permanent home?

Her next step was to understand—from the point of view of a homeless person, as a potential user of her facility—what services were needed. See Figure 6.2. Her target audience could be sorted by a common characteristic: homelessness. But there was a variety of other factors: physical disabilities, mental health, age, sex, ethnic background. While on a guided tour of the

Figure 6.2 An example of a potential end user for a homeless shelter would be a person living on the street.

homeless shelter, she learned that homeless persons who did not live at the shelter lined up for free breakfast in a certain location. There would be approximately two hundred people in line on any given morning. The rest of the afternoon, these people would congregate in a nearby park, waiting for dinner to be served. To try to find out what a homeless person thought, believed, expected, and wanted, the student decided to interview some of the people in this group directly. She came up with a list of eight questions. The first two questions were general "icebreaker" or "warm-up" questions, intended to put the interviewee at ease. Notice the use of broad, open-ended questions. Was this a good strategy?

> Hi, my name is Dalia. I am a student at a local design school. I am researching the problem of homelessness in San Diego for a school project, and I am trying to understand what it is like to be homeless. May I ask you a few questions about yourself? Anything you tell me will be strictly confidential. I will not share this with anyone else.
>
> 1. Can you tell me a little about your life?
> 2. Can you describe for me a typical day you may have?
> 3. Where do you eat?
> 4. Where do you sleep?
> 5. Have you ever stayed in a shelter?
> 6. Would you like to work?
> 7. If you could change one thing, what would it be?
> 8. What do you feel would truly help you?

Dalia described some of the pitfalls of her interviews. At one point, waiting in a line of hundreds for breakfast to be served, she decided to ask her questions to a woman next to her. As the woman started to answer, a man in line interjected, "Why are you lying?" and a verbal argument ensued. Dalia quickly thanked the woman for her time and ended the interview. Steps were taken in the future to approach the subject in a more private location (not within earshot of other people) in order to encourage truthful answers and to avoid conflict.

Expert Interviews

Interior designers need to gain information on a topic or project type from relevant experts. For example, when designing a spiritual space, it may be important to ask questions of a member of the clergy, or when designing a dental office it may be important to interview a dental hygienist. Experts in a particular field will have insights and knowledge that will be essential to the success of your design.

Professional Interviews

Interior designers often use interviews to gain information about a specific professional or technical skill related to the area of design. You could interview a structural engineer when designing a mezzanine in a retail space; a Leadership in Energy and Environmental Design (LEED)–certified professional when considering sustainable features in your project; or a woodworker about fabrication techniques, properties of wood, and joinery when designing wood furniture.

Successful Interviews

There are four stages to a successful interview:

1. Preparation
2. Arranging
3. Conducting
4. Recording (this last stage is sometimes referred to as "reconstruction")

Preparation involves collecting background information on your subject matter as well as your interviewee. It is essential to familiarize yourself with terminology and acronyms. In order to get people to open up to you, you must know their lingo. For example, when a student was interviewing postal workers for a post office redesign, it quickly became apparent that there were many acronyms that she had to be familiar with in order to communicate fluently with the workers. You must identify your interviewee and anticipate the type of information that person will bring to your project.

Preparation also involves making a list of questions, putting the questions in a logical order, and orchestrating the format of the interview—formal or informal. The list of questions is called a **questionnaire**. You might administer these questions aloud in an interview. Alternatively, you could print the list of questions and distribute the list to a larger audience of people to fill out—this would be called a survey.

Before you choose your interviewees, ask yourself the following questions:

- Why am I conducting this interview rather than gathering information from other sources?
- Who are ideal candidates to be interviewed? A professional who works in the field? An academic who studies the issue? A published author who has already written books on the topic? A person in the local community who has dealt with this issue in his or her personal life? (Wheeler, 2008)
- Is the person available for an interview?

- Do I have a solid base of knowledge about the topic that will enhance my credibility with interviewees?

Arranging involves contacting the interviewee and communicating your intent and your passion for the project as well as your respect for the interviewee's knowledge and participation. Arranging also involves selecting an appropriate location and time for the interview to take place. Sometimes the interview will be face-to-face, but often it can be a conference call (at a prespecified time over the phone) or via Web-based telecommunication. The following is a checklist of questions to ask yourself as you arrange an interview:

- *Am I able to approach the interviewee from a positive standpoint, assuming that she or he will have time to talk with me?*—Keep in mind that most people are usually flattered by the attention and are willing to participate in an information interview, particularly if they know you're a student.
- *Can I choose a location that is comfortable for the interviewee?*—Generally, people are much more willing to participate in an information interview if the setting is a comfortable and familiar one. Many professional interviewers suggest choosing the interviewee's office or a public location near their office (with few distractions), as the interviewee may be more comfortable in familiar surroundings.
- *Have I addressed issues of confidentiality? Have I gotten written permission to use the information I receive from the interview?*—See the example of an "Informed Consent" form to be completed by the interviewee.

Sample "Informed Consent" Form
(WHEELER, 2008)

"I _____ [respondent's name] hereby give my permission for _____ [student's name] to interview me and quote my responses in a scholarly research paper. I understand that this research paper will be submitted to an instructor at _____ [school name]. I understand that I waive any claim to copyright to this material should the student ever publish it in a scholarly journal or in electronic format online. I understand that the author [will / will not] maintain my anonymity as a part of this interview. I hereby give my permission in the form of my signature below."

Signature _____ Date _____

Conducting the interview involves arriving on time, dressed appropriately and prepared with tools to record the interview. It also involves establishing a rapport with the interviewee (or the staff of the interviewee if you meet at the interviewee's office), remaining focused and attentive to your surroundings, and picking up nonverbal cues about the interviewee. Before starting the interview, ask yourself these questions:

- *Can I get a site tour before the start of the interview?* (A tour may help inspire questions you hadn't thought of before.)
- *Have I established myself as a trustworthy and reliable person to the staff or receptionist (the "gatekeeper"), and have I instilled confidence in the interviewee?*
- *Am I wearing professional attire in keeping with the office environment? If I am interviewing someone who may be intimidated by professional attire (children, elderly, homeless), am I appropriately dressed? Does my attire match the cultural expectations of my interviewee?*

Recording could be as simple as audiotaping or videotaping the interview. But sometimes these methods can make the interviewee uncomfortable or can be prohibitively disruptive. If you are going to audiotape or videotape the interview, it is imperative to get permission when you set up the interview, or at least prior to the interview. Recall the Sample "Informed Consent" Form presented earlier.

Other recording methods include making notes on paper, bringing along a friend to transcribe the exchange, or having interviewees write or type their answers. Depending on your typing skills, you could bring a laptop computer to the interview and type while the interviewee is speaking. (You may want to practice this skill beforehand.)

Below is a list of questions to ask yourself during the interview:

- *Do I understand what the interviewee is saying?*—Don't be afraid to ask for clarification of terminology that you may be unfamiliar with.
- *Do my body language and facial expressions remain open yet neutral to avoid intimidating the interviewee or influencing the responses?* —You may want to ask yourself your questions in front of a mirror to practice remaining neutral.
- *Have I reacted with surprise or strong emotion to any of the interviewee's answers?*—Have you remained attentive and reacted appropriately, so that the interviewee knows you are still listening with a certain degree of detachment? A good trick is to maintain an attitude of "I've heard it all before."
- *Are the questions flowing in a logical way?*—If the interview is not going as planned, you may need to improvise the order or wording of the questions.

- *Do I feel that the interviewee is being truthful? Am I getting the responses I need?*
- *Have I left my contact information with the interviewee for future questions or information?*
- *Have I expressed my appreciation?*—In addition to a simple spoken "Thank you so much for your time," you are strongly encouraged to send a handwritten thank-you note in the mail.
- *Have I gotten the information I need?*—Check to make sure the tape recording was successful. If you are using handwritten notes as a recording method, you may want to reconstruct the interview by writing out the responses in full sentences immediately after the interview ends—while the comments are still fresh in your mind. One last thing: If you don't have it already, ask for a mailing address so you can send that thank-you note.

Degrees of Formality

Interviews range in formality and structure, depending upon the situation. Note the progression of interview types displayed in Figure 6.3. The most casual type of interview is the **informal conversation**, in which no predetermined questions are asked, in order to remain as open and adaptable as possible to the interviewee's nature and priorities. A researcher happens upon the subject without prearrangement and asks a few warm-up questions; then, during the interview, the researcher "goes with the flow." For example, as you enter a building, you encounter a resident and ask how many people live in the building. In the elevator, you ask another resident her opinion about the building's current occupants. And as you are leaving, you ask a person living in the building next door to give you his opinion of the neighborhood. All of these interviews are chance occurrences that yield a cursory opinion from a singular subject. Keep your eyes open for opportunities that arise on guided tours or in public places.

The **generally guided** approach utilizes a list of topics to be covered. This approach is intended to ensure that the same general areas of information

Figure 6.3 As described in-depth in this chapter, interview types can range from a casual conversation to a formal, structured interaction.

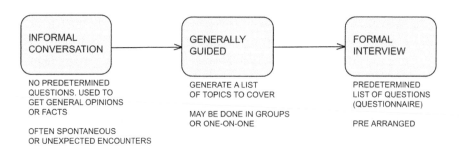

INFORMAL CONVERSATION

NO PREDETERMINED QUESTIONS. USED TO GET GENERAL OPINIONS OR FACTS

OFTEN SPONTANEOUS OR UNEXPECTED ENCOUNTERS

GENERALLY GUIDED

GENERATE A LIST OF TOPICS TO COVER

MAY BE DONE IN GROUPS OR ONE-ON-ONE

FORMAL INTERVIEW

PREDETERMINED LIST OF QUESTIONS (QUESTIONNAIRE)

PRE ARRANGED

are collected from each interviewee, but it allows for a degree of freedom and adaptability in getting this information. For example, to determine the public's opinion about the way-finding/signage system currently used in a local hospital, you informally survey random staff members, patients, and visitors in the waiting room. You ask each person about (1) their ease in locating destinations; (2) their opinions of the signage, wording, graphics, mounting heights, and location; and (3) possible suggestions for improvement. You do not ask everyone the questions in exactly the same way; you vary them depending on whom you are asking.

In a **formal interview**, a **standardized questionnaire** (a prepared list of questions) is presented to an interviewee at a prearranged time and place. The interviewee is prepared to answer the questions. The questionnaire can consist of all types of questions, as outlined in the following section.

The Questions You Ask

Interviews are distinctly different from social conversation. Although we may make polite conversation in interviews and ask questions in social interactions, all interviews are purposive and goal-directed. Questions are the heart of any interview. Three points determine the structure of the interview:

- Types of questions
- Phrasing of questions
- Question order

Types of Questions

There are different types of questions. Questions may be **primary** and **secondary** (see Table 6.1); or a range, from **open-ended** to **closed-ended** (as in Table 6.2); or **neutral**. Typically, the questions you ask in the information interview are neutral. For example: What is your favorite color? How much does the product cost? Where were you born?

There are also certain types of questions to avoid, including **leading** or **loaded questions** and **compound questions** as well as **tagged statements**. (See Table 6.3.)

Sometimes, the most effective type of follow-up question is not a question, but a **probe**. "A *probe* is the interviewer's prompting for further elaboration of an answer" (Zeisel, 1984). The most powerful probe is *silence*. Most people are uncomfortable with silence, so they will try to "fill" it by talking. As the interviewer, resist the inclination to talk; instead, wait for the interviewee to continue. You can increase the effectiveness of the silence with nonverbal cues such as a slight nod or an attentive, expectant facial expression and eye contact.

Table 6.1 Primary and Secondary Questions

Primary Question	Response	Secondary (Follow-Up) Question
Purpose: To introduce the topic		Purpose: To attempt to elicit further information
"How did you first get interested in surfing?"	"My parents lived by the ocean and gave me a surfboard for my fourth birthday."	"What happened then?"
"Are you satisfied with your office space?"	"No. I can't seem to get much work done."	"Why do you feel that is?"

Probes are not usually part of the list of questions. That is, they are not usually scripted. However, a novice interviewer may plan ahead and identify what kinds of probes may be necessary after certain questions. Experienced interviewers have developed a skill for using different probes "on the fly" to encourage more from the interview. There are names for different types of probes. See Table 6.4 on page 154 for a list of probes from Coopman's On-line Tutorial, *Conducting the Information Interview* (2006), along with examples to illustrate each type of probe.

The final question type that you may use is "Why?" Use of this type of question should be limited, because too many "Why?" questions may make interviewees defensive as they seek to justify a claim they have made or be-

Table 6.2 Questions Ranging from Open-Ended to Closed-Ended

Highly Open-Ended	Moderately Open-Ended	Extended Bipolar	Moderately Closed-Ended	Highly Closed-Ended
Broad, without restriction	Restricted to topic	Purpose: Requires a yes or no answer with elaboration	Asks for specific information	Predetermined list of choices of answer
"What don't you like about your kitchen?"	"How do you prepare meals?"	"Will this stove meet your needs? Why or why not?"	"How many cooks use this kitchen?"	"Is this a one-cook or two-cook kitchen?"
"What is a typical day in the office?"	"What is your role in the office?"	"Do you have enough privacy for meetings?"	"What are the qualifications for your position?"	"Would you describe your workspace as (a) excellent, (b) good, or (c) poor?"

Table 6.3 Types of Questions to Avoid

Question to Avoid	Reason	Examples
Leading Question	Implies that you expect a certain answer that can skew your findings	"Would you agree that child safety is the first priority?" "Does the office seem too small to you?" "Are you ever going to organize this place?"
Loaded Question	Implies a certain answer and an underlying negative belief	"Don't you think this color scheme seems dated?" "Are those no-good teenagers responsible for this damage?" "Do you think management is lacking leadership abilities?"
Tag Lines	Inserted at the end of a question, which tends to weaken or confuse	"You are planning to remodel your kitchen, right?" "I feel this is the right decision, don't you?" "I am going to draw it this way, okay?"
Compound, Multiple, or Double-Barreled Questions	Two or more questions combined into one question, which does not allow each question to be answered separately	"What is the best part of this job and how often do you get to do it?" "Who usually visits the museum during the day and in the evening?" "Why did you choose this location? Is it because of the view, the access to the park, or the building's historic value?"

cause such questions may frustrate them when they cannot explain why they feel a particular way. Also, if you ask too many "Why?" questions, interviewees may start to speculate or fabricate information because they may not want to admit that they don't know the answer. If you were being interviewed, how would you feel if asked these questions?

- Why have so many employees been terminated at your workplace?
- Why weren't you consulted on the color of your office?
- Why don't you like this color?

Phrasing of Questions

Carefully worded questions can motivate interviewees to answer freely, accurately, and thoughtfully. There are three factors to consider when phrasing questions: Language, Information Level, and Complexity. Use words that interviewees will understand, but don't be overly simplistic. Be specific,

Table 6.4 Probes

Type of Probe	When to Use	Examples
Nudge or Addition	To encourage interviewee to continue talking, but not in any specific direction (enhanced by nod and/or raised eyebrows)	"I see." "Go on." "Really?"
Clearinghouse	To make sure you have gotten all of the information on that topic	"Is there anything else?" "Are there questions I should have asked but didn't?" "Was there something you would like to add?"
Depth	To elicit greater detail	"What happened after you found your old guitar in the attic?" "Tell me more about your experience as a bicycle messenger in New York." "Please explain the installation process in greater detail."
Clarity	To understand the use of a particular word or phrase	"What do you mean by 'incompetent'?" "How are you defining excellence?" "Is it the hue that you don't like or the intensity of the color?"
Feelings	To explore emotions	"Why do you think you feel that way?" "What were you feeling at the time?" "Why did it make you happy?"
Focus	To get back on track when the conversation is drifting	"Let's return to your years as an editor." "You began by talking about your lack of storage space."

precise, and concrete and always take care to avoid language or terminology that will offend or insult interviewees. Do not ask questions for which interviewees do not have the information. Do not ask questions that insult interviewees' intelligence. Phrase questions so that they are simple, clear requests for limited amounts of information.

Question Order

Like speeches, interviews have an opening, a body, and a closing. As the interviewer, you want to begin the interview in a way that facilitates the interview process, ask questions that assist all parties in achieving their goals, and end the interview on a positive note.

The interview's opening, sometimes referred to as "breaking the ice," usually sets the tone for the remainder of the interview. Your goal is to establish a productive climate so both you and your interviewee will participate

Type of Probe	When to Use	Examples
Accuracy	To verify information	"Was that in 1988 or in 1998?" "How do you spell their name?" "Did you say the color was 'old' or 'bold'?"
Hypothetical	To propose something based on the interviewee's previous response	"What would you have done differently? "What advice can you offer?" "What would have been a better alternative?"
Reactive	To give the interviewee another chance to elaborate or react	"How do you explain that?" "What do you think about that?" "What is your response to that statement?"
Self-Descriptive	To find an underlying cause	"So did growing up in the South influence your choice of house?" "Was there an influential person in your life?" "What do you think happened to make you feel that way?"
Echo	An active listening technique that involves literally repeating back what was said	
Summary	Paraphrasing the response to make sure you understand it	"So what I'm hearing you say is that you like the first option." "Like you said, you need more privacy." "Let me check to see if I understand your points . . ."

freely and communicate accurately. You may want to demonstrate your knowledge of the subject matter by summarizing your research up to this point. For example, "I have read your article entitled 'Legal Assistance for Victims of Domestic Violence' and I have visited a local shelter for victims of domestic violence. I would like to ask you a few questions so I can better understand the services available."

The body of the interview is the series of questions and responses that aim to collect the information. There are different "shapes" to an interview, as described below and made visual in Figure 6.4:

- **Funnel**—Use this question sequence when the interviewee knows the topic well and feels free to talk about it, or when the person wants to express strong feelings. This is the most common of all question sequences for all types of interviews. In this sequence, the interviewer begins with broad, open-ended questions and moves to narrower,

Figure 6.4 To help you visualize which overall strategy of question order would work best for you, consider these interview structures: the Funnel, the Inverted Funnel, and the Tunnel.

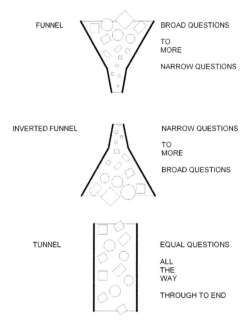

FUNNEL — BROAD QUESTIONS TO MORE NARROW QUESTIONS

INVERTED FUNNEL — NARROW QUESTIONS TO MORE BROAD QUESTIONS

TUNNEL — EQUAL QUESTIONS ALL THE WAY THROUGH TO END

closed-ended questions. The interviewer may also begin with more general questions and gradually ask more specific questions.

- **Inverted Funnel**—This question sequence is effective when an interviewee needs help remembering something or to motivate an interviewee to talk. In this sequence, the interviewer begins with narrow, closed-ended questions and moves to broader, open-ended questions. The interviewer may also begin with more specific questions and gradually ask more general questions, as the interviewee becomes more comfortable.
- **Tunnel**—In this sequence, all questions have the same degree of openness. Also called the "string of beads" questions sequence, the tunnel sequence allows for little probing and variation in question structure. It can be useful for simple interviews seeking surface-level information, but not for in-depth interviews.

According to Carter McNamara (1999), question order is essential to getting the maximum benefit. He has a few additional tips:

1. *Ask about facts before asking about controversial matters (such as feelings or beliefs).* With this approach, interviewees can more easily engage in the interview before warming up to more personal matters.
2. *Intersperse fact-based questions throughout the interview.* Long lists of fact-based questions tend to leave interviewees disengaged.
3. *Ask questions about the present before questions about the past or future.*

It's usually easier for interviewees to talk about the present and then work into the past or future, especially if the topic is a sensitive or emotional one.

Concluding and Reconstructing the Interview

Upon conclusion of the interview, your goal is to leave the interviewee feeling positive and satisfied with the interview. The interviewer is responsible for signaling the upcoming conclusion, as with "My final question . . ."

A **final summary** is a consolidation of the entire interview, and it provides a test of your listening and note-taking skills. As your conversation with the interviewee ends:

- Highlight key aspects and overall conclusions.
- Point out areas of agreement and disagreement.
- Ask the interviewee about the accuracy of your summary.
- Close your notebook, turn off the tape recorder, etc.
- If necessary, restate the confidential nature of the interview—and the purpose and use of the information.
- Be alert to other bits and pieces of information, as the interviewee may relax and relay important information as part of an informal chat.
- A sincere farewell marks the end of a post-interview discussion.

To emphasize the importance of the interview, Dr. L. Kip Wheeler, an English professor at Carson–Newman College, has this message for students (2006):

> Congratulations. You have engaged in firsthand research, and found information that may never have been recorded before in any publication. You are one step closer to becoming an authoritative writer on this topic. Other writers may end up quoting you and your publications on this matter.

There are several ways to compose a **post-interview record**. If the interview was audiotaped, you may want to type a written **transcription**. If you took notes during the interview, you may want to write out the responses in full sentences *as soon as possible* while the conversation is still fresh in your mind. You may also summarize the interview in a report using direct quotes from the interviewee or paraphrasing what the interviewee said. All of these methods correspond to a **reconstruction**. Make sure to record all of the technical information necessary to cite the interview in your working bibliography, including the proper spelling of the interviewee's name, appellations, affiliations, and the date of the interview.

Often we enter a situation without considering that something may not go as planned. Recently a client, Jorge Rodriguez, contacted an interior designer for design advice. Jorge needed to create a more supportive living environment in his home for his elderly mother. Since this interior designer had designed the client's home originally, she had all of the measurements and physical data of the existing house. Now she needed to collect information about the client's mother—her wants and needs. The designer planned to gather this information by interviewing Jorge's mother at the house.

Upon arriving at the Rodriguez home, the designer realized her plan was not going to be easily accomplished. Jorge's mother did not speak English! The designer had to have Jorge translate her questions to his mother and then translate his mother's answers to the designer. This disconnection was awkward, and the designer was unable to establish a trusting rapport between herself and the interviewee. There were topics of conversation about daily habits and lifestyle that were not easy for the woman to say, especially in front of her son. When it became apparent that an interview was not going to yield any in-depth or useful information, the designer decided that the only way to get this valuable information would be to observe the woman in her daily rituals—to see, firsthand, how she used the space and what might be lacking. The designer obtained the woman's permission to observe her over the course of one day. The story of this experience is continued in Chapter 8: "Observation." Look for the box titled "A Day in the Life. . . ."

In addition to documenting the interview, you may want to do a **post-interview assessment**. Your objective in this assessment is to evaluate the information you have just obtained for accuracy, relevance, and completeness. Can you verify the facts you have collected?

As stated earlier, it is customary to thank your interviewee with a follow-up card or a handwritten note.

Current Trends in Alternative Interviewing Techniques—Non-Verbal or Image-Based Interviews

Graphic representations were used in an interview setting back in 1921, with the Rorschach inkblot test, which evaluated the psychological interpretation of an inkblot, seeking to show the correlation between an image and the projection of the respondent's thoughts, emotions, and beliefs onto the image. During the 1940s and 1950s, the pioneer sociologist Robert Merton

Figure 6.5 In 1993, at Tomasita Elementary School, in Albuquerque, New Mexico, students were asked to draw some ideas for a new school building. Of course, there were pictures of computers, books, and furniture. Many of the students drew pictures of kids on bikes and tricycles. One of the tricycle drawings was instrumental in designing a tricycle "street" in the tot lot, equipped with center stripe and stop signs.

often used images and photos in "focused interviews" to help elicit feelings about war from war veterans, with the belief that people are sometimes moved more by an image than a word. In his book *Inquiry by Design*, John Zeisel (1984) also mentions using photos or drawings as a non-verbal probe—for example, to assist in getting a respondent to more clearly visualize something that happened in the past (such as showing a victim in a police interrogation a photo of the crime scene), or to get office workers to think more spatially about a room or an environment (for example, showing a photo of a doorway or a lock on the door). The architectural researcher Edith Cherry pioneered the concept of participant end user involvement. She writes extensively about involving end users (schoolchildren) in the design process by having them participate in creative drawing exercises to envision their ideal school. See Figure 6.5.

> The measure of the exercise is not so much in whether the ideas make their way into the final design, but did we have a good time? And did the kids feel that they had made a contribution? Did they get excited about their new school? Did we as designers form a commitment to do a good project for them? (Cherry, personal communication, June 4, 2008)

See Figure 6.6 for another gathering of participant end users.

Sorting Techniques

Edith Cherry advises you to orchestrate categories or headings to organize group interview situations. "Adults usually do not like to draw. Instead we

Figure 6.6 In this photo taken at the Girl Scout Headquarters Building in 1998, participants sat around a large table. They were shown layouts of the site and asked to draw ideas for the project.

use idea cards. Give the group a ten-minute deadline and have them put them up on the wall" (Cherry, personal communication, June 4, 2008). For projects that have multiple points of view, many different staff types, or complex issues, this kind of communal, unrestricted session is a great idea. Headings on the wall, for a school project, might include "Activities," "Operation," "Aesthetics," "Recreational," and "Educational." As school administrators, faculty, and staff fill out the cards, you can pin up the cards under the appropriate heading. Always include a category called "Other" to welcome ideas or issues that do not fall under any identified category. This activity allows user groups of all sorts to see what ideas or issues are faced by other users of the space. For a complex project such as designing a detention center, there are all kinds of staff members who may be able to provide valuable input. Workers on the night shift may face different problems than those on the day shift. The corrections officers would see things differently than would the cooks. This kind of session could help you—as well as the entire staff—examine the design challenges from multiple points of view. Figure 6.7 shows such a gathering.

Interactive Interviewing Trends: User-Generated Imagery

People tend to assign meaning to images. Therefore, designers may use images in the interview process to get interviewees to go deeper, into regions to which words cannot take us. To get a clearer picture of a client's mental images of style, a kitchen designer may ask the client to collect clippings from design magazines. The word *modern* may mean something different to a designer than it means to a client, so images tend to help clarify discrepancies in historical styles. Henry Sanoff, in his book *Visual Research Methods in Design* (1991), talks about extracting cognitive information by asking the subject to record **self-reports**. The form of these reports may be verbal, written (in a diary format), or visual (through photographs or artwork).

Figure 6.7 Programmer Edith Cherry explained, "Adults usually do not like to draw. Instead we use idea cards" (personal communication, June 4, 2008). As this photo shows, idea cards can be used instead, and displayed and sorted under various headings.

In her initial meetings with a client, Jennifer Luce spends much of the time using creative techniques to try to determine the client's needs. For Jennifer, an interview is an interactive effort in which she tries to get at the client's underlying values or needs, ones that the client may not be able to articulate. "We give our clients assignments to express themselves. This exercise immediately breaks down barriers and opens doors. . . . During this unique interview process with residential projects, we have a very important goal: to discover the deep-seated desires and personality of the client" (J. Luce, personal communication, January 3, 2008). The following excerpt is taken from a story in the *New York Times* about working with Luce's client, Greg Lemke, a scientist in La Jolla, California.

> After their first meeting, Ms. Luce asked Dr. Lemke to create a work, in any medium, that would reveal his sensibility. "The idea was to really get to know how he thinks," said Ms. Luce. As Dr. Lemke recalls it, "Jennifer auditioned me as a client."
>
> Dr. Lemke, a lover of classical music (and an amateur composer), made a tape of several of his favorite fugues, including one by Shostakovich.
>
> The fugue, Ms. Luce realized, is about variation on a theme. With a basic structure in place, the composer can go off in unexpected, sometimes even whimsical, directions.
>
> With that realization, Ms. Luce came up with the idea of building a spine down the middle of the house, as a kind of structure from which she could explore architectural variations. The spine contains storage for everything from clothes to music to Dr. Lemke's research notes. Its doors are a mosaic of weathered zinc, hot rolled steel and lacquered wood." (Bernstein, 2007)

Another example of a self-report is: the practice at many weddings of scattering disposable cameras on the tables and inviting guests to take photos. This is a good way for the wedding party to get an insight into the subjective experience of their guests. Instead of relying solely on the professional photographer to capture the day, the wedding party seeks alternative perspectives from the point of view of their guests. We can use similar techniques to gather information from our subjects, by having them photograph what is important to them about their environments.

The architect Jennifer Luce gave disposable cameras to employees of a furniture showroom and asked them to photograph what was most important or inspiring to them about the products they sold and about their work environment. She collected more than 500 photographs that included details of the furniture, views of nature, and artistic interpretations of the existing workplace. She posted many of them on a tackable wall surface in her office for a meeting with the client, the owner of the showroom, to give the client a sense of what the employees envisioned for the new showroom, as well as to provide a jumping-off point for her own ideas. "When you look at it all on the wall, all the info—there is the kernel of a really strong innovative and new idea" (J. Luce, personal communication, January 3, 2008).

An innovative, research-based design company, fathom, asks the client to bring in stacks of images that evoke feelings, wants, and needs for the facility. (This is just one of the one-on-one interview techniques that fathom uses. They also couple these interviews with ethnography [observation], photo documentation, color and sensory analysis, and interactive discovery sessions, to name a few.) The fathom interviewer asks the client-participant a series of questions to help the participant explain what the images represent to him or her. Through these probing questions, the interviewer helps the participant uncover deeper thoughts and feelings than if the interviewer had simply asked, "What does this image mean to you?"

A fathom graphic designer then manipulates and arranges the images into unique collages that reflect the client's underlying desires. Researchers then study the images, along with the participant's verbal explanation, to derive a **metaphor**. A *metaphor* is the expression of an understanding of one concept in terms of another concept, where there is some similarity or correlation between the two through the use of a poetic device—for example, "All the world's a stage." In this case, researchers seek to understand the wants and needs of the client on a deeper, subconscious level, and they strive to create a mutual understanding through a combination of symbolic words and images. Figure 6.8, parts a, b, and c, are materials prepared by fathom to help clients understand the fathom process and see the results it brings.

Practicing What You've Learned

This discussion of interviewing techniques concludes with a series of activities you can do as a "warm-up" before going out into the world. Each Activity is designed to target a step in the four-stage process: Preparation, Arranging, Conducting, and Recording. As you focus on each step in the process, you will discover that you are gaining confidence in your interviewing skills— through understanding your interviewee, using appropriate terminology, posing questions in a logical order, exhibiting a professional demeanor, and being able to elicit accurate and useful information to add to the data you are compiling for your project.

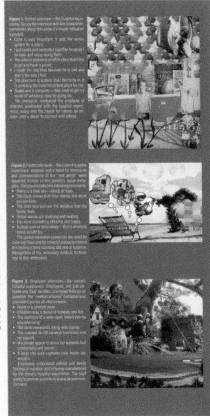

Figure 6. Proposed patient room. Design solutions were prioritized based on both patients' and families' desires for each of the key domains of Control, Energy, and Connection. All elements support the theme of transformation:
- Daybed and window seat valences; inset area carpet tile
- Sleeper lounge chair
- Separation for privacy and family area
- Table for games and dining
- Moveable work area and hidden medical gases
- All fabrics and colors more "homelike"

Figure 6.8a (above left) Brochure page from fathom explaining the ZMET process, which is used to obtain subconscious information from end users through the use and manipulation of images.

Figure 6.8b (above right) Brochure page from fathom explaining how the interview process leads to design inspiration.

Figure 6.8c (left) Proposed design solution for a patient room that incorporates end user input obtained by the ZMET process.

⊛ ACTIVITY 6.1 Seeking Out the Experts

Purpose: **To identify ideal candidates for an interview.**

1. Using a research topic from one of your classes, identify three individuals or groups who would be potential interviewees.
2. In one or two sentences, describe the ideal person or group of persons.
3. Find three individuals who fit the description. You can use the Internet or the library, or you can make use of faculty contacts, colleagues where you work, or contacts provided by fellow students. For example, if you are interested in finding out more about the airline industry, you may want to interview an airline employee such as a pilot or a flight attendant. You may be surprised at how quickly you will find that one of your coworkers or classmates knows someone in that industry.
4. Provide the name, qualifications, and contact information (phone number, mailing address, e-mail address, and/or Web site) of each person you may seek to interview.

Interviewee Name	Qualifications or Position	Contact Info

⊛ ACTIVITY 6.2 Composing the Hypothetical Interview

Purpose: **To practice putting together a questionnaire.**

1. Generate a list of five or six questions for each interviewee you listed in Activity 6.1. Apply the wording techniques and question order discussed in this chapter.
2. Break into teams of two and conduct mock interviews in class with your fellow students. Use probes during your session.
3. Record the mock interview using the note-taking and reconstruction method.
4. When you have concluded the interview, ask for feedback from your

interviewee. Did he or she feel your questions were appropriate? Can your interviewee offer any insight into improving the content or format of the questions?

ACTIVITY 6.3 Distinguishing Truth from Falsehood

Purpose: **To practice reading body language to determine whether an interviewee is being truthful.**

1. Create a list of questions regarding personal experience in the past. Examples: Have you ever been involved in a car accident? Have you ever lied to someone to get them to do something? What is your most vivid memory from elementary school? Did you use public transportation to come to school today? Or the interviewer can ask the interviewee to recount a story or an anecdote based on a suggested topic.
2. Break into teams of two and conduct informal interviews. The interviewee will attempt to answer the question with either a truth or a falsehood. The interviewer should observe the body language of the interviewee to help determine whether the interviewee is telling the truth or is lying.

ACTIVITY 6.4 The Practiced Art of Body Language

Purpose: **To practice developing neutral body language for an interview setting.**

Ask your questions in front of a mirror. This may be a difficult or emotional experience for some people. Notice your facial expressions and body language. Make adjustments so that you exhibit neutral body language yet remain engaged. You are almost ready!

Purpose: **To practice the art of setting up an interview.**

1. Contact the interviewees identified in Activity 6.1.
2. For each of those interviewees, set up an interview that would be convenient for both of you at an appropriate location.
3. Fill out the table below and provide the date/time/place scheduled for the interview.

Interviewee Name	Contact Info	Date/Time/Place of Interview

4. Armed with your list of questions that you pretested in Activity 6.2, conduct an interview with each interviewee.
5. Record your experience with each interviewee, as well as their responses.
6. Also write about your feelings during the interview—what worked and what seemed awkward.
7. Prepare to share the experience with your class.

Conclusion

As an interior designer, you are going to be expected to interview clients, users, and experts on a regular basis. It is important to become a confident interviewer. Knowing when an interview needs to take place, identifying candidates for the interview, and then convincing the potential interviewee to give you the information is the first task. The second task is to properly prepare a list of intelligent questions, meet the person in an appropriate manner, and accurately record the information. Not only will acquiring this series of skills allow you to gather usable information, it also will instill in you a sense of confidence about interacting with clients and design professionals in the future.

Look for potential interviews everywhere. If you simply talk to people whom you know, it is remarkable how quickly you'll find that a friend, a neighbor, an instructor, or a family member knows someone who may have information about your topic. For example, a student interested in airport design announced her intention in class but lamented that she didn't know anyone in that industry. Within minutes, she had a short list of potential interviewees: one student's father was a pilot (potential end user) and another student had an internship at a firm that specialized in airport design (expert).

Interviews are the perfect opportunity for meeting new people, understanding another person's perspective, establishing a professional contact, and setting the stage for a future relationship. The interviewee could serve as a jury member at your final presentation, could be a future employer, or could be a future client when you are in the professional arena.

View the interview not as an isolated event but as the beginning of a relationship. For example, the exhibit planner Alice Parman was one of the author's interviewees for her thesis project at the University of Oregon. Ms. Parman attended her final presentation and then became a reference for her first internship.

References

Bernstein, F. A. (2007, August 23). From modest to modernist. *New York Times*. Retrieved May 9, 2009 from http://www.nytimes.com/2007/08/23/garden/23luce.html

Coopman, S. J. (2006). *Conducting the information interview*. Online tutorial, San José State University. Retrieved May 9, 2009 from http://www.roguecom.com/interview

Kinsey, A. (1948–1953). *The Kinsey Reports on human sexual behavior*. New York: Signet.

McNamara, C. (1999). *General guidelines for conducting interviews*. Minneapolis: Authenticity Consulting.

Merton, R., Fiske, M., & Kendall, P. (1990). *The focused interview: A manual of problems and procedures* (2nd ed.). New York: Free Press.

Parman, A. The Big Picture: Strategic Planning and Interpretive Master Planning. Retrieved May 9, 2009, from http://www.aparman.com

Patton, M. (1990). *Qualitative evaluation and research methods*. Thousand Oaks, CA: Sage.

Ronner, H., & Jhaveri, S. (1974). *Louis I Kahn complete works 1935–1974*. Boston: Birkhäuser Basel.

Sanoff, H. (1980). *Methods of architectural programming*. New York: John Wiley.

Sanoff, H. (1991). *Visual research methods in design*. New York: John Wiley.

Wheeler, L. K. Research Assignment #3. English Department, Carson–Newman College. Retrieved April 20, 2008, from http://web.cn.edu/kwheeler/researchassignment3.html

Zeisel, J. (1984). *Inquiry by Design: Tools for environment–behaviour research*. Cambridge, England: Cambridge University Press.

7 Surveys

CHAPTER OBJECTIVES

When you complete this chapter you should be able to do the following:

- Understand the purpose, content, composition, and distribution methods of surveys using standardized questionnaires.
- Define a sample.
- Prepare a predetermined list of questions for distribution.
- Distribute a survey, record the data gathered in it, and analyze the results.
- Represent data both graphically and in written form.
- Evaluate the information collected in the survey, and incorporate the information into the body of research for your project.

KEY TERMS

Bar graph

Bias

Check-all-that-apply

Client questionnaire

Client satisfaction survey

Coding

Contingency question

Convenience sample

Demographic data

Descriptive statistics

End user questionnaire

Exhaustive

Focus group

Focus group questionnaire

Forced-choice

Inferential statistics

Interval categories

Likert Attitude Scale

Line graph

Multiple-choice question

Mutually exclusive

Nominal categories

Nonstructured question

Open-ended question

Ordinal scale

Pie chart

Popular opinion questionnaire

Population

Purposive sample

Qualifier

Qualifier question

Questionnaire

Random sample

Ranking

Ratings scale

Sample

Semantic differentials

Sentence completion question

Standardized questionnaire

Statistic

Stratified random sample

Subject

Summary statement

Survey

Target market questionnaire

User profile

Visual interpretation question

X–Y plot

In general, to **survey** means to query (someone) in order to collect data for the analysis of some aspect of a group or an area. In an even more technical sense, to survey means to do a statistical study of a sample population by asking questions about knowledge, opinions, preferences, and other aspects of people's lives. For the purposes of interior design, to survey means to reach out to people to obtain information that is essential to the programming and design process. Like interviews, surveys attempt to get information from people through the use of a list of questions—very often a written list, which is usually referred to as a **client questionnaire**. Both interviews and surveys are a type of personal report.

The difference between interviews and surveys is that you would use a survey when there are too many subjects for you to interview personally, or when you need to get the opinions of a majority of users. For example, you could interview an instructor to get the opinion of a single user, but you would need to conduct a survey in order to get the opinions of all of the faculty members at a school. You would choose to prepare and conduct a survey when your task is to turn qualitative information (opinions, feelings, and beliefs) into quantitative information (statistics). To do this, you must design a standardized questionnaire made up of questions that can turn opinions into numbers or percentages. It is not an easy task, but when it is done correctly it can yield very useful data for your project.

According to InformeDesign, a **questionnaire** is a series of topic-related questions written to help you discover subjects' opinions (Sommer & Sommer, 2002). The reasons for using a **standardized questionnaire**—an identical series of questions distributed to a group of people—are (1) to survey as many people as possible with the most timely and efficient means and then (2) to be able to turn those people's responses (raw data/qualitative data) into quantities such as percentages or majorities. This numerical statistical data has a variety of uses, but primarily it is used to form a substantial basis for future design decisions. This chapter will take you from collecting the raw data by conducting a survey to communicating the results (including guidance on representing the data through graphic or visual means such as graphs, charts, and tables). We will also explore the process of analyzing the results and the different ways of interpreting the statistical data.

Types of Questionnaires for Interior Design

As interior designers, we can survey clients to understand trends in a client base, or we can survey end users and communicate this information to clients to support or refute previously supposed theories. We can survey potential users to help determine the direction of a proposed program or a space that has not existed before. This section of the chapter explores the different audiences you might want to reach—and the tool you would design to do that.

Client (or Potential Client) Questionnaires

Interior designers can poll residential clients before a project begins, to find out their basic information, project scope, budget, goals, and such fundamental demographic information as name, address, and family size. For example, for new or potential clients living in a new development in Mexico, the interior design firm Define Design set up an online survey (see Figure 7.1) that addresses this type of information-gathering.

If the client, or the decision-making agency, is more than one person, a survey allows the individual members of the group to anonymously voice their opinions about their personal goals or priorities. The designer can then share the findings with the rest of the group as part of a quest to ascertain the priorities or establish the goals of the collective. One goal might be to uncover which key personnel the group believes the designer should interview in order to gather more in-depth information.

The exhibit planner Alice Parman calls this questionnaire her "Start-Up Agenda." For her interview process, presented in Chapter 6, she asks a series of mainly open-ended questions designed to delineate a clear agenda for the project. But for a survey, more detailed questions are needed. In her statement (on page 172) addressed to her audience directly, Alice outlines the purpose of having the whole group participate in the survey.

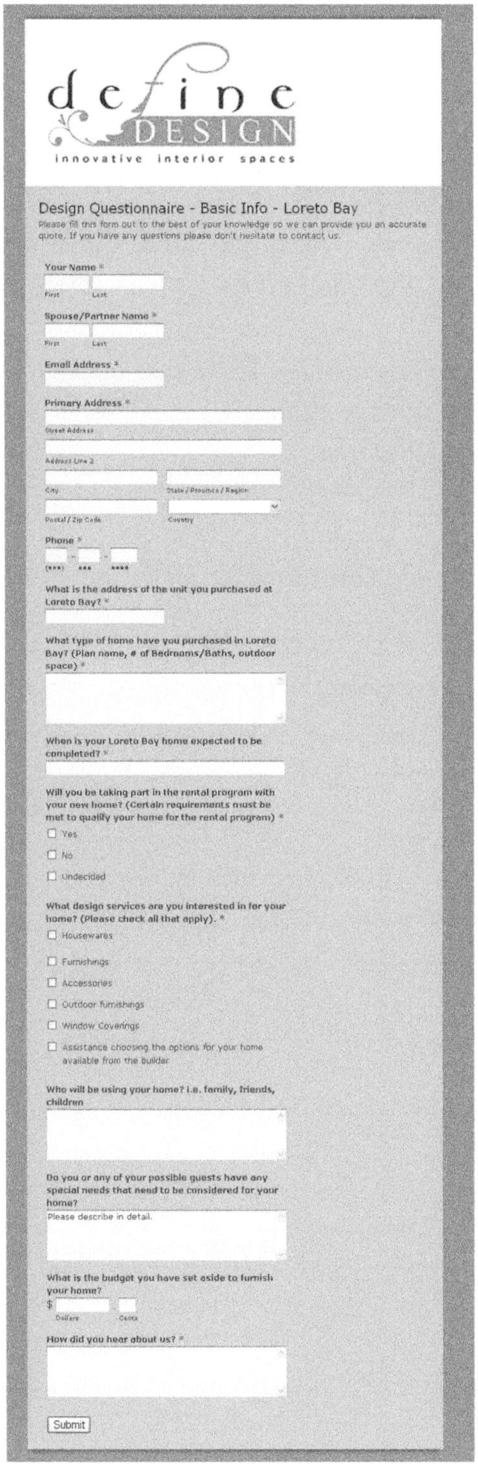

Figure 7.1 Professionals often give new clients standard questionnaires to help clarify the scope of work, the budget, and other important information. The interior design firm Define Design has set up an online survey for new or potential clients living in a new development in Mexico. Survey data is stored and used to track trends.

These concepts and values will guide me as I design and fulfill a planning process that is customized to your situation, resources, and project goals. Interpretive planning is grounded in the mission, vision, and identity of your institution. One of my most important responsibilities as a facilitator and planner is to continually advocate for actual and potential audience members. [My goal is to] create a plan that is energizing and inspiring, yet realistic and doable within the institution's capacity and your community context (Parman, 2008).

Below is a sample survey, adapted from a document titled "Exhibit Makeover Worksheets," that Alice might ask her clients to complete to help her get a design project underway.

⊙ Sample Questions for an Exhibit Makeover

MAIN FACTS

What are the juiciest, most compelling facts about our subject matter?

_____

_____

_____

What are the two or three most important facts people need to know about our subject matter?

_____

_____

_____

What are the most frequent questions people ask about our subject matter?

_____

_____

_____

The following is an example of a checklist of possible preliminary conceptual design directions for an exhibit. A survey can often be more helpful if there is a limited number of options to choose from.

---

⑨ The Museum's Community Role: *We Make a Difference*

COMMUNITY ROLE OF _____ (YOUR MUSEUM)

Review each description as it might apply to your museum today. Check the descriptions that you think best match how your community *now* views your museum. Rank order each description on a scale of 1 to 5 (1 = perfect match; 5 = not at all like us).

____Visitor attraction: The museum is the "front porch" of the community, welcoming visitors and giving them an overview of what's special and unique about this place.

____ Catalyst for change: The museum exists to deliver a message that will encourage people to think differently about their relationship to others or to the world.

____ Center of creativity: The museum engages visitors in activities where they make and do things. Visitors, rather than the museum, determine the outcomes.

____Memory bank: The museum displays aspects of the history of a place, person, cultural tradition, etc.

____Storyteller: The museum interprets the history of a place, person, cultural tradition, etc., in ways that relate the past to the present—and even to the future.

____ Attic: The museum preserves objects and images that would otherwise have been discarded.

____ Treasure trove: The museum preserves valuable, meaningful, and/or rare and unusual objects and images.

____ Shrine/hall of fame: The museum honors a particular group or individual and assumes that visitors have a built-in interest in this topic.

____ Exclusive club: Although open to the public, the museum is primarily aimed at people with special interests in and knowledge of the topic.

In order to evaluate client satisfaction, we can also set up a list of questions to be answered at the completion of a project. Usually, this list of questions is referred to as a **Client Satisfaction Survey** or *Exit Poll*. This information could be used to improve customer service or collect references for future projects.

End User Questionnaires

Are the employees of the company satisfied with their work environment? Can they offer any suggestions for improvement? An **end user questionnaire** is aimed at uncovering raw data that would support or refute any preconceived notion or theory the client has about the experience of the users of the space. This kind of questionnaire must guarantee absolute anonymity so that the respondents can answer the questions honestly and without fear that giving a negative response would affect their job security or otherwise put them at risk. Many times an end user has valuable information or feedback about the current space that would then require more in-depth study through direct observation or one-on-one interviews.

An example of an end user questionnaire used to survey faculty members for a redesign of their faculty workspace appears on the following page.

Target Market Questionnaires

A **target market questionnaire** might be used to help you identify your end user group when the group is not known. Who would most likely use your new facility? This kind of questionnaire enables you to generate a **user profile**—or to elaborate on a user profile if a vague notion of who would use the space has already been determined. For example, if your client would like to open an alternative birthing clinic, what are the characteristics of the target audience? Obviously, the target audience would be pregnant women or women who are planning to become pregnant, but how can you more fully detail your user profile in order to design a space that would cater to this user group's specific needs and closely align with their sense of aesthetics?

The first couple of questions in this type of questionnaire would be **qualifier questions**; that is, they would focus on whether the respondent fits the overall target audience. Is the respondent a woman? Is she of child-bearing age? Is she married or in a committed relationship? Is she planning to have a child or additional children? And would she consider using the alternative birthing methods your client is planning to offer at the facility?

Once the respondent's applicability is determined, the next part of the questionnaire would focus on the respondent's demographic information, such as where she lives, what her income level is, and what her cultural background may be—to give substance to the user profile. In the remainder of the questions, you would be asking about her expectations and desires for

⊛ Faculty Workspace Questionnaire

In order to develop a supportive new workspace for our school, we are interested in knowing what you, the faculty, may need in the new space in terms of storage and work area.

Please rank the following in order of priority from 1 to 5 (1 = lowest priority; 5 = highest priority). Please add comments as necessary to explain your needs more fully.

____ Individual Storage Units for Each Faculty Member
Comments: _____
_____
_____

____ Additional Computer Workstations
Comments: _____
_____
_____

____ Layout Area to Grade and Sort Student Work
Comments: _____
_____
_____

____ Informal Conversation Areas (sofa/lounge chairs)
Comments: _____
_____
_____

____ Meeting Tables
Comments: _____
_____
_____

____ Other (Is there an area of need that we have not addressed?)
Comments: _____
_____
_____

Please put this survey in the box marked FACULTY WORKROOM COMPLETED SURVEY in the mailroom by _____.

the ideal alternative birthing clinic, from functional qualities to aesthetic ones. This last kind of question may include many descriptive words (often referred to as **semantic differentials**) and images to help direct the design concepts at a later date.

Focus Group Questionnaires

If you have already identified your target market and you know the user profile, you might use a **focus group questionnaire** to gather opinions about potential users of the space, such as visitors, patrons, or customers. The group of potential users you would assemble for a group discussion is called a **focus group**. The concept of the focus group was presented in Chapter 6 with regard to interviews, because a focus group can be viewed as an in-depth interview of multiple people simultaneously. However, if you wanted to quantify the responses in order to draw a conclusion based on multiple interviews, this process may fall into the survey category.

Popular Opinion Questionnaires

Sometimes it is necessary to get a sense of what people think about a proposal or an existing condition, even if these people will not be clients or end users of a space. These people are neighbors, or anyone else who could be affected by the proposed design—including those people who may perceive your project as competition. Acknowledging and understanding the opposition to your project may be just as important to the project's success as rallying those who favor the project. This group may also include those who have expert opinions that could help improve your design. Expanding on the example of the alternative birthing clinic, respondents to a **popular opinion questionnaire** may include midwives at other alternative birthing clinics or doctors who favor traditional medical practices (so that you can at least understand the concerns of a divergent opinion). Questions in this type of survey include qualifiers that establish the person's education level or areas of expertise, followed by opinion questions. Sometimes, incorporating these people into the planning process will open doors that seem to have been closed, or it will establish a dialog that will allow your project to proceed more easily.

Questionnaire Design and Distribution Methods (The Act of Surveying)

The graphic layout of a questionnaire is very important. The questionnaire should not appear long, intimidating, or confusing. It should be clear, concise, and inviting to the respondent. Several items must be stated clearly at the outset: (1) why people are being surveyed, (2) how long the questionnaire should take to complete, (3) instructions on how to fill out the questions (with pencil or pen), and (4) what to do with the completed questionnaire.

You might offer incentives for completing the survey, such as a coupon for a free coffee or snack, or a gift certificate, or the promise to be entered into a raffle for a prize. Professional survey companies often have respondents earn points for completing surveys.

A questionnaire can be written, oral (the researcher can ask the respondent the questions and record the respondent's answers), or electronic (distributed via the Internet or through e-mail). Written surveys can be mailed to the respondents, or distributed via mailboxes at work, or they can be left in a public area along with a drop box for returning completed surveys. It is important to get permission when distributing a survey in this last manner. You cannot simply go into a classroom or wait outside a business without securing permission. In fact, it is important to understand the difference between private property and public spaces. While free speech is protected under the U.S. Constitution, interfering with business could be a complicated issue; so it is important to obtain written permission from the businesses you may affect when you're attempting to collect information from subjects in a survey.

The most popular and promising method of distribution is through the Internet. Web sites such as SurveyMonkey.com and Wufoo.com offer students a way to customize a questionnaire and distribute it to a list of e-mail addresses. The respondents are assured anonymity and can respond at their own convenience. The limitation to this method is that you can collect data only from persons who have an e-mail address or access to a computer.

How can you reach your intended audience? Distributing or conducting a survey involves a certain degree of salesmanship and optimism, as well as an abundance of energy and courage. Doing a survey in person requires a great deal of time and legwork. For example, if you are trying to collect information about shopping habits in a grocery store, you may need to stand outside as people are entering or exiting in order to ask your questions. If you are planning to survey students in the student lounge, you must prepare a sign and a drop box and plan to be there to answer questions when the lounge is full of students.

It is often difficult to overcome people's suspicions about how you are going to use their information. So you must establish a rapport with your survey subjects. Whether by speaking to potential subjects personally or by writing a clear and compelling introduction to the survey, you need to (1) establish that you are a student, (2) assure their anonymity and confidentiality, and (3) pinpoint your project goals.

Sampling—Establishing a Sample

Population includes all the members of a particular group of individuals that you have decided to study or to describe. It is usually very difficult or impossible to study an entire population (Fraenkel, Wallen, & Sawin, 1999). Consider these examples of *entire* populations:

- All persons who have a family member who has been diagnosed with autism
- All women who are experiencing or have experienced infertility
- All preteens in the United States who play video games
- All teachers, staff, and students of a particular school
- All persons who live or work in a certain part of town

A **sample** is a subgroup of a population that is thought or meant to be representative of the population (Fraenkel et al., 1999). An individual member of the sample group would be called a **subject** or respondent.

The most common method of selecting a sample group of subjects is a **random sample**: selecting people by chance. The idea is that each member of the population has an equal probability of being selected, which reduces the likelihood of a sample being biased (Fraenkel et al., 1999). This is depicted in Figure 7.2a.

You could use the questionnaire as a standardized list of questions and personally survey your sample group. If you stood outside a grocery store to conduct your survey, your sample population would be any shoppers who might stop to answer a few questions. This would be called a **convenience sample**, because the subjects were chosen based on the fact that they were the closest to you or easiest to gather. (See Figure 7.2b.) If you approached only those people who looked to you as though they bought a lot of groceries or bought a certain item, you would obtain a **purposive sample**; that means the subjects were selected deliberately and therefore may not reflect the characteristics of the population as a whole (Fraenkel et al., 1999).

Whether you choose a convenience sample or a random sample (as in Figure 7.2c) or a **stratified random sample** (this last type is a sample adjusted

Figure 7.2 Illustrated in the group on the left, the population is all of the children in a playground (30 children). A sample would be a few selected at random (six children) who would represent all of the children. The group in the middle illustrates a convenience sample of the six children selected who are nearest to the researcher. In the group on the right, a random sample would be six children selected from various locations around the playground.

for percentages), your goal is to reduce or minimize **bias** (a systematic mistake based on prejudice) and to represent the entire population as accurately as possible, identifying and adjusting for variables. (Recall the discussion of variables in Chapter 3.)

Types of Questions

Survey question types should be mostly closed-ended, because a large number of people are being consulted and it is easier to quantify information that has a limited number of choices. You must know *exactly* what you are trying to find out and what your goals for the questionnaire are, so that you ask questions that are specific and you quickly get to the point of what you are trying to accomplish. You may want to use different types of questions to verify an answer. Asking a question in more than one way will help limit the chance that your results will be skewed because your audience was confused by a particular question. Your questionnaire not only needs to present your questions, it needs to identify the characteristics of the subject so that you can more easily see whether you are reaching your end user or target market. To achieve this, make sure you integrate the following kinds of identifying questions in your questionnaire.

Qualifiers are questions that test whether the respondent fits a list of certain predetermined qualifications. You may want to ask these questions upfront, because they will determine whether the respondent fits the user profile of the population. You'll need to collect simple **demographic data**—such as age, gender, education level, occupation, and mobility/ability levels—that would qualify the subject as a member of your defined population. These human characteristics help you to build a demographic profile, which is a collection of attributes assigned to a particular population. Qualifiers can also be questions about the person's lifestyle, habits, and preferences. For example, if you are looking for people who frequent hair salons more than once a month, you may have to compose two questions: one that asks whether respondents have ever been to a salon, then a follow-up question regarding intervals of frequency—less than once a month, once a month, and more than once a month.

Open-ended or **nonstructured questions** should be used only (1) when the sample population is small or (2) as a follow-up to a series of closed-ended questions as an opportunity to gather clarification for answers. It is generally too difficult to translate the many answers generated by open-ended questions into statistics that would identify trends. Imagine tallying election results if all the candidates were write-ins!

For initial information-gathering, you may not know enough about the subject to develop other types of questions, so a preliminary survey may include only open-ended questions. Interior design student Jennifer Kautz was interested in gathering general information on a sensitive subject: people's experience with contemporary funeral services in the United States. In order to accommodate a variety of possible answers, Jennifer put together the following questionnaire. Notice how the questions are subdivided, and how the intent of the questions is stated to help ensure clarity.

The results of this open-ended questionnaire identified many issues, including the respondents' desire to participate more in preparing the body for burial, their desire for funerals to be more spiritual and earthly than religious and formal, and the surprising number of respondents who wished to be cremated rather than buried. Responses to questions 7 through 9 allowed the student to project what the funeral of the future would look like, and the responses influenced her decision to create a more sustainable and earth-friendly project situated in a nondenominational, parklike setting.

ⓠ Sample Open-Ended Question Survey

(Kautz, personal communication, 2008)

For questions 1 through 3, I would like for you to consider what you know and have experienced for funerary services in general.

1. In your experience, what has been the most helpful aspect of funerary services in dealing with your grief over the loss of a loved one?
2. What has been the least helpful aspect?
3. If you could change anything about the funeral service industry, what would it be?

Questions 4 through 6 are more specific to one particular loss that has affected you.

1. What was your relation to the deceased?
2. What kind of ceremony, if any, accompanied the funeral services?
3. Did you participate in the ceremony? If so, in what capacity did you participate?

Lastly, in questions 7 through 9, I would like to know what you might have considered for your own funeral arrangements.

1. Would you prefer cremation, burial, or some other way of caring for your remains at the end of your life?
2. What kind of services and/or ceremonies would you like for your own funeral? Why?
3. Is there a special place you would prefer to have your remains scattered, buried, enclosed, or memorialized? If so, where and why?

Multiple-choice questions can come in two varieties: **forced-choice** and **check-all-that-apply**. When giving a person a multiple-choice question with only one response required, you want to make sure that the categories are **mutually exclusive**—that is, that your categories do not overlap. This can be a simple yes/no question. Or it can have different categories, as in age ranges. For example, the age categories "under 11, 11 to 20, 21 to 40, 41 and over" are mutually exclusive (Zeisel, 1984, p. 164). Determining how to partition responses into groups is called **coding** (Zeisel, p. 164). There is an art to dividing up possible answers, as there are several different types of data: nominal, interval, and ordinal.

Nominal categories are different possible answers based on *names* of things, such as kinds of furniture (*chair, table,* or *desk*); or *descriptive* words, such as *curved, active,* or *busy*; or *adjectives* to describe the way a space feels, such as *intimidating, powerful,* or *comforting*. If you wanted to know the types of activities that a person does in a room, you could generate a list for the respondent to choose from, such as "Sleep, Eat, Study, Entertain, Relax, Play, Work. . . ." When a question is a list, you want to make sure it is **exhaustive**—which means that you have listed all of the possible responses. This mistake is often found in questionnaires developed by students. If respondents can think of another option as a response to a question, they may become annoyed or frustrated. In addition, your data will not be accurate. To make an incomplete list exhaustive, researchers add an "Other" category (Zeisel, 1984, p. 164).

Interval categories involve numbers, such as the example of age ranges used above. Some additional examples are number of hours, size of office, or ranges in income level. Usually the items are divided into increments that make sense to the user.

When you want responses that indicate frequency, intensity of feeling, or degree to which respondents agree or disagree with a statement, you will want to use a **ratings scale**. Usually the question type involves creating categories along an **ordinal scale**—a ranking of measurement that ranges from "low to high," "least to most," or "agree to disagree." A typical example is the **Likert Attitude Scale**. This is a widely used scale in which respondents are given a list of statements and asked whether they "strongly agree," "agree," are "undecided," are "neutral," "disagree," or "strongly disagree." These are used to measure attitudes (Fraenkel et al., 1999). It is a good idea to group all of these questions together under a single heading so that the respondent becomes familiar with the scale and can move more quickly through the questions (Zeisel, 1984). Should there be an odd number of divisions or an even number of divisions? An odd number of divisions gives a "neutral" center value, while an even number of divisions forces respondents to take a non-neutral position.

Another type of question that uses an ordinal scale is **ranking** in order of importance or priority. These types of questions are often difficult to answer.

Example: Rank in order of importance the following aspects of your work environment:

_____ Privacy

_____ Storage

_____ Low Noise Level

_____ View

_____ Temperature

_____ Work Surface

To make ranking questions conceptually easier, you could vary them by, for example, allocating a percentage or a fixed amount to each category.

Example: What percentage of your total budget do you envision spending on each of the following kitchen components? Must total 100 percent.

_____ Cabinets

_____ Appliances

_____ Flooring

_____ Countertops

_____ Backsplash

_____ Fixtures/Hardware

Another variation would be to have respondents select the top three categories that correspond with their priorities. It may be less intimidating to the respondent to just choose a few items from the list.

Sentence completion questions are open-ended questions that give the respondent an opportunity to answer in a creative way. These questions can be used judiciously to spark a different kind of response that might influence your design immensely. Or they can be used as a fun, light-hearted way to establish a rapport with an unknown respondent—to humanize the anonymous responses.

Examples:

If I could be someone famous for a day, I would be _____.

My biggest guilty pleasure is _____.

If I were a cartoon character, I would be _____.

If I were a box of cereal, I would be _____.

The thing most people don't know about me is _____.

When I was young, _____.

If I won a million dollars, I would _____.

My greatest fear is _____.

Visual interpretation questions allow respondents to respond to an image (a photograph, drawing, or diagram) or to compare a series of photographs.

For example, one student wanted to explore what types of space were most conducive to studying. Using her knowledge of environmental psychology, she selected photos of spaces, each with one variable: size of room, ceiling height, amount of sunlight. She posed questions that had a choice of three photographs each, and she asked the respondent to select the photograph whose content was most conducive to studying. She then increased the complexity by showing photographs of furniture pieces and asking which would accommodate the respondent's needs for studying. She found that most students preferred to use a bed rather than a chair or a desk for studying.

You may find yourself using all of these question types in your survey. For example, see Figure 7.3. You can explore an issue through a series of questions or overlapping questions to test the same concept.

There are, of course, some question types that you probably should avoid. The first type is simply *weak questions*. For example, "What is your favorite

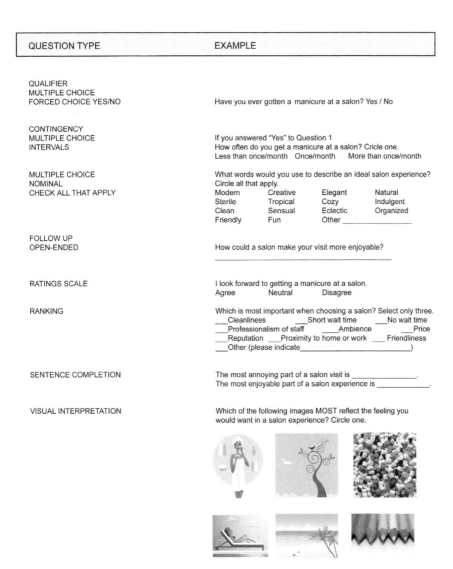

Figure 7.3 The sample survey uses a variety of question types.

color?" is a weak question because there are too many ways to interpret or apply the question. It is not specific enough to yield a valid answer. Are you asking a person about her favorite color for a wall in an office or her favorite color for a cocktail dress? This example illustrates an important part of composing a survey: Specificity! Answers would differ depending on the context and the object that is to be colored.

Another type of question to avoid is one that *assumes there is a universal meaning to subjective words,* like design terms and adjectives. A good example would be the use of the word *comfortable* in a question. For some people, a "comfortable" space is open, free of clutter, streamlined. Other people would describe "comfortable" as plush, cozy, and full of personal items.

You may not be able to use answers that come from *questions about general likes and dislikes.* Questions like "Do you like your job; why or why not?" and "Do you like to drink wine?" leave too much room for misinterpretation, because they combine feeling, thoughts, beliefs, and actions. Rework these questions to ask about *behavior.* For example, you can ask, "Do you drink wine?" followed by a **contingency question** about how often or in what situations the respondent drinks wine. Then you can ask specifically about a feeling or belief about alcohol consumption.

The final question type to avoid is *questions that make assumptions* or lead respondents to take an obvious side on an issue. An example would be "Wouldn't you recycle more often if bins were provided in the cafeteria?" Who would answer "no" to that kind of question?

Pretesting Your Questionnaire

Once you've completed the first draft of your questionnaire, it is advisable to test the questionnaire (1) for the length of time it takes to complete and (2) for clarity. "Make a few copies of your first-draft questionnaire, and then ask at least three readers to complete it. Time them as they respond. . . . Discuss with them any confusion or problems they experience" (Axelrod & Cooper, 2008, p. 699).

Consider assembling a focus group just for the purpose of pretesting the questionnaire. Did you get the kind of responses you were seeking? Did the group misunderstand any of the questions? Review the group's answers with them to determine whether the intent of each question was clear. Keep in mind that you may have to revise the wording of a question, the order of the questions, or the type of question. You may have to add further instructions. For example, a questionnaire recently distributed at a school failed to tell respondents what to do with the survey after they completed it! Believe it or not, this kind of error occurs quite often because the researcher is so caught up in the content that simple logistical tactics often go overlooked.

Analyzing the Data

It is important to keep careful records of your survey data. Most researchers recommend using a computer spreadsheet to help you sort and organize the data. Your questionnaire doesn't do you any good if you can't draw new conclusions from the data. After the survey is completed and the data collected, you'll need to assemble the results in some usable format that allows comparison within the subject group, between groups, or both.

Statistics

Drawing conclusions depends on your interpretation of statistics. A **statistic** is a numerical characteristic of the sample that measures relationships, such as percentages, averages, and tendencies. "**Descriptive statistics** refers to a variety of methods that are used to simplify, summarize, organize, and identify relationships among quantitative data and sometimes to visually display such data" (Fraenkel et al., 1999, p. 20). As William Trochim (2006) explains, **inferential statistics** are used "to reach conclusions that extend beyond the immediate data alone." He continues:

> For instance, we use inferential statistics to try to infer from the sample data what the population might think. Or, we use inferential statistics to make judgments of the probability that an observed difference between groups is a dependable one or one that might have happened by chance in this study. Thus, we use inferential statistics to make inferences from our data to more general conditions; we use descriptive statistics simply to describe what's going on in our data (Trochim, 2006).

Summary Statements

The way that interior designers most often summarize their survey results is in a text format called a **Summary Statement**. A typical Summary Statement might be "Survey results showed the majority of workers ranked personal storage space as their highest priority and lounge seating as the lowest priority." When you prepare a Summary Statement, be specific, and acknowledge inherent weakness in your findings, if necessary. Let readers draw their own conclusions about the possible causes, or let them at the very least remain neutral about the possible cause or solution at this point. Another sample Summary Statement might be "Out of 250 faculty, only 36 responded to the online survey. Of those surveyed, only 3 people, less than 10 percent, were satisfied with their workspace. One could infer that the remaining staff members were satisfied, but the few who were asked informally why they didn't take the online survey most often said they were just too busy."

The following Summary Statement was made by an interior designer to the administration of a school. The statement summarized the findings of an informal survey that had been distributed via faculty mailboxes at the school. The questionnaire presented a list of areas of concern, and the faculty members were asked (1) to rank the areas in order of priority to them and (2) to make suggestions for improving the faculty workspace. Included in the designer's report was a floor plan that served to reflect, graphically and spatially, the findings of the survey. This floor plan was not intended to be the final design; rather, it was included to provide clarity in terms of physical relationships, quantities, lengths, constraints of the space, and clearances. (The floor plan is reproduced in Figure 7.4.)

A Sample Summary Statement

I received 35 feedback forms in my mailbox out of 60 possible respondents, which represents 58 percent of the total user population. Below is a summary of their comments listed in order of priority from highest to lowest.

AREA OF CONCERN: INDIVIDUAL STORAGE UNITS FOR EACH FACULTY MEMBER

This was the highest priority. But there seemed to be a variety of storage needs that would be supported by a combination of lockers, flat files, and locked shelving, as well as file cabinets. Tall faculty members were worried that they would be assigned to a drawer that would be too low for them. I was inspired by the way the faculty mailroom is set up with flat files below and shelving at eye height. In the scheme provided, a faculty member could elect to have a combination of locker, flat file, and shelving. Interior design faculty members wanted there to be desk-height table space near the lockers on which to lay stuff down as they load or unload their binders. Also, to make sure that all of the aisles are accessible, there was concern for a minimum width. This has been adjusted in the new plan. (Note how this is represented in Figure 7.4.)

AREA OF CONCERN: ADDITIONAL COMPUTER WORKSTATIONS

The additional computer workstations were the next highest priority. Faculty seemed to like the placement of the computers near the door so they could look through the glass to see if there were any computers available. Many faculty members only make use of the room when they need to use a computer. Faculty requested that wi-fi be available at all times. They also wanted to see an additional photocopy machine with paper storage placed near the printer, which was not originally thought of as an area of concern.

AREA OF CONCERN: LAYOUT AREA TO GRADE AND SORT STUDENT WORK

Most faculty grade the work in the classrooms, but they valued a work surface for other work. I provided a few mobile tables that can be used, as well as additional workspace at each computer for paper/book/project layout. The current computer carrels do not provide any clear desk space adjacent to the computer. One faculty member was vehemently opposed to sharing workspace with any other faculty member. I think this has to be addressed in order for the room to work.

AREA OF CONCERN: INFORMAL CONVERSATION AREAS

Although this was not high-priority, most faculty agreed that a place to sit and relax was a good idea, especially because there is no nurse's office. There was a suggestion for more than two comfortable lounge chairs (I have provided four) and for increasing the length of the sofa (instead of a love seat), so that two people would feel more comfortable sitting there, or someone could lie down if they had a headache.

AREA OF CONCERN: MEETING TABLES

This was also not high-priority, but it could serve as an informal meeting space or additional layout space. Someone suggested meeting with students there, but it is my understanding that this room is just for faculty.

The following floor plan (Figure 7.4) provides a visual representation of the areas described above.

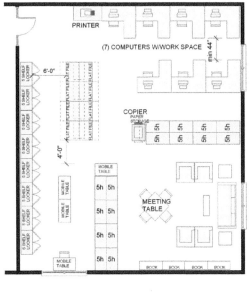

Figure 7.4 Sometimes an analysis of data includes a graphic representation such as a floor plan. This is not necessarily a final design, but it helps explain the data gathered and the conclusions drawn from the written survey.

STORAGE

DESK HEIGHT WORK SURFACE

SEATING

Use **line graphs** (as in Figure 7.5) to track changes over short and long periods of time. When smaller changes exist, line graphs are better to use than bar graphs. Line graphs can also be used to compare changes over the same period of time for more than one group.

Pie charts (as in Figure 7.6) do not show changes over time. Instead, use pie charts when you are trying to compare parts of a whole.

Use **bar graphs** (as in Figure 7.7) to compare items across different groups or to track changes over time. However, when you're trying to measure changes over time, bar graphs are best used when changes are larger.

Use **X–Y plots** (visually very similar to line graphs) to determine relationships between two different things. The *x*-axis is used to measure one event (or variable), and the *y*-axis is used to measure the other. If both variables increase at the same time, the variables have a positive relationship or correlation. If one variable increases while the other decreases, the variables are said to have a negative relationship. Sometimes the variables follow no pattern and are said to be unrelated. Note: Be cautious about assuming that a correlation is a causal relationship. That is, just because two variables have a relationship

Figure 7.5 (below left) Learning Line Graphs

Figure 7.6 (below right) Perfecting Pie Charts

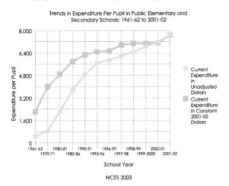

LEARNING LINE GRAPHS

Line graphs can be used to show how something changes over time. Line graphs are good for plotting data that has peaks (ups) and valleys (downs), or that was collected in a short time period. The following pages describe the different parts of a line graph.

Trends in Expenditure Per Pupil in Public Elementary and Secondary Schools: 1961-62 to 2001-02

NCES 2003

THE TITLE

The title offers a short explanation of what is in your graph. This helps the reader identify what they are about to look at. It can be creative or simple as long as it tells what is in the graph. The title of this graph tells the reader that the graph contains information about the changes in money spent on students of elementary and secondary schools from 1961 to 2002.

THE LEGEND

The legend tells what each line represents. Just like on a map, the legend helps the reader understand what they are looking at. This legend tells us that the green line represents the actual dollar amount spent on each child and the purple line represents the amount spent when adjusted for inflation.

THE SOURCE

The source explains where you found the information that is in your graph. It is important to give credit to those who collected your data! In this graph, the source tells us that we found our information from NCES.

CREATE A GRAPH TUTORIAL | 9

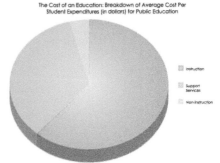

PERFECTING PIE CHARTS

Pie charts can be used to show percentages of a whole, and represents percentages at a set point in time. Unlike bar graphs and line graphs, pie charts do not show changes over time. The following pages describe the different parts of a pie chart.

The Cost of an Education: Breakdown of Average Cost Per Student Expenditures (in dollars) for Public Education

NCES Common Core Data (CCD) 2002-03

THE TITLE

The title offers a short explanation of what is in your graph. This helps the reader identify what they are about to look at. It can be creative or simple as long as it tells what is in the chart. The title of this chart tells the reader that the graph contains information about how money is spent for public education for the average student.

THE LEGEND

The legend tells what each slice represents. Just like on a map, the legend helps the reader understand what they are looking at. This legend tells us that the green slice represents money spent on instruction, the blue slice represents money spent on support services, and the orange slice represents money spent on non-instruction activities.

THE SOURCE

The source explains where you found the information that is in your graph. It is important to give credit to those who collected your data! In this graph, the source tells us that we found our information from the NCES Common Core of Data.

CREATE A GRAPH TUTORIAL | 11

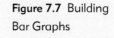
Figure 7.7 Building Bar Graphs

BUILDING BAR GRAPHS

Bar graphs can be used to show how something changes over time or to compare different times. Bar graphs are good for plotting data that spans many years (or days, weeks . . .), has really big changes from year to year (or day to day . . .), or they can be used for comparing different items in a related category (for example: comparing something between different states). The following pages describe the different parts of a bar graph.

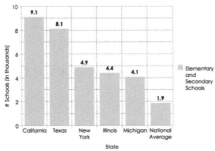

Top 5 States with the Most Elementray and Secondary Schools

NCES Common Core of Data (CCD) 2002-03

THE TITLE

The title offers a short explanation of what is in your graph. This helps the reader identify what they are about to look at. It can be creative or simple as long as it tells what is in the graph. The title of this graph tells the reader that the graph contains information about the states with the most elementary and secondary schools, and how many schools each of those states has.

THE LEGEND

The legend tells us what each bar represents. Just like on a map, the legend helps the reader understand what they are looking at. This legend tells us that the blue bars represent elementary and secondary schools. If a graph has more than one color bar, the legend will have more than one entry.

CREATE A GRAPH TUTORIAL | 6

with each other, one variable did not necessarily cause the other. Simply because the age of the respondent had a positive correlation to the income level of the respondent, do not conclude that aging *causes* income level to rise. The data indicated only that these two characteristics were related in *some* way.

Consider using graphs, charts, tables, and other graphical materials to help you organize and summarize your data. Visuals can be very compelling and informative when properly done. To help you build a graph, explore online tools such as the one available at the National Center for Education Statistics (NCES) Web site: http://nces.ed.gov/nceskids/createagraph.

Practicing What You've Learned

This chapter concludes with several Activities to prepare you to translate survey data into a usable representation for presenting to your instructor and the public. Once you get used to the basics of tabulating and representing data, you can be more innovative.

⊕ ACTIVITY 7.1 Compose a Simple Survey

Purpose: **To practice writing simple questions that target specific types of data collection.**

In this Activity, you will design a questionnaire to collect data for a cafeteria design for a school. The task is to query students who go to school (anticipant end users) for the purpose of understanding which cafeteria amenities are used most, liked most, used least, and liked least. Use the table below to compose a simple survey of nine questions. The first two questions should be qualifier questions. The remaining questions should range from broad to specific, investigating the respondent's interaction with each type of existing cafeteria furniture, fixtures, and equipment (FF&E), and helping you gather innovative ideas for future cafeteria FF&E as well as ideas for a supportive layout.

Question type	Purpose	Write your questions here:
Qualifier	To determine the age or education level of the respondent	
Qualifier	To determine the respondent's experience with cafeterias	
Open-Ended	To determine cafeteria behavior or preferences	
Multiple-Choice	To determine behavior or preferences	
Ranking/Scale	To determine preferences	

Question type	Purpose	Write your questions here:
Sentence Completion	To collect innovative ideas	
Visual Interpretation	To find deeply rooted or subconscious desires	
Other	To collect additional data	
Other	To collect additional data	

ACTIVITY 7.2 Conducting a Simple Survey

Purpose: **To implement a survey. To collect and record sample data.**

Obtain permission from a local school to survey the students. Distribute the survey that you composed in Activity 7.1 to a sample of children on the school playground. Provide them with instructions on how to fill out the form and what to do with it when completed. Provide incentives, such as candy or stickers, and see if you can motivate the children to respond freely and honestly.

Purpose: **To graphically represent data collected from administering a simple survey.**

Tabulate the answers to the survey from Activity 7.2. Turn each finding into a number. Represent your findings using a line graph, pie chart, or bar graph. Then try to represent your data in an innovative way, such as a 3-D model or a drawing. The more creative, the better. Present your survey results to the class.

Conclusion

When there are too many people for you to be able to interview each one personally, or when you need to convert the opinions of many people into a quantity or a statistic, surveys are an effective way to collect that information. In the interview process (covered in Chapter 6), you gather introductory information that can help you create a survey. In a survey, you're trying to accomplish only a few focused goals or trying to get an answer to a very specific question. The interview helps you to understand what your question is, then your survey targets getting that question answered.

A survey can be designed just like any other creative task. For example, Chapter 6 concluded with a story about one designer's interview with an elderly Mexican woman (see the section titled "An Unexpected Twist"). The designer could take the information she gathered from that one-on-one experience and apply it to a larger or community-based project, such as an assisted-living facility for single, elderly, Mexican women. How would you go about getting responses from one hundred potential end users? The interview experience described in Chapter 6 showed that sometimes there may be a language barrier, which enables you to set up a survey with an awareness that you did not have before. Perhaps the questions would be written in Spanish, or given verbally, or visually rather than textual. As you'll see in Chapter 8, sometimes your survey must be immediately followed up with direct observation, as people's actions often speak louder than their words.

References

Axelrod, R. B., & Cooper, C. R. (2008). *The St. Martin's guide to writing* (8th ed.). Boston: Bedford/St. Martin's.

Fraenkel, J., Wallen, N., & Sawin, E. I. (1999). *Visual statistics: A conceptual primer*. Needham Heights, MA: Allyn & Bacon.

National Center for Education Statistics (NCES). (2008). *Graphing tutorial*. U.S. Department of Education. Retrieved June 2008 from http://nces.ed.gov/nceskids/createagraph/default. aspx

Parman, A. (2008). *Museum consultant and organizational coach*. Retrieved from www.aparman. com/

Sommer R., & Sommer, B. (2002). *A practical guide to behavioral research tools and techniques* (5th ed.). New York: Oxford University Press.

Trochim, W. M. K. (2006). *Research methods knowledge base*. Retrieved May 2008 from http://www.socialresearchmethods.net/kb/statinf.php

Wheeler, L. K. (2008). *Research assignment #3*. English Department, Carson–Newman College. Retrieved April 2008 from http://web.cn.edu/kwheeler/researchassignment3.html

Zeisel, J. (1984). *Inquiry by design: Tools for environment-behavior research*. Cambridge: Cambridge University Press.

8 Observation

When you complete this chapter you should be able to do the following:

- Understand the importance of observation in the information-gathering process for design.
- Be aware of the varying types of observation techniques.
- Choose and employ the appropriate observation techniques for your project.
- Evaluate the information collected and incorporate it into the body of research for your project.

KEY TERMS

Accretion traces

Anonymous observer

Artifacts

Behavioral mapping

Case study

Casual observation

Codify

Control group

Cultural milieu

Data sheets

Environment-Behavior

Erosion traces

Ethnography

Experiments

Extraneous variables

Genius loci

Hidden Observer

Historic precedent

Hypothesis

Identified Observer

Mental mapping

Observation

Paradigmatic case

Participant observation

Person-centered mapping

Place-centered mapping

Precedent study

Proposal study

Scientific method

Self-reports

Shadowing

Simulation

Systematic observation

Trace observation

Visual notation

> Once you understand the elements which seem almost mundane, they become the building blocks, the basis for understanding. Without a foundation of information, you don't have the right to create something new (J. Luce, personal communication, January 3, 2008).

As we have seen, a design project does not begin with a design. It begins with data collection and analysis, which can be creative endeavors as well—not separate from the design process, but an integral part. As the award-winning architect and designer Jennifer Luce observed, "I once took a seminar in landscape design in which students spent the first week measuring things: the width of a street, height of a tree, the number of people that cross the street in one hour. It was put on by a company called West 8 in Rotterdam, the Netherlands (http://www.west8.nl). I asked myself, 'What is this method, this process, going to do for the student?' Basically, it lays the cards on the table. Once you understand the elements which seem almost mundane, they become the building blocks, the basis for understanding. Without a foundation of information, you don't have the right to create something new" (J. Luce, personal communication, January 3, 2008).

We are constantly gathering information about our environment. When you take a dog for a walk, for example, he uses his senses of smell, touch, sight, and hearing to gather important information about his environment. This is also true of humans. As a child, you may know your grandmother's kitchen from the smell of cookies baking or you might know your school by the color and texture of the brick. For people with limited vision, the senses of hearing, touch, and smell are elevated. To locate a bus stop, these people may rely on the sound of the traffic, the texture of the pavement, and the smell of exhaust.

Gathering Evidence: Past and Present

Like a dog sniffing to see who has passed, we use our senses to obtain information about the current situation as well as events that may have happened in the past. This chapter will focus on **observation**: the use of one or more of the senses to obtain and record information on individuals, objects, or events, as a method of gathering information for interior design (Fraenkel, Wallen, & Sawin, 1999). As suggested in Table 2.2 in Chapter 2, observation is a broad category containing anthropological studies (observation of people and their behaviors) as well as observations of the physical world. In interior design, **Environment-Behavior** research is one way to study how people interact with their environment. We can observe people casually, using journaling or informal people-watching; we can systematize our observation, using **behavioral mapping** or **shadowing** techniques; we can construct models or prototypes that create **simulations** of reality; we can go further by setting up controlled environments to conduct **experiments** to observe how people act under given conditions.

For the purpose of interior design, there is much information that is *essential* to our understanding that we can gather *only* by directly observing the existing environment (Site Analysis—to be explored in depth in Chapter 11) and the activity of the end users (Environment-Behavior). In addition, it is important to examine previously completed projects that are similar in scope, program, or project type (case studies).

Types of Observation

Casual Observation

Casual observation may be a chance occurrence in which something in the environment catches your attention and warrants further investigation. For

Figure 8.1 "Types of Observation" Matrix

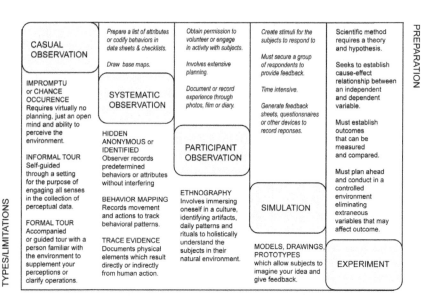

example, you may notice that the entrance to a supermarket seems to conflict with vehicular traffic in the parking lot, or that the entrance to an emergency room is particularly hard to find. (See Figure 8.1.)

Casual observation could also take the form of an informal or formal tour of a space. If you are taken on a guided tour, the behaviors you see may be modified because the subjects know that they are being watched. An informal tour would be one that is self-guided and as unobtrusive as possible. The purpose of your observations on an information-gathering tour would be to get a firsthand, direct experience of the space and subjects in question. Pay attention to your senses of sight, sound, smell, and touch (for this last one, think of textures, temperature, etc.). You can even incorporate the fifth sense, taste, in your observations, when appropriate. (Consider the taste of local cuisine or the taste of the back of a postage stamp!) Because taste often depends on smell, it can be very relevant, for example, in cafeteria design for a health care site. Or envision the difference between (1) providing patients just a cup of coffee as refreshment while they're waiting to see their doctor and (2) creating a "tea experience" where they can select their tea, pour hot water over it into a nice cup, then sit and smell and taste the tea to help them relax a little before their appointment. Or think of it like this: When patients walk in the office they could be smelling chai rather than antiseptic cleaners.

The combination of experiences from your senses results in what landscape architects call the **genius loci**, the spirit of the place. The roots of this term lie in Roman mythology. In contemporary usage, *genius loci* usually refers to a location's distinctive atmosphere, and it infers that designs should always be adapted to the context, to support the essence of the place (Norberg-Schulz, 1980).

It can be impossible to capture or comprehend the essence of a place solely from the photographs, maps, or textual accounts you find in your literature review. Can you understand how it feels to be on a cliff overlooking the ocean if you haven't been there? To record a casual observation, you might make a mental note, written notes, a video, or still photography. Later you can organize the photos and notes in a sequence that corresponds to what you observed, to help you recall the experience and communicate it to others.

Consider this example of gathering casual observations. Interior designer Annahi Barce studied the behavior of her nephews at her mother's house. Her mother asked her to redesign an outdoor space that the boys would use when they stayed over. Over the course of several visits, Annahi observed the boys' behavior. She discovered that the boys did not sit still to play with their toys as she had assumed. They were very active, and their activities included rearranging their large toys, playing with gardening equipment, jumping, and fighting with each other. Analyzing her observations led her to conclude

Figure 8.2 Casual observation of her nephews at play yielded information that helped the designer Annahi Barce understand how they actually used the space. The photo on the right shows the boys' redesigned play space, which now uses diffuse light, artwork, and furniture to support focused activities.

that the existing, undifferentiated play space did not encourage focused activities such as reading, writing, or making art. Annahi designed a semi-enclosed indoor/outdoor space that diffused the light. Taking cues from traditional "school" design, she provided seating and tables, a storage space for toys, and colorful objects for inspiration. The space was transformed into a play space that encouraged focused play, which was warmly received by the client and happily used by the boys. See the results in Figure 8.2.

Systematic Observation

Systematic observation usually occurs *after* casual observation, when a situation needs more in-depth observation and you have already compiled lists of predetermined attributes or behaviors. There are many different systematic observation techniques, each designed to focus the researcher's attention on certain aspects of the people or the environment. The first step is to **codify** the process—that is, to come up with a series of symbols or words, a kind of shorthand—to represent both the attributes and the activities of the subjects. Concerning attributes, for example, if you wanted to divide a group of children by gender, you could use symbols on your map, such as a triangle to represent a boy and a circle to represent a girl. **Visual notation** is the shorthand technique that you will use to codify the attributes and activities of the subjects. It could be as simple as color-coding the activity. If you were observing people in a gym, in your notation you might use a red pen to represent people who are running, a blue marker for those lifting weights, and a green marker for people who are resting between exercises. Or the notation could use descriptive abbreviations: "run," "wts," and "rest." Once you have established a list of what you are looking for, you will want to show how these behaviors occur in the room or space.

Behavioral mapping is just one technique used to obtain more specific data about the behaviors in a space or about the relationships between people in a given space. If you wanted to study the behavior of children on a public playground or in a classroom, or worshippers in a church, you may want to go out into the field, do some direct observation, and diagram or map your observations. You may also want to study a given space over time—for example, the different interactions of people in a hotel lobby or in an airport waiting area—or compare inhabitants of a local park during the day to the inhabitants and activities in the evening. There are basically two types of behavior maps: place-centered and person-centered.

Place-Centered Mapping

Place-centered mapping involves making a base drawing of the space prior to the observation period, showing physical objects: barriers (full-height

Jorge Rodriguez's elderly mother had been staying at his home in a temporary situation, so the family had set up a bed in the recreation room. Jorge wanted to make this space a permanent residence for her, and he sought a solution from an interior designer. When the designer got to the house, she was expecting to *interview* the woman to find out her preferences. However, the elderly woman did not speak English and was too shy to have her son translate. (See "An Unexpected Twist" in Chapter 6.) So, with her permission, the designer *observed* her for the remainder of the day.

This experience allowed the designer to see, firsthand, how the woman used the existing space. Observing her gave insights that the designer never would have gleaned from simply interviewing her or her son. The designer observed how the woman used furniture to support herself while moving around the room: how she used the arms of her sturdy armchair to slowly lower herself to a seated position and how she retrieved her knitting supplies hidden in the cushions! The designer realized that the placement of the chair allowed the woman the best view of the home's long driveway so that she could see when family members were returning home, and she saw that the chair's high back and pillows allowed the woman to take a nap while seated in her watching post.

Jorge had pointed out that games and puzzles were an important part of his mother's day. But observation allowed the designer to understand how the round game table offered no dangerous corners, how the woman chose a seating position diagonally opposite the entry door so that she could easily see entering family members, and how the table allowed her to leave a puzzle partially completed and then return at a later time. Multiple chairs enabled her to interact with her grandson through board and card games.

The designer also observed the woman at her daily prayers at the foot of the bed: how she carefully lowered herself to a kneeling position and used the bed to rest her elbows. The placement of the bed allowed her to look up at the sky through the existing skylight, which, her son confirmed, was essential to her daily ritual. While she was lying in bed, she often looked at the many photos, which were all visible to her from that position. Jorge offered the possible explanation that she said "Goodnight" to all of the photos.

To analyze the use of space, the designer used place-centered behavioral mapping—translating the woman's activities into a graphic form and codifying the behavior. Thus,

walls, partial-height walls, glass or translucent partitions), furniture, ceiling height changes, material changes, lighting levels, and so on. Then you would map a subject's behaviors within or through the space. This type of map indicates flow patterns of certain types of user, reveals major circulation paths, and could expose conflicts between types of users. For example, in a restau-

the designer recorded the woman's main paths of travel, using a red dot to mark the places where she stood or sat for more than 15 minutes and using a yellow line to map the direction she was looking in. It became possible to see the parts of the room that were most important: the parts providing (1) visual access to the driveway to see when family members were coming home, (2) physical access to the window to open and close the drapery, and (3) visual access to photos from a sleeping position. During the designer's visit, the woman made one spoken request: privacy "curtinas" to be made by her son-in-law, which would mean more to her than anything purchased at a store. The designer made note of this on the map as well. (See Figure 8.3.)

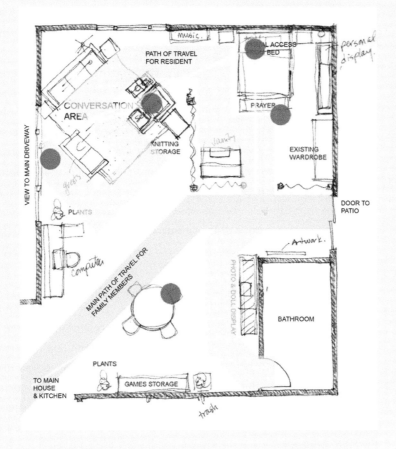

Figure 8.3 This place-centered behavioral map of an elderly woman's living space attempts to record her main paths of travel and favored seating locations (in red). Further notes such as visual access, placement of personal items, and requested privacy curtains have also been recorded on the plan.

rant, you may want to observe the way different users—wait staff, patrons, and kitchen staff—use the front lobby. Does the path of the wait person ever intersect the path of a patron, or does the path the kitchen staff takes to the dumpster interfere with the delivery of food by the wait staff?

Person-centered mapping involves selecting an individual to follow for a given period of time in order to obtain information about how that person uses or interacts in a space. Basically, this kind of mapping involves tracking your subject and making notes about location, movement, and activities, taking into account the length of time for each activity. **Shadowing** is a type of person-centered tracking in which you observe naturally occurring behavior in a natural environment over several days. For example, this technique could be used to identify the tasks that a typical office employee performs, the amount of time required to do the tasks, and the way the employee uses the space. At the same time, it could help identify problems that may be interfering with office efficiency and productivity. The observer follows an employee through the workday and records every movement to gain a clear picture of how that employee uses the space.

Consider this example: A company was preparing for a redesign. The interior design firm performed its initial research, which included shadowing an employee for a day. To minimize the potential observer effect (discussed in Chapter 2), the shadower maintained a considerable distance so as not to influence the employee's behavior. The shadower did such a great job, in fact, that the employee forgot he was being observed until he went into a small supply closet to get a ream of paper, turned around to leave, and was startled to find himself nose to nose with his shadower. The shadower had been able to watch from a distance throughout the day, but in an effort to be thorough and not take his eyes off of his subject, he had inadvertently stepped into the supply closet, startling his subject!

In the **Hidden Observer** method, subjects are unaware that they are being watched. The researcher might use a one-way mirror or a hidden camera, both of which raise some ethical questions. This technique is often used by toy manufacturers to observe a focus group of children testing out a manufacturer's products. It is also employed in police interrogations. In interior design applications, the observer may also be slightly removed from the action—for example, on a mezzanine looking down on an interior mall space, or on a rooftop observing the playground below. In any of these cases, the hidden observer may not be close enough to the subjects to be able to observe details or may not be able to use all of her senses (hearing, smelling, touching) to fully record all of the nonvisual details. But it can provide a sufficient overview.

An **Anonymous Observer** is one who blends in with the other subjects in an environment: like another patient in a waiting room, another subway passenger, or another art student in the park (Zeisel, 1997). Zeisel refers to this kind of observer as a "marginal participant," and includes deliberate choice of clothing, posture, and the objects you are carrying such as a camera for a tourist, a notebook for a student, and a sketchpad for an artist. This kind of observation can be very successful, as long as the observer is self-aware and sensitive to the environment.

An **Identified Observer** is one who is clearly observing yet has the potential to remain neutral and not interfere with the natural behavior. An example would be a college student observing a classroom at a grade school. The teacher introduces the observer to the children and briefly explains that the observer is interested in observing the class. Although the subjects are aware that they are being observed, it is assumed that, over time, they will resume their normal activity and allow the observer to view natural environment behavior. Remaining unobtrusive may require some skill on the observer's part. With older subjects, the risk is that the observer may be viewed negatively as a spy; steps should be taken to make clear that the observer is not going to relay information to management, law enforcement, or any agency the subjects may perceive as threatening.

In Chapter 2, we talked a bit about the effect the observer may have on the observed. The *Hawthorne Effect* is a tendency for subjects in an experiment or other type of study to change their behavior just because they are being studied (Fraenkel et al., 1999).

As interior designers, we also are very interested in the physical environment itself: the spaces, the objects, and the relationships between them. We can observe what exists, or how things change over time. And we can also take note of what is missing in an environment, something designers often refer to as "the presence of absence."

Trace Observation

"In addition to the immediate and obvious technique of observing behavior in progress, observation methods can include studying the physical evidence left by the interaction of people and the environment" (Sanoff, 1991). This trace evidence—the objects manipulated, left behind, or taken away—gives an indication of patterns of behavior or attitudes toward the environment. Similar to the approach taken on the television series *CSI: Crime Scene Investigation,* this method is investigative and demands that you look for indications of earlier activity and seek to interpret those findings. For example, in a school library, what does the lack of dust, a worn path in the flooring tile, or the chipped edges of desks mean to an interior designer? What does the presence of graffiti on a schoolyard wall, broken windows, or an abundance of trash indicate? "This type of research is critical to the designer because it gives you an opportunity to know what often goes unsaid by clients and users. There are two types of traces that are measured, erosion and accretion" (Guerin & Dohr, 2007, p. 5). "**Erosion traces** are shown by deterioration or wear that provides a look at the usage pattern. **Accretion traces** are a build-up of a residue or an interaction. These traces are added to the environment and show how the user has changed an environment" (Sommer & Sommer, 2002, cited by Guerin & Dohr, p. 5). Trace evidence could also show up as manipulation or adaptation. For example, the reconfiguration of chairs in a classroom to a circle may indicate a group discussion in which everyone was encouraged to participate.

Regardless of which type of *systematic* observation technique you use, you need to decide how to record the data. One method is to construct preprinted **data sheets** with places for the date, time, and setting, as well as checklists for behaviors to be identified or quantities to be indicated (Sanoff, 1991). These sheets could have different symbols or words to abbreviate types of users and activities observed. There could be blank spaces on which to record details, such as the number of people, the type of activity, and the duration of the activity. Also, there should be predetermined categories that focus your observation. For example, if you are observing people waiting in a birthing clinic, you may identify subcategories of users as (a) pregnant women, (b) children, and (c) other adults (clearly not pregnant); or as (a) couples, (b) single women, and (c) families; or as (a) first-time visitors, (b) return visitors, and (c) emergency visitors (in labor). These categories could be listed on preprinted sheets so that you can simply enter check marks during the observation period. It's a good idea to have a column or area for notes that may occur to you on the fly, such as "Expectant mother observed panicking when her child was out of sight" or "Noticed there was always someone waiting outside the single restroom."

ACTIVITY 8.1 Defining the Public

Purpose: **To sort/categorize subjects to discover the many ways of categorizing people.**

Visit a public place—such as a museum, zoo, park, airport, plaza, or store—in which there are many different types of people. As you watch the people engaged in various activities, list as many different categories as possible. At first, your categories may be based on very obvious, *inherent* physical characteristics such as age, gender, or race. But as you observe the people in this space, see how many other categories you can name. You can sort your subjects based on other *applied* physical characteristics, such as whether or not they are wearing a hat, and *activity-based* categories, such as whether or not they are carrying a small child. Can you observe physical details that would allow you to sort people into possible *invisible* categories, such as religious beliefs or political affiliation or education level? Use the table below as your starting point. Name at least 10, and preferably 20, categories not already listed, and indicate the kind of category for each one.

	Category	Inherent	Applied	Activity-Based	Other
1	Age	X			
2	Gender	X			
3	Race	X			
4	Wearing a hat?		X		
5	Carrying a child?			X	
6	Religion				X
7	Political affiliation				X
8	Education level				X

ACTIVITY 8.2 Developing a Data Sheet

Purpose: **To put together a preprinted form that will allow you to record data easily.**

Using the categories developed in Activity 8.1, compose a matrix or sheet on which you can record the number of people in each category quickly and easily. Maybe you can have a separate piece of paper for each category and you make a check mark for each person you observed who belongs in that category. Or you can list categories in a column on the left and provide space to record in a column on the right. Or you can limit your categories to just a few and arrange the boxes graphically on a page. How can you represent individuals who fall into more than one category?

Purpose: To explore how observation requires patience and time in order for you to absorb the layers of details for information.

Take a photo of an exterior or interior space that shows evidence of recent activity or neglect, such as an empty classroom, the front yard of a residence, or a store parking lot. Bring the photo to class and switch it with another student's. Spend at least ten minutes looking at the photo, uncovering evidence by observation. How many instances of trace evidence can you find in the photo? Determine whether each trace is attributable to accretion or to erosion. Which ones are adaptations?

ACTIVITY 8.4 Identifying Trace
Evidence
in the Field

Purpose: To explore how observation requires patience and time to absorb the layers of details for information.

PART ONE

Go to a friend's kitchen and note all of the physical traces that indicate the kind of behavior that previously occurred in the space. Create a list including accretion traces, objects (dishes, crumbs, cigarette butts, handwritten notes, clothing), erosion traces (items that are worn or missing), and indications of adaption (closed blinds, open cabinets). After each item, list implications, behavior, or beliefs that could have caused the trace evidence. For example, the large number of beer bottles in the kitchen might lead you to assume that there had been a party the night before. When you have finished, ask your friend if your interpretations are correct.

PART TWO

With your friend's permission, document your observations through photos, drawings, and video or audiotape. Present your findings to the class, and discuss when your assumptions were correct and when they were not.

Participant Observation and Ethnography

Participant observation occurs when the observer is interacting with the subjects in some way. There are varying degrees of interaction, and each level involves the risk of observer effect (the observer somehow influencing the observed) and subjective interpretation by the observer. From Chapter 2, recall that in quantum physics it is understood that the act of measuring influences the measure. For example, if you try to pick something out of the water, the act of your hand going into the water has an effect on the objects in the water. Some scientists believe that *any* act of measuring has an effect on the objects being measured. A researcher or designer engaged in participant observation is aware that his or her behavior will have an effect—but the subjective nature of the study will not be compromised, as the intent is to understand through activity.

Ethnography is what a cultural anthropologist specializes in. It is the intensive study of a particular culture, society, or community through fieldwork, which usually involves living or working with the people being studied in order to learn about their way of life. Ethnography examines, in a holistic, comprehensive, and interactive way, the daily rituals and patterns that make up a culture. Ethnographers are the most involved participant observers; they take part in the activities with the subject in order to increase understanding of the behavior, which is a complexity of thought and action.

> If you want to understand what motivates a guy to pick up skateboarding, you could bring him into a sterile laboratory and interrogate him . . . or you could spend a week in a skatepark observing him interacting with his friends, practicing new skills and having fun. Ethnography is observing people's behavior in their own environment so you can get a holistic understanding of their world—one that you can intuit on a deeply personal level (LiAnne Yu, cultural anthropologist, quoted in AIGA, 2009, p. 4).

Examples of ethnography that pertain to interior design would be to participate in a drum circle for several weeks in a local park to understand the culture of the park-goers, as part of redesigning the park; to volunteer at an animal shelter in order to understand the process of rescuing animals, as part of planning a rescue facility; or to serve meals in a local soup kitchen in order to understand the complexity of planning a new dining room for a church.

Ethnography is not just about observing. It is also about immersing oneself in a **cultural milieu** in which a person's behaviors are not merely recorded as a series of codified behaviors but are given meaning. One of the ways ethnographers discover meaning is by examining **artifacts**, to learn what people value and hold dear (AIGA, 2009, p. 7). Artifacts are objects

Artifacts are objects that have meaning within a culture. For ritual—both public and private—in daily life, an artifact is any object made or modified by a human culture. These objects usually include but are not limited to tools, weapons, clothing, furniture, objects used for ritual, artwork, and decorative items and useful crafts. The meanings assigned to artifacts are usually emotional as well as reflecting a set of values or beliefs. For example, a tombstone, a wristwatch, and a flag all have meaning beyond their physical appearance. The tombstone marks the passing of a loved one and denotes the physical presence of that person's remains. The wristwatch may have been given to someone by his grandfather, who has passed away. A flag symbolizes a nation, a culture, or an ideology that a person may be willing to die for. The significance of an artifact goes far beyond the item's material value or worth. The artifact has meaning that may not be apparent at first. What the observer may view as a rag could be a remnant of a baby blanket, or a piece of a woman's wedding dress. Memories, which are intangible, become more real to a person in the presence of such an object.

Your notes about an object should go beyond describing its physical appearance. You should also explore how the object is used, stored, and cared for. In addition, consider the impact of the object in the room in terms of its placement among other objects. Is it prominent or relatively obscure among similar objects? A description of a candle means nothing without mention of its placement on an altar, whether it is symmetrically balanced with a similar candle, its height in the room, and when it is lit.

In the case of Jorge's mother, about whom we spoke earlier in the chapter, artifacts observed in her room were a cross hanging on the wall, her rosary beads, an old Bible, a hand-knitted blanket, her antique doll collection, and photos of family members who were no longer living. The curtains that she requested be made by her son-in-law would serve as a future artifact. It is clear that this client valued handmade objects, especially crafted for her by a family member.

that have spiritual, emotional, or historical meaning to a person or a group of people. A collective may assign significance to architectural elements, such as the columns and arches in an Islamic mosque, or in the Mexican culture significance might be assigned to photos, skulls, and fruit in a Day of the Dead altar.

Mental Mapping

Mental mapping, which was pioneered by Kevin Lynch in 1960 in his landmark book *Image of the City*, is a process by which the subject is asked to draw a map or plan of his or her environment. This process is discussed in detail in Chapter 11 as it relates to data-gathering and analysis of the site you've chosen

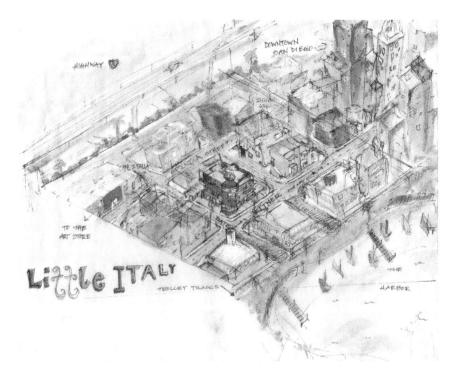

Figure 8.4 Leanna Duncan's conceptual sketch of Little Italy, a neighborhood in San Diego, California, where she has her office. Note which places are emphasized and how she attempts to describe access to her office through highways and other forms of transportation.

for your project. Here in Chapter 8, we explore the potential of mental mapping as a way to gather information about how a person perceives, understands, and uses a space. The subjective way in which the subject communicates this information can illustrate priorities, as well as subtle, subconscious wants and needs that go beyond observable behavior. In fact, mental mapping can be seen as a way to observe the mind of the subject, as the drawing that the subject produces is a reflection of that person's thoughts, knowledge, and emotion about an interior space. Consider Figure 8.4. (Note: Mental Mapping is different from the Concept Mapping we explored in Chapter 3.)

⊛ ACTIVITY 8.5 Mental Mapping

Purpose: **To see firsthand how a subject perceives his environment.**

Ask a friend (who is not studying interior design) to draw a plan of her home, or the home she grew up in, and to identify the most important elements of that residence, as well as to indicate her likes and dislikes about the spaces. Has she included outdoor spaces? Which spaces are most detailed and which are left as vague outlines? Which room is drawn the largest? After your friend has drawn the plan, ask her questions about it to increase your understanding of how people tend to represent their feelings about space on paper. The outcome of this Activity will be discussed in detail in Chapter 11.

Self-Reports, Simulations, and Experiments

Self-reports—activity logs or diaries, in which the subjects themselves log events at specific time intervals—can be very informative. For example, if you were studying the behavior of overweight adults in order to design a medical health spa, it would make sense to have them record all the food they eat during the course of a day, as well as to record the circumstances (their activity, thought, or emotion) surrounding the activity. Note: Researchers have found that this method alone is rarely accurate, as people tend not to tell the whole truth on self-reports. It is recommended that you follow up with direct observation of your subjects' behavior, or with trace observation, which would support or refute their reports.

As interior designers, we use the technique of **simulation** all of the time. Every time we draw a perspective drawing to *represent* a three-dimensional space or any time we construct a virtual or physical scale model, we are asking our viewers to *imagine* that our design is reality and to respond accordingly. The difference between a simulation and an experiment is that the simulation involves the subject's imagination. The subject knows that the design is not reality. A simulated client meeting, for example, would mean that someone is acting as a client to replicate an actual client meeting. The simulation is the act of re-creating a condition that occurs, perhaps, daily for the purpose of recording responses, yet the subject is aware that this particular occurrence is not reality. A scale model allows the viewer to imagine what occupying the space would be like, so that too is a simulation, as is a card-

Figure 8.5 As a student, Leanna Duncan constructed a scale model of her museum project to analyze the quality of light and the effect of the landscaping on the interior gallery space. A scale model is used to simulate the actual experience of walking through the museum since the viewer of the model must imagine being inside the space.

The Albuquerque Main Library, built in 1972, had not had a major remodel in more than 25 years. Much had changed in library service, especially with computerized book check-out and other electronic services. Part of the remodeling project was to redesign the double entry to emphasize one entry only, for control. This main entry was to have a new Circulation Desk. The Information Desk would also be new. From previous work with clients and casework drawings, the design team knew that laypeople have a hard time understanding plans and elevations of casework. To address this communication problem, the team drew up, conventionally (plan, interior elevation, exterior elevation) their best guess at the program for these major desks. They then cut out these images and taped them together into a study model of the two desks. (See Figure 8.6.) In the three dimensions, the librarians were able to imagine themselves using the desks. They could decide where they needed keyboards, CPUs, printers, phones, faxes, reference shelves, and all the other items that would require shelving, drawers, power, and data lines. The design team could discuss where to lower the counters for ADA compliance, sight lines, access and egress, knee spaces, drawer location and drawer inserts, etc. (E. Cherry, personal communication, June 4, 2008).

Figure 8.6 Librarians at the Albuquerque Library review a mock-up of the circulation desk.

board mock-up of a chair or a taped outline of a room on the floor. Check out the example in Figure 8.5.

As discussed in Chapter 3, an *experiment* involves conducting observation in a controlled environment using the **scientific method**. "An experiment is a type of study in which a researcher deliberately manipulates an independent variable . . . to observe what changes occur in one or more dependent variables" (Fraenkel et al., 1999). This study assumes cause-and-effect. For example, if the independent variable (see Chapter 3 for an introduction to this concept) is arrangement of furniture and the dependent variable is socializing, you can control the arrangement of furniture in a room with human subjects and record their degree of socialization. In this example, you may also need a **control group** and to account for the **extraneous variables**—that is, the variables you have not accounted for that may affect your outcomes, such as the degree to which the subjects know one another. If the subjects are friends, they may socialize regardless of furniture arrangement. An experiment starts with a **hypothesis**, which is what the researcher thinks is true. For example, a student thinks that the reason many students are not using the library to study is that the library is too noisy. Her experiment is to temporarily reduce the noise in the library by putting up acoustic treatment. If the number of students who study in the library increases as a result of her intervention, her hypothesis is supported. The trick is to make sure there are no other variables that may have been the cause of the increase—for example, that the time of year is closer to finals or that the student lounge, where most of the students usually study, is closed. (For another example, see Figure 8.7.)

In an experiment, there is an inherent need to measure and compare. In the example just mentioned, the *number* of people is being measured. But you could also measure *length of time* spent in the library. For the socializing experiment, you could have measured the *distance* between people. Other measurements in interior design experiments could be *temperature, cost,* or *weight*.

Figure 8.7 Students test the bearing capacity of the model bridges they built from foam core and balsa wood. The bricks represent a standard unit of weight. The simulation becomes an experiment when the added elements of hypothesis and comparative measure are introduced.

Case Studies

This chapter concludes with a look at a comprehensive kind of investigation called a **case study**. The term *case study* is used in many fields. In the medical field, a case study would be a comprehensive look at a singular instance of a person who exhibited all of the classic symptoms of a certain affliction. The story of the "elephant man" was a case study in which a man was afflicted with an extreme form of the disease called neurofibromatosis. Documentation of the way his body was deformed, the way he lived, and the way he died served to inform medical science. Even after his death, his remains, and the detailed story of his life, still serve to inform science.

In the field of interior design, the case study is an in-depth examination of a previously completed project (or a previously proposed project) that has conditions related to your own project, so that it can serve as a prototype or an example of either a successful or an unsuccessful design solution. There are different kinds of case studies to explore. A **precedent study** usually refers to a project that exemplifies innovation in architecture or design, such as in its structural, technological, or formal (related to form) exploration.

> The goal of precedent research in architecture is to have an understanding of what has come before, and use that knowledge to help define and develop your design concepts. As a designer, your background and experiences are extremely important, as these experiences become influences you will bring to each design you produce. Precedent research is meant as a way to expand and supplement these personal experiences. As you know more and understand what other architects have proposed, and why, you will be capable of producing a richer and more meaningful design solution (Pearson, 2008, p. 1).

Another particular type of case study is the **historic precedent**, as we often go back in time to the first project of its kind: an archetype, an architectural icon, or a pioneer study that led the way. Or we examine a project that exemplifies a certain historic style or time period.

We can also use recent or cutting-edge projects as examples to illustrate technological breakthroughs and possibilities or trends in philosophy and design theory. When many designers point to a project as an icon, it operates as a reference point and may function as a focus for the founding of schools of thought. Such a project is often referred to as a **paradigmatic case**. A good example is Le Corbusier's Villa Savoye (1929–1931). This building illustrated the five points of modern architecture as stipulated in Le Corbusier's manifesto, published in 1926. Its construction ushered in a whole new understanding of modern architecture. Thus, a case study can serve as a singular example that says, "Here I am. Learn from me."

Sometimes, the term *case study* refers specifically to an interior design project that solves a social problem or that benefits society, such as an innovative institutional program. The case study in this instance could also be used to document and explore how a project offered a unique solution to a problem faced by a certain user group or in a particular area—for example, a museum for the visually impaired or temporary housing in a disaster-stricken community.

Table 8.1 describes the standard types of case study and provides an example of each one.

The terms *document* and *explore* are used over and over in this section. That is because the key to doing a case study is that you must collect data and then analyze it using one or more of the techniques discussed in this chapter to accomplish a multifaceted understanding of the project: textual descriptions in related publications, archived documents such as floor plans and maps (to be discussed in Chapter 11), interviews with people related to the project, and direct observation. A case study acknowledges the individuality and uniqueness of the participants and the setting (Guerin & Dohr, 2007) with a comparable project type, user group, or program and generalizes its applicability to the larger field of interior design.

An underlying assumption in science is that if you dissect something, you can find out the inner workings of an organism or discover how it functions in its environment. Case studies can be used in socioeconomic research, Environment-Behavior research, and comparative and interpretive studies. They can be used to compare the quality of designed environments, to track current design trends, or to provide an historical framework for your proposal. Or they can be centered around a new material, new use of technology, new construction method, or new design principle such as sustainable design.

To fully understand your project type, you may need to visit a few existing projects that are similar in scope, or that serve the same function or have the same user group or are located in the neighborhood. When you find one that is innovative or has accomplished its goal successfully, you have found a subject for your case study. Next, you must document all the parameters of the project you found and dissect the project. What makes this project unique and a success? Or, on the flip side, what makes it a complete failure? We can also learn a great deal from another designer's mistakes, inappropriate use of color or materials, poor spatial configurations, or misguided assumptions about the way the users would use the space.

The following outline represents a good format for an interior design case study:

1. Project Basics
   - Project location
   - Completion date

Table 8.1 Projects to Examine (Comparable to Your Project Type)

Historic Precedent	Precedent Study	Case Study	Paradigmatic Case	Proposal Study
Refers to a project that has stood the test of time and is viewed as an icon that typifies a particular style, time period, or designer's work.	Usually refers to an innovation in design, such as in its structure, form, its use of technology, or its testing of a theory of design.	Usually refers to a social aspect of a project, such as how an institutional design benefits society. May exemplify a solution to a problem faced by a certain user group or may have social significance due to function or location.	Usually refers to a recently completed project that utilizes the newest theories or technologies and seeks to break from tradition or from the past.	This is a study of a project that has not yet been realized in physical form. Can be an idea or a concept, or a fully developed set of drawings or models.
Value: Historic value may be about an event that occurred there.	*Value:* Serves as a prototype to document or demonstrate innovation on a technical or functional level.	*Value:* Its value as a case study may lie in the program or spaces.	*Value:* Serves to promote a revolution in thought or action. Initiates change in perspective just by its existence.	*Value:* Informs future generations of designers even though it has not yet been implemented.
Example: The classic courtroom that is designed to follow court procedure	*Example:* A University of Oxford project where art was used in the laboratories to inspire creativity in scientists	*Example:* The design of St. Vincent de Paul/Father Joe's Villages, in San Diego, California, is a complex of spaces providing services for the homeless based on the idea that people deserve to be treated with dignity while acquiring job training and life skills to reintegrate them into society.	*Example:* W hotels began putting the bar in the middle of the lobby, which changed the paradigm of contemporary hotels. This move was based on the idea that every square foot of the hotel had the potential to generate revenue.	*Example:* The "Aeroscraft," a concept for a flying luxury hotel (http://www.popsci.com/aeros/article/2006-02/flying-luxury-hotel)

- Building type
- Square footage
- Client
- User group
- Design team

2. Background and Context
   - Goals, mission, philosophy
   - Budget
   - Background of client
   - Background of designer(s)
   - Timeline of construction or relevant details
   - Historic or cultural milieu, design movement or time period

3. Function and Physical Appearance
   - Program
   - Floor plans, sections, elevations, site map
   - Models, drawings, diagrams, and preliminary design sketches produced by design team
   - Photos of exterior and interior
   - Other physical documentation, such as dimensions, FF&E
   - Key design features and/or strategies to achieve design

4. Implications for the Future
   - Performance studies, if any
   - Impact on surroundings, neighborhood, environment
   - Influence on other designers

5. Summary
   - Applicability to your project
   - Anything else that you have learned

6. References
   - Cite all sources.

Three Interior Design
Case Studies
(written by students)

Example of an Historic Precedent

MORGANS HOTEL NEW YORK
New York, New York 10016
By Student Sergio Murguia

PROJECT BASICS

- Owner: Morgans Hotel Group
- Total Square Footage: 72,000
- Meeting Square Footage: 6,400
- Number of Floors: 20
- Number of Rooms: 113
- Banquet Capacity: 190
- Year Built: 1929
- Year Remodeled: 1984
- Overall Design: Andrée Putman

General Background: In 1984, Morgans Hotel Group created a hotel so *avant-garde* that it revolutionized the hospitality industry. Banishing tradition, they introduced the concept of the "Boutique Hotel," characterized by personalized service and home-away-from-home ambience in a setting of timeless elegance.

With interiors by the renowned French designer Andrée Putman, Morgans' chic, decidedly residential feel created a sensation in the hotel industry when it opened 23 years ago, and it is still the choice for discerning travelers seeking the very best.

Design Concepts: The design update of Morgans presented an intriguing new challenge: Instead of beginning with a "blank canvas," Morgans Hotel Group asked Ms. Putman to add luster to one that had already been enormously successful and well-received. With a new color palette, unconventional and "un-hotel-like" new materials, and meticulously chosen design finishes that are vintage Putman, Morgans remains a modern classic, seamlessly melding understatement and simplicity with cutting-edge style.

Public Spaces: New design features are evident throughout Morgans' public spaces. The "Living Room" Lobby, which is both sophisticated and homey, features textured taupe-colored glass walls with overlaid bronze mullions and a custom Putman-designed wool rug of black, rich camel, and taupe in a bold three-dimensional Cubist pattern. The floors are covered with three varied shades of imported Italian granite in different finishes. There are intimate groupings of antique French leather club chairs and dark end tables with antique lamps. The Living Room has the feel of a cozy library and is an ideal place to relax, watch a movie, read a book, chat with a friend, or play a computer game. Complimentary tea, coffee, and light fare are offered throughout the day.

The hotel's restaurant, Asia de Cuba, serves Asian and Latino cuisines in a soaring and beautifully theatrical Philippe Starck–designed space. It features a 30-foot-long illuminated marble communal table that runs through the dining room, a 15-foot-tall photo lightbox with a "running waterfall," ultra-comfortable high-backed white banquettes, and cozy living room areas with fireplaces. It is a clean-line contemporary design with a touch of some traditional elements. The feeling is both elegant and tranquil.

Guest Accommodations: Breaking all industry rules by veering sharply away from formulaic institutional design, the guest rooms are modern, homey, informal, and replete with elegant and unusual design flourishes. To update guest lodgings, Ms. Putman began in the hotel corridors, which are covered in a Putman-designed 100 percent wool carpet in rich taupe with a black-and-white checkerboard-patterned border. Guest room doors are of French custom bird's-eye maple, above which sit custom-built incandescent light fixtures that cast a soothing glow. With only four to eight rooms per floor, each hallway contributes to the hotel's intimate residential feel.

The guest rooms present an immediately pleasing atmosphere of elegant informality and unfussy style. With a palette of taupe, camel, and ivory, and materials such as corduroys, suede, and silks, the rooms are simple yet remarkably rich in texture. The walls are painted with a mixture of four muted tones, producing the effect as that of an Impressionist wall painting. Robert Mapplethorpe's black-and-white photos adorn the walls.

Club chairs and ottomans are covered in wide-wale corduroy, as are the roman shades in all the windows. Bird's-eye maple custom-built window seats are upholstered in taupe suede with throw pillows covered in subtly patterned handwoven silk. In addition to a regular closet, each room features a four-drawer dresser cabinet with a full-length lighted wardrobe mirror. Flat-screen televisions rest on sleek, nontraditional stands.

Bathroom walls are covered with black-and-white matte Japanese tiles in a checkerboard design and a mosaic of Venetian glass border. Unconventional features include customized stainless-steel airplanelike sinks and hospital fixtures, floor-to-ceiling shower doors and partitions in ¾-inch glass, and poured-in-place seamless granite floors.

Elements of Morgans Hotel Design That Inspire My Project: I really like the three-dimensional, geometric design of the floors and the angled tables in the dining room and meeting room. I would like to incorporate the clean, uncluttered look of the guest suites and the soft, informal fabrics that make the rooms homey. The Living Room is an interesting concept that I might like to incorporate into a club room rather than in the lobby (Murguia, 2008).

Bibliography

Baksa, A. (2008, April 23). *On the boards.* Retrieved April 2008 from http://www.arpad-baksa-architect.com/

Beatyman, M. (2007, May 1). New York's first green boutique hotel slated for 2008. *Interior Design.* Retrieved April 2008 from http://www.interiordesign.net/id_newsarticle/CA6438137.html

Curbed. (2007, May 1). Chelsea's narrow 19-foot site revealed as greenhouse 26. Retrieved April 2008 from http://curbed.com/archives/2007/05/01/chelseas_narrow_19foot_site_revealed_as_greenhouse_26.php

Daly, M. (1988, July 22). The comeback kids. *New York Times Magazine.*

"Euroflash." (1984, December). *Vanity Fair.*

Hospitality Design. (2007, April 26). New York City to welcome first green boutique hotel. Retrieved April 2008 from http://www.hdmag.com/hospitalitydesign/content_display/design-news/e3if6c28ca5b32761d8f839d04903b6eb9c?imw=Y

Monaghan, C. (1986, November). Hotels go intimate: The new breed is luxurious, small and sometimes suite. *Travel & Leisure.*

Morgans. *Explore our hotels.* Retrieved April 30, 2008, from http://www.morganshotelgroup.com/company.html

Morgans New York. *Morgans New York Hotel.* Retrieved April 30, 2006, from http://www.morganshotel.com/

Plumb, B. (1985). French designer Andrée Putman applies her special wizardry to a Manhattan hotel that caters to a discriminating, international clientele. *Vogue Living.*

Slesin, S. (1984, September 20). Design ideas in 2 new small hotels. *New York Times.*

Weinraub, J. (1985, January 10). Breaking the rules with Andrée Putman and Steve Rubell: An old hotel with a bold new look. *Washington Post.*

Example of a Case Study

HARRIS FAMILY CHILDREN'S CENTER
Exeter, New Hampshire
By Student Jessica Herndon

PROJECT BASICS

- Location: New Hampshire
- Building Type: Early Education School

- Square Footage: 8,160
- Completion: 2006
- Client: Harris Family Children's Center
- Design Team: Bargmann Hendrie & Archetype, Inc.

Background and Context: The facility incorporates principles from the Reggio Emilia Schools in Italy, providing great outdoor and indoor learning experiences for infants to children five years old. These schools place great value in the role of the environment as a motivating force in creating space for relations, options, and emotional and cognitive situations that produce a sense of well-being and security (Harris Family Children's Center, 2007).

The school's mission is also to expose children to appreciation of the arts and sciences, and give them opportunities to explore and experiment, while connecting and respecting the environment. (See Figure 8.8.)

The outdoor learning environment is an integral part of the learning process. Here, it serves as an extension to the classroom. Children can spend time outdoors observing nature and documenting their findings.

In the Reggio Emilia schools, the physical environment acts as the "third teacher" (Harris Family Children's Center, 2007), communicating the importance of the effectiveness and functionality of a space to facilitate learning.

Design Intent and Validation: The design of the building was intended to be functional as well as flexible to serve a wide range of students, from six weeks through five years of age. After-school care for elementary school students is also provided. During the summer months, the building accommodates 40 students for camp. (See Figure 8.9.)

The designers felt the need to create an environment that was aesthetically pleasing to both children and adults, with the main idea that parents can spend some time with their children throughout the day. The space has unique architectural and educational features, such as the "living room," a circular entry which acts to ease the transition into school. It has built-in benches, where even theatre or story time can take place. (See Figure 8.10.)

Centrality was also an important feature, such as the entry lobby that connects the two wings of the school. Here, a sense of community and public identity are encouraged. Skylights and a large window wall let vast amounts of daylight in, making a smooth transition from the outdoors to indoors as well as giving students the opportunity to watch the passing of time and

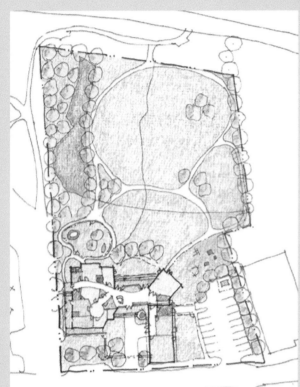

Figure 8.8 The site plan of Harris Family Children's Center was included in the case study because the concept of this facility provides outdoor learning experience and derives some of the interior concepts from the surrounding landscape.

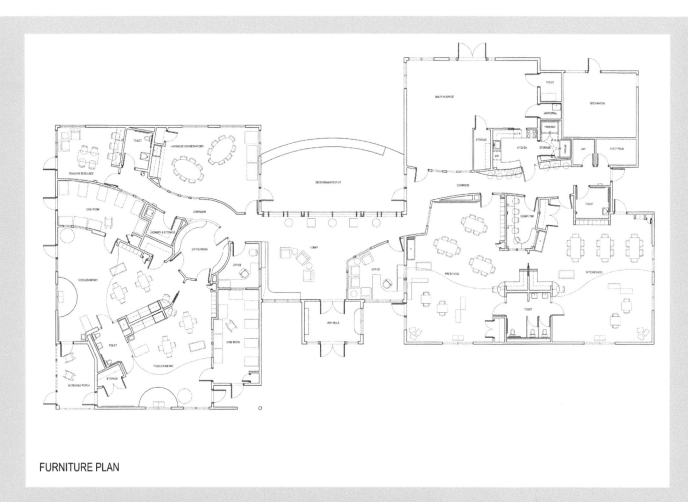

FURNITURE PLAN

Figure 8.9 (above) A furniture plan was essential to include as part of this case study as there are many unique features to consider. Note the circular space with benches at the classroom entrance, which eases transition to this area.

Figure 8.10 (left) Harris Family Children's Center interior of classroom shows cathedral ceilings and large windows so that students feel connected to the outdoors.

change of seasons. The large window wall offers a view of the lawn and the river, and the flooring, carpet, and curved walls mimic the flow of the river.

Features of the space include cathedral ceilings, participatory kitchen, built-in sinks, arts and science room, screened porch with hammock, natural light, soft and natural colors and textures, and more (Herndon, 2008).

Bibliography

Harris Family Children's Center. (2007). DesignShare.com. Retrieved April 29, 2008, from http://www.designshare.com/index.php/projects/harris-family-childrens-center/narratives

Lion's Eye. (2006, October 11). *New Harris Family Children's Center opens*. Phillips Exeter Academy. Retrieved April 2008 from http://www.exeter.edu/news_and_events/news_events_3771.aspx

Example of a Paradigmatic Case

THE LIGHTHOUSE
London, England
By Student Jennifer Newton

PROJECT BASICS

- Name: The Lighthouse
- Location: London, England
- Building Type: Residential
- Square Footage: around 1,000
- Number of Stories: 3
- Completion Date: 2016
- Client: Potton
- Design Team: Sheppard Robson

Background and Context: The UK recently published the Code for Sustainable Homes, a standard in which all homes in the UK must be constructed by 2016. This code consists of six levels, six being the highest level of sustainability. The Lighthouse was an ambitious project by architecture firm Sheppard Robson to meet Level Six and is the UK's first net zero-carbon house. It is expected that these homes will sell for around $350,000 in American dollars; certainly not a cheap investment for its modest 1,000-square-foot size. However, it will cost only around $60 per year in American dollars to run the house after it's built. The idea is that while the up-front cost is high, the building will pay for itself over time and in the long run be an extremely affordable house. Sheppard Robson's main goal with this project was to create a home where the environmental systems and construction methods didn't compromise the quality of lifestyle but added to it. Another key factor to this project was to make the space attractive and up to today's standards for modern living. The client, Potton, is the largest self-build package provider in the UK and has over forty years of building experience. They teamed up with architecture firm Sheppard Robson, recognized for their environmental sustainable design, to help create the Lighthouse.

Design Intent and Validation: As mentioned, the Lighthouse meets Level Six of the Code for Sustainable Homes published by the UK; this was the ultimate goal for this project. The requirements to reach Level Six were researched and will be presented here. First, the home must be completely zero-carbon (zero net emissions of carbon dioxide from all energy use). The home will also have to be designed to use no more than 80 liters (or 20 gallons) of water per person per day. Items to achieve this can include a 6/4 dual flush toilet, flow reducing/aerating traps throughout, and smaller-shaped bathtubs that require less water to fill. Along with this requirement is another, which requires that at least 30 percent of all water used come from nonpotable sources such as rainwater harvesting systems or gray water recycling systems. Surface water management is also required for a Level Six house, which could refer to area of porous paving. Also, a minimum number of materials (an exact number wasn't found) must meet at least a "D" grade in the Building Research Establishment's Green Guide (materials are rated from A+ to E). A site management plan must be in place during the home's construction, and space for waste storage during its use must also be considered. In addition to these requirements, 90 percent of the Code of Sustainable Homes must be achieved; this includes energy efficient appliances, minimizing construction waste, an accessible provision for recycling, and improving daylighting.

Key Design Strategies: The Lighthouse implements several sustainable ideas. First, the sloping 40-degree pitched roof integrates a photovoltaic field with SIPs (structural insulated panels). The timber framing used for the house gives this project an attractive exterior, an important factor Sheppard Robson considered in the design of the Lighthouse. Another unique feature with this project is the interior layout. The sleeping quarters were placed on the ground floor and the living areas were placed above. The reason for this was to give the most heavily trafficked rooms maximum exposure to sunlight; double-height windows and a rooftop light shaft supply this exposure.

One of the most unique features of this project is what is referred to as the "windcatcher," defined as a "low-tech passive cooling system that has been around for millennia." This system works like a chimney and allows cool air in and lets hot air out. On each floor of the house, the windcatcher has shuttered apertures that can be opened or closed as needed, depending on the season. This is used in conjunction with the windows on the outside of the house and with the doors in the central corridor. This system allows ultimate flexibility for the residents in regards to the flow of air and results in no need for electricity. This system works because of natural gradations in temperature: the idea that hot air rises and cold air settles toward the ground.

More details are given here:

1. **Windcatcher:** The ventilation shafts of the windcatcher reach several feet above the roof to allow cooler air to reach the inside.
2. **Photovoltaic array:** Solar panels extend down the sloped roof and thus capture energy for heating and lighting the house.
3. **Efficient insulation:** The building uses extremely efficient insulation and adds to the home's overall efficiency.
4. **Biomass boilers:** These run on low-cost, renewable organic waste material, such as compressed sawdust discarded by the timber industry.

Performance Studies: An initial concern with the Lighthouse regards the windcatcher itself. It could potentially attract dust, bugs, and possibly birds as well. A solution found to remedy the problem involves installing filters and screens to maintain the interaction with the air outside but keep out pests and unwanted particles. Another remedy to this problem lies in a more traditional approach where the shaft is wider at the base than at the top; this slows down the breeze at the base and allows the dust to settle (also known as an internal dust sill). Currently, the Lighthouse is uninhabited so it can undergo more monitoring and research. At the end of 2007, the prototype fell short of the British construction standards for zero-carbon homes. Another problem that surfaced was keeping the building's air tightness with such a unique shape. Air tightness is an important concern as it increases the efficiency of the building itself. The architects plan on working out these problems and making it available for sale. When it is 100 percent effective, the Lighthouse will be nearly free to operate and maintain.

How Do Elements of This Project Inspire or Relate to My Own Project? Several features attracted me to the Lighthouse. The windcatcher idea was incredibly inspiring; it would be really great if I could incorporate something similar into this in my project. The fact that the architecture firm designing this house wanted to incorporate attractive, modern elements with sustainable design is another reason why I chose this project; this is exactly the direction I want my project to go. I also noticed that the plan seemed to have the feeling of "here and there," as described by NextHouse designer Joel Turkel. The space is open yet retains privacy; this is something I will definitely model my own project after. Overall, the design is contemporary and clean-lined and I was especially drawn to this.

Bibliography

Farr, D. (2008). *Sustainable urbanism: Urban design with nature*. New York: John Wiley.

Halliday, S. (2008). *Sustainable construction*. New York: Butterworth Heinemann. *Lighthouse by Potton*. Retrieved June 2008 from http://www.thelighthousebypotton.co.uk/Press/LighthouseBrochure.pdf

Lighthouse is shining example of eco building. (2007, September 24). Timber and sustainable building. Retrieved June 2008 from http://www.timber-building.com/news/fullstory.php/aid/183/Lighthouse_is_shining_example_of_eco_building.html

Manaugh, G. (2008, May). London cooling. *Dwell*, pp. 100, 102, 104.

✹ ACTIVITY 8.6 Case Study Through Direct Observation

Purpose: To experience, document, and analyze a particular piece of design work, interior space, or exterior space. (It could also be an artifact, a piece of furniture, or a sculpture.) It will serve as the object of a case study, which means that by fully understanding it, you will be able to apply what you've learned to a future project.

1. Choose a space to do a case study on. The place you choose should be something that you have access to—for example, a local business, a public market, a park, or a historical landmark or monument.

2. Fully document the existing space through photographs, floor plans, elevations, detailed sketches, or videotape.

3. Collect archive data such as drawings (plans, sections, elevations, etc.) and three-dimensional representations of your project that you can reproduce. If drawings for your particular project are not available, you will have to construct them to scale from context clues of your research.

4. Find out who designed the item, and collect any kind of documentation of the designer's thoughts or influences. You may find previously documented interviews, videos, and articles, or you may have to contact the designer directly and ask your own questions!

5. Prepare one 20 × 20-inch-square presentation board to distill all of the information down to the most essential aspects, influences, and consequences of the design.
6. Present your case study to the class.

As examples of case studies, you have now seen just a few of the projects that students have used. There is a tendency in interior design to also group case studies into project types. The three student case studies fit into these types:

- Commercial: retail, hospitality, office
- Institutional: educational, health care, museum
- Residential: single family, multi-unit, emergency shelter

This convention makes it easy to reference case studies when you are searching for a project type.

Conclusion

To be a good observer and to learn from your observation, you must call on all of your available resources, including all of your five senses. Like getting multiple perspectives (as was discussed in the "Narrowing Your Research Topic" section of Chapter 4), observation requires gathering multiple perspectives from many points of view and many sources as well as gathering them over time. The mapping techniques and the historical precedent both illustrate that time is an important factor in observation. As you evolve as a designer, observation techniques will expand and develop. Just be sure to keep a fresh, open perspective and never take anything for granted.

References

American Institute of Graphic Arts (AIGA). (2009). *An ethnography primer.* Retrieved January 30, 2009, from http://www.aiga.org/resources/content/3/7/4/5/documents/ethnography_primer.pdf

Fraenkel, J., Wallen, N., & Sawin, E. I. (1999). *Visual statistics: A conceptual primer.* Boston: Allyn & Bacon.

Guerin, D., & Dohr, J. (2007). *Research 101 tutorial: Part III, research methods.* InformeDesign, University of Minnesota. Retrieved December 25, 2007, from http://www.informedesign.umn.edu

Herndon, J. (2008). *Case study: Harris Family Children's Center.* Unpublished master's thesis. The Art Institute of California, San Diego.

Murguia, S. (2008). *Case study: Morgans Hotel.* Unpublished master's thesis. The Art Institute of California, San Diego.

Norberg-Schulz, C. (1980). *Genius loci: Towards a phenomenology of architecture*. New York: Rizzoli.

Pearson, M. A. (2008). *Precedent study 3*. Retrieved January 30, 2009, from www.cod.edu/people/faculty/pearson/Images/2201-3.pdf

Sanoff, H. (1991). *Visual research methods in design*. New York: Van Nostrand Reinhold.

Sommer, R., & Sommer, B. (2002). *A practical guide to behavioral research tools and techniques* (5th ed.). New York: Oxford University Press.

Zeisel, J. (1997). *Inquiry by design: Tools for Environment-Behavior research*. Cambridge: Cambridge University Press.

Part Three

Programming

Part Three of *Research-Inspired Design* is a step-by-step approach to translating the collected information into a written program. Creating your written program is a process that is the heart of this book—the pivotal document that, along with site analysis, seeks to encourage innovation in the design solution.

9 Research-Inspired Design

When you complete this chapter, you should be able to do the following:

- Create a thesis statement that answers your research question.
- Develop a detailed thesis proposal identifying the problem to be solved, your research conclusions, your project intentions, and your goals.
- Identify the issues common to your project type.
- Interpret information gathered through research to create a comprehensive client profile and end user profile.

KEY TERMS

Acronym	Photo study
Client profile	Project type
End user profile	Research question
Ethnography study	Scale
Full-time user	Scope
Knowledge visualization	Thesis
Part-time user	Thesis defense

Your research is going to lead you to conclusions. How you assemble and present all of your information will determine whether others will get onboard with your conclusions. This chapter will walk you through the process of translating your information-gathering about the design problem, theories, solutions, and research into one cohesive body of work called your *thesis*. The thesis will make an argument for your conclusions; and if it is done correctly, it will result in enriching the knowledge available to all interior designers. Although your studio class might be referred to as a *senior project*, a *graduate project*, or a *capstone project*, you will likely be developing a thesis as part of the process.

The Interior Design Thesis

An interior design **thesis** is an argument or a position that a designer develops and supports through a provocative and complex interior design project. There are three organizational parts to an interior design thesis:

- The **thesis statement**—the identification of a problem and proposed solution,
- The **thesis proposal**, or *statement of intent*, which clarifies the details of the proposed thesis solution and outlines the project proposal, and
- The **thesis project**, where you apply the proposed solution in a real-world design scenario.

What Is a Thesis?

A thesis always includes the identification of a problem and a proposed solution to the problem, which is then tested through the thesis project (Hodge & Pollak, 1996). Your thesis project should be a synthesis of everything you have taken from your education thus far, allowing you to draw upon your skills in a complex and challenging application. "A wise student recognizes relationships between one semester's studio project and the last, and predicts issues and interests for exploration in the next; each project stands on its own as well as within a body of work" (Hodge & Pollak, p. 8).

Often an analogy is drawn between a hypothesis and a thesis, and it's true that they're very similar, with each of them involving the testing of an idea.

However, a thesis exists on a larger scale, with a hypothesis acting as one of the many tools used to direct, develop, and strengthen the thesis. The thesis is not just the solution; it also includes all of the research and influences that came together to prove the solution to the problem.

Figure 9.1 exhibits how your thesis statement might relate to a hypothesis, design theory, and design philosophy, as discussed in Chapter 3.

As you develop your interior design thesis, keep in mind these five basic principles:

1. Your thesis is not a statement of fact or an observation, but rather an *assertion* about the facts you have gathered and observations you have conducted. For example, to say that people use many toxic cleaning supplies is to state a fact. A thesis about this topic would first identify a problem: people are poisoning the environment with chemicals to keep their homes and buildings clean. Then it would present a solution: the specification of materials that are durable, stain-resistant, and easy to clean—materials that will reduce the excessive use of toxic cleaners (LEO, 2003).

2. A thesis is research-based. It uses outside sources, including all of those discussed thus far—literature reviews, personal reports, observation, case studies, experimentation, and the development of hypotheses.

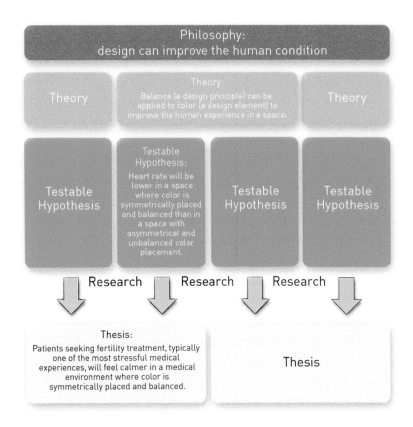

Philosophy:
design can improve the human condition

Theory

Theory:
Balance (a design principle) can be applied to color (a design element) to improve the human experience in a space.

Theory

Testable Hypothesis

Testable Hypothesis:
Heart rate will be lower in a space where color is symmetrically placed and balanced than in a space with asymmetrical and unbalanced color placement.

Testable Hypothesis

Testable Hypothesis

Research   Research   Research

Thesis:
Patients seeking fertility treatment, typically one of the most stressful medical experiences, will feel calmer in a medical environment where color is symmetrically placed and balanced.

Thesis

Figure 9.1 Embedded within your thesis will be the influences of philosophy, theory, and one or more testable hypotheses that have helped you build your argument.

- Keep a small notepad or a stack of index cards handy at all times. Some people use their computer, but your computer likely isn't easy to consult in the aisles of a bookstore or library when an unexpected source arises. When a source looks promising, record the author, title, place of publication, publisher, date of publication, ISBN or call number, library or bookstore where you found the source, and some quick analysis of the source's relevance or importance to your project. This will help you keep track of resources you want to consult as well as those you have already used. Never discard these notes! Keep them so that you know what resources you have explored and so that you don't repeat yourself or waste time tracking down a book you already deemed irrelevant.

- While writing your preliminary draft of your thesis proposal, color code the text in the word-processing file, using a different color for each of your main sources. That way if you forget to cite the source at the time or if you move text around in the editing process, you won't lose track of where your information came from and you can easily identify the source to cite at a later time. Remember to change all of your text back to black before submitting your work.

Also, the direction your research takes will be greatly influenced by your adopted philosophies and theories.

3. The depth of research supporting your thesis project should make you an authority or expert on some focused element of the design field. Thus, you want to take on a topic and project for which you have some kind of personal and professional interest, such as lighting design, exhibit design, or green design.

4. The thesis project should have a current and relevant purpose and use that can be applied as a contribution to the expanding body of knowledge available in the field.

5. The thesis has a working bibliography that allows you to keep an organized record of your research.

Developing a Thesis Statement

Most often, the *thesis statement* is a two- or three-sentence declarative statement—positioned near the end of the first paragraph of the thesis proposal or statement of intent—that explicitly outlines the purpose or point of your project and makes a claim that you will support and defend with your research. A good analogy is that a thesis statement is to a thesis project as a topic sentence is to a paragraph. Usually, the thesis statement comprises three parts: problem, theory, and solution. You state the problem or issue you have identified, then your theory about this problem, and finally your proposed solution to the problem. The problem is *why* you have chosen this thesis. The solution is *what* will solve the problem. The theory connects the two by telling *how* the solution will solve the problem. Your research will either support this model or weaken it.

You may be more comfortable treating your thesis statement as a statement, but it can also be posed as a **thesis question**. The question "Is this the right solution to the problem?" would be answered through a series of unfolding revelations that progress toward a conclusion that finally answers the question. If you want to try this format, don't lose sight of your content in the process of rewording it. Try turning some practice statements into questions before tackling your thesis statement.

For some students the thesis is a series of statements, followed by thought-provoking questions to reinforce the research direction. The following is an example of student Jennifer Newton's thesis statement:

> Houses are no longer compartmentalized. Instead, they encourage discovery and social interaction. This social interaction extends to several relationships: How residents interact with their physical space (bringing in the idea of the relationship between a building and its users), how residents interact with each other, and how residents interact with nature.
>
> What principles define the ideal living environment? How then can the typical home environment be reinterpreted to encourage social and spatial interaction and include these ideal principles?

Your thesis statement is a response to an open-ended **research question** (discussed in Chapters 4 and 5) that motivates your research process. Your research reveals many potential answers or solutions to your research question, and the thesis statement selects one of the potential solutions and says, "This one is the right one!" (See Figure 9.2.) Your thesis statement will present your knowledge in a well-written, coherent format, and it will establish the foundation of your thesis project. It must include the following elements: (1) the identification of a current and relevant design problem and (2) a proposed design solution to the problem. Often it is bracketed by an opening explanation of what inspired the project or by clarification of the context of the problem, as well as a clear closing statement of the designer's goals for the project. By solving the problem, what do you hope to accomplish? Finally, your thesis statement must also take a stand, declaring that this one solution over all others is the correct one.

Figure 9.2 The thesis statement chooses one solution out of many possibilities and says, "This one is the right one!"

Turning Your Research Question into a Thesis Statement

Purpose: **To turn your open-ended research question into a declarative statement or statements that communicate the problem, your theory, and the solution that your thesis project will explore.**

The thesis statement must be clear and concise, and approaching it step by step is essential to capturing that clarity and focus. Use the chart below to help you maintain a methodical approach.

1. *Identify your research question.* This is the question that motivated you to begin researching a topic in the first place.
2. *Identify the problem.* Be careful that you identify not the symptoms of the problem, but the problem itself. This is where focus is essential. You will not be able to solve the problem if you haven't correctly identified it.
3. *Identify the solution you have selected. This is also the answer to the research question.* This is where you are stating the solution to the problem.
4. *State your theory about the problem. This theory must also support the solution.* This is where you summarize your theory about the topics and issues of the thesis. Why do you think this is the right solution? How do you think your solution solves the problem?
5. *Create a declarative sentence or sentences combining steps 2, 3, and 4.* This is your thesis statement. It will have embedded in it the context of the thesis, the problem, the theory you are applying to the problem, and the solution.

(1) Question	Your research question. What are you studying?
(2) Problem	Problem that you have identified.
(3) Solution	Solution you have selected to answer the research question.
(4) Theory	Your theory about the problem; supports your solution.
(5) Statement	Declarative sentence or phrase combining items 2, 3, and 4.

Your thesis statement must be written with careful deliberation and polished until it finally encompasses the central idea of your thesis project, summarizing your research in two or three concise sentences. The following are some principles (adapted from Owl at Purdue, 2008) to follow when writing a thesis statement:

- It is not a fact or casual observation; it must beg to be proved. Someone should be able to theoretically argue against it. How successfully they argue will depend, of course, on how persuasive you are.
- It takes a position on a topic rather than simply announcing that the project is about a topic. Clearly taking a stand may encourage controversy or inspire other points of view.
- It should call attention to the innovation in your project.
- It argues one main point, which may be followed by a few, specific supporting points that will also be addressed.
- Most important, it passes the "So What?" test: Tell us something new about something we care about.

ACTIVITY 9.2 Knowledge Visualization for Communicating Ideas with Imagery

Purpose: To communicate your thesis statement in a graphic format.

Sometimes we can develop, communicate, or reinforce our ideas, concepts, and knowledge more effectively through images, a technique sometimes referred to as **knowledge visualization**. This tool is especially useful when you are trying to capture the essence of insight, experience, attitudes, values, perspectives, opinions, and predictions.

1. Collect three images to present as part of your thesis proposal.
   - *A Found Photograph (to illustrate the problem)*—Find a photo that is a visual representation of your design problem or issue. Be creative. What would express the essence of the problem? Look at the list of inspirations at the end of Chapter 3 for ideas on where to look for this image.
   - *An Image of a Hand (to illustrate your theory)*—To graphically represent your theory, produce a photograph of a hand. In this image, document a hand engaged in a way that reflects your theory about the problem and/or the solution to the problem. You can photograph the image yourself or have a friend take the photo. The important thing is that the hand is the subject of the image. The hand embodies action, and your theory is essentially a call for action to solve the problem. Remember this: Your solution is what you will do, but the theory embodies how you will do it.
   - *A Line Drawing, Diagram, or Object (to illustrate the solution)*—Find a line drawing, a diagram, or an object that is an expression of your solution. This could be something you make or something you find. Again, just let it be an expression of your vision of how your goal would be accomplished. This is not meant to be a design drawing for the project. It is an expression of the meaning behind the solution.

2. Present your three images to the class along with your thesis statement. Get feedback on the clarity of your ideas. Do the images you selected support the nature and goals of the project? Figure 9.3 presents an example of knowledge visualization applied to a thesis statement.

Figure 9.3 This series of images: a child riding a bike, a hand holding an egg, and a sketch illustrating the concept of a "safety bubble" represents a thesis exploring a safe play environment for children and poses the question, "Have play environments for children become too safe?" This thesis studies the relationship of safety and the concept of challenge in a play environment for children, seeking the ideal balance of safety and challenge.

As you develop your thesis statement, use the following questions to test your statement:

- *Complexity:* Does my thesis question answer or explore a challenging design question?
- *Relevance:* Is the point I am making one that would generate thought-provoking discussion or argument?
- *Scope:* Is my thesis too vague? Too general? Should I focus on a more specific aspect of my topic?
- *Objectivity:* Does my thesis deal objectively with the topic at hand, or is it an emotional declaration of my personal feelings?
- *Professional Context:* Does my introduction place my thesis within the larger, ongoing scholarly discussion about my topic?

The following are examples of thesis projects and the statements and questions that were proposed by the interior design thesis students who developed them:

- Green Apartment complex for employees of Toyota: Is the answer to sustainable design found in the past rather than the future? Can looking to traditional Japanese architecture help us find the answers to today's environmental needs and challenges? (Yuki Endo)
- Museum of Religion and Spirituality: Can a church become a museum, or will it always be seen as a church? Is our connection to iconography and symbolism so embedded in our collective consciousness that a sacred space cannot become a secular space?
- Redesign of the local Humane Society animal habitat: More cats and dogs are euthanized each year due to lack of proper socialization than due to lack of space or funding. This can be changed if we rethink and redesign the typical human society model of housing dogs in cages. Isolation in cages creates socially deprived and stressed animals. An interactive, homelike environment can increase adoptions and decrease rates of euthanization. (Michelle Hill Gilles)
- Redesign of Terminal 1, Lindbergh Field, San Diego, California: San Diego's airport, Lindbergh Field, is face-to-face with frustration as the density of passengers has increased but the building has not and cannot due to space limitations. Can we explore the idea of physical density versus psychological density to provide a more comfortable airport experience for passengers and staff of the airport? (Kelly Powell)

Think of your thesis statement as a "working thesis statement," as it often shifts and evolves in response to your programming process, which will be discussed further in Chapter 10.

Writing Your Thesis Proposal

The *thesis proposal* is a critical element that creates a link between your research and the programming phase of your thesis project. It explains the research about the problem, the influences on the problem, and the proposed solutions to the problem. At many schools, it is a written document and verbal presentation that must be approved before the student is allowed to move forward. Your thesis proposal is the gateway to thesis design and the rest of the thesis process. Because of this, it is important to approach your thesis proposal with the same consideration you would give a position paper or persuasive speech. You should be clear, thorough, and, most of all, confident and enthusiastic about your ideas.

The thesis proposal must get the attention of the audience. It is up to you to establish your audience's interest in your project and get them to relate to at least some part of your project. Usually the best way to do this is by sharing your inspiration for the project. There is a good chance that the reasons you care will also be the reasons the audience will care. Your proposal must be very clear, communicating your ideas effectively. Plus, you must establish your academic and professional credibility with the breadth and thoroughness of your research and the thoughtfulness of your solutions.

Table 9.1 provides a format to follow to ensure that the thesis proposal covers all critical points. Manipulate the format here and there to tailor it to your unique project criteria. Remember, this is the core of your project intentions and ideas: the Who, What, Where, and Why of your project! To relate the thesis proposal to an application in the professional world, a project proposal is often how you get the funding for your great ideas. So don't leave anything out. Do not assume that because the instructor has been meeting with you throughout the quarter, thoroughness is not an issue. Write your proposal as though the reader knows *nothing* about your project. In some institutions, the instructor is not the person who approves the proposal, so if something is not in your document and presentation, your reviewers, critics, or jury might never see it!

Your thesis proposal likely will not be presented in chart or table format, but instead will be a well-written academic paper and bibliography. The table format used below is simply intended to delineate between the different elements you will be discussing.

Once you've written the thesis proposal and designed the thesis project, the breadth and thoroughness of your research and your subsequent conclusions should stand on their own: capable of being used by others, independent of you. Your conclusions will add to the body of interior design knowledge, and another researcher should be able to pick up where you left off and build upon your conclusions (Groat & Wang, 2002, p. 46).

Table 9.1 The Thesis Proposal

Section #	Section Title	Goals	Questions to Answer	Tips
1	Introductory Sentence and Paragraph	Catch the attention of the audience that will experience your project.	What inspired you to pursue this thesis? What is/are the problem(s) you have identified and are investigating? How does this thesis relate to the larger context of interior design?	Show your passion for your topic, but maintain objectivity. Thesis is not the place to make an emotional argument.
2	Thesis Statement and Supporting Context	Identify the problem, and propose your solution. You can also use this as a transition into your project type and title.	What is the problem? What is your solution? What are your goals for the project? What do you hope to accomplish with this solution?	Usually located at the end of the first paragraph. Present it in boldface type, or separate it from the main body of the text.
3	Your Project Type and Title	Establish the unique identity of your project.	What is the name of your project? What is your client profile? What is your client's motivation for investing in this project?	Keep it simple: "In order to explore the previous statement, I am creating a _____. It is called _____." Then develop this further.
4	Your Poetic Concept or Theme	Use this to hook the audience and draw them further into exploring your vision for your project.	What is this project and space about? What are your creative and conceptual ideas? What makes this place unique?	Include any quotes, images, or other inspirations here to help explain and sell your ideas. Use Activity 9.2 to help you.
5	Area of Professional Focus	Identify the two or three categories of interior design that you will apply to exploring your thesis.	What area of interior design will you become an expert in as you design this project?	This should relate to your professional goals, as it will give you a thorough skill set that might steer the direction of your career. For example, if you want to work in museums, an area of professional focus should be exhibit design.

continued

Section #	Section Title	Goals	Questions to Answer	Tips
6	End User Profile	Establish the complex identity of your end user or user group.	Who is this place for? What is the demographic of your user? Does the user have special wants or needs? What influence does your user have on your project?	Understanding your end user is key to the success of any project. Take the time to truly "know" your end user. Use techniques from this chapter as well as from Chapters 3, 4, and 6.
7	Activity Requirements	Define the overall functions and primary uses of the space or building.	What is the overall function of the place? What primary end user activities will you be designing for?	Activities should define a space, not a preconceived notion of what a space should be. (This is the foundation for "Activity-Based Programming," discussed in Chapter 10.)
8	Programmatic Requirements	Establish the objective and goals of the project, and provide a space-by-space breakdown.	What are the square footage requirements? What is the overall organization of the space? What are the individual spaces? What are the primary relationships between spaces? How will the place be used?	This portion is not just an itemized list, but your opportunity to connect the user to the space: to tell your reader how the spaces will be used, and what the choreography of the user experience will be.
9	Spaces of Focus	To help you define the scope, identify spaces or areas of the project that apply to your thesis.	What spaces within this project will you be designing in detail? If you are designing a pediatric cancer treatment center this might include one floor of the building, which houses the private patient rooms, nurse's stations, and the infusion unit.	This is especially significant if you have a very large-scale or small-scale project. Know your time frame and what you can accomplish. Do not expect to design everything. Instead, identify the areas that are essential to exploring your thesis.
10	Site Selection	Share existing site and building conditions and any contextual factors, such as historical, cultural, or regional information.	Where is this building? What is the regional, local, and site context? What are the significant features of the site or building? Does the building hold historical significance?	This is the "nuts and bolts" of the site. Share any significant building features that will help you to explore your thesis and project goals.

Section #	Section Title	Goals	Questions to Answer	Tips
11	A Sense of Place	Place the site within a larger context.	Why did you select this place, and why is it suitable to your project? Does the building fit the program? How are you improving the site with your project? Will you make it a better place? How will you give character and add enrichment and expression to the place?	Share your general intention or vision about the place or space, so that the reader understands what makes this building appropriate in relation to your goals.
12	Identify and address any consistent or anticipated questions or challenges to your thesis.	Prepare yourself to defend your thesis to a wide variety of critics, peers, and professionals.	What are the questions thus far, and what are the answers? Where are the holes in your argument? How does your research address these issues? What are the foundations of your ideas?	This is your chance to strengthen your argument by arming yourself with the tools to confidently defend your ideas. Defending a thesis is always challenging, but your preparation will support your reasons for persistence.
The End	Bibliography	Show the depth and breadth of your research process, and give credit to the sources that built your argument.	What format will be required by your instructor? What are your literary sources? Did you watch any films or speak with any experts you should credit? Have you thoroughly documented each and every source so as to avoid unintentional plagiarism?	This bibliography will serve as a resource for future researchers who will build their own research upon your conclusions and what you have contributed to the interior design field.

Develop the ability to recognize which ideas are worth pursuing and the ability to persuade others of the value of your ideas. Don't get so overburdened by your research about the topic or the interior design field that the weight of the information and knowledge interferes with the creative interpretation and generation of new ideas. Be open-minded, think independently, and be prepared to potentially defy the crowd and advocate ideas that you believe in but others may not agree with. Remember, a project that creates a little controversy can be a good thing. It means your audience is engaged; it means they care (Weisberg, 2006, p. 100).

Using Research to Develop
Your Thesis Project Type

Embedded somewhere in the thesis proposal will be the identification of your **project type**, which usually defines the primary function of the space. It is important to develop your research, identify the problem, and propose the solution before selecting your project type. Although you may have an idea of where the project type is headed, simply by the focus of your research, the identity of the project should emerge out of a response to the problem. Otherwise, you may end up with a "square peg in a round hole" situation, where you limit the potential of what your project type could be by forcing it to be something you are already familiar with.

Once you have identified your project type, you will need to familiarize yourself with the programming and design issues associated with the project type, such as sustainability, budgets, social responsibility, needs and requirements, terminology, controversy, and innovation. "Every project type has a history of development and its own vocabulary. There are theories or philosophies associated with each building type that you need to understand . . . [In the real world], your client already knows many of these things, and in order for you to communicate, you have to speak the language" (Cherry, 1999, p. 87).

You should also have an understanding of the context of the project type: political, social, geographical, or historical (Cherry, 1999). When designing a restaurant, for example, you might want to know about the dramatic origins of the restaurant in France after the French Revolution—as a place that served *essences,* broths made primarily from chicken and beef and served to restore strength to the sick. Knowing this historical reference might help to enrich your programming and design process and add meaning to your design decisions.

Use the case studies and techniques discussed in Chapter 8 to familiarize yourself with your project type and to help you identify issues common to the project type. In the book *Programming for Design*, Edith Cherry uses the example of a museum. Regardless of the uniqueness of a particular museum project, the museum project type always addresses issues of flow and how museum patrons will circulate through the building and the exhibits. Your project research should alert you to this issue, so that the issue can inform your thesis proposal and programming process (Cherry, 1999).

Another example related to museums and other large institutional projects involves the use of project-specific terminology and **acronyms** (abbreviations made by the first letter of a series of words; for example, in health care design, an M.O.B. refers to a "medical office building," while in commercial projects a T.I. project is a "tenant improvement project." It is likely that when you are in practice and you attend a start-up meeting, your client will use terms that are unfamiliar to you. Sometimes it can feel like everyone around the table is speaking a different language! Familiarize yourself with these terms before meeting with the client, and don't be afraid to ask for clarification. This may happen in your interviews, observation, or literature review, so the point is equally important. Your knowledge of professional terms will increase your level of professional credibility with the client or end users.

Scale Versus Scope

A project type question that students often ask is, "How big does my project have to be?" This is a valid question, but at this point the project is not concerned with **scale**, or *size*. During the thesis development, there is no requirement for how many square feet the project has to be. What matters is how in-depth you go. In a thesis project, **scope,** or the depth and detail of the project, is everything. For example, an industrial designer could be given the task of designing a backpack, a seemingly small design project. However, the industrial designer could spend months designing the backpack if he integrates innovations such as a solar panel (like the one shown in Figure 9.4) that collects energy to power a small reading light, or a waterproofing technique to allow the pack to be submerged in water (Smithsonian Institution, 2007). After the Columbine school shooting in April 1999, some backpacks were designed with Kevlar to be bulletproof in the case of another shooting, and after the attacks on the Twin Towers in New York City you could find an executive backpack that included a parachute! More recent is the development of a backpack with an ergonomic shape and a suspension system to reduce the impact of the backpack's weight on the body (Binns, 2007).

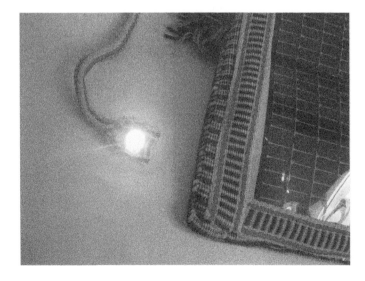

Figure 9.4 As the size of a project gets smaller, the scope can get larger. This small handbag was a complex innovation to bring reading lights to children who are seeking to get a better education in nonindustrialized countries. It includes solar panels to collect energy during the day and a small flexible reading light for use at night (Smithsonian, 2007). The Portable Light Project was established by MATx, the material-research unit of KVA (Kennedy and Violich Architecture), in Sierra Madre, Mexico.

Rather than focusing on the size of the project type, focus on the scope and on what you can accomplish in the time frame allotted with your classes. If you select a small single-family dwelling, the small size could prompt you to increase the level of detail in order to increase the scope of the project. If you are designing an airport, the large size means you would need to focus on carefully chosen areas to reduce the scope of the project.

Developing a Client Profile

As discussed in Chapter 6, the client is the person who hires you and provides the funding for your project. In the professional world, the client typically comes to you. When you're developing an academic project, however, unless the instructor provides you with a client it is up to you to decide who that person or group of people might be. As Edith Cherry puts it, "Self-awareness is the first step to understanding your client and their thought process" (1999, p. 21).

When seeking out a client for your thesis, ask yourself, "Who would be willing to invest in what I am proposing?" For example, if you are creating a women's shelter, your client might be the American Red Cross. If you are designing a museum of religion and spirituality, your client might be the Smithsonian Institution.

Your client could be an individual, such as Oprah Winfrey; a company, such as GAP; an organization, such as the American Red Cross; an institution, such as a university; or a foundation; such as the Getty Foundation. Regardless of size or visibility, the client is the ultimate decision-maker for the project.

The client and the end user are often the same person, as in the case of a residential project or when a CEO or university president hires you to design his or her personal office. Some of the most dynamic thesis projects are those in which the student has identified a real person to approach as a client and has the opportunity to interview and observe the person and then use this information to develop a very realistic client profile and/or user profile. Other times the client is completely separate from the end user. Most commonly the client is one of many end users in a project—such as a couple who hires you to design a home for themselves and their five children, in which case they are two of seven end users. A partner in a law firm might hire you to redesign the firm's offices, in which case the partner would be one end user and the staff and clients would be the other end users.

You can apply the information-gathering techniques you mastered in Chapters 6, 7, and 8 to create a comprehensive client profile for your thesis project. For example, as previously discussed, the company fathom (spelled with a lowercase letter "f") uses innovative techniques to understand its residential clients, taking the clients through a rigorous process of delving into the subconscious to extract deep-seated wants and needs—a process that fathom calls the "deep design process."

For example, a typical fathom client might experience the following process: First the client is asked to collect eight metaphorical images expressing how he feels about his home office. Over the next few weeks, the company takes him through a process that includes the following information-gathering techniques: an extensive 90-minute ZMET (Zaltman Metaphor Eliciting Technique) interview, a brainstorming session, and psychological exercises that come together to produce "design objectives." Part of the interviewing process (performed by Olson Zaltman Associates in Boston) involves creating a short story with characters representing the client, his current office, and his ideal office, as well as creating a collage that serves as his summary statement for the process (see the collage in Figure 9.5). The brainstorming session and psychological exercises (performed at fathom's office in Pittsburgh) include the client sorting preselected images into piles representing his thoughts and feelings about an ideal office. He also participates in PPG's Color Sense Game™, an online color game that reveals what colors he is most compatible with. All of these information-gathering techniques play a part in creating an in-depth and insightful client profile that will serve as inspiration for the final home office (Berdik, 2005), shown in Figure 9.6.

Familiarize yourself with the impact your client will have on the project. The client holds the keys, so to speak, so all design decisions must be made in response to your client's requests. The greatest influence the client has is usually on the project's budget. A recreation center sponsored by Nike is going to have a different design direction (and budget) than one run by a city government or one started by a local businessperson.

Figure 9.5 (below left) A collage created with a patented process called ZMET (Zaltman Metaphor Elicitating Technique) used to extract "hidden knowledge" locked deep inside our heads (Berdik, 2005).

Figure 9.6 (below right) The results of fathom's creative information-gathering process: a home office with a bay window to provide short breaks, a skylight, and flexible work spaces to support the client's multitasking work process (Berdik, 2005).

Sometimes a students says, "My boss really wants to redesign her shop," and asks, "Can I make her my client and redesign the store as my thesis project?" Hiring on to design a space for someone (usually without being paid) and then turning the work into your thesis project is not the same as selecting a client through the research process and making the experience an opportunity to deepen the thesis exploration. An academic studio is a place for exploring the realm of possibilities and creating ideas, not for creating a product. To hire yourself out often dilutes your academic potential by removing control of your thesis proposal from you and placing it in the hands of your "boss."

When you present your design project, critics might point out that given your particular client, some furniture or finish selections would be unrealistic. As you select your client, take some time to analyze the resources the individual or organization might have. This doesn't mean you should automatically select a wealthy client so that you "don't have to worry about budget." Be true to the project, and remember that budget is not a limitation but an opportunity to be creative. In today's world, some of the most provocative projects are made out of recycled license plates and reclaimed barn wood.

What Should Your Client Profile Include?

To create your **client profile**, at a minimum include the following (if your client is your end user, please refer to the following section called "Developing a User Profile" for more in-depth development):

1. Name of the individual or organization
2. Name of the decision-maker within the organization
3. Logo if applicable
4. Location
5. Company organization and background
6. Budget constraints
7. Previous involvement with similar projects
8. Statement discussing the client's reason for investing in this project
9. Summary of the client's goals, wants, and needs

Developing a client profile is one task for which the Internet can be especially helpful. You can begin by searching online to brainstorm the options for a project client. Once you have identified a client, there is often a wealth of important information about the client on the Internet, as well as ideas for how and where you might dig deeper. For example, you may learn on a Web site that your client has had books or articles published, so you might track down her publications. Or you might discover that your client's place of business is very near you, so you can arrange a site visit or even an observation session. Many students interview their hypothetical project client to get feedback directly from the source. In this case, the client may even attend the student's final **thesis defense**, or the final *thesis presentation*, to offer feedback. If you are not able to get an interview with your client's leaders or other management, there is still a good chance you could talk with another representative of the company or organization. This can be just as valuable, especially if that representative is also part of your user group.

Developing a User Profile

The traditional methods used to develop a design, although valuable as a "starting point," do not allow the architect or designer to connect with the end user on a profound level. That is why we need more meaningful research techniques, such as those discussed in the earlier chapters of this book, to help us create the end user profile. Louis D. Astorino, founder of Astorino, an architecture and engineering company that specializes in using design to enhance the quality of the human experience, explains the situation like this:

> Traditionally, architects achieve great design that supports established relevant goals. Design elements are selected based upon the design team's experience, as well as client needs assessments, interviews and surveys conducted during pre-design. While these planning tools offer insights as a starting point for determining necessary physical attributes, they do not enable the architect to connect with the end users on a profound emotional, intellectual or experiential level (Ilov, 2008).

Using research to develop your user profile can be one of the most exciting parts of a design project. The company fathom believes that a project's success depends upon the designer's understanding of the end users. Christine Astorino of fathom explains: "Our process is founded in the belief that a project's success depends on truly understanding the users—the challenges they face, the goals and dreams they hold close and the type of environment that will help them succeed" (Ilov, 2008).

"Because fathom avoids 'that's the way it is always done,' the research techniques used to understand the client are based on the principle that people can't communicate things they haven't seen before" (Ilov, 2008). So, as a designer, how do you get that deeper information from a user, when in truth they may not know what they don't know? In addition to techniques mentioned previously, fathom uses background research, one-on-one interviews, ethnography and photo studies, color studies, and personal profiles. Figures 9.7, 9.8, and 9.9 represent the information-gathering phase, the interpretation, and the design application, respectively, for an individual dwelling.

For every project, fathom brings together a variety of experts, specialists, and consultants such as industrial designers, graphic designers, interior designers, color specialists, anthropologists, psychologists, and neuroscien-

Figure 9.7 (right) Information-gathering: A collage of images selected by a client to represent his subconscious design ideals (Conley, 2006).

Figure 9.8 (below left) Interpretation: Notes and early sketches from fathom's brainstorming process. Notice how the step-by-step process unfolds from general issue, to specific issue, to design objectives and the designer's thoughts (Conley, 2006).

Figure 9.9 (below right) Design application and presentation: A computer rendering of the client's new home, designed based on the information extracted during the extensive research process (Conley, 2006).

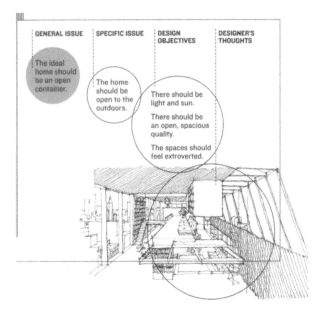

tists. This dynamic team reviews all of the complex information gathered and interprets it with a variety of unique perspectives in order to best determine the programming and design criteria that will respond to create that feeling.

Within a single project you can have great user diversity. So how do you counterbalance that? By making no assumptions, taking time to get to know your user, being thoughtful, and being insightful. Understanding your user is your opportunity to turn interior design into a means of bettering the human experience. Take advantage of being a part of something bigger!

The best way to start your **end user profile** is with an attitude of empathy. Empathy goes beyond sympathy in that it is the ability to actually put yourself "in the other person's shoes" and truly see things through that person's "lens of experience." Thoughtfully interpret the information you gather about the end users to help you feel what they feel, see what they see, and experience what they experience. The result of this will be a clear insight into your user's wants and needs.

While conducting a photo study of a local hospital, a student documented a large clock on the footwall of a patient's room. The student's immediate interpretation was that the clock must be very discouraging to the patient as it slowly ticked away the minutes of the day. A follow-up interview with the patient revealed that the clock was actually comforting to the patient. If she was hungry she could see when lunch would arrive; if she was in pain she could see when pain medication would be delivered; and most important, it let her know when her next visitor would arrive. Knowing this allowed the student to thoughtfully and accurately interpret the information gathered during the photo study.

When fathom was developing the program for a Veterans Administration hospital called Veterans' Recovery Center, they asked this question: "How can we allow our nation's veterans to help change the face of the VA?" The answer was to let the veterans tell their own stories. For example, one of the end users was a homeless veteran who was suffering from a mental illness. At one time he had been a special agent in the armed forces and had earned several medals for serving his country. As a designer, you have an opportunity to recognize that this end user is not simply a homeless person. This is not how he started out, and in fact he has done amazing things in his life. So knowing this, can you let him help you design his space?

What Should Your User Profile Include?

Your information-gathering no doubt reveals such statistical information as age, sex, and ethnicity. However, there is no formulaic system for telling the story of another human being, as each project and each user and user group will be different. It is up to you to develop a personal profile for your users both at the group level and at the individual level. Start with the general and then move into the more specific as time and resources allow.

First, separate the **full-time users** from the **part-time users** to make the process more manageable. Full-time users are the people who use the space a significant amount of time at regular and frequent intervals. For example, in a museum the full-time users would be the staff and administration who work there all day every day. Your part-time users are the individuals who use the space intermittently. In the museum, the part-time users would be the visitors or researchers. Keep in mind that you can have multiple types of full-time or part-time users in any project. For example, a museum might have a curatorial staff as well as an administrative staff. Both groups are full-time users; however, they might have very different needs.

At the large or general scale, use data about demographics, trends, target markets, etc., to identify the following characteristics:

- Age
- Sex/gender
- Socioeconomics/Class/Income
- Personal interests/Affiliations
- Ethnicity/religion/culture
- Physical characteristics/Health status/Abilities
- Politics
- Profession

Next, if you have multiple user groups, identify them and shift your focus to these groups. Characterize the demographic differences between the groups, as well as the differences in how the groups will use the space. For example, in a high-end retail shop located in a mall, the demographics of the full-time employee user group will likely be different from those of the part-time customer user group. There will also be differences in which spaces each group uses and how. For example, the customers will use the dressing rooms differently than the employees do, and the customers will not be using the break room. Identify these differences so you know how to design for both.

When working at this scale, also identify the relationships between the users and user groups. Is there a hierarchy? Are there issues of public space and private space? Are there patterns of people-grouping? For example, in an advertising agency, the creative team might be grouped separately from the graphics and technology team. Again, you must know and understand the reasons for these relationships so you can design for them.

In most architecture and interiors firms, it is common to separate the architecture and interiors professionals into separate units. OPX, a strategy and architecture company in Washington, D.C., uses an open floor plan, free of hierarchy or divisions between Architecture and Interiors. This design solution accomplishes a dynamic of interaction and open communication that makes everyone an equal partner on a project with an equal sense of personal responsibility for the project's success.

The final step is to explore the user at the individual level in order to gain a deeper insight into the process. Here, creativity is a key component when you are interpreting, communicating, and translating information into design.

An innovative technique for both gathering information and interpreting it is to use an anthropological approach. An **ethnography study**, previously discussed in Chapter 8, is a descriptive anthropological technique that involves the study and documentation of a culture. In other words, ethnography tells the story of a people. As interior designers, we can apply the same storytelling techniques to understand and communicate information about our end users. An ethnography study can help you go beyond mere statistics to accomplish the following:

- Identify patterns in behavior.
- See "backstage."
- Capture emotional expression.
- Tell a story.
- Pay attention to detail.
- See from a new perspective.

Ethnography uses many of the same techniques we have already discussed, such as interviews and observation, but it also uses creative documentation to extract the meaning of the information gathered.

One of those creative documentation techniques is a **photo study**. A photo study for interior design documents the interaction between people and their environment. You can either take the photos yourself, or offer the user or user group a disposable camera and ask them to take pictures of "a day in their life." Sometimes this second option works better, since you will see the experience directly through the eyes of the end user. You can focus a photo study in various ways: take images of only the space itself, of objects in the space, of people in the space, of activities in the space, or a combination of all of these. The key is to remain open-minded. Photograph whatever seems significant at the time, free of interpretation. You can extract meaning and draw conclusions later.

ACTIVITY 9.3 "Points of View"—Documenting and Interpreting the User's Wants and Needs Through a Photo Study

Purpose: **To add a layer of objectivity to your observation process by performing your observation technique through the eyes of a camera.**

By removing yourself from the situation now and reviewing the images later, you can often see things you would not have seen in the moment.

1. Select one of the following people:
   - A creative professional
   - A college student
   - A construction worker
   - A firefighter or other service person
   - A priest, minister, rabbi, or other spiritual teacher
   - A homeless person
   - A new mother
   - A patient in a hospital
   - A bride or groom preparing for the wedding
   - Or . . . a prototype of your typical user

2. Using a disposable or digital camera and using photographs only, create a photo montage expressing "a day in the life."

3. **Rule for this photo study:** Do not take pictures of the person. Only take pictures of the artifacts or objects in the environment and trace evidence of the person's interaction with the environment. (Recall the discussion of trace evidence in Chapter 8.) Keep in mind that an object you photograph, such as a shoe, could be connected to a person, but the subject of the photo must be what is significant about the shoe, not what is significant about the person.

4. Print your images and assemble them on a piece of matte board. Arrange them in meaningful relationships. As you create the montage, consider the story you want to tell. What images capture the reality, the feeling, the emotion, the relics and objects, the interactions with people or things? How does the person leave the mark of his day on the spaces around him?

5. Share your montage with the class. Tell them what you have learned and get their feedback. Do they see something that you did not? Getting a variety of opinions on your photo study is essential to an accurate interpretation.

Now, for your thesis project do the same for your end user!

Similar to developing your client profile, developing your user profile offers an opportunity to identify a real person or group of people to serve as a prototype of your typical user. You can then use these techniques to build your user profile and your thesis proposal.

Case Study
Exploring the User Experience

It is essential that you understand the differences among information-gathering, documentation, interpretation, and presentation. In their project at Mellon Arena, home of the Pittsburgh Penguins in Pittsburgh, Pennsylvania, fathom used interviews and observation to collect information, and then they used thorough notes and a photo study to document the information. They interpreted the results by categorizing the user experience into phases and extracting an interpretation of what that phase of the experience meant to the user. Finally, they presented a well-thought-out selection of images and quotes, arranged in a meaningful montage.

Users are sometimes resistant to change in their conditions or environment. According to fathom, the best way to deal with this resistance is to get your users on board by involving them in the process. The following photo studies and interviews with the staff and fans at Mellon Arena comprehensively tell the story of the Penguins fans. Fathom understands that for the devoted Penguins fan, nostalgia and pride can create an attachment to the existing arena and a resistance to change. They also understand that the fan experience begins long before the fans actually walk into the arena building.

The following pages (Figure 9.10) tell the story of the Penguins fans' experience, organizing it into six phases, beginning with the moment of the ticket purchase and lasting until the post-game events.

Fathom's presentation method successfully translates the emotion and excitement of the fan experience to the programming and design team, adding insight to the design process and creating a new arena that embodies the essence of the Penguins fan experience and responds to the pride the fans feel for their team.

Figure 9.10 Nostalgia and pride can make sports fans very attached to their local sports arena. When designing the new Mellon Arena in Pittsburgh, Pennsylvania, fathom understood this and found fans to be more receptive to change if they were part of the process. Fathom separated the fan experience into seven stages and used quotes from fans, descriptive imagery, and a clear definition of project goals to create a storyboard that describes the fan experience and helps designers consider design decisions from the fan perspective.

"...the stresses of everyday life that all of us have in our jobs and whatnot, and families and bills and all that stuff, and you go to a hockey game, or any other sport for that matter, and *it just takes you away* and gets you thinking about something else for a couple of hours." —*Penguins fan*

"I guess just by going and supporting them *I feel like in some insignificant, tiny way I've contributed* to help achieve and so I feel proud." —*Penguins fan*

ticket purchase

Make the process convenient whether online, by phone or at the box office and create a sense of anticipation during the ticket purchase. Instill a sense of curiosity and pride in the arena for non-fans as well.

fathom THE PITTSBURGH PENGUINS

pre-turnstile

The pre-turnstile process begins when one departs home or work for the arena. Things like parking, using public transportation, walking to the arena, shopping or dining in the city beforehand are part of the pre-turnstile experience. There are different forms of energy—focused energy around the arena/concourses, and intense energy in the bowl. How do we enhance this part of the experience and create hope in the team and anticipation in the city?

"...people when they come out of the office they're still connected to the office. All the things that they're thinking about all day long. As they get a little further away, they're still thinking about how I forgot to do this, I forgot to do that, then they get closer and they see the building. It kind of washes some of that away. You know, you're about to go into the arena and then they pull their ticket out of their pocket and that feels like **this is something that's going to change me...**" —Penguins staff

"...imagine walking into the plaza or any of the plazas and having hidden speakers, kind of like what you see at Epcot, that have different sounds... and it being something as subtle as us recording a youth hockey practice with no yelling or screaming or talking, but it's just **the sound of blades cutting through the ice**, sticks tapping on the ice, pucks being hit into the nets..." —Penguins staff

"It's very cold looking, it's not very inviting...**it's not really something that says, 'come up here and check this out.'**" —Penguins staff

[talking about another arena]...It kind of represented that you were going into something and **you could see that there was excitement inside**, where not so much in the arena because there's very limited view into the actual building from the outside. I know what's going on in there, so I'm excited to go in, but if you didn't - it's just not an inviting building." —Penguins fan

fathom THE PITTSBURGH PENGUINS

arrival

Arrival is the initial impression one has upon entering the arena. How can we enhance it to immerse each person in the experience instead of being a mere spectator? Welcome each fan and create a sense of anticipation with things like programs, giveaways, signage as well as sights, smells and sounds.

"And they all funnel in Gate Three because that's where a lot of the people are walking up from because that's where most of the parking is except for the surface lots. And they're trying to come in and they're met with this wall and the choice of two escalators. And they've got to choose." —Penguins fan

"Then as you get into the building, you take that experience maybe up a notch and you hear an announcer in the background again, and then **you build up to a crescendo**, because as you go into this building, your experience is also one of dealing with different elevations." —Penguins staff

pre-game/ event

How can we enhance or improve the process of getting to one's seat before the game or event begins? Concourses, exhibits, vendors and ushers should all be taken into consideration and help to reinforce the entire Penguin game fan experience.

"...the moment they walk in the door from the moment they get to their seat. Right now it's basically just a hallway to get from one to the other, a vestibule to get from one to the other, whereas I think **in the new arena, they're going to be hit with an experience quite frankly as soon as they hit the exterior plazas, and it's going to build to a crescendo by the time they get into their seats,** and that's even before the guys hit the ice." —Penguins Staff

"If you are like me and you run late for everything, you want to try and get to the event as fast as possible and find your seats and I just think it is hard to get to places there, to get to your seat."
—Other event user

"At Mellon Arena, it's crowded, you're squeezing through areas. You want to get something to eat, you're squeezed... If you come into the main entrance to Mellon Arena and there is a giveaway like last night, there's boxes stacked to the ceiling, there's this little alleyway between the boxes that you come in, then you're in there, there's ten feet, you make a right or a left or you go straight and then there's another souvenir stand there and you're crushed in and you look for your seat. You go up the ramps and then your seats are small. So you're still constrained. **If you're constrained physically, you're going to feel constrained emotionally** like you were at work." —Penguins staff

EXISTING CONDITIONS

QUOTES

"...You're into the game. You're into it, my kids are into it, you know, you high-five strangers, you high-five your kids..." —Penguins staff

"...when one person starts going, "let's go Pens!" and everyone starts chanting and they do the wave and everyone is standing up... it's just a level of excitement..." —Penguins fan

"You get a buzz from the crowd, a certain energy that the crowd produces, and you can kind of get a feel that maybe the players are sensing something from the crowd as well..." —Penguins fan

the game/event

When someone is in the bowl, at the game, at the concert, they should feel like they are in the middle of it. Fan participation, game rituals, energizing music and lighting are all part of the game experience.

fathom THE PITTSBURGH PENGUINS

intermission

Intermission activities happen on and off the ice. How can we enhance this time for event attendees, make it more convenient, efficient and fun, while at the same time generating revenue? Fan participation in activities on the ice, videos of Penguins history and key players all encourage a sense of connection.

"Once you're in your seat in Mellon Arena, it doesn't matter, you can't really tell when you're watching the ice whether you're in the nicest facility in the world or in Johnstown War Memorial. You're so many feet away from the ice and you're watching a performance and you're fixated on that. What separates you is what happens between the time you get from your car to your seat and whenever you leave your seat between breaks in the performance or breaks in the hockey game, and I think that's what will separate the experience." —Penguins staff

fathom THE PITTSBURGH PENGUINS

post-game/event

Are there changes we can make within or outside the arena that will allows fans to stay until the end of the game or event? Can we keep them even longer? Traffic flow inside and outside and last-minute purchases or post-game drinks/meals are things to consider.

"...obviously you're going to have hockey, you're going to have these events, but I think it could be something that you do, it [could be] an everyday place. You know, **every day it's one of the stops when you come here to Pittsburgh.**" —Penguins staff

"You get outside and you've got to walk halfway around the arena before you can get anywhere. So I come out of my seat and okay well I can't go out these doors even though there are doors here and I can't get out of this crazy crowd of people, I've got to funnel into an escalator. A one-person-wide escalator. And then finally get down and **spew out the doors and everyone kind of explodes at that point and there's this mass of people.**" —Penguins fan

ARAMARK

Conclusion

When you prepare and present your thesis proposal you should be able to answer two questions:

1. Tell us why you care.
2. Tell us why we should care.

Your thesis project must pass the "So What?" test. You must teach your audience something new about something they care about, be it the topic, your users, your site or building, or some other aspect of your project. Your information must be current, relevant, and engaging and exciting to your audience. If you know the answer to the two questions above, then your project has likely passed the test.

In Chapter 10 you will learn how to unite all of the information you have collected into the project program. The project program is a detailed document that clearly identifies the problems you have identified and your strategies for solving the problems with your design project. It also establishes your scope of work and goals for your design.

References

Berdik, C. (2005, October 30). Office of my dreams. *Boston Sunday Globe*, pp. E1, E5.

Binns, C. (2007, March 12). Bungee backpack. *Science World*.

Cherry, E. (1999). *Programming for design: From theory to practice*. New York: John Wiley.

Conley, L. (2006, June). My dream home. *Fast Company*.

Groat, L., & Wang, D. (2002). *Architectural research methods*. New York: John Wiley.

Hodge, B., & Pollak, L. (1996). *Studio works 4*. Cambridge, MA: President and Fellows of Harvard University.

Ilov, A. (2008, July). fathom.

Literary Education Online (LEO). (2003, October 14). Literacy Education Online. "Thesis statement." Retrieved 2008 from http://leo.stcloudstate.edu/acadwrite/thesistatement.html

Owl at Purdue. (2008). Purdue University. Retrieved June 20, 2008, from http://owl.english.purdue.edu/owl/resource/589/02/

Smithsonian Institution. (2007). *Design for the other 90%*. New York: Cooper Hewitt, National Design Museum.

Weisberg, R. (2006). *Creativity: Understanding innovation in problem solving, science, invention, and the arts*. New York: John Wiley.

10 The Written Program

CHAPTER OBJECTIVES

When you complete this chapter you should be able to do the following:

- Define the problems to be solved with design.
- Identify the five steps of the programming process.
- Understand how form, function, economy, and time are going to be addressed in programming.
- Use information-gathering techniques to develop the project program.
- Identify programmatic concepts or strategies that solve the problems you have identified.
- Synthesize all the information that you have gathered into an organized and detailed project program.

KEY TERMS

Activity-based programming
Adjacency matrix
Criteria matrix

Dynamic dimensions
Equipment list
Occupancy load factor

Primary activities

Problem statement

Programmatic concepts

Programming

Project program

Relationship diagram

Secondary activities

Spatially based programming

Static dimensions

Closing the "Synthesis Gap"

In *Programming for Design*, Edith Cherry (1999) uses the following definition for **programming**: "Programming is the research and decision-making process that defines the problem to be solved by design." As discussed in Chapter 1, programming is the first phase in the Interior Design Process (see Figure 10.1), and it serves as a bridge between research and design excellence. The more thorough your programming process, the smaller the gap between programming and design. This void between the completed project program and the design process is referred to as the "synthesis gap" (Karlen, Ruggeri, & Hahn, 2004, p. 4).

In this chapter you will experience a cycle of *analysis*, dissecting your body of research into its parts, and *synthesis*, recombining and organizing the information into meaningful categories in order to identify the design problem and develop *strategies* or **programmatic concepts** for solving the problem.

According to the widely accepted programming process presented by Pena and Parshall in *Problem Seeking* (2001), programming includes the following steps (p. 12):

1. Establish goals
2. Collect and analyze facts
3. Uncover and test concepts
4. Determine needs
5. State the problem

The end product is a highly detailed written document called a **project program**, or *programming document*, which assimilates this information and serves as a sort of guide or manual throughout the design process.

Figure 10.1 Programming begins when the client and designer both agree there is a problem to solve. It ends at schematics, when you impose the program upon a specific base plan.

Because the essence of programming is to define a problem and seek a solution, before you read further in this chapter you are encouraged to revisit "Design as Creative Problem-Solving" in Chapter 1.

What Is Programming?

Similar to the thesis statement, programming identifies the design problem and provides strategies for solving it. However, while thesis is a sort of testing ground for ideas, programming is the application of the ideas. As a student, when you make the transition from your thesis proposal to your thesis project, you will create a project program that synthesizes what you learned from the research that you used to develop your thesis proposal.

While thesis is an academic process, programming is a professional skill that you practice while in school, similar to the way you practice your drafting skills, design skills, or computer skills. Just as your thesis proposal serves as the gateway to thesis design, in the professional world your project program is a contract that must be approved and signed off by the client, signifying the end of the programming phase and the beginning of the schematic design phase. Your presentation of the program to the client tells them you have listened to them, have correctly identified their wants and needs, and have "identified broader issues related to the project, such as human factors, environmental responsibility and social and cultural influences on the design" (Ballast, 2006, p. 1).

In programming, you predetermine the activities and behavior that will occur within the building, keeping in mind the emotional responses and feelings that might be evoked in the user, and you provide the spaces in which these events occur. In other words, like the choreographer of a graceful performance guiding the dancers as to what to do, and how to do it, you have control over the movements and behavior within the spaces you program. The nature of the performance is up to you.

Programming is a very considerate process as well as a technical one, but it should not be seen as a means of imposing constraints on the project. Instead, see it as a process of guiding the project in a direction that will give it many exciting opportunities along that path. "A problem statement which is too limited inhibits creative ability" (Adams, 2001, p. 32).

ACTIVITY 10.1 Identifying Problems and Exploring Multiple Solutions

(Inspired by Adams, 2001)

Purpose: To think about the design problems you experience every day and to brainstorm how many different ways those problems could be solved.

1. Grab a pen and small pocket-sized notebook and over the course of a day make a list of all of the problems you encounter. Every time you see a problem—be it in your home, yard, school, or place of work, or someone else's home, yard, and so on—jot it down on your list.
2. At the end of the day, look at the list. Using a highlighter or other marking tool, identify the problems that could be solved with design. You may highlight everything on your list or you may find there are only a few items. The goal is to learn to identify design problems.
3. Now, select one of those design problems and come up with three possible design solutions to the problem. Your solutions should be creative and diverse, expressing an effort to "think outside the box."
4. Document your three design solutions on your notepad or in a sketchbook, and share them with the class. Let your solutions be a conversation starter and see how many more solutions you can come up with as a group. Exhaust all of the possibilities!
5. Ask yourself the following question: Was the first solution actually the best one, or did pushing yourself a bit further help you come up with something that solved the problem more elegantly, efficiently, inexpensively, etc.?

What Is a Program?

A project program identifies and accurately describes the problems to be solved. It documents the programming process and contains an "analysis of the project goals and objectives, aesthetic considerations, organizing concepts, the existing building, activities and relationships, space needs, adjacency requirements, code review, budget requirements and scheduling requirements" (Ballast, 2006).

The program also clearly defines your focus for the project, as well as defining the scale and scope (discussed in Chapter 9). If you are developing your thesis, your program will establish that you have enough body to your project to fit a scale appropriate for a thesis project. If your thesis project is enormous in size, then you cannot expect to design everything. The program presents the overall context for the project and then carefully "draws a line around" your areas of focus. The same principle applies to the professional project program. Once a client has signed off on the program, establishing the parameters of the project and your responsibility, they cannot require additional work without incurring additional fees.

There is quite a bit of variety in the scope of project programs. The program could be a simple contract, stating the terms of agreement, or it could be an elaborate, multipage document that details everything. For a residential project, it might be a very simple statement of goals and a list of spaces and furniture and equipment to be included. On a larger project, the program might be a large, bound volume, used by all team members to guide not only current needs of the project and organization but future needs as well (Ballast, 2006). Once that document is signed, whether small or large, it is legally binding for all parties involved.

Just as with your thesis proposal, your program should integrate all of the research you have done for a project, as that research has guided your programmatic decisions. This includes writing in an understanding of your client's values. This can be difficult to do. It is not unusual to see programs containing a list of requirements but omitting the essence of the project, which would be the key to its solution. "This search for values is a programming, *not* a design, activity" (Hershberger, 1985, p. 42). For example, when Louis Kahn was programming the Salk Institute, Dr. Salk wanted "a place where Picasso would feel welcome." How can one articulate the aesthetic requirements of a space? This information must be stated somewhere, so that the designer can make subsequent choices that are in keeping with the client's wishes—ones that may not fall into the categories of furniture, fixtures and equipment, programming concepts, or spatial allocations.

This thoughtfulness and level of detail essentially means that you should be able to hand your program over to another designer and they should be able to design the project with nothing but that document to guide them. In the real world, it is common for one person or team to program a project and then pass that programming document off to another designer or design team. That programming document becomes the guide that provides all relevant information and necessary guidance for the rest of the project. This does not mean that the program cannot be changed or adjusted once you enter the design phase. According to Pena and Parshall (2001), programming is a two-step process that gets refined during design development. You can see your program as a living document: inherently flexible, responding to the design, and subject to change with the client's approval.

In our Thesis Programming course we sometimes suggest to the students that upon the completion of Thesis Programming and on the first day of the Thesis Design course we will not be handing back their programming documents. Instead we will distribute the documents randomly. Whichever program a student receives is the project that the student will design. As you can imagine, this always elicits emotional outbursts from students who are not willing to relinquish their programs to another designer. So we ask why, and they always reply, "Because I worked so hard on this! I put my heart and soul into that program!"

We use this example to illustrate how rich with information the project program must be, but also how the programming document should be viewed as separate from the design. A program should be viewed as an objective guide to be used by *any* designer. The knowledge, passion, and vision you have for a project must be embedded in the program, or you run the risk that your ideas will be lost in translation from programming to design.

In the professional arena, a program may be written by someone other than a designer, such as a facilities manager, an owner, or a professional programmer. Or a designer may be called on just to write a program (for a project to be designed in the future by a different designer). In school, we are writing the program that we ultimately are designing. As designers, we need to understand the programming process and how it relates to the design process, but it is rare for a designer to write his or her own program and then design it.

The rule of thumb is that you should write your program as if someone else will be designing the project. Ask yourself the following questions: Have I embedded all of the relevant information into the program? Have I embedded my client's values? Would my instructor or another student be able to design the project from this document?

Programming Step by Step

The Cycles of Analysis and Synthesis

In *Problem Seeking* (2001), Pena and Parshall refer to programming as analysis and design as synthesis. Programming dissects the project context, and design brings the parts together to create something new. It is true, however, that there are multiple layers of analysis and synthesis in any design project, and we are constantly cycling through analysis and synthesis at the research level, the programming level, and the design level. Pena and Parshall's five-step programming process can be different in an academic environment than in a professional context (Table 10.1).

During the research phase you assimilate information or facts and piece them together to develop new ideas, leading to new design philosophies, theories, and conclusions. In programming you will again analyze information

Table 10.1 The Five Steps of Programming

Step	The Pena and Parshall Problem-Seeking Format	Common Academic Format	Common Professional Format
1	Establish Goals	Collect and Analyze Facts (Analysis)	Establish Goals (Analysis)
2	Collect and Analyze Facts	Establish Goals (Analysis)	Collect and Analyze Facts (Analysis)
3	Uncover and Test Concepts	Determine Needs (Analysis)	Determine Needs (Analysis)
4	Determine Needs	Uncover and Test Concepts (Synthesis)	Uncover and Test Concepts (Synthesis)
5	State the Problem	State the Problem (Synthesis)	State the Problem (Synthesis)

and facts in order to identify a design problem; then you will group and organize the information into meaningful categories and patterns that allow you to synthesize it into programmatic concepts (strategies) that will solve the problem. In design you will analyze the multiple organizational options as well as the multiple design solutions available for every programmatic concept, and you'll synthesize this into a design solution that will solve the design problem (Cherry, 1999).

In this chapter you'll walk through the five steps of programming, identifying at each point where you are in this cycle of analysis and synthesis. No two interior design projects are exactly alike, so the order of steps frequently changes or overlaps to accommodate the project conditions. For purposes of this book, the steps are presented in an order common to an academic format. In school it makes sense to begin with a literature review in order to orient and familiarize ourselves with the topics and issues at hand, but in the profession, programming usually begins with a start-up meeting where the client and designer clearly establish the goals and objectives for the project.

Form, Function, Economy, Time

In *Problem Seeking* (2001), Pena and Parshall suggest that in each of the five steps of the programming process you should address the issues of form, function, economy, and time.

- *Form* concerns the existing conditions of the site and building, the physical and psychological environment of the interior, and the quality of construction (to be discussed further in Chapter 11).
- *Function* pertains to the people using the space, or the end users; the activities to be performed in that space; and the relationship of spaces

to each other. We will discuss activity-based programming later in this chapter.

- *Economy* concerns money and the initial cost of the interior, operating costs, and lifecycle costs.
- *Time* refers to ideas of past, present, and future as they affect form, function, and economy (for example, the project schedule or the organization's plans for future growth) (Ballast, 2006).

Figure 10.2 shows a tool that one design company uses to obtain needed information about these four issues.

MICRO PROGRAMMING QUESTIONNAIRE
PERSONNEL AND SPACE REQUIREMENTS FORECAST

Figure 10.2 The architecture and interior design company WDG, in Washington, D.C., uses this Micro Programming Questionnaire to identify the client's current needs as well as their plans for future growth.

| Client Name: | Date: |

Name of Person Interviewed:	Telephone Number:
Title:	Fax Number:
Location (Floor/Exposure):	

SURVEY OBJECTIVE: To determine current and future detailed staffing and space requirements.

I. PERSONNEL REQUIREMENTS
- Identify personnel by functional titles.

WORKSPACE PROJECTIONS:

Personnel by Functional Title (& Name for Senior Personnel)	Current Quantity of Positions 2008	Future Quantity (Year End)		Total Workspace To Be Planned For		Private Office or WS/ Special Equipment Requirements
		09	10	SF Each	Total USF	

VISITORS
Identify the number and origin of visitors your unit receives (per day):

From other groups/departments:	From outside the Company (clients, etc.):

ADJACENCIES
Primary:_____
_____

Secondary:_____

SECURITY REQUIREMENTS_____

ELECTRICAL/DATA/TELEPHONE
REQUIREMENTS_____
_____
_____
_____

Figure 10.2 (continued)

MICRO PROGRAMMING QUESTIONNAIRE
PERSONNEL AND SPACE REQUIREMENTS FORECAST

II. MEETING ROOMS

Please identify the types of support rooms required by this department, including frequency of use.

Description	Quantity at Year End			Avg. hours per day used?	Share with other groups?	Comments
	2008	2008	2010			
Conference, Presentation, Training & Multipurpose Rooms:						
225sf (Seats 10-15)						

Technology Required:
  __Advanced (with Lap-tops, etc.)
  __Normal (Projector/Screen)
  __None (Meetings Only)						

150sf (Seats 6-8)						

Technology Required:
  __Advanced (with Lap-tops, etc.)
  __Normal (Projector/Screen)
  __None (Meetings Only)						

Open Meeting Area 80sf +						
(Seats 4-6) Technology Required:						
Other						
Technology Required: Seats _____ (# of people)						

III. DEPARTMENTAL SUPPORT SPACE REQUIREMENTS

SUPPORT SPACE	2008	2009	2010	Size/Seating/Adjacencies/Special Needs
Separate Reception Area				
Separate Photocopy Room				
Visitor Workspace				
Mailroom				
Workroom / War Room				
Library/Resource				
Kitchen/Break Areas				
Storage Closets				

EQUIPMENT	Indicate Quantity Required				Comments/Adjacencies
Individual/Department	Fax	Printer	Copier	Other	

Pena and Parshall use a chart similar to Table 10.2 to show the relationships between (1) the five steps of the programming process and (2) issues of form, function, economy, and time (2001, p. 30).

Exploring the Five Steps of Programming

Step One: Collecting and Analyzing Facts

In the first step of programming you will review your body of research and determine the following: What do I know? What is given? What are my unknowns? (Pena & Parshall, 2001, p. 25)

Figure 10.2 (continued)

MICRO PROGRAMMING QUESTIONNAIRE
PERSONNEL AND SPACE REQUIREMENTS FORECAST

IV. FILES & STORAGE CABINETS

<u>Do not include</u> those files located within offices or workstations.

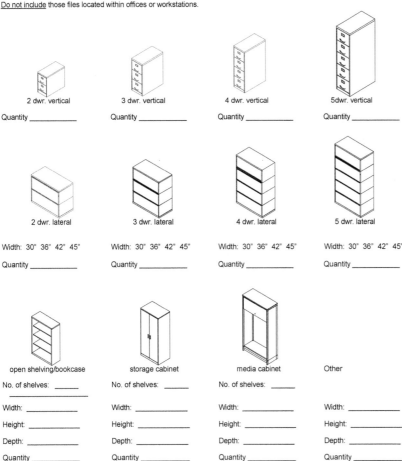

Your research likely has produced a huge pile of information. Now you must organize the data you have collected—placing it into meaningful and sequential formats and clearly summarizing confirmed quantitative data (Karlen et al., 2004). For example, after interviewing and observing employees of a large company, you might analyze your data and combine any patterns that you find into a chart or *matrix*, such as the scenario planning matrix shown in Figure 10.3.

Establish the existing context and requirements of the problem, such as the number of people to be accommodated, special adjacencies, user characteristics, the existing building conditions, and anything else of significance gathered in your research process.

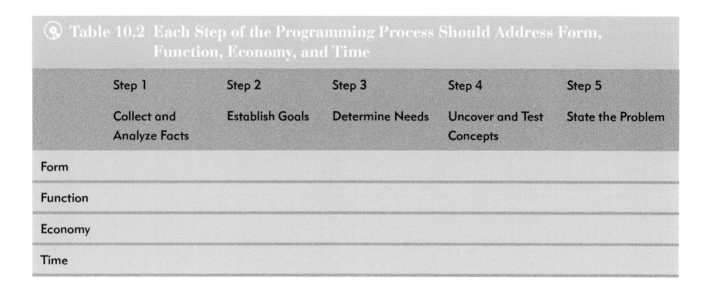

Table 10.2 Each Step of the Programming Process Should Address Form, Function, Economy, and Time

	Step 1 Collect and Analyze Facts	Step 2 Establish Goals	Step 3 Determine Needs	Step 4 Uncover and Test Concepts	Step 5 State the Problem
Form					
Function					
Economy					
Time					

The information you gather during this step is often your opportunity to educate your clients and users as well. According to Steve Polo, a partner at the company OPX in Washington, D.C., "Every company has an 'operating system,' but many companies don't actually know what it is. The result is that how they do things around the office stops being intentional" (personal communication, July 2008). Like placing the client in front of a mirror, your information can help the client better understand the reality of the existing conditions.

Figure 10.3 The company OPX uses this matrix to summarize quantitative data into a format that can be easily analyzed and communicated to other designers and to the client. Copyright OPX, 2008, all rights reserved. Used by permission.

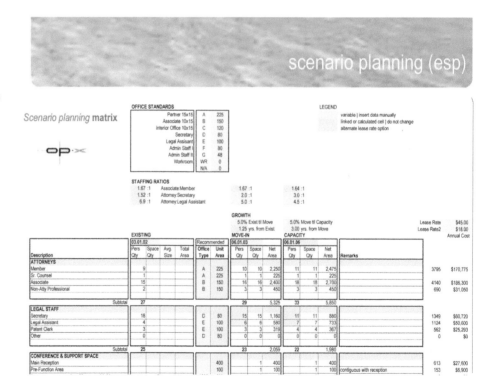

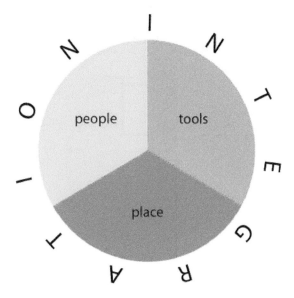

As a "design solutions company," OPX uses a fact-collecting process called an "integration audit" (Figure 10.4). In an integration audit, OPX looks at three areas of the organization's business practices—people (users), tools (technology), and place (spaces)—in order to identify any gaps or misalignments. OPX maps out their findings in a graphic format that they can share with the client. For many organizations, what was thought to be a five-step business process turns out in reality to be a 50-plus-step process, wasting a significant amount of time and money.

For example, in one large organization, the programmer who was focusing on evaluating tools and technology found within the organization's computer system 50 different versions of the same letter. What was supposed to be one "Activity Memo"—written by an employee, passed to management for a round of revisions, and then sent right back to the employee to be mailed—went through 50 revisions and took nine months to get out the door.

What should have taken one week took nine months! Imagine the impact on organizational efficiency when OPX identified this issue, isolated the real problems causing the issue—such as training problems, trust issues, and turf battles between management and employees—and identified strategies to solve those problems. (See Figure 10.5.)

When you're working with a large body of information and facts, carefully filter the important and useful information from the rest. Otherwise you or the designer might become overwhelmed with the amount of data. This does not mean you have to discard all information that does not immediately apply, for it may become relevant at a later date. Edith Cherry (1999) suggests that you create an easily accessible appendix for your programming document that houses articles and information that at the moment seem superfluous but might be relevant at some point.

Sample Process Map

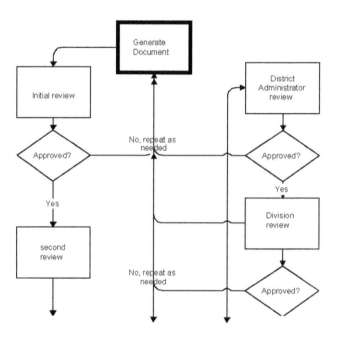

(Inspired by Pena and Parshall, 2001)

Purpose: **To practice isolating the most important information and filtering out the superfluous.**

Looking at your body of research—the information, facts, and ideas—can you identify the information relevant to each of these four categories: function, form, economy, and time? Use the chart below as a place to list this information, or create a similar chart.

Step One	Form	Function	Economy	Time
Collect and	1.	1.	1.	1.
Analyze Facts	2.	2.	2.	2.
	3.	3.	3.	3.
	4.	4.	4.	4.
	5.	5.	5.	5.

Step Two: Establishing Goals (Analysis)

In this step you will identify the following: What does the client want to achieve and why? (Pena & Parshall, 2001) It is not enough to simply list the types of spaces and the required square footage. You must also identify problems and issues that are relevant to the space and you must know what objectives the client is trying to reach with those spaces (Ballast, 2006). Some programmers refer to this as a mission statement (Cherry, 1999, p. 99). Your understanding of those goals will drive the direction of the programmatic concepts and strategies you employ.

Just as some organizations are not aware of their operating system, some organizations are not clear about their goals. So you have to provide them some tools to assist in the process. When identifying your client's goals regarding the form or aesthetics for their spaces, you can use some of the creative information-gathering techniques discussed in Part Two of this book.

You can also use similar techniques for identifying client goals related to function, budget, and time. For example, the company WDG Architects in Washington, D.C., uses a macro programming questionnaire—covering 14 main operational points such as square footage standards, storage requirements, adjacency issues, and security issues—to help corporate clients identify specific goals and objectives related to their new space. This can be seen in the questionnaire in Figure 10.6.

Establishing project goals determines the scope of the project. All subsequent steps happen within the realm of the goals and objectives established by the client up front (Cherry, 1999).

MACRO PROGRAMMING QUESTIONNAIRE

Client Name: Date:

Name of Person Interviewed: Telephone Number:

Title: Fax Number:

SURVEY OBJECTIVE: To determine high-level goals and objectives for new space

1. **Project Goals**

    a. Image/Culture   _____

          Internal (employee amenities/retention)   _____

          External (public space/guest arrival)   _____

2. **Square Footage Standards and Planning Policies for the Office Area**

    a. Investigate New Workplace Strategies   _____
    or stay with existing Standards?   _____

Figure 10.6 The company WDG uses the "Macro Programming Questionnaire" to extract critical facts about their client's business practices that will reveal goals and objectives of the client.

Figure 10.6 (continued)

b. Existing/Desired Workplace Culture

    1. Hierarchical of Flat? _____

    2. Autonomous vs. Interactive Job _____
       Functions _____

    3. Policies regarding Office vs. _____
       Workstation assignments _____

    4. Offices assigned based on title or _____
       function? _____

    5. Policies regarding Centralized vs. _____
       Decentralized Management as it _____
       relates to placement of Offices _____
       (Executive Areas or Decentralized _____
       Management) _____

    6. Rate of Churn as it relates to _____
       Reorganizations and Promotions _____

3. **Headcount**

  a. Existing (broken down by sf standards _____
    and Departments) _____

  b. Projected (broken down by sf _____
    standards and Departments) _____

  c. Telecommuting Goals and _____
    Accommodations _____

  d. Part-time Staff, Consultants and _____
    Special Projects _____

4. **Mail Services**

  a. Main Incoming and Distribution Point _____

  b. Satellite Mail Distribution Areas _____

5. **Reproduction Services**

  a. Central Reproductive Services _____

  b. Satellite Copy Areas _____

6. **Food Service**

  a. Main Food Service Facility _____

  b. Satellite Food Service Areas (Pantries, _____
    Coffee Bars) _____

  c. Food Service for Conference and _____
    Training Room Functions _____

7. **Conference Rooms**

  a. Centralized vs. Decentralized _____

    1. AV _____

  b. Informal Conferencing _____

Figure 10.6 (continued)

8. **Files/Storage Requirements**

    a.   Central File Requirements   _____

         1. High Density Files   _____

    b.   Library Functions   _____

    c.   Departmental File Requirements   _____

         1. Ratio of File Drawer to Person   _____

9. **Other Amenity and Support Functions**

    a.   Company Store   _____

    b.   Training   _____

         1. AV   _____

    c.   Auditorium/Great Room   _____

         1. AV   _____

    d.   Client Dining Facilities   _____

    e.   Demonstration Room   _____

    f.   Learning Center   _____

    g.   Fitness Center   _____

    h.   Day Care   _____

    i.   Lactation Room   _____

    j.   Workroom / War Room   _____

10. **Adjacency Issues**

    a.   Departmental   _____

    b.   Support Functions   _____

11. **Telecommunications Systems**

    a.   Main Distribution Frame   _____

    b.   IDF Closets   _____

    c.   Server Farms/Computer Rooms   _____

    d.   Tech Labs   _____

12. **Building System/Infrastructure Issues**

    a.   24/7 Program Requirements   _____

    b.   Typical hours of Operation   _____

    c.   Raised flooring   _____

    d.   Lighting (direct/indirect)   _____

13. **Security Issues**

    a.   Front door   _____

    b.   Departmental   _____

    c.   Support Functions   _____

Figure 10.6 (continued)

14. **Existing Manufacturer/Vendor Relationships**

    a. Facilities Management Software   ————————————————

    b. Furniture Manufacturers/Dealers   ————————————————

    c. Demountable Partitions   ————————————————

    d. Carpet   ————————————————

⊗ ACTIVITY 10.3   Identifying Goals and Objectives

(Inspired by Pena & Parshall, 2001)

Purpose: **To identify the goals and objectives for your project.**

Using your understanding of the client and end users to help guide you, take a few moments to identify the goals and objectives for your project.

Step 2	Form	Function	Economy	Time
Identifying Goals and Objectives	1.	1.	1.	1.
	2.	2.	2.	2.
	3.	3.	3.	3.
	4.	4.	4.	4.
	5.	5.	5.	5.

Step Three: Determining Needs (Analysis)

In Step Three you determine the following information about the client: How much money and space are available and needed? What level of quality is required or requested? (Pena & Parshall, 2001) In this step you also determine what the client's priorities are. Steve Polo, a partner at OPX, observes:

> To find out what the client needs you have to ask questions. You have to ask the right questions, and you have to ask questions interesting enough to elicit a response you can use. Then you have to come to an agreement about what it all means, and a solution must be extracted. If

In every project we are essentially laying three things on the table in front of the client—time, budget, and quality—and we tell them to choose two of these as priorities. If they choose less time and higher quality, meaning they want it done fast and done well, it will cost them. If they choose less time and an affordable budget, then the quality will suffer. And if they want an affordable budget and high quality, then the project will take more time to complete. Being up front with the client helps them sort through and determine their priorities.

you miss one piece you will miss the right answer. You will get an answer, but it is just an answer, not necessarily the right answer (personal communication, July 2008).

Determining the client's needs balances the desires of the client against the available budget or establishes a budget based on the defined goals and needs. As you determine client needs, you are primarily dealing with quality, quantity, budget, and time (Ballast, 2006).

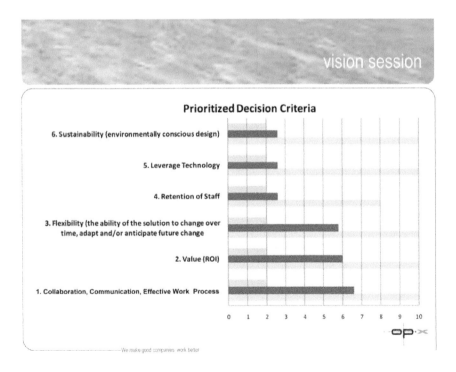

Figure 10.7 Using a Web-based facilitation process for all project stakeholders, OPX graphs "prioritized decision criteria" in a bar graph format. This becomes an "agreed-upon" decision-making guide for the entire project team. Copyright OPX, 2008, all rights reserved. Used by permission.

Most clients want it all, including more than they can afford (Ballast, 2006), but in reality they can't have it all, so you must guide them in selecting priorities and separating wants from needs. This provides you or your design team with guidelines for making decisions throughout all phases of the Interior Design Process.

As an example, on one FF&E project for a high-profile dentist in San Diego, California, the client was concerned with projecting an image of being on top of the most current trends and technology in the dental field. This meant reflecting the most current trends in design as well. In this instance, the client prioritized image and quality over budget. For the designer, this information was very helpful when it came to deciding which furniture to specify for the project. The client would want furniture pieces selected for style rather than for their lower price. In more complex projects, compiling the list of wants and needs and establishing priorities can be a much more complex process. It is important that this information is communicated very clearly among that client, programmer, and designer so that everyone is "on the same page." Figure 10.7 provides an example of how OPX communicates their understanding of client priorities with the project team.

⊛ ACTIVITY 10.4 Determining Needs

(Inspired by Pena & Parshall, 2001)

Purpose: **To help you learn to identify priorities, which will help you make appropriate design decisions.**

Take a few moments to identify the needs of your project's client and end user, being careful to separate wants from needs in the process. Rank each item from most important to least important as you complete this exercise.

Step 3	Form	Function	Economy	Time
Determining	1.	1.	1.	1.
Needs	2.	2.	2.	2.
	3.	3.	3.	3.
	4.	4.	4.	4.
	5.	5.	5.	5.

In Step Four you will identify how the client wants to achieve their goals and you will develop a strategy for achieving those goals, also referred to as programmatic concepts (Pena & Parshall, 2001). As Edith Cherry (1999) puts it, "What are the ways we can do what we want to do (goals and objectives) given what we know now?"

This is the most creative phase of programming. It is where you take your insights about the problem and develop programmatic concepts as solutions. It is important to understand the difference between programmatic concepts and design concepts. Ballast (2006) explains that a programming concept is not a physical solution, but rather a performance requirement related to methods of solving problems or satisfying a need. A design concept is the specific physical response that attempts to achieve a programmatic concept. Programmatic concepts become the basis for later design concepts.

According to Pena and Parshall (2001), "Programming deals with abstract ideas known as programmatic concepts, which are intended mainly as operational solutions to a client's performance problems, without regard to the physical design response." They refer to this as the "principle of abstract thinking."

When you look at the research web diagram shown in Figure 10.8 (introduced in Chapter 1), you can see how research, programmatic concepts, design concepts, and design solutions all fit together. If you skip ahead and select a design solution before you have chosen the right program, programming concepts, and design concepts, your prematurely identified design solution could dilute the effectiveness of the solutions naturally evolving from the program you eventually select and develop.

An example of a programmatic concept in a retail project would be to provide a medium level of security to protect against theft of merchandise without making the security methods obvious. Design concepts that could achieve this programmatic concept would be to provide a central cash/wrap at exit, to tag all merchandise with concealed electronic identifiers and install a detection device at the exit, or to display only samples of merchandise as a basis for buying and have purchases delivered to the customer from a storage room (Ballast, 2006).

Understanding Programmatic Concepts

To review, a programmatic concept is a written description of an abstract strategy for achieving a performance requirement. You are not stating a design solution that would limit the creative thinking of the designer. Figure 10.9 shows how multiple programmatic concepts can be explored and translated into design solutions.

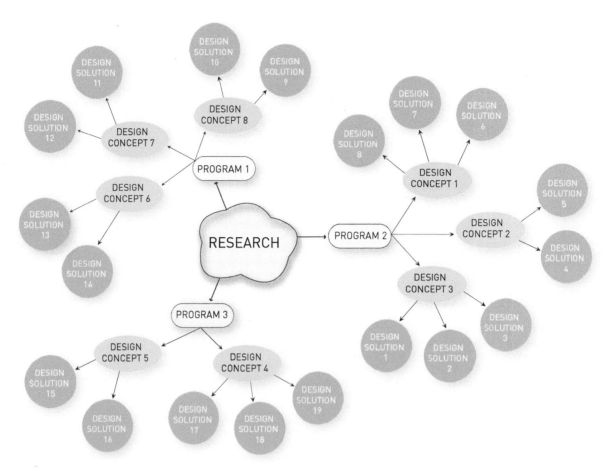

Figure 10.8 Design solutions should evolve in response to the specific project program you have developed. Skipping ahead to design solutions while your project is still in the programming phase can dilute the effectiveness of the solutions. As this diagram shows, we see that the same body of research can generate multiple programs which, in turn, can inspire multiple design solutions.

Table 10.3 is a list of the programmatic concepts identified by Pena and Parshall in *Problem Seeking* (2001). It should not be considered a complete list, as there are surely others you could identify, but it is a very thorough list and should be considered a place to start when exploring programmatic concepts.

As mentioned previously, this should not be considered a complete list as there are many other programmatic concepts you can explore. Programmatic concepts can be applied at varying levels of influence—from very broad concepts, such as people groupings, to more specific concepts, such as privacy. As you read through the continuing list of programmatic concepts in Table 10.4 (page 293), try developing your own list of programmatic concepts. How might you apply your own list to your project program?

Programmatic concepts can also serve as aesthetic guidelines. The following are aesthetically based programmatic concepts:

- Inspiring
- Intimidating
- Mysterious
- Eclectic

Table 10.3 Defining Programmatic Concepts

Programmatic Concept	Definition of Concept	Examples and Tips
Priority	Evokes questions about the order of importance, such as relative position, size, and social value. The concept reflects how to accomplish a goal based on a ranking of value and places a higher value on one thing than another.	A school might choose to specify lower-cost library furniture as budget might take priority over style. It is often difficult to get a client to establish and commit to project priorities.
Hierarchy	Related to a goal about the exercise of authority; expressed in symbols of authority	A company might choose to reduce a sense of hierarchy between management and other employees by eliminating closed offices and providing only open workstations for all employees.
Character	Concerns the image the client wants to project in terms of values and the general value of the space	Does the character of the building or space express what is happening there? Some buildings, such as an art school, a natural foods market, or an office building on Wall Street in New York City, might express a strong and unmistakable character.
Density	Can be low, medium, or high—a goal for efficient use of land or space, a goal for high degrees of interaction.	A frequently used computer lab at your school might be high-density, or a bustling school corridor might be high-density between class times and low-density while classes are in session.
Service Groupings	Should services be centralized or decentralized? Each service should be centralized or decentralized for a definite reason, to accomplish a specific goal.	In hospitals, it is common to have one centralized nurse's station per hospital unit or floor and smaller, decentralized nurse's stations positioned at intervals around patient rooms to increase convenience and efficiency of administration and treatment.
Activity Grouping	Should activities be compartmentalized or integrated? Closely related activities can be integrated to promote interaction, while needs for privacy would call for compartmentalization.	A creative office environment might use open office stations to promote interaction, while patient rooms in a hospital are compartmentalized to provide patient privacy.

continued

Programmatic Concept	Definition of Concept	Examples and Tips
People Grouping	This concept states degree of massing of people in a space and is derived from the physical, social, and emotional characteristics of the group (Ballast, 2006).	Public spaces, such as a museum or stadium, group together large numbers of strangers, while a residence groups together people who are well acquainted or related.
Home Base	This is related to the idea of territoriality, and it results in an easily defined space where a person can maintain his or her individuality.	In a shared dormitory room, residents will often personalize their beds and desks to create a sense of defined territory within the confined space.
Relationships	The correct interrelation of spaces promotes efficiency and effectiveness of people and their activities. The concept of functional affinities is the most common programmatic concept and is usually developed through the relationship diagram.	This concept most directly affects the organization of spaces and rooms (Ballast, 2006). For example, in a museum it is common for exhibits to be grouped together, for retail spaces to be grouped with food services, and for administration and fund-raising staff to be grouped together. The curatorial department is often grouped with the collections storage or secure vault.
Communication	A goal to promote the effective exchange of information or ideas in an organization may call for networks or patterns of communication. Who communicates with whom? When? How often?	How can you design a nurse's station to promote the effective exchange of patient information and updates when a shift change occurs?
Neighbors	Is there a goal for sociability? Will the project be completely independent, or is there a mutual desire to be interdependent and to cooperate with neighbors?	In a library, individual semiprivate carrels prevent sociability between patrons while large, open worktables with multiple seating arrangements promote sociability.

Programmatic Concept	Definition of Concept	Examples and Tips
Accessibility	Can first-time visitors find where to enter the project? What visual cues help visitors locate the main entrance of a public building? Should there be multiple entrances? Does the building feel welcoming or exclusive? This also applies to provisions for the disabled beyond signs and symbols.	Due to heightened security measures, museums that used to feel welcoming and accessible to all have a new sense of inaccessibility, as you must wait in security lines and pass through metal detectors to enter.
Separated Flow	This circulation pattern causes segregation of traffic flow in a space.	This could pertain to flow of people, service access, and other activities of a space or place (Ballast, 2006). This might also define how you separate the front-of-house services from the back-of-house spaces, which are not open to clients or visitors.
Mixed Flow	This circulation pattern calls for multi-directional, multi-purpose traffic.	Responds to the goal of promoting interaction among people. Sometimes it is a goal to not have mixed flow (Ballast, 2006). In an airport security line, the goal is to not have mixed flow as people line up one or two at a time and waiting lines are organized by type of ticket or by type of traveler—for example, families versus business travelers.
Sequential Flow	In this circulation pattern, the progression of people and things must be carefully planned.	Many history or themed museums create a sequential flow that takes visitors through a choreographed experience so as to present information in a certain order, such as chronological. This helps enhance learning and understanding of the information presented.
Orientation	Provides a bearing or a point of reference within a building, a campus, or a city. Relating periodically to a recognizable space, thing, or structure can prevent a feeling of being lost in large buildings.	In museums, providing a recurring connection to an atrium or a view of an easily identified landmark prevents feelings of being overwhelmed or disoriented.

continued

Programmatic Concept	Definition of Concept	Examples and Tips
Flexibility	To some, this concept means that the building can accommodate growth through expansion. To others, it means that the building can allow for changes in function through the conversion of spaces. To still others, it means that the building provides the most for the money through multifunctional spaces. Flexibility really covers all three: expansibility, convertibility, and versatility.	Open workstations in a corporate environment provide for maximized flexibility, as configurations can be manipulated to accommodate future growth or downsizing. They can also adapt to changing organizational structure within the company. As departments are created, shrink, or grow, the flexible systems furniture configurations can change with them.
Tolerance	Is a space specifically tailored precisely for a static activity, or is it provided with a loose fit for dynamic activity that is likely to change?	A phone booth is low-tolerance as it is designed for one function only: making a phone call. A school gym is high-tolerance as it could be used for many activities, such as basketball games, school dances, or assemblies.
Safety	Which ideas will implement the goal for life safety? Look to codes and safety precautions for form-giving ideas.	The application of durable materials capable of withstanding bleach and other cleansers helps hospitals maintain a sterile environment and protect patients from dangerous microorganisms.
Security Controls	The degree of security control varies from minimum to medium to maximum depending on the value of the potential loss. These controls are used to protect property and life and to guide personnel movement.	Spaces with high levels of visibility, such as the main entrance of a government building, are usually more secure than those with a low level of visibility, such as an enclosed stair. On the other hand, low visibility—such as a bank vault remotely located below ground level of the bank—could serve to prevent traffic flow and increase security.

Programmatic Concept	Definition of Concept	Examples and Tips
Energy Conservation	This minimized the use of mechanical systems to control the interior environment and comfort of a building. This can be achieved in several ways.	The number of mechanically heated spaces can be kept to a minimum through the use of insulation, correct orientation to sun and wind, compactness, sun controls and shading, wind controls, and reflective surfaces. The designer can also specify materials produced using comparatively lower amounts of energy, using recycled materials, and using recyclable materials (Ballast, 2006).
Environmental Controls	What controls for air temperature, light, and sound will be required in order to provide for people's physical comfort?	Explores the kind of controls necessary to meet human comfort needs, including air temperature, light levels, sound, and humidity. This includes building mechanical systems as well as providing natural or passive means to achieve climate control (Ballast, 2006).
Phasing	Will phasing of construction be required to complete the project on a time-and-cost schedule?	Determines if a project must be completed in stages to meet time and cost schedules. Also states whether the project can be based on linear scheduling or must provide for concurrent scheduling to meet urgent occupancy requirements (Ballast, 2006). The Getty Museum in Los Angeles was being built on a fast track that started the construction phase before the construction documents phase was completed.
Cost Control	A search for economic ideas that will lead to a realistic preview of costs in order to meet the extent of available funds and budget (Ballast, 2006)	If a project comes in over budget, the project team will meet to explore value engineering options that will reduce the project costs while still achieving client priorities.

Note: Concept definitions (center column) from *Interior Design Reference Manual: A Guide to the NCIDQ Exam* (3rd ed.), by D. K. Ballast, 2006, Belmont, CA: Professional Publications and *Problem Seeking: An Architectural Programming Primer,* by W. M. Pena and S. A. Parshall, 2001, New York: John Wiley.

Table 10.4 Additional Programmatic Concepts

Programmatic Concept	Explanation
Expansion	As a space goes from being dark or enclosed to bright or more open, the end user experiences expansion. Expansion could result from many design solutions, such as a raised ceiling, extensive windows, or a skylight. Expansion in a space communicates messages, such as increased public access, spatial hierarchy, or a mixed flow of users.
Compression	As a space goes from being bright and open to being comparatively darker or more enclosed, the end user experiences compression. Compression could result from design solutions, such as a lowered ceiling, more narrow corridors, or smaller spaces. Compression communicates messages, such as increased privacy, increased security, or reduced public access.
Transparency	Transparency is a visual continuity between two spaces that suggests a sense of wholeness or unity between the spaces, be it connections between indoor spaces or a connection between indoor and outdoor spaces. Transparency could be used to reinforce relationships, influence environmental controls, increase spatial flexibility, or reduce privacy.
Authenticity	Authenticity refers to the accuracy of a representation and might apply in the case of historic preservation. It might also apply to genuineness or honesty in design, such as the "honesty of materials" referred to in Chapter 3 with regard to the design of the Salk Institute and the expression of the true nature of the materials used in construction.
Comfort	Comfort can hold various interpretations, so it is important to identify what the comfort goals are before applying the concept. Comfort is most commonly applied to environmental systems, but it could also apply to safety and security, orientation, people, and service groupings or density of spaces, to name a few.
Privacy	Privacy could be visual, acoustical, or physical and can vary from a complete lack of privacy, such as a busy street intersection, to total privacy, such as an acoustically isolated meeting room. Privacy is important when you're working with relationships, people groupings, home base or territoriality, security, and density.
Utility	Utility refers to the usefulness or purpose of a space or an object and can involve prioritizing function over form. Utility might be important when you're considering issues of safety or security, choosing project priorities, or defining the character of a space.

- Generic
- Complex
- Practical
- Sterile
- Empowering

How do these concepts impact your project? This is where you go beyond performance criteria to express meaning, aesthetics, and poetic quality, allowing you to embed your personal values in the project, as discussed in Chapter 2.

ACTIVITY 10.5 Uncovering Programmatic Concepts

(Inspired by Pena & Parshall, 2001)

Purpose: **To explore which programmatic concepts apply to your project in each of the four categories of form, function, economy, and time.**

Review the tables you prepared in Activities 10.4 and 10.5. Think creatively here, focusing not only on functional applications, but upon influences of meaning and poetry as well. Use the examples provided in Tables 10.3 and 10.4, but don't be afraid to test out your own programmatic concepts as well.

Step 4	Form	Function	Economy	Time
Uncovering	1.	1.	1.	1.
Concepts	2.	2.	2.	2.
	3.	3.	3.	3.
	4.	4.	4.	4.
	5.	5.	5.	5.

In 1995, the bombing of the Oklahoma City Alfred P. Murrah Federal Building killed 168 people and carved a semicircular blast radius out of all floors of the façade, extending through more than half of the depth of the building. Planning for the design of the new Federal Building presented the challenge of balancing the programming concepts of security, accessibility, and building character. How do you create a building with maximum security that looks and feels like minimum security, in order to preserve the building's image of public service? The final solution treated three sides of the building as concrete façades, appearing strong and impenetrable, and finished with an approachable and transparent glass curtain as its entrance façade. Security was maintained on the entrance side by replacing street access and vehicular traffic with a pedestrian lawn that provides a secure zone. The semicircular design of the entrance sequence in the otherwise rectangular floor plan conceptually pays tribute to the fate of the original federal building, and the glass walls symbolically expose the "soft underbelly" of the building. In the images presented in Figure 10.9, you can see the juxtaposition of the strong concrete materials and the more delicate glass.

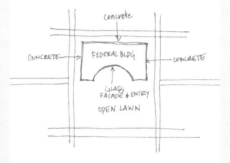

Figure 10.9 In the restoration of the Oklahoma City Alfred P. Murrah Federal Building, multiple programmatic concepts were explored and translated into design solutions.

⊛ ACTIVITY 10.6 Understanding Programmatic Concepts

(Inspired by Pena & Parshall, 2001)

Purpose: **To practice expressing ideas using images instead of words.**

Knowledge visualization—using images instead of words—can make it easier to express abstract ideas. This Activity applies this theory to the understanding of programmatic concepts.

1. The class divides into groups of two or three. Each group is assigned two of the programmatic concepts explained in this section and is provided with brief descriptions of the assigned concepts.
2. Each group is to do the following:
    - Develop an explanation for your assigned programmatic concept *in your own words.*
    - Come up with a real-life application of that concept that your classmates can relate to or identify. Examples from the school building or well-known city landmarks or famous examples work best.
    - Diagram the programmatic concept, expressing it through a simple line drawing that can be communicated on the whiteboard or chalkboard.
3. As a group, present your ideas to the class by drawing your diagram on the board and sharing your definition with the class, along with the real-world example you chose to illustrate your point. (See Figure 10.10.)
4. As a class, use this as a conversation starter to draw out other examples and ensure that all students understand the concept.

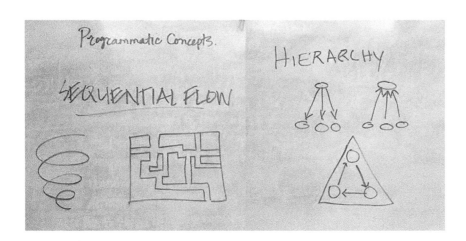

Figure 10.10 In these examples of classroom activity, students were asked to create visual representations or diagrams of various programmatic concepts.

In Step Five you will identify the following (Pena & Parshall, 2001):

- What are the significant conditions affecting the design of the space?
- What are the general directions the design should take?

In this step you will state the essence of the design problem from which to create a **problem statement**. Problem statements are the bridge between programming and design and are agreed upon by both client and user. In Activity 10.7, develop a minimum of four problem statements—one each for form, function, economy, and time (Ballast, 2006).

⊙ ACTIVITY 10.7 Stating the Problem

(Inspired by Pena & Parshall, 2001)

Purpose: **To practice applying programmatic concepts to solve specific problems.**

Building on Activity 10.6, in which you practiced identifying programmatic concepts, in this Activity you will apply those concepts to solve specific problems. As stated above, list at least four problems: one for each category. Then apply the two questions to each problem.

Step 5	Form	Function	Economy	Time
State the Problem				
What is the programmatic concept that will solve the problem?				
How will the programmatic concept be applied to solve the problem?				

Professional Program Formats

Just as there are multiple approaches to the programming process, there are many different formats for the programming document. For some interior design firms the programming document is a spreadsheet, for others it is a list of bullet points, and for still others it is a descriptive narrative. Figure 10.11 provides one example.

In *Architectural Programming: Creative Techniques for Design Professionals* (1995), Robert Kumlin presents the following checklist of information that should be included in a programming document:

1. Priority statement
2. Issues, program objectives, and program concepts
3. Space standards
4. Organizational diagrams
5. Space lists or required square footage
6. Affinities and grouping or adjacencies
7. Flow diagrams
8. Room data sheets
9. Architectural and engineering criteria (environmental requirements)
10. Codes, ordinances, regulations
11. General criteria and standards (relating to the project as a whole)
12. Equipment data sheets
13. Site evaluation
14. Existing facility analysis
15. Cost evaluation and budget analysis
16. Schedule
17. Unresolved issues
18. Other information (design guidelines)
19. Site/building selection criteria

Table 10.5 presents a suggested format for a programming document. Each category will be explained in more detail later in the chapter, with specific explanations and tips. As mentioned earlier, the programming document can vary from project to project, school to school, and office to office. No one format is the "correct one." For example, interior designer Denise Guerin uses the following program format to "inform, entice, and excite" the interior design project:

1. Introduction
2. Literature Review
3. Methods
4. Program (Findings)
5. Design Solutions

HUMANE SOCIETY & ANIMAL COMMUNITY CENTER	Room Number	Count of Rooms	Occupancy Load x sq ft	Dimension W	Dimension L	Size (sq ft)	Size (sq ft)	Total for all Room Count	Occupancy / Activities / Function /Usage	Acoustics	Atmosphere / Environment	Colors
reception area	1	1	5x100	20	25	500	500	500	greeting, directing clients, register	protected from dog habitat	welcoming, friendly	strong, saturated colors (jewel tones)
dog habitat	2	30	100x50	6	9	54	50	1,500	pet habitat	keep sound in	utilitarian for dog feeding and sleeping but with residential feel	strong, saturated colors
adoption viewing	3	3	100x20	40	50	2000	2,000	6,000	looking for or adopting a pet	keep sound in	residential in feel, comfortable, interactive	strong, saturated colors
veterinary clinic	4	1	100x50	50	100	5000	5,000	5,000	utilizing vet services, pet grooming	exam rooms acoustically protected	inviting, not clinical	neutral
veterinary exam room	5	4	5' x 10'	5	10	50	50	200	preliminary exam of dog	keep sound in	basic room with little diversions	neutral, calming
retail and thrift shop	6	1	30x100	40	70	2800	3,000	3,000	shopping, retail and thrift store	acoustically protected from animal area	inviting, innovative, interactive, whimsical "Muttropolis"	neutrals to feature products, with saturated accents
classroom arena	7	2	100x20			0	2,000	4,000	attending classes	keep sound in	outdoor, spacious	none, outdoors
cafe	8	1	15x75			0	2,000	2,000	eating/socializing	acoustically protected from animal area	inviting, open to dogs, casual	strong, saturated colors
dog park (1 acre outdoors)	9	1	100x435			0	43,560	43,560	dog exercise and play	outdoor, none needed	park-like	none, outdoors
restrooms	10	3	20x15'			0	300	900	restrooms	keep sound in	upscale	neutral, with saturated colors
corridors	11	1				0		5,600	circulation	none needed	intuitive way finding, curved and "path-like"	neutral
retail storage room	12	1	300x2 people			0	600	600	store overstock	none needed	utilitarian for storage	neutral
utility closet	13	3	50x1			0	50	150	store cleaning supplies	none needed	utilitarian for cleaning supplies	neutral
laundry room	14	1	50x1			0	50	50	store cleaning supplies	keep sound in	utilitarian for laundry	neutral
						Total sq ft	74,010					

Figure 10.11 Some interior designers will summarize the programming information in an easy-to-read programming spreadsheet, sometimes referred to as a criteria matrix. Courtesy interior design student Michelle Hill Gilles.

Before beginning your interior design programming document, it is a good idea to confirm the required format and content for your project program.

Each part of this document is essential. However, students often find the "Long Program" to be the most time-consuming, as it takes you through the building space by space, almost like a conceptual walkthrough. Remember, though, that nowhere in this document will you be providing design solutions. Instead, you are providing conceptual strategies for solving the problem and achieving the predetermined goals and objectives for the project.

Activity-Based Program Versus Spatially Based Program

Before moving on, let's take a moment to discuss a programmatic approach called **activity-based programming**. Student designers tend to use **spatially**

Electronic Equipment	Finishes or Materials	Fixtures / Plumbing	Flooring	Furniture / Furnishings	Lighting (all on automatic dimmers when possible)	Privacy	Storage	Outdoor Views
copy machine, telephone, fax, tv monitor for security camera rotating through spaces	recycled materials for countertops, flooring, etc	none needed	resilient to wear, vct or coved sheet vinyl	desk, office chair(s), transaction counter, file cabinets,	natural lighting, task lighting	none needed	office supplies, paperwork, client files	needed
tv monitors, sound system	all resilient to wear; recycled whenever possible	drain in floor, water spout	resilient to wear, vct or coved sheet vinyl	dog bed, dog water and food dish, picture frame for dog photo on entry	natural lighting as well as fluorescent, skylight	none needed	dog bedding, extra dishes	none needed, skylight if possible or open to courtyard
tv monitors, sound system	all resilient to wear; recycled whenever possible	drain in floor, water spout	artificial grass turf	residential furniture, chairs, sofas, tables,	natural lighting as well as fluorescent, skylight	each area physically segregated but visually open	some toys, leashes	none needed, skylight if possible or open courtyard
full surgical suite of equipment	all resilient to wear; recycled whenever possible	water access in dog grooming area	resilient to wear, vct or coved sheet vinyl	front desk, waiting area seating, exam tables, desk chairs		doctor area private from exam room and entry	medical supplies, dog food, office supplies	none needed
computer in ea exam room with large wall display	all resilient to wear; recycled whenever possible	none needed	resilient to wear, vct or coved sheet vinyl	bench for pet owner(s), cabinet for storage	fluorescent, natural color lighting	each room private with entrance and exit back to clinic area	small cabinet for supplies	none needed
cash register, telephone, fax	recycled, bamboo for shelving and displays	none needed	rubber recycled flooring	front desk, counter stools, seating area for reading, display shelves, display podiums	natural lighting as well as fluorescent, skylight	none needed	overstock storage	none needed
tv monitor with dvd/vcr player	all resilient to wear; recycled whenever possible	drain in floor, water spout	artificial grass turf	chairs for class participants (folding chairs)	outdoors, natural lights, if indoor arena natural lighting	keep dogs in fenced area	toys and props, folding chairs	outdoors, if indoors none needed
cash register, telephone, fax	all resilient to wear; recycled whenever possible	sinks, refrigerators, ice machine, water dispenser	linoleum - custom pattern	42" café tables, chairs, transaction counter for cash register, counters for beverage dispenser	natural lighting as well as can down lights for evening, pendant lighting over tables, skylight	none needed	extra deli food, utensils, dishware	needed, tables by full windows, skylights
none needed	all resilient to wear; recycled whenever possible	access to water for dog fountain, water spout	natural grass	benches, outdoor seating, picnic tables, pooper scoopers	post street lamps with automatic on/off	fenced in area with two-way secure gate	none needed	provide hearty landscaping
none needed	all resilient to wear; recycled whenever possible	4 toilets, 2 lavatories, drain in floor	ceramic tile	waste baskets, vanity, paper towel dispenser, toilet tissue holder	can down lighting, sconces around vanity mirror, timer	full privacy needed	paper supplies	none needed
sound system	all resilient to wear; recycled whenever possible	drinking fountain(s)	resilient to wear, vct or coved sheet vinyl	intermittent seating for staff or clients	sconces, sky lighting	none needed	none needed	none needed
none needed	all resilient to wear; recycled whenever possible	none needed	resilient to wear, vct or coved sheet vinyl	work tables, storage shelving	fluorescent, w/ timer	lockable and secure from public	overstock, supplies	none needed
none needed	all resilient to wear; recycled whenever possible	utility sink, drain in floor	resilient to wear, vct or coved sheet vinyl	mop, bucket, cleaning supplies	fluorescent, w/ timer	lockable and secure from public	cleaning supplies, linens	none needed
none needed	all resilient to wear; recycled whenever possible	drain in floor, water access for washer and dryer	resilient to wear, vct or coved sheet vinyl	shelving	fluorescent, w/ timer	lockable and secure from public	linens/dog bedding, soiled and clean	none needed

Figure 10.11 (continued)

based programming, meaning that they define spaces based on their preconceived notion of what spaces that project type *should* hold. For example, with spatially-based programming, in the design of a restaurant you need a hostess stand, bar, dining room, kitchen, and restrooms, and in the design of a house you need a living room, dining room, kitchen, bedrooms, and bathrooms. Activity-based programming, on the other hand, defines spaces based on the activities, behaviors, and functions that will occur in the space. Recall the discussion of underlying assumptions in Chapter 2.

Ask yourself the following questions to identify the activities happening within your project spaces:

1. How many different activities take place within the space or building?
2. What are these activities? Make a thorough list.
3. What are the **primary activities**? These are the activities occurring on a full-time, frequent, and regular basis.

Table 10.5 Organizational Outline of Programming Document

	Cover Page
	Table of Contents (including each section and page numbers)
Section 1	Project Proposal (also called an Executive Summary, Statement of Intent, or Priority Statement)
Section 2	Project Design Philosophy (or Mission Statement)
Section 3	Project Goals and Objectives 1) Form and Aesthetics Goals 2) Functional Goals 3) Economic Goals 4) Time Goals
Section 4	Codes and Building Occupancy Classifications
Section 5	Equipment List
Section 6	Overlying Programmatic Concepts
Section 7	Existing Site and Building Conditions Report
Section 8	Short Program: "At-a-Glance" Summary of Spaces
Section 9	Long Program: Activity-based programming for space-by-space development, including programmatic concepts applicable to each space
Section 10	Appendix (for potentially important information not yet applied)

4. What are the **secondary activities**? These are the activities that support the primary activities and that occur on a part-time, infrequent, or irregular basis.

⚙ ACTIVITY 10.8 Activity Based Programming

Purpose: **To understand how activities can shape and define a space.**

Pick a building (or a project) and collect or draw pictures or take photographs to illustrate all of the activities happening within the building or space. Then answer the following questions to supplement your images.

It's All in the Name

In a written program, each space or area is given a name. Naming each space may seem like a simple thing to do, but is it very important that you understand the significance of naming each space. A room's name often determines many assumptions or preconceptions about that room's design and function. A codes official will often base his entire evaluation of the code compliance of the room based solely on the room's name shown on the resulting plan. For example, when you name a room a "bedroom," the codes official will assume that people will sleep there, and will therefore require operable windows. If a room is named a "kitchen," you will not be permitted to exit through that room as one of the means of egress.

Even beyond the codes issues are other preconceptions. For example, if you name a room a "bedroom," your resulting design will most likely be a room with a bed in it. If you name that room "sleeping accommodations for two," you may end up with a completely different design solution. Subtle changes in language may also help you later to think outside the box. Consider the different connotations of the following room names: "cafeteria," "dining area," "eating lounge," "banquet hall," or "snacking station." Can you think of areas in your program that would benefit from reinterpreting (or reinventing) the room names?

A student, Machiko Ichimaru, wrote a program for a children's daycare center. She selected room names that would allow the children to be more creative and understand the space for themselves. The large motor skills play space was called "The Power Room," while the snack area was dubbed "The Refueling Station." Names such as these also helped the guest critics understand the playful nature of the space and the student's willingness to explore innovation within the typical daycare program.

1. In order, from most common to least common, how would you rank the activities?
2. Where in the building or space are the activities occurring?
3. Is the space appropriate to accommodate the activity, how many people were involved, and what equipment was used?
4. Were you surprised at how many different activities happen in one building?
5. Can you categorize the activities or group them in any way?
6. Can you identify how the building or space supported the activities within? Are there any situations where the building or space was not appropriate for the activities? How was the space adapted to better suit the activities?

Purpose: **To understand the nature of each activity taking place within your project and the required relationships between these activities.**

Use the four questions listed just before Activity 10.8 to help you make a specific and thorough list of all the activities that will be happening within the spaces you are designing. Once you have identified the activities that take place in the building, use the following questions to help you more thoroughly understand the nature of each activity taking place within the space or building so that you will know how to design for it. Make copies of the questions as needed in order to cover all of the activities within your individual project.

1. What is the activity?
2. Is the activity primary or secondary? Full-time or part-time?
3. What is the nature of the activity? Is it physical, sedentary, guided, etc.?
4. At what time of day or night does the activity take place? (Hours of Operation)
5. How often is the activity performed—number of times per day or week and so on?
6. Is the activity done by people alone, in small groups, or large groups?
7. Who is involved in the activity?
8. Does the activity share space with other activities?
9. Are there any special environmental requirements for the activity— lighting, cooling, ventilation, acoustics?
10. Are there special security requirements for the activity?

On a separate sheet, create a "Relationship Diagram" reflecting the relationships between the activities you listed in Activity 10.9. Please note: This is not a relationship diagram between "spaces"; it's between activities only. Use color and other methods of annotation to help you identify and separate the most important relationships from those that are less critical. The next step will be to define, or to "re-define," the spaces within which these activities take place, allowing each space to develop in direct response to the activities it will be supporting.

Creating a Programming Document

Similar to the methods used to develop the thesis proposal, Table 10.6 walks you through every section of the programming document, offering tips and advice. Check on the required format from either your instructor or your boss. Every class is different, and firms usually have a standard format they use for all projects. It is not the format that is essential, but the thoroughness of the detail. Remember, you should be able to hand this document to another designer and walk away from the project, leaving behind all of the tools and information a designer would need in order to proceed to schematics.

Table 10.6 The Programming Document

Section #	Section Name	Elements to Include	Tips
	Cover Page	1) Name of Project 2) Location of Project (address) 3) Your name 4) Date 5) Project or client logo or other graphics you wish to include	Take the time to create a pleasing graphic layout. Everything you do as a designer is a visual presentation, so wow your client or instructor with your attention to detail.
	Table of Contents	Including each section number and name and corresponding page numbers	This is how your client or instructor navigates this often large document. Save your readers time by setting up your document so they don't have to search for anything.
1	Project Proposal	This is also called the *Executive Summary, Statement of Intent,* or *Priority Statement.* At a minimum, include the following: 1) Project Inspiration 2) Statement of the Problem 3) Priority Statement 4) Summary of Project Intentions and Goals 5) Summary of Issues and Conflicts	If you are developing a thesis, you can insert your thesis proposal here. If not, the outline of the thesis proposal provided in Chapter 9 is a good guide for writing a project proposal. Simply adjust it to meet your specific project conditions.

continued

Section #	Section Name	Elements to Include	Tips
2	Project Design Philosophy or Mission Statement	See Chapter 3 and the discussion on developing a philosophy.	Remember the discussion about Louis Kahn and the Salk Institute? Kahn applied the philosophy that the research institute should be like a monastery, with the scientists similar to monks in that they were dedicating their lives exclusively to benefiting humankind.

3	Project Goals and Objectives	1) Functional Goals
		    a) For People
		    b) For Objects
		    c) For Activities
		2) Form & Aesthetics Goals
		    a) For Site
		    b) For Building
		    c) For Environment
		    d) For Quality of Interiors
		3) Economic Goals
		    a) Initial budget considerations and constraints based on nature of the client and the client's resources
		4) Time Goals
		    a) Future Intentions
		    b) Project Scheduling
			Remember that these refer not to existing conditions but to goals for the new project.

4	Codes and Building Occupancy	1) List all codes and regulations applicable to the project 2) Identify Occupancy Classification(s)	See the discussion in Chapter 13 regarding building codes.
5	Equipment List	1) List all equipment required, including relevant specifications that will influence the design, such as dimensions and safety precautions	See the example provided in Table 10.7.

Section #	Section Name	Elements to Include	Tips
6	Overlying Programmatic Concepts	Once you have identified the problems or issues, use Tables 10.3 and 10.4 to help you identify which strategies or programmatic concepts you will apply to solve the problems.	This is a great place to insert your images from Activity 10.6. It is not enough to simply state "Hierarchy." Instead, you must explain how hierarchy will achieve the client's goals. Is it by creating spaces that exaggerate hierarchy among employees, as is the case with many government organizations, or is it by eliminating a sense of hierarchy to create a team environment?

7	Existing Site and Building Conditions Report	1) Location and Address (include a map as a supplement, clearly indicating north)
		2) The building's square footage, broken down by floors
		3) Exterior building conditions
		  a) Images of neighborhood context
		  b) Exterior materials
		  c) Any comments on architectural style, if relevant
		  d) Historic Preservation regulations and considerations, if applicable
		  e) Images of exterior of building
		  f) Adjacent businesses
		  g) Adjacent transportation
		  h) Intended relationship to community (tell how it either turns toward the community or away from it)
		  i) Exterior circulation as related to site access (cars, bus, etc.)
		  j) Exterior as related to building access (people, supplies, ADA, etc.)
			Remember that this report is answering the question "Does the building fit the program?" Don't just provide documentation. Also use diagrams, overlays, and notes to show the designer what is significant and appropriate about the building.

continued

Section #	Section Name	Elements to Include	Tips

		4) Interior building conditions
		  a) Structural system of building, including essential structural elements called out on floor plan
		  b) 8" × 11" or 11" × 17" image of floor plan(s)
		  c) Images of any other building drawings you have access to, such as RCP, elevations, or building section
		  d) Interior images
		  e) Indication of important views
		  f) Service functions and locations (trash, recycling, deliveries, etc.)
		  g) Maximum ceiling height
		  h) Windows: any typical features such as sill or header height
		  i) Other major building features
		5) Diagrams of site selection criteria and what conclusions you have drawn through your information-gathering process	

8	Short Program	Organized in a grid format: 1) Provide a list of spaces, organized in a rational way. 2) List occupancy (refer back to your codes textbook for occupancy load requirements, especially in areas such as assembly spaces). Also see Chapter 13 for more discussion about "occupancy load factor." 3) Number of units 4) Unit square footage 5) Overall square footage (number of units × unit square footage) 6) Circulation percent 7) Number of restrooms required for each area or for project based on project occupancy loads 8) Total square footage needed for the entire project (This number is critical as it will be the driving factor behind the selection of an appropriate building.)	This is an "At-a-Glance" Summary of the building and spaces. Your innovation should be evident just from scanning your Short Program, as the organization and definition of spaces will show how this project is different from those that have come before. Tools for calculating square footage: a) Consider the number of people present b) Consider the size of furniture, known equipment, or other elements you already know will be in the space. c) The required occupancy load factor based on code requirements d) Prototypes of similar spaces in other projects or found in the built environment around you

Section #	Section Name	Elements to Include	Tips
9	Long Program	1) List space 2) List square footage 3) List users 4) List of activities, including description 5) Equipment requirements, including sizes (don't forget Audio/Visual) 6) Any furniture or materials performance requirements (**Note:** You don't have to give the furniture or material selection, just performance requirements, such as "nonslip flooring." Students often include art requirements here as well.) 7) Lighting and acoustical requirements 8) Storage Requirements (how much and what is being stored) 9) Any required adjacencies 10) Identify problems to be addressed in the space and programmatic concepts (strategies) for solving the problem.	Developed in response to activity-based programming using activity requirements to define spaces. Organize your Long Program exactly as you organized your Short Program, by overall function (for example, administration versus classrooms when designing a school). Do not rely on simple one-word bullet points and lists, but explain your intentions for each space. You are basically providing a virtual walkthrough of the project. When you're developing the Long Program, it is important to know your scope of work or focus so you don't waste time developing spaces that are not part of your job requirements.
10	Appendix	This can be a new section you create that is unique to your project type and might not apply to every project, or this can be a place where you insert articles or data that might not apply at the moment but might become important at a later date.	You might have more than one appendix for your project. If this is the case, simply label them Appendix 1, Appendix 2, and so on.

Tips on Developing the Equipment List

For each space in the project, you should identify the equipment required in an **equipment list**—both the existing equipment as well as the equipment requested by the client. Be very specific. You may create your own chart for this process, listing each space and providing the required information, or you may use a format similar to the example by student Lauren Komera for the lobby of a boutique hotel. (See Table 10.7.) Once this chart is completed, you can use it to assist you in developing the square footage requirements listed in the Short Program.

Table 10.7 Sample Equipment List for the Lobby of a Boutique Hotel

Space	Equipment Required (Name and Manufacturer)	Dimensions	Required Adjacencies or Clearances Between Equipment
Lobby	Computer System—Dell Optiplex 960	15.79" × 7.36" × 17.24"	Adj. to computer screens, check in/out stations and server
Lobby	Server—Dell 2900 III	18.85" × 8.92" × 26.55"	Adj. to computer screens, check in/out stations and server
Lobby	LCD Monitors—Planar PL1711M 17" dual input monitor with stand	16.1" × 14.4" × 8.6"	Adj. to CPU, check in/out stations and server
Lobby	Touch Screen Check In/Out System—Planar PT1910MX 19" touch screen	16" × 17.2" × 10.5"	Adj. to CPU, computer screens, and server
Lobby	Card System—See appendix for more information	TBD	Adj. to CPU compter screens and server
Lobby	Living Wall System—Gsky Active Living Wall System (including panel system, thermostat, humidistat, fans and irrigation system	TBD—units come customizable—see appendix for schematics and specifications	HVAC system and drainage

Five Ways to Calculate Square Footage

Determining space allocation is a skill that gets easier over time. Eventually you will have an instinctual sense of the difference between 100 square feet, 500 square feet, and 1,000 square feet. In the meantime, here are some tips to help you make educated square footage calculations.

Step 1: Occupancy Load Factor. Determine the minimum number of square feet required by each occupant, based on the Occupancy Load Factor (O.L.F.). This is discussed at length in Chapter 13. Multiply the O.L.F. by the number of people expected to use the space, and this gives you a minimum required square footage as a place to start.

Next, consider the impact of human factors and proxemic relationships. A person in a wheelchair takes up a different amount of space than a person who is standing, and people of different cultures are comfortable with varying amounts of personal space between themselves and other individuals. Also consider that in space-planning there is a difference between **static dimensions** and **dynamic dimensions**. Think about your seat in one of your classes. You take up a different amount of space depending on whether you are (1) sitting up in your chair, paying attention, or (2) lounging back, with your ankles crossed out in front of you, staring at something outside the window. Another example: When you are focused and working hard at your drafting table, you take up much less space than when you are frantically whisking about your desk, trying to make the deadline for a final presentation. When you are calculating square footages, you should consider not only the static dimensions within the space but also the dynamic dimensions; then accommodate for that heightened level of activity.

Step 2: Equipment and Clearances. Calculate the square footage required to accommodate required equipment or furniture in the space. Don't forget to account for the required clearance around the equipment. For example, a massage table may be 2 feet wide and 6 feet long, or 12 square feet. But you must also include the 3 feet of open circulation space required on all sides of the massage table. In reality, the square footage requirement for a massage table is actually 8 feet wide by 12 feet long, or 96 square feet. That's a huge difference!

The equipment list to be discussed later in this chapter will give you the sizes of the relevant equipment to be used in the project. Knowing the sizes of the equipment and any existing or required furniture, such as systems furniture, will help you develop your calculations. This is a great approach for commercial kitchens with large appliances, medical spaces with large equipment, and office spaces that will be using systems furniture. The book *Interior Graphic and Design Standards*, by S. C. Reznikoff (1986), is a great tool for finding typical sizes of equipment and furniture when using this approach.

Step 3: Identify Standard Dimensions. Some spaces, such as a basketball court in the United States, are based on accepted or required standard dimensions. Whether you are designing for a half court or a full court, there is a culturally established set of rules for the space that you will need to abide by.

Step 4: Percentage of the Whole. If you already know the overall available square footage for the project, you can use an understanding of your priorities or spatial hierarchy to determine how you want to divide the space. For example, if you are designing a 1,000-square-foot Buddhist retreat, you might know that you want 50 percent of the square footage, or 500 square feet, to be dedicated to the meditation space; 25 percent, or 250 square feet, dedicated to a retail space such as a bookstore; and the remaining 25 percent, or 250 square feet, dedicated to back-of-house services.

Step 5: Applying Prototypical Sizes. You can use information from your precedent or case studies (refer back to Chapter 8) to identify prototypical or appropriate sizes for spaces that are similar to those you are creating. Study the floor plans of other projects to see how the designer has used space. You could even interview people within a space and ask if the size is appropriate for the function. Keep in mind that you are looking for the most appropriate amount of space for the activity, which may, in fact, differ from the prototype.

After finalizing your calculations, verify them and your conclusions with the client before moving forward.

Tips on Developing the Short Program

The Short Program is very concise. It is a simple, "at-a-glance" summary of the project program, but it contains some critical information. For example, see Table 10.8. First, like a bird's-eye view, it shows the grouping of spaces and overall organization and relationships of the project. Second, the Short Program lists all spaces within the program, the number of occupants, and the square footage required for each space. These numbers help you to identify codes relevant to your project and to determine other information, such as the number of restrooms required, the percentage of circulation required, and the total square footage. This information is essential if you are responsible for selecting an appropriate building or space for the project.

Table 10.8 illustrates in very simple terms how you might format the Short Program in a grid format. Once you have identified all space types, the number of units, the number of occupants per unit, and the square footage per unit, you can add up your total occupants and your total square footage and use this to calculate the number of toilets required per codes; to check your **occupancy load factor**, discussed further in Chapter 13; and to establish the amount of circulation required. Add that information to your square footage requirements to get the final required square footage for the project. Figure 10.12 (page 309) illustrates the Short Program format for an airport project.

Table 10.8 The Short Program

Type of Space	# of Units	Occupants per Unit	Total Number of Occupants	Unit Square Feet	Total Square Feet
Management office	4	3	(4 × 3) 12	150 sq. ft.	(4 × 150) 600 sq. ft.
Open workstations	10	1	(10 × 1) 10	70 sq. ft.	(10 × 70) 700 sq. ft.
Totals			(12 + 10) 22 occupants		(600 + 700) 1300 sq. ft.

ACTIVITY 10.10 The Art of "Guesstimating"

Purpose: **To help you get an idea of the sizes of spaces in order to help you with your own space allocation calculations.**

1. Close your eyes and guess the size of the classroom you are in right now.

2. Once you have come to a conclusion, use the ceiling tiles or other modular units in the space to confirm the actual size of the space. For example, every standard acoustic ceiling tile (A.C.T.) is either 24" × 24" or 24" × 48". How close were you?

3. Now go out in the world and try to guesstimate the square footage of all the spaces you occupy that day, from public to private. How about a coffee house? a church? an elevator? a plaza? In each space, see if you can find a way to confirm how accurate you were in your guesses. You can use the ceiling tile or other modular elements, such as regularly sized floor tiles or bricks, as long as you can easily identify the size of the modular unit. After a while you will get a sense for the size of spaces, and your guesses will become pretty good estimates!

At a Glance Program

Passenger Relations Process Spaces

	Activity	Space	Occupancy / Unit (Average)	# of Units	Unit Square Ft	Total S.F.
1	Drop off	Curb Side	---	1060' linear	Existing	Existing
2	Luggage Check- In/ Ticket Purchase	Counter	3 (1 employee, 2 passengers)	12	80	960
3	Luggage Check- In	Waiting	---	---	---	3,000
4	Boarding Pass Printing	Kiosk	3	6	50	300
5	Eating	Eateries	~20	9	1,500	13,500
6	Coffee Drinking	Coffee Shop	~10	3	800	2,400
7	Bar	Bar	~20	3	900	2,700
8	Lounging	Lounge	80	1	3,000	3,000
9	Child Education/ Play	Children's	~20	1	1,000	1,000
10	Shopping	Retail Shop	10	9	500	4,500
11	Restroom Use	Restroom	30	2M 2F	1000	4,000
12	Immigration Status Check	Customs	2	1	100	100
13	International Money Exchange	Money Exchange	2	1	100	100
14	Security Screening, Waiting	Security Suite	---	1	4,000	4,000
15	Waiting to Board	Open Seating	400 (plane capacity)	1/ gate (8)	15,000	120,000
16	Boarding/ Deplane	Connection Tunnel	0-30	1/ gate (8)	200	1,600
17	Luggage Claim	Claim Area	1/ Flight (400)	3	500	1,500
18	Pick-up	Curb Side	---	1060' linear	Existing	Existing
19	Waiting for Pick-up	Inside Waiting	100	1	300	300

Figure 10.12 This Short Program—prepared by interior design student Kelly Powell—gives an overview of the project program and organization, as well as critical information such as square footage and space occupancy loads.

The Long Program is where you identify the spaces and the activities occurring in the spaces, applying your activities analysis and activity relationship diagram discussed in Activity 10.8, and letting the activities and function define the space. The Long Program should establish the relationships between spaces and the relationship between people and spaces. You do not have to use the word *room,* as the word *space* leaves more flexibility to respond with creativity. Remember from Chapter 2 the example of the dining room versus the entertaining space? Because a family might do more in the space than dine, why should that be the limiting factor?

Be careful not to provide design solutions in your Long Program, but only programmatic concepts and strategies. For example, a company occupying two floors in an office building might need a way to circulate between floors (*the design problem*). The programmatic solution would be "vertical circulation." This programmatic solution leaves the door open for many different design solutions, such as a stair, an elevator, an escalator, a rope ladder, a firefighter's pole, or even a jet pack. This flexibility allows you to select the most appropriate design solution in the design development phase.

Consider an example from the offices of a well-known Internet company. With a large office space, the company had to solve the problem of productive time lost walking back and forth from space to space. What was their design solution? Scooters and "Segways" to move people along the corridors twice as fast and with twice as much fun!

ACTIVITY 10.11 Redefining the Chair

Purpose: **To understand how one programmatic concept can lead to many different design solutions.**

The Long Program for an advertising firm calls for a teaming area with a large, durable work surface and flexible seating for six to eight employees.

If "flexible seating" is the *programmatic concept,* what would you select as the design solution? How many different design solutions can you come up with to achieve the programmatic concept of "flexible seating for six to eight employees"? Here's a hint: Have you ever seen office employees sitting on a yoga ball as their office chair? You can get really creative with this Activity!

Your Long Program should use clear, expressive, and technical language. Table 10.9 is a sample excerpt from a Long Program, which gives you an idea of the level of detail, the information included, and the language used. The example is for a teaming space in an advertising agency. (Notice we did not use the word *room* to describe the space.) Remember that this is only one space in a larger project. The length of your Long Program will depend on the number of spaces and the scope of the project.

If you are developing a thesis project, use this as an opportunity to focus your project and identify activities and spaces that will best support your thesis statement and explore the field of design you are most interested in. As discussed earlier, the grid is meant to clarify the information and is not necessarily the intended format.

Establishing Relationships: Criteria Matrix and Relationship Diagrams

To achieve the functional objectives and goals for a project, you need to decide and graphically indicate which spaces should be convenient to each other to best facilitate the relationships among people, objects, and activities. **Relationship diagrams**, like the one shown in Figure 10.13, are a great way to identify (1) the location of critical spatial relationships and (2) the types of relationships between spaces, from immediately adjacent to no adjacency required. Arrange for the relative sizes of the bubbles to reflect the sizes of the spaces, and include a key that determines direct adjacency, convenient access, no-access, and the various ways that adjacency and access

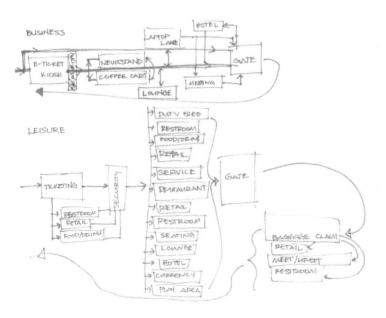
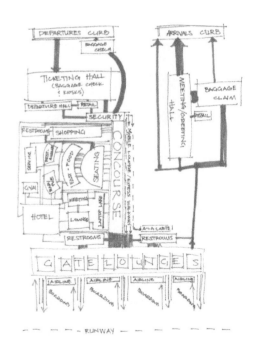

Figure 10.13 Relationship and other programming diagrams for a thesis project program for an airport. Courtesy interior design student Morgan Greenseth.

Table 10.9 The Long Program for a Teaming Area in an Advertising Firm

Space Name	Teaming Area
Square Footage	200 square feet
End Users	Employees of all levels, often including management
Activities (Tip: Don't forget to include specific quantitative data, such as the number of people involved. Also, for an activity in an advertising firm, don't just say "team meetings.")	Four to six persons meeting in teams for brainstorming and concept development. This might include large-scale diagramming, mapping storyboards on a tackboard, or using other creative tools that require large work surfaces and pin-up space.
Equipment Requirements, including sizes and clearances. (Tip: If you have provided a detailed equipment list elsewhere, that would suffice.)	Ten linear feet of vertical display space (such as tackboard or magnets), dry-erase board, laptop computers, overhead multimedia projector (Hewlett-Packard NEC VT700-LCD projector: 12.2" × 10.2" × 4.4"), projection screen (size to be based on final dimensions of the room and location of seating: Width = Distance of Center Line of Seating from Screen / 2), telephone with conferencing capacity
Furniture and Material Performance Requirements (Tip: You don't have to give the design solution yet!)	Large work surface with washable and durable surface material, flexible seating for up to six persons. Some sound-absorbing materials either in floor or ceilings, washable wall covering

can be represented. You can use lines of varying weight, colored lines, or dashed lines. Unlike a "bubble diagram," the relationship diagram is independent from the base plan and scale. A well-thought-out relationship diagram will help you to shorten the gap between programming and schematic space-planning.

Many interior designers also use a matrix—either an **adjacency matrix** or a **criteria matrix** that includes an adjacency portion—to document required spatial relationships. An adjacency matrix focuses solely on the nature of spatial relationships, while a criteria matrix also addresses needs and requirements for each space, such as electrical or day lighting needs. (See Figure 10.14.) Also, look again at Figure 10.11, which is an example of a very complex criteria matrix, addressing all the programming requirements for a Humane Society project.

For your own project, create a relationship diagram and adjacency matrix to help you explore all of the critical relationships in your project.

Lighting and Acoustical Requirements	Task lighting (preferably ceiling-mounted to avoid obstruction), wall washers for vertical display space, natural light preferred but not required (This space does not need complete privacy, only enough acoustical isolation to prevent noise pollution in adjacent spaces.)
Storage Requirements (how much and what is being stored)	Drawer storage for pens and markers, large-scale work pads (24" × 36"). Also provide small-scale organizer for tacks, magnets, Post-its, etc.
Required Adjacencies	Preferably this space will have adjacency to main circulation route with some acoustical separation but visual connection in order to promote team-building atmosphere
Design Problems and Programmatic Concepts (Strategies)	The client wants to create a direct connection between this space and the rest of the office to encourage an "open forum" culture. However, teaming sessions can get rowdy, so acoustical separation is a must. Also, the space is for everyone and it should reflect that. • *Relationships:* The space could be centrally located, accessible to both management and other employees. • *Communication:* The space could provide for impromptu interaction and communication, yet the opportunity to acoustically isolate if necessary. • *Flexibility:* The space could adapt to the employees and the task at hand. • *Accessibility:* Create an "open forum."

Effective Communication of the Program

In the game of "Telephone," poorly communicated ideas can result in a garbled mess at the end. It is the same with your programming document. Every individual on the project team must be able to use the program as a guide, so you need to know your audience and how to "speak" to them. Much of the programming document is in a written format, and the same writing guidelines you would use in a history course or an English course would apply here. Proper grammar and spelling are essential to ensuring your great ideas are not lost in the translation of your writing.

Sometimes, the presentation of your programmatic conclusions and ideas will benefit from images, sketches, or diagrams that help clarify your words. Clients tend to respond well to images, especially those in 3-D, as the images will bring your ideas to life and help the client visualize the future project. When you use diagrams to communicate with other people, there are two kinds—rough and finished—and both can be equally beneficial as

Figure 10.14 Adjacency matrix for the same airport shown in Figure 10.13. Courtesy interior design student Morgan Greenseth.

The flow of the airport is predetermined by the FAA, which creates mandatory adjacencies and strict design layouts.

The mandatory spaces may need additional spaces to suit the needs of passengers, guests, and employees. These may be added in addition, as long as the typical airport flow is not disturbed.

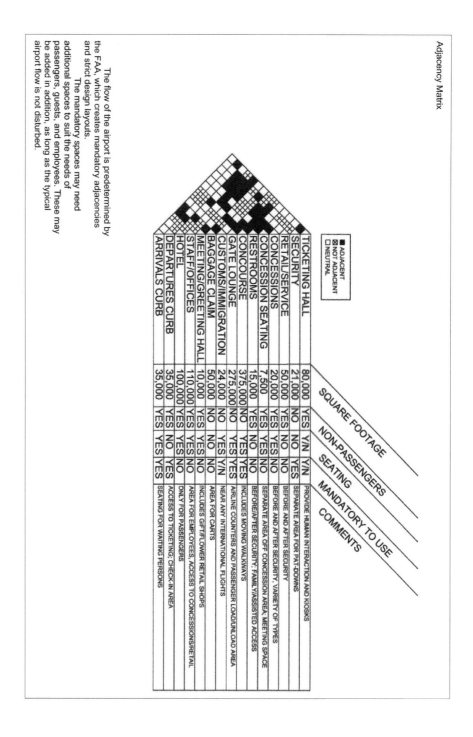

Legend: ■ ADJACENT ⊠ NOT ADJACENT ☐ NEUTRAL

	SQUARE FOOTAGE	NON-PASSENGERS	SEATING	MANDATORY TO USE	COMMENTS
TICKETING HALL	80,000	YES	Y/N	YES	PROVIDE HUMAN INTERACTION AND KIOSKS
SECURITY	21,000	NO	NO	YES	SEPARATE AREA FOR PAT-DOWNS
RETAIL/SERVICE	50,000	YES	NO	NO	BEFORE AND AFTER SECURITY
CONCESSIONS	20,000	YES	YES	NO	BEFORE AND AFTER SECURITY, VARIETY OF TYPES
CONCESSION SEATING	7,500	YES	YES	NO	SEPARATE AREA OFF CONCESSION AREA, MEETING SPACE
RESTROOMS	15,000	YES	NO	NO	BEFORE/AFTER SECURITY; FAMILY/ASSISTED ACCESS
CONCOURSE	375,000	NO	YES	YES	INCLUDES MOVING WALKWAYS
GATE LOUNGE	275,000	NO	YES	YES	AIRLINE COUNTERS AND PASSENGER LOAD/UNLOAD AREA
CUSTOMS/IMMIGRATION	24,000	NO	YES	Y/N	NEAR ANY INTERNATIONAL FLIGHTS
BAGGAGE CLAIM	50,000	NO	NO	NO	AREA FOR CARTS
MEETING/GREETING HALL	10,000	YES	YES	NO	INCLUDES GIFT/FLOWER RETAIL SHOPS
STAFF/OFFICES	110,000	YES	YES	NO	AREA FOR EMPLOYEES, ACCESS TO CONCESSIONS/RETAIL
HOTEL	100,000	YES	YES	NO	ONLY FOR PASSENGERS
DEPARTURES CURB	35,000	YES	NO	YES	ACCESS TO TICKETING; CHECK-IN AREA
ARRIVALS CURB	35,000	YES	YES	YES	SEATING FOR WAITING PERSONS

long as they are clear. You can also use your diagrams to communicate with other designers or project team members.

Designers also communicate the program through verbal presentation, which varies depending on the type of program being presented. A programming presentation for a residential client might be informally presented in the client's home or over your office desk, while a commercial or institutional program might be presented to a group of stakeholders at a conference table or in a more formal PowerPoint presentation. Either way, your verbal communication must be professional and must communicate to the client that you have listened to them; that you understand their wants, needs, and goals; and that you have provided strategies for accomplishing those goals.

Conclusion

Interior design does not happen in a vacuum. You can identify the design problems to be solved, but the programming process illustrates the importance of understanding the context around the problem. That context includes the client and other persons involved in the project, the site, and any other influencing factors. So you must understand the design problem from multiple perspectives. Your solutions might be the best ones for the client, but what about the other people involved, such as the end users, contractor, subcontractors, neighboring people or businesses, or professional critics? It's a lot to balance, but juggling so many individual needs usually leads to a more thoughtful solution. Don't fight the context of the project and see it as an imposition on your creativity. Instead, see it as a challenging opportunity (Adams, 2001).

In the film *The Building of the Getty*, Richard Meier juggles an ever-expanding list of influences on his project, from the reticent neighbors occupying the slopes of the building site, to the conflict between his personal design philosophies and the aesthetic expectations of the client, to the conflict between Richard's expectations for the site and those of the landscape architect. In your own projects, you need to acknowledge and address these types of influences at the programming level so that in schematics and design development you solve the client's design problem within the rich context where it resides.

References

Adams, J. L. (2001). *Conceptual blockbusting: A guide to better ideas*. Cambridge, MA: Basic Books.

Ballast, D. K. (2006). *Interior design reference manual: A guide to the NCIDQ exam* (3rd ed.). Belmont, CA: Professional.

Cherry, E. (1999). *Programming for design*. New York: John Wiley.

Hershberger, R. G. (1985). Values: A theoretical foundation for architectural programming. In W. Preiser (editor), *Programming the Built Environment*. New York: Van Nostrand Reinhold.

Karlen, M., Ruggeri, K., & Hahn, P. (2004). *Space planning basics*. New York: Wiley.

Kumlin, R. (1995). *Architectural programming: Creative techniques for design professionals*. New York: McGraw-Hill.

Pena, W. M., & Parshall, S. A. (2001). *Problem seeking: An architectural programming primer*. New York: John Wiley.

Reznikoff, S. C. (1986). *Interior graphic and design standards*. New York: Whitney Library of Design.

11 Site Selection and Analysis

CHAPTER OBJECTIVES

When you complete this chapter you should be able to do the following:

- Understand the relationship between the project site and the building for interior design.
- Collect site and building shell information from a variety of sources, including maps, city records, Internet sources, existing plans, and field surveys.
- Analyze the site in terms of physical possibilities and constraints.
- Analyze the site in terms of social, economic, cultural, and historic context.
- Become familiar with terminology associated with site analysis.

KEY TERMS

Accessibility

Adaptive reuse

Addition

Anthropological

As-built drawing

Basement

Beams

Building system

Bulk

Caissons

Cartographers

Climate map

Column

Column bays

Context

Cover sheet

Crawl space

Curtain wall

Demographic

Density

District

Economic or resource map

Edge

Existing condition

Feasibility study

FF&E Inventory

Field survey

Foundation

Geographic

Hardscape

Land use map

Landmark

Load-bearing

Mental map

Metes and bounds

New building

Node

North arrow

Paths

Pedestrian

Physical map

Piles

Place legibility

Psychographic variable

Qualitative information

Quantitative information

Road map

Rural

Sanborn map

Satellite imagery

Seismic

Site analysis diagram

Site plan

Slab on grade

Softscape

Solar orientation

Structural system

Suburban

Sun path

Tenant improvement

Topographic features

Topographic map

Trusses

Urban

Vicinity map

Vignette

Zoning

The site is the one unique thing to every project. There are two places inspiration comes from: the site and the client. And there's the unique combination of the two (J. Luce, personal communication, January 3, 2008).

When we start a new project, we must gather information about the site. (See Figure 11.1.) The interior design of a space depends on the exterior. In fact, in most cases the interior of a building is inextricably linked to the exterior. Your building is not hermetically sealed from the environment. It is organically and structurally connected to its surroundings.

Does Your Building Fit Your Program?

All buildings are like living creatures. They take in nutrients (deliveries, entrance of occupants, fresh air), they give off by-products (trash removal, plumbing waste, off-gassing), and they change over time (deterioration, future growth, and alteration). Viewing the building as an organic entity will help you to envision the type of information you need to collect before starting the project. For example, if you had the background plans for a building shell and did not gather information about the exterior environment as well as the interior, you might not know that the view of the ocean is to the west, the parking lot is on the north, and there is a very noisy school playground to the south. Without this information to inform your design of a corporate office, you might inadvertently locate the storage room to the west, the front entrance on the east, and the director's office to the south. Do you think the director would be happy with her office far from the view and adjacent to the noise? So you must look outside the building first to determine the constraints and possibilities of the site. In the context of the interior design studio project, there are several different ways you may approach site selection:

- *Scenario 1(a)*—The instructor may have already assigned you a site. There may be documentation of the site, such as a site plan, an existing conditions plan, a satellite view, a verbal description, and/or photographs. In this case, you are primarily responsible for interpreting the given evidence and responding to the site conditions with your design solution.
- *Scenario 1(b)*—Sometimes the instructor assigns a location, but obtaining the documentation is the responsibility of the student, which involves a site visit or field trip. In this case, the student is responsible for collecting data about the site and then analyzing the data.

This Note describes an "inspiration or starting point" experienced by one of the authors of this textbook. She writes: "When I was in college, I was struck by the university's misuse of a beautiful, historic residence, The Sage House, as office space. I documented the ill fit with photographs of file cabinets in the hallways, wires running across a beautiful stained glass window at the front of the house, and the like. It seemed to me that the house should be reverted to residential use, and I determined that due to its size and configuration, it would make an excellent bed and breakfast. I also determined, through analyzing the site as well as interviewing school authorities, that it would be an ideal housing facility for visiting faculty who traveled from various countries and who would stay varying lengths of time due to their teaching schedules—a few days if giving a lecture, or perhaps a few weeks, a few months, even an entire semester." From this example, you can see how the site was the catalyst for a new idea. Analysis of the site (The Sage House) led to an idea for a program (a bed and breakfast) and then to the user group (visiting faculty).

- *Scenario 2*—In advanced studios, you may already have a user group (for example, autistic children) and/or a program (supervised play and treatment area for autistic children), but no assigned site or location. This would allow you to choose a building or space for your project. One possible assignment is *site selection*, which involves a combination of documentation and site data collection, as well as analysis to select the perfect site. An appropriate assignment in a Thesis Programming class might be for each student to document three possible sites for a project, present the sites to the class, and have the class decide which site is most suitable for that student's project. Further along in this chapter you'll get some guidance on what makes a site "suitable" for a given program.
- *Scenario 3*—In some instances, a site can be the inspiration or starting point for the whole project. See "A Note from the Authors," above.

In the professional environment, many times it is the client who determines the site, because the client has already purchased or leased a property or wants to renovate a home that the family has lived in for years. But frequently, in both commercial and institutional design, a client will look to the designer to determine the best location for the project. The client may have a real estate agent assemble several choices for the designer's consideration. This kind of service is called a **feasibility study**. A designer not only determines whether the building is physically suitable to accommodate the needs of the program, but also may determine whether the local demographics (characteristics of the population living and working in the area) will support the new project, or whether the existing services (plumbing/sewer/electrical) will support the new function, as in converting a shoe store into a restaurant.

Site Selection

In site selection, as in apartment-hunting, you start with a list of parameters or criteria. For example, when you are looking for a place to live you may want to start with a list of the things that are most important: proximity to school, access to natural light, minimum square feet, number of rooms, cost or rent per month, accommodate pets, quiet. You could also include a "wish list" of amenities that you would love to have but that are not absolutely necessary, such as a view of the ocean, a fireplace, a balcony. You may then further assign value by ranking the items. (Recall the presentation in Chapter 1 called "Applying Research to the Search for a New Apartment.")

You can do the same exercise with your site selection process: set parameters. The parameters are going to be different for a commercial project than they would be for a residential project. You will want to determine, first, if the site's setting should be **urban, suburban,** or **rural.** Each of these types of areas has pros and cons. Urban environments are characterized by high density (number of people per square unit of measure), access to public transportation, and a variety of cultures, yet these positives may be offset by noise, pollution, and crowds. Suburban environments have less density and fewer people, but they may be farther from public transportation and not subject to a high volume of foot traffic. A rural environment is prized for its access to open spaces and the natural landscape, but it may be difficult for people to access. See Figure 11.2 for a comparison of the three settings in the context of density.

Figure 11.2 Population density is the number of people living per unit of area. It is one important site characteristic. This diagram compares, side by side, the relative density of typical rural, suburban, and urban areas.

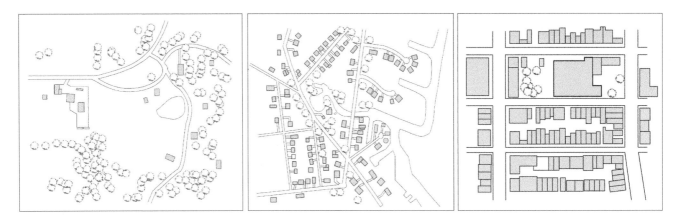

The perfect site for your studio project may be more obvious than you think. It may be the vacant lot across from the school, a property in the mountains that your aunt has owned for years, the airport that you fly into when you go home for break, or even an abandoned warehouse that you drive by every day. For a school project, the best site is one that you are somewhat familiar with and/or one that is easily accessible. The issue of accessibility arises because there are some kinds of information that you can collect only by visiting the site. You may be able to determine many things by examining satellite imagery, photos, and as-built plans, but you may also want to experience the smells, sounds, and spirit of the place (its *genius loci*; see Chapter 8), which can only be explored on-site.

The Nature of the Site: Surrounding Influences

Information-gathering can be done on many levels. The space in question is conceptually embedded in a series of concentric circles representing boundaries that expand outward. Figure 11.3 illustrates this.

"Site-Specific" Versus "Siteless"

Most projects are called "site-specific" because they are designed with a particular site in mind. But not all projects have a site. If you are designing a prototype or an interior space that can be applicable in more than one loca-

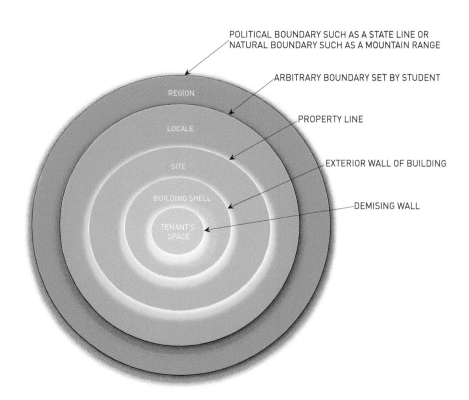

Figure 11.3 Imagine that the interior space is nestled within a series of concentric boundaries: within a structure (building shell), which is inside a property line (the building site); surrounded by a larger sphere of influence, such as a district or area (the locale); which is in a larger, politically demarcated or economic sphere (the region).

POLITICAL BOUNDARY SUCH AS A STATE LINE OR NATURAL BOUNDARY SUCH AS A MOUNTAIN RANGE

ARBITRARY BOUNDARY SET BY STUDENT

PROPERTY LINE

EXTERIOR WALL OF BUILDING

DEMISING WALL

REGION

LOCALE

SITE

BUILDING SHELL

TENANT'S SPACE

tion, you may have a "siteless" project and would have to provide for general site conditions, but not for conditions that are specific to any particular area. For example, if you are designing emergency housing that can be shipped to a disaster area, your project would be independent of the site.

Site Data Collection

Gathering information about a site can be very exciting and rewarding. All buildings are rooted in a context—whether it relates to natural features such as the sun, the ocean, or existing trees, as in a rural or country environment; or whether it has a relationship nestled between other houses in a suburban neighborhood; or whether it finds itself in the urban landscape surrounded by a "concrete jungle."

Because no two objects can occupy the same place at the same time, each site is unique. Each site has particular zoning restrictions and building codes to follow, distinctive views, and so on. Table 11.1 serves as a menu from which to choose as you begin your research of the site (or plan your research strategy). Not all records exist for all sites, and not all forms of data need to be collected for all sites. Since no site exists independent of its environment, a designer will want to become as familiar as possible about all aspects, physical and otherwise, of the project's location. Even information that seems unrelated to the project can have an impact or allow you to make better design decisions later in the process.

The planning of an interior space begins with a thorough understanding of the site. How far away from the building should you start your information-gathering? Table 11.1 gives you some answers to that question.

The Region: Site Data Collection for Context

How far away from the building should you start? This question can be answered in a number of different ways depending on the nature of the project, but usually it is important to get a sense of the **context** of the neighborhood. What do you want to know? How about who lives there? **Anthropological** information includes all aspects of human life: how people live, what they think, their customs and lifestyles. You may want to know about the culture (or cultures), local customs, lifestyle, and religious beliefs of people living in the region. Regional areas are often defined by boundaries, such as a city limit or state line—a formal legal border that would allow you to start your search for information by gathering political, social, and economic data. You can begin to collect statistical **demographic** information about the inhabitants of the region, such as their language, age, occupations, family structure, and income level.

Table 11.1 Site Information Sources

What	How	Where do you find it?
Regional	Maps Census Descriptive Text	Library Internet Travel Books History Books Articles
Locale	Satellite Images Direct Observation	Google Earth On location
The Building Site	Site Plan Direct Observation	Owner, Designer, Real Estate Agent, or local Building Department Records Office On location
Within Building Shell	As-Built Documents Field Measurements	Owner, Designer, Real Estate Agent, or local Building Department Records Office On location

You can also gather regional information from the standpoint of a physical **geographic** boundary, such as a river or a coastline. Geographic factors within a region include the local climate, topography, and natural resources. The **topographic features** that determine the growth of the area include the shape of the visible landscape, such as mountains, cliffs, valleys, forests, and bodies of water. Other physical regional information includes the climate (annual average temperatures and rainfall), local industries, food sources, and man-made features such as transportation hubs like airports, ports, and train stations.

If a project is in New York City, you might start by looking at maps of the island of Manhattan. Maps would show that Manhattan is surrounded by the Hudson River to the west and the East River to the east. By noting these physical boundaries, you can start to understand the various ways that commuters travel into the city via bridges, tunnels, and ferry lines; this, in turn, can help you select a site based on ease of access. A regional view of the island of Manhattan reveals the natural edges or boundaries of the surrounding rivers and the man-made bridges and tunnels that provide access from the surrounding boroughs. (See Figure 11.4.)

A site in New York City relies heavily on public transportation and **pedestrian** (walking) traffic. You may want to know where the nearest bus stop or subway station is located. In what direction does the traffic flow? What is the zoning (commercial, industrial, or residential)? This kind of information is

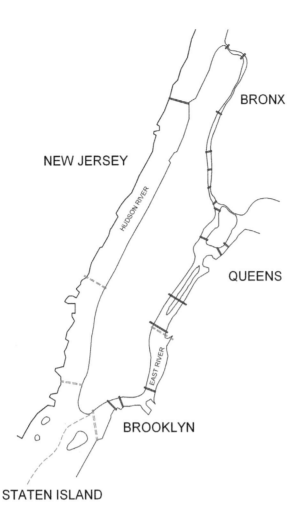

NEW JERSEY

BRONX

HUDSON RIVER

QUEENS

EAST RIVER

BROOKLYN

STATEN ISLAND

Figure 11.4 A regional view of the island of Manhattan reveals the natural edges or boundaries of the surrounding rivers and the man-made bridges and tunnels that provide access from the surrounding boroughs.

essential to finding out whether your project would even be allowed in the location you have selected.

Regional information gives a broad understanding of an area socially, economically, and geographically. The following is a list of items or issues you may want to look at within the boundaries of the region:

- *Climate*—Usually identified by annual rainfall, temperatures
- *Natural resources/products of the region*—If an area is known for an abundance of rock quarries producing stone or for pine trees producing wood, this information may be useful later when you're selecting building material or finish.
- *(Potential) Sources of pollution*—Industrial areas
- *Natural hazards*—**Seismic** (earthquake zone) or flood plain
- *Cultural/historic implications*—Past inhabitants, former uses of the region, political struggles, cultural significance of region

- *Current regional ecosystem*—Economic influence of the region on surrounding regions. We live in a web of interrelation with our surroundings, a four-dimensional network. For example, a dam in one location can prevent water from reaching another location downstream. Information gathered about this will lead to awareness of the cause and effect of our design decisions.
- *Demographics*—Languages, ethnicities, ages, income levels, education levels, values
- *Neighborhood/quality of life issues*—Local landmarks, sources of community pride or lack of pride, gangs, local community centers
- *Zoning*—Is the area zoned for commercial use, industrial use, or residential use?

The Locale: Site Data Collection Within a Small Radius Around the Property in Question

Once you have collected data on the region, it is critical to focus on the more immediate area surrounding the project. The radius around the site varies from project to project. For a rural site along a river, for example, you may want to look at all of the adjacent properties for possible sources of view, noise, or pollution. This area could be a mile or so in diameter. For a suburban site, the area might be just the radius of one block in all directions for the sources of view, noise, or pollution. For the urban site, it may be more critical to study the height or use of the buildings directly adjacent to your site. The following is a list of items or issues you may want to look at within the boundaries of the locale:

- *Landscaping*—**Hardscape** (concrete, stone, and brick paving that must pitch to a drain) versus **softscape** (grass lawns, soil, and vegetation that permits natural water permeation)
- *Water and wind*—Site's proximity to bodies of water and prevailing winds
- *Adjacent uses*—Compatibility of uses of nearby properties with planned use of the site
- *Adjacent structures*—Their height and configuration
- *Adjacent tenants*—Thoughts of people living or working nearby who may be affected by development of the site
- *Utilities infrastructure*—Water, sewer, electricity
- *Traffic types and patterns*—Pedestrian/access by car/public transportation. Identify main access or high-traffic streets, back alleys, direction of traffic flow (one-way or two-way streets), bus stops, subway stations, and bike paths.
- *(Potential) Sources of pollution*—Noise, odors, and other nonvisual qualities

Since the site's locale extends a shorter distance than the regional area, designers usually find this information by direct observation techniques, site-specific behavioral mapping (discussed in Chapter 8), and detailed photographic surveys. Also, since the smaller area involves a more limited population, you can distribute questionnaires to adjacent residents or business owners to find out demographic information or public opinion in the immediate vicinity. Qualitative data such as views, odors, and noise can only really be obtained by direct observation and descriptive journals.

The Building Site: Data Collection Within Property Boundaries

Once you have collected information on a region and your locale, you need to collect information about the **existing conditions** of the property to be developed (if it's a **new building**), expanded (an **addition**), renovated (a **tenant improvement**), retrofitted for a new use (an **adaptive reuse**), or demolished. Construction documents can be obtained from a variety of sources depending on the building's type and age and the record-keeping habits of the previous owner. The following is a list of items or issues you may want to look at within the boundaries of the building site:

- *Existing structures within property lines*—This includes buildings, outbuildings, storage sheds, garages, and other structures. This information would be found on a site plan, sometimes referred to as a *plot plan*. A site plan should be an aerial view of the site, showing either the roof plans or building outlines of the existing structures. The property line is usually indicated with a standard dash-dot-dot-dash line style and sometimes by the **metes and bounds**. (This is a technical term used by surveyors to indicate the exact locations and angles, or corners, between points on the land. The points may be marked on the earth with wooden stakes, brightly colored plastic tape, or metal markers embedded in the asphalt on a neighborhood street or the concrete plaza around an urban building.)
- *Existing natural and man-made site features*—The locations of trees, rock formations, ponds, paths, and other such features should be documented. For example, the design of Frank Lloyd Wright's Fallingwater was influenced by the existing spring and waterfall on the property.
- *Existing access and entry points into the site*—This would include curb cuts and driveways for vehicular traffic. Also important is to locate fences and walls that prohibit entry, as well as the gates and openings that would allow people or goods to get in and out. Existing traffic patterns within a site are important, for example, in the case of a supermarket or similar property. Mapping the patterns of vehicular traffic—for example, indicating delivery trucks in red, vehicles carrying customers in blue, and people walking in yellow—allows the designer to clearly

identify potential problems with the existing entry layout and perhaps to reroute traffic patterns so that future traffic may flow more easily.

- *ADA/Universal Design*—**Accessibility** to front entrance, height of curbs, path of travel from accessible parking to accessible spaces, existing changes in level that may require a ramp or an elevator
- *Parking*—This can be determined from the site plan.
- *Building orientation with respect to the sun*—**Solar orientation** and the determination of the **sun path** are essential pieces of information that will affect your building in terms of solar heat gain and glare from direct sunlight. You can obtain this information by looking at satellite imagery or the site plan to determine compass direction (**north arrow** or *compass rose*) and then tracking the sun's rising and setting through the use of a solar chart or computer software that simulates the location's latitude and calendar date. (See Figure 11.5.)
- *Views*—"A visual analysis . . . is useful in determining the visual character of the site itself as viewed from the outside as well as the visual impact of its surroundings upon potential on-site development. Factors to be examined include mass and space definition from natural

Figure 11.5 This diagram illustrates the "solar path" or sun movement during different times of the year. The movement of the sun around your site is important to understand in order to predict potential solar heat gain, glare, and how shadows are cast.

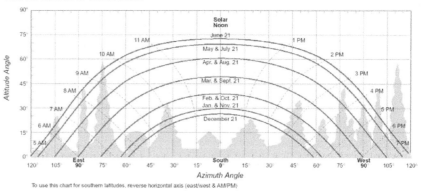

Sun Path Chart for 40° North Latitude

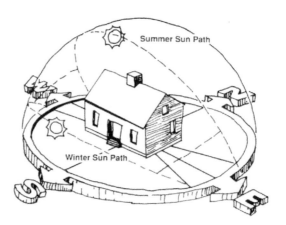

and man-made elements, off-site views to be accentuated or screened, and on-site view opportunities or problems" (McBride, 2006).

- *Maintenance considerations/trash removal/deliveries*—All buildings receive deliveries and generate trash. Understanding the site can make it easier to plan your space's public and private entrances and to keep them separated when necessary. For example, the visitor's entrance to a mortuary should be remote from the service entrance.

- *Use and abuse considerations*—All buildings are subject to deterioration, whether by natural causes or man-made ones. Public institutions such as schools, prisons, and hospitals require that security measures be taken to ensure safety of occupants and long life of the building. These considerations are related not just to the site, but also to the user group and maintenance. Site-related issues include observation of existing evidence of *accretion* (traces of elements added to the site), such as graffiti or litter, as well as evidence of *erosion* (traces of wear or removal of elements from the site), such as vandalism, theft, and termite damage. See Chapter 8 for more detailed explanations of *accretion* and *erosion*.

- *Flexibility considerations (future use of building? changing technology)*—These are multifaceted analyses of the physical constraints of the site, including the amount of open space on the property that can be used for expansion of/additions to the existing building. This includes collecting data on required setbacks, easements, and elements on the property that would be costly to relocate or environmentally sensitive. You can also determine this flexibility by looking closely at the building shell, the structure, and materials of the existing building.

The Interior Space: Site Data Collection Within Building Shell

As an interior designer, you are looking to collect data on existing conditions of the physical aspects of the building as well as the subjective or experiential ones, in order to determine constraints, possibilities, and sources of inspiration for your design. For example, determining which walls are load-bearing and which walls are non-load-bearing will be essential for determining the ease of potential reconfiguration of the space at minimal cost or disruption. Determining the locations of existing plumbing fixtures as well as the sanitary drain locations will allow you to later make informed decisions about possible locations of new fixtures at a minimal cost. You'll want to consider **quantitative information**, such as the number of windows (quantity) or the sill height of windows (numerical measurement). These are both examples of physical constraints.

There are equally important **qualitative information** items to document, such as the quality of the light (natural and artificial), temperature, ventilation, humidity, acoustics, and ergonomics of the space.

Part of site documentation could include doing an inventory of existing furniture, fixtures, and equipment—including historic elements or materials to be preserved, relocated, and reused or removed for salvage. For a designer who had the opportunity to turn an old farmhouse in Maryland into a bed and breakfast, **FF&E Inventory** constituted a bound book of all the existing furnishings. Each furnishing had a separate page dedicated to it. The page included a photograph, a text description, dimensions (length x width x height), and an evaluation of the condition of the piece. Each piece of furniture was assigned a key number. Later, during the design process, the designer was able to incorporate the pieces into the furniture layout, labeled with the corresponding key code. She was also able to use the inventory document to determine the budget, basing estimates on how many pieces needed to be refinished and the extent of the refurbishment. Having this level of detail available helped the designer when she had to determine yardage for those pieces that needed to be reupholstered, and also helped her determine whether the remaining unused pieces could be sold to local antique shops.

The following is a discussion of building systems you may want to analyze for their condition and applicability to your program.

Understanding the Building

What kind of information is essential within the building shell? For most interior design projects, information gathered about the configuration, condition, and qualities of the building shell may be the most important information about the site. A building is not just a structure; it is a collection of building systems. **Building systems** can be visualized like various systems in the human body. As in the human body, the systems are usually dependent on one another to perform their assigned functions.

Imagine the building as a living thing—say, a very large animal. The **structural system** is like the animal's skeleton, holding the building up and giving it its underlying form. The skeleton, or framework, may be apparent on the exterior, as for a crab or a starfish, or hidden, as in a human being. The bones of the building may be steel, concrete, or wood members connected in such a way as to transfer the loads all the way to the earth.

The other systems operate within the structural framework. A building breathes: It takes in outside air and gives off exhaust air. The respiratory system of a building is its form of ventilation, which is natural (through open windows, louvers, and vents) or mechanically operated (through ducts and HVAC equipment). A building also has a circulatory system, to keep it warm or cool, and a plumbing system, to carry hot and cold water in and out. It has muscles that allow it to move goods or people through it via conveyance systems such as stairs and elevators. A building's nervous system is its electrical system, as well as its security system or fire alarm system that alerts the building to potential danger. A final analogy is that the building has a skin: a cladding system that encloses the structure to make the spaces truly interior and to regulate the temperature, mitigate the effects of weather, and protect the inhabitants from rain, wind, unwanted intruders, and other environmental factors. A designer must consider each of these systems when evaluating the building for a potential use, as in a feasibility study.

Structural Systems

The fundamental (and often hidden) structural system of a building is the foundation. **Foundation** systems can be shallow, composed of a **slab on grade**, a **crawl space**, or a **basement**. Deep foundations include **piles** and **caissons**.

Structural framing systems are usually made of steel, wood, concrete, or masonry units, which utilize a series of **load-bearing** walls or columns. How do you determine the existing structural system? The easiest way is to sit down with an architect or an engineer and review the as-built plans and sections to identify the structural system. Is a particular building's structural system a steel frame with glass **curtain walls**? Or is it composed of cast-in-place concrete load-bearing walls? Perhaps it has large overhead **trusses** or deep **beams** that span long distances and rest on **columns**.

About those columns: Regardless of the material the columns are made of, it is important to identify the column grid. You may be able to look at existing floor plans and sections to determine the column grid. Measure the distance between columns to determine the **column bays**. Why would the column bays or column-spacing be important? Column-spacing establishes a rhythm in the building. A good interior designer understands this rhythm and plans the new walls or furniture systems to fit within this grid. The existence of columns also limits what types of functions can take place in the room. For example, a building that has a column every 20 feet will not be able to accommodate an indoor soccer field. If the column grid is not clearly identifiable, you may need to consult a structural engineer in order to determine which walls are load-bearing and which ones are non-load-bearing interior partitions. Figure 11.6 will give you a clear idea of this.

Structural systems have a meaning that is not only functional but also historical and cultural. While it is important to understand the physical limitations of the structure, it is also a good idea to collect data on the cultural associations or historical origins of the structural system or spatial

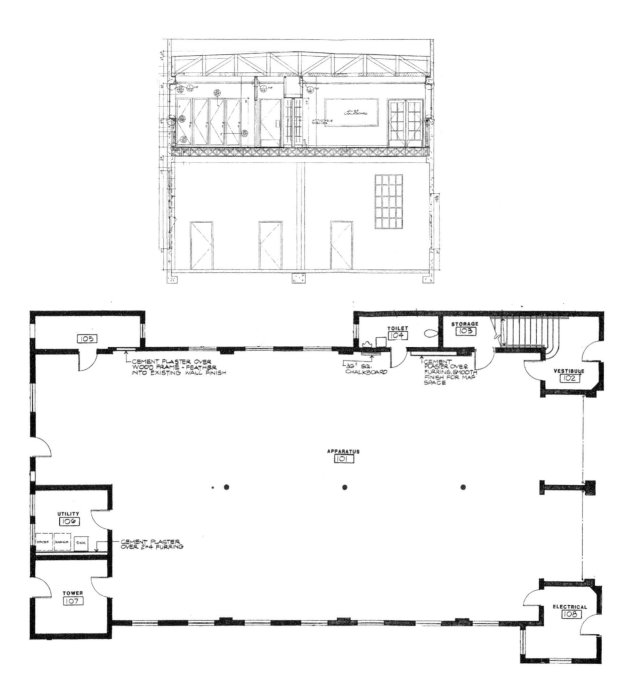

Figure 11.6 We can analyze this building shell of a firehouse to gather information about its structure. The floor plan reveals a perimeter load-bearing wall and three columns that go right down the center of the floor plan. The section shown above the floor plan shows that there are trusses that span the width of the building.

configuration. For example, a hacienda-style house has it roots in a Mexican traditional way of life, and the materials used—wood and plaster—have been selected because they are readily available in the region and they respond well to the climate. Islamic architecture utilizes towers—iconic "minarets"— as well as wind scoops as part of the natural ventilation system. Columns and arches in Islamic architecture also have cultural meanings that go well beyond the physical properties of holding up the structure.

If your program calls for a large open space for recreation, you may be looking for structural members that will span long distances, such as the overhead trusses used in a warehouse. If your program calls for large exterior or storefront windows, you may be looking for a steel frame with moment connections, or a steel-framed building clad with glass curtain walls. If your program calls for a series of smaller spaces with good acoustical properties between one space and the next, you may be looking for a concrete masonry unit (CMU) or concrete load-bearing walls. Keep in mind that while adaptive reuse—using a structure for a purpose other than the original intended use—is a great idea, your program must fit the existing structural system.

Once you have identified all of the structural components, you must analyze the building for possibilities and constraints. Measure the usable floor area. Usable floor area excludes items such as the thickness of walls or uninhabitable shafts for plumbing. Measure the size of the windows and the width of the window mullions. Would you be able to put an interior partition between two existing windows? Identify stair and elevator locations and the existing corridors leading to building exits. Look at the section of the building to determine the existing ceiling heights and any structural elements that are not visible on the floor plan.

Sources of Site Data

Sources for Regional Data

Maps—The Broadest Resource

When seeking information about a region, you will probably want to start with primary sources such as maps. There are several useful types of map, and each type presents different information. Most maps include a compass rose, which indicates the directions north, south, east, and west. Most maps also include a scale so you can estimate distances. Here's a look at some different types of maps:

- **Climate maps** give general information about the climate and precipitation (rain and snow) of a region. **Cartographers**, or mapmakers, use colors to show different climate or precipitation zones.
- **Economic or resource maps** feature the type of natural resources or economic activity that dominates an area. Symbols are used to indicate the kind of resource or product that is manufactured there. For example, oranges on a map of Florida tell you that oranges are grown there. Business Improvement Districts (BIDs) use economic resource maps to impart a vision that's intended to improve business in the area.
- **Physical maps** illustrate the physical features of an area, such as its mountains, rivers, and lakes. The water is usually shown in blue. Colors

are used to show *relief,* or differences in land elevations. Typically, shades of green are used to show lower elevations, and shades of orange or brown indicate higher elevations.

- **Road maps** show major—and some minor—highways as well as roads, airports, railroad tracks, cities, and other points of interest in an area. Interior designers would use this kind of map primarily to create the **vicinity map** for the cover sheet of the construction document set. Building officials use vicinity maps to determine zoning, and contractors use them for driving directions to find the project's location during the construction phase. It is important not to confuse a vicinity map with a site plan, which will be discussed later in this chapter.

- **Topographic maps** use contour lines to show the shape and elevation of an area. Lines that are close together indicate steep terrain, and lines that are far apart indicate flat terrain (Fact Monster, 2007).

- **Satellite imagery** at the Google Earth Web site offers maps and satellite images for complex or pinpointed regional searches. The images allow you to see characteristics of the neighborhood that traditional maps cannot—such as shadows cast by adjacent buildings, the quality of open spaces, and possible views. The Web site's tools allow you to search for public amenities such as schools, parks, restaurants, hotels, and public transportation hubs.

- **Zoning** and **Land use maps** are an indispensable tool for urban planning. According to the New York City Department of City Planning Web site, "Zoning shapes the city" (NYC DCP, 2009). **Zoning** primarily determines two important things that can affect your project: (1) allowed *uses* (see Chapter 13 for a discussion of occupancy classifications) of buildings in a particular area (Residential, Commercial, Industrial, etc.) and (2) the **density** (number of people per square unit of land) or **bulk** (number of square feet allowed to be built on a particular lot). District regulations may also apply that control specific characteristics of a neighborhood, such as the materials that can be used on a building's façade, the number of parking spaces required, the amount of open space required, and the minimum distance required between buildings. Ordinarily, an architect would be responsible for obtaining this kind of information for a new building, but if the project is a tenant improvement or adaptive reuse project, an interior designer may be called upon to collect this kind of data. Figure 11.7 shows a zoning map for an area of New York City.

- A **Sanborn map** is a kind of historical map that was created for cities during the late 1800s and early 1900s. Scaled at 50 feet to 1 inch (1:600), these maps contain an enormous amount of information, including outlines of each building, building heights, property boundaries, street names, location of utilities such as sewers, and even the

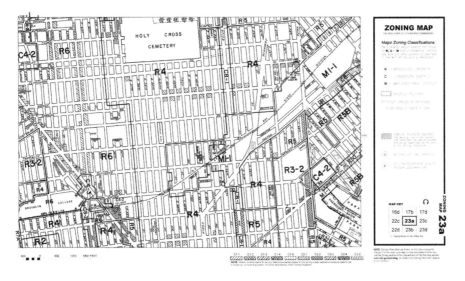

Figure 11.7 A zoning map may be obtained at the city's offices. This map, for example, was found on the New York City Department of Building Web site.

names of such public buildings as schools and churches. These maps are found primarily in archives and special collections in public and university libraries, but sometimes they are available in city offices as well (Sanborn Fire Insurance Maps, 2003).

Another Kind of Map

Mental maps are drawn representations of the way individuals perceive their own environment (Rosenberg, 1998). Such "maps" are not necessarily accurate, nor are they to-scale. In addition, they may use all kinds of personalized graphic notations to represent roads, buildings, signage, trees, mountains, etc.

In 1960, a researcher named Kevin Lynch pioneered the use of mental maps to illustrate a new concept: **place legibility**. He published his findings in a book titled *The Image of the City*. In this landmark book, he explained that all people rely on certain overriding types of navigational tools. He identified and defined these elements: paths, edges, nodes, districts, and landmarks.

- **Paths** are occupiable and are identified as places that can be traversed as in a sidewalk or corridor.
- An **edge** is a boundary. In interior design, this could be a wall, a flooring transition between two materials, or a ceiling height change.
- A **node** is a decision-making point. Usually, it is at the intersection of two paths. An example would be an entry lobby, from which a visitor has the option of several destinations.
- A **district** is an area that someone can mentally go inside of. If it's an exterior space, the architectural details, lighting levels, or building

Figure 11.8 This drawing, created by a student to represent her hometown of New Orleans, shares the mental image she has of the city and of navigational tools such as landmarks. Drawn by interior design student Heather Williams.

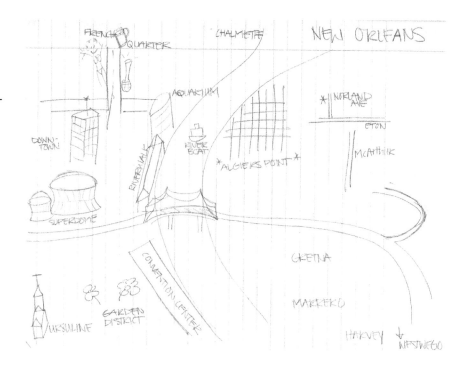

functions would be similar, as in a city's "gaslamp district"; in interiors it could be the staff area or the food court.

- A **landmark** is a distinct and unique external navigational tool that can be at any scale. A landmark can be a piece of artwork, a sign, or anything else that stands out as memorable. If the receptionist tells a visitor to "turn left at the red wall," the red wall would be the landmark.

You can investigate someone's mental map by asking that person for directions to a landmark, or by asking someone to draw a sketch map of an area. A designer can draw her own map of an area or region, which would reflect her own perception of the environment. When would this kind of information be valuable? Consider Figure 11.8.

⊛ ACTIVITY 11.1 Mental Mapping

Purpose: **To understand how people store and represent navigational information.**

1. Think back to when you were a child. When you have a clear mental image of your neighborhood where you grew up, start to draw a map.

What were the cues in your environment that led you home? That led you to the park, the school, or a friend's house? Were there other points of interest that you would like to identify: places or objects of meaning? Did you have a historical landmark in your hometown, or a ballpark? Where did you go to meet your friends or hang out? Draw a map of your hometown, using graphic devices (color, hatches, sketches, text, etc.) to illustrate how a friend might find your house and some of these key points of interest. Indicate other neighborhoods or areas with common characteristics, such as "downtown" or "the gaslamp district" or "the east side." Indicate natural features—such as woods, mountains, and lakes, and man-made features such as railroad tracks, signs, fountains, and clock towers—that helped you navigate your world.

2. Pin up the hand-drawn maps, and have the class members present their maps to the rest of the class. Identify and discuss the use of paths, edges, districts, nodes, and landmarks. Note: Most people rely on paths and landmarks mainly to navigate. Encourage the use of more difficult way-finding concepts, such as districts and nodes.

Other Sources of Data

Maps, of course, will not tell you everything you want to know about a region. For demographic information, such as number of people, ages of people, and income levels, you will want to look at census data, which is available at www.census.gov. This Web site contains many powerful tools for collecting statistical data on your region, including population growth and other demographic trends, special maps, and articles related to demographics that highlight trends across the country. Which city is the fastest growing? Which city has the largest percentage of women with college degrees? Which city has the largest percentage of people living below the U.S. poverty level? Statistics are an important tool to use when determining the ideal region in which to set your project, or they can act as supplemental data to support the choice of site.

You can also find regional site information on some real estate Web sites. (As discussed in Chapter 5, this kind of information is secondary and therefore subject to interpretation or exaggeration.) *Yahoo! Real Estate* provides **vignettes**: holistic, multifaceted neighborhood profiles that provide a snapshot of the life of the area. Information includes cost of living, school statistics, crime rate, and local climate/weather. Demographic data include median age, marital status, unemployment rates, political affiliations, and education levels of inhabitants.

On the Fox television network's show *Kitchen Nightmares,* Gordon Ramsay helps failing restaurants become successful. One of the first things Ramsay does is to look around for other restaurants in the neighborhood. He uses that information to determine what does NOT exist, so that the new restaurant will enjoy freedom from competition. It is notable that often what is NOT observed is just as important as what IS observed—if not more so.

One of this textbook's authors was commissioned to design a tile showroom in Manhattan. She tells this story: "The first thing I did was visit all of the other tile showrooms in Manhattan. Each had a different way of displaying tile, and each had a different target audience. One used large full-scale vignettes of kitchens and bathrooms to illustrate how that store's tile could be used. With permission, I documented that showroom as a case study through floor plan sketches and photographs. Another tile showroom used small wood boards, approximately 12" wide x 18" high, to illustrate different tile patterns and materials. These boards were hung by cleats from continuous wood strips that ran the length of the room, allowing customers to view a variety of small amounts of tile. Seeing that these could be easily removed from the wall, I reached to take one down. Immediately, a salesperson came over and asked if she could help me. From this interaction, I realized that my gut instinct was to touch the tile and 'play' with it, which was not allowed in this store. Suddenly, I realized what was missing from the competition: a showroom that invited customers to 'play' with the tile." The design concept was born: "An interactive playground for designers." (See Figure 11.9.)

Figure 11.9 From market research, Bella Tile's interactive Velcro walls are covered with tile samples that beckon designers to come and play with the tile.

Psychographic variables are any attributes relating to personality, values, attitudes, interests, social class, or lifestyles. They are also called IAO variables (for "Interests, Attitudes, and Opinions"). They can be contrasted with demographic variables (such as age and gender) and behavioral variables (such as crime rate and education level). Psychographic profiles are used in market segmentation and advertising. This kind of information, along with other pertinent household information, allows you to formulate a qualitative, subjective description of the place.

Another secondary source, Property I.D., is a company that collects and organizes a variety of information from a city's archival records, building department records, and maps. Occasionally, secondary sources will be more relevant or easier to digest than data from a more primary source such as a map or government census documents. For more qualitative data, you may want to wander through the neighborhood by car, bus, or bicycle, or on foot, using unstructured or structured observation techniques and plenty of photographs, sketches, and textual descriptions.

Sources for Locale Data

Since the site's locale involves a smaller area than the regional area, designers usually find this information by direct-observation techniques, site-specific behavioral-mapping (discussed in Chapter 8), and detailed photographic surveys. Also, since the population of a locale is more limited, you can distribute questionnaires to adjacent residents or business owners to gather demographic information or check out the public's opinion in the immediate vicinity. You can really only obtain qualitative data such as views, odors, and noise by direct observation and descriptive journals.

Sources for Property Data

For information specific to the property in question, you will want to obtain any existing records or construction documents. On the **cover sheet** or *title sheet* of the construction document set, you would find the project data: information such as street address, block or lot number, total square feet, occupancy classifications, owners, previous designers, and any consultants (structural engineers, mechanical engineers, lighting consultants, plumbers, landscape designers, and so on) who worked on the project previously. You would also find out pertinent historical information about the dates on which the documents were prepared, submitted, revised, and approved.

Sources for Data Within the Building Shell

Usually, the set of plans for a building have been prepared according to prescribed professional standards upheld by design practitioners, but not always. As a conscientious designer, you must conduct a **field survey** to document all of the existing building conditions visually and with a tape measure, in order to determine the accuracy of the **as-built drawings**. But generally, the as-built plans are essential to include in your data-gathering and for your preliminary analysis of the site. A full set would provide the following:

The **site plan** shows the existing and proposed conditions on the lot(s), including:

- Property lines, setbacks, easements
- Access to the site: street names, driveway, parking, sidewalks, fences, gates
- Adjacent buildings (if applicable) or adjacent natural features, such as waterways
- Landscaping elements, including hardscape, fountains, trees, shrubs, lawns, and paths
- Building footprint OR Building roof (NOT THE FLOOR PLAN)
- Entrances marked with red arrows
- North symbol
- Scale (if applicable), usually in engineering scales—1:20, 1:50, 1:100
- Views (indicated with arrows, if applicable)
- AREA OF WORK or SCOPE OF PROJECT, indicated with hatch pattern, color, or bold outlines

Figure 11.10 provides examples of these conditions. You can determine most of the conditions by examining the site plan, which you should be able to obtain from the building's owner or property management company. This information can also be found in the records department at a local building department; the city government usually keeps these records. A less formal way to gather the information would be to look at satellite images. Whether using the site plan or satellite images, a designer would definitely supplement this kind of research with direct observation, photographs, and a textual description of the site.

Demolition Plan, Architectural Floor Plans, Structural, Mechanical, Plumbing, Electrical Plans, Reflected Ceiling Plans, Exterior Elevations, Building Sections, Interior Elevations, Details, Door and Window Schedules, Finish Schedules, and Specifications.

How to Obtain Background Plans

Ideally, in terms of a base building plan, what you want is an editable CAD file that can be immediately opened and used. You may be able to obtain a native design document from its original source, the design firm that created it. With a little research, you may be able to locate the architect or designer and obtain the firm's written permission to use the file in your school project. Even if you are able to obtain this kind of file, however, you may want to ascertain the validity of the construction drawings by conducting a field survey and taking your own accurate measurements of the building.

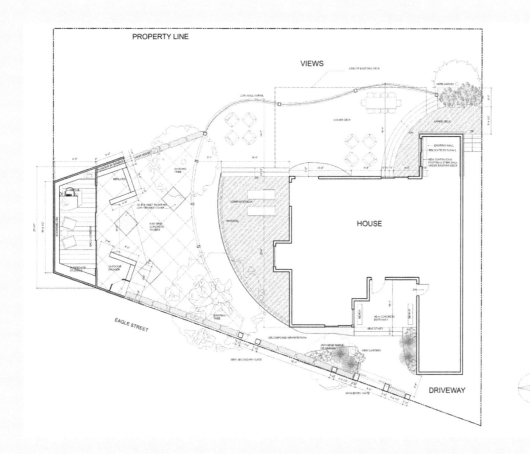

Figure 11.10 This is a typical residential site plan, showing how a house is situated with respect to the property boundaries, the landscaping, and the views. Note the inclusion of the North symbol.

Oftentimes, buildings are not built exactly as called for in the plan. Other times, a design firm will issue "as-built" plans that reflect how the building was actually built. Keep in mind that the design firm may not want to release the file to you due to cost and liability. These CAD files are protected by copyright law, which prohibits their use without the express written permission of the author of the original document. Be respectful when requesting this type of document, and emphasize that you are using the file only for a school project and not for profit.

If you cannot obtain the editable CAD file, the next best thing would be the blueprints or copies of the construction documents. For most commercial sites, these documents would be part of the public record, kept by the local building or planning department in their records department. These documents can be located by their address or block/lot number and can be viewed via microfiche. Sometimes you can get printed copies. Again, the copyright laws protect the original designer, so in many cases you will be asked to fill out a form requesting the original designer's permission to copy the files. Allow time for this process to occur, as it can take up to 30 days.

If these documents are not available through the city's records department, brainstorm about who might have these documents. Contractors, consultants who worked on the project, or the building's owner or property management company may have them. If the property is for sale or lease, the real estate agent or leasing agent may have floor plans.

If none of these sources has the information you need, here are a few questions to ask yourself:

- Is the building historically significant? If it is, you may want to try your local historical society.
- Is the building part of the city's infrastructure of public services, such as a firehouse or a building within a city-operated park? Some city agencies maintain records of their own buildings and would be able to supply you with a copy.
- As a last resort, does the building have a posted Building Exit Plan that would give you an idea of the shape of the building and the location of elevators, stairs, and exits? You could use this information as a starting point for creating your own documents from field measurements.

Tips on Field Measurements

Even if you are able to get a complete set of construction documents, you should double-check the information in the documents against the actual field measurements to verify the accuracy of the as-built plans. Professional designers may refer to the information on the existing plans that were prepared by previous designers, architects, and engineers, but they are legally responsible for generating their own drawings based on field measurements taken by themselves or their staff.

There is an industry-specific, prescribed way to document existing conditions on a field survey. First, have a team of at least two people, if not three, each with a designated job.

- One person will be responsible for notations.
- The other two will do the measurements with a tape measure.
- One person will be responsible for holding the end of the tape measure and calling out what he is holding it next to ("to wall," "to door opening," "from sill to floor").
- The person at the other end of the tape measure will be responsible for calling out the numerical value in a consistent format. Decide, in ad-

vance, whether it will be in units of inches or feet-and-inches (centimeters or meters-and-centimeters), and try not to mix the two.

The person responsible for recording the measurements should decide which will be easier to interpret or which will be easier to enter into the computer when drafting. (Note: Inches tend to work better than feet-and-inches.) Many professional firms have replaced the traditional tape measure with laser measuring devices that give precise lengths.

Use a mechanical pencil with an eraser. A mechanical pencil needs no sharpening; just make sure you have enough lead. Use 8½ × 11-inch or 11 × 17-inch graph paper to sketch out each floor plan to fit on its own sheet of paper. For better results, put a sheet of graph paper underneath a sheet of vellum on a large clipboard and do your sketching on that. Pick one spot as the origin and use that spot to begin all of the measurements for that wall. In a multiple-story building, the spot should be structurally consistent on all floors. The following are standard abbreviations:

- M.O.   Masonry Opening
- W.H.   Window Height
- S.H.   Sill Height
- C.L.   Centerline
- B.O.   Bottom Of
- O.A.   Over All
- C.H.   Ceiling Height
- A.F.F.   Above Finished Floor

It is usual to measure to the centerline of a window and then measure the width of the window. Another industry standard is to put ceiling heights in an oval. List objects measured in a consistent order: first by length, then by width, and finally by height. Wear protective clothing and comfortable shoes or boots. (You never know the condition of the existing building. You may find yourself crawling into a dusty attic or wading through unexpected ponds on the roof.) Figure 11.11 is an example of a field measurements document you might create.

Site Summary

The document a student of interior design would be asked to produce is a written research paper that includes a textual summary of the information gathered about the site, along with visuals including photos, maps, and other research data. The following is one student's existing conditions report for her senior project.

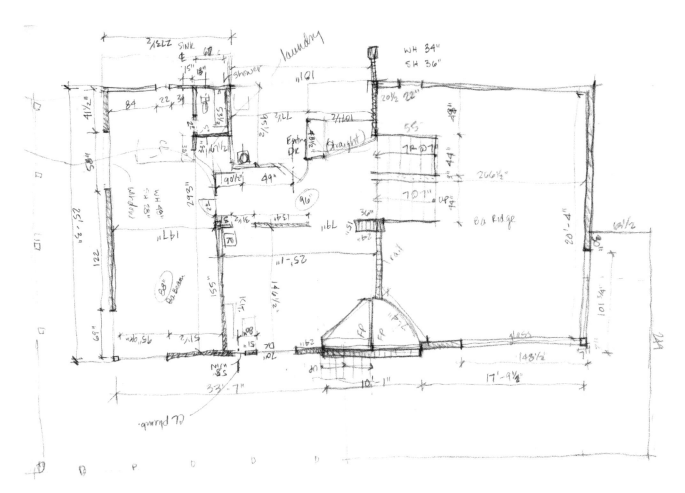

Figure 11.11 This is an example of field measurements. Note the use of a sketched plan, overall measurements for each room, and the ceiling height measurement in an oval. Sill height and window height are also indicated in a conventional manner.

Case Study:
Existing Conditions Report

by Sara Plaisted

After researching three possible locations for mixed-use zones in Barrio Logan, I have concluded that the building is best facing west on a corner for maximum sun and prospect exposure. Two of the three possible sites either had a commercial coffee house or housing. The site I chose is located a little farther east than I originally wanted, but the limitations the site presents are inspiring. There are options for parking if the empty lots are developed or the site is structurally sound to construct underground parking.

I had originally planned to include a market in one of the three retail spaces; however, by surveying the neighborhood I found a very large market within walking distance down the street.

Absorbing the texture of the neighborhood, I found much inspiration for my design: metal, rust, concrete, wood, steel, chain-link fencing, shipping containers in the nearby port, cars (headlights, tires, mirrors, grille, exhaust pipes, etc.), railroad tracks, the Coronado Bridge floating just above eye level, local art.

- The site is located on the northeast corner of Beardsley and National in Barrio Logan in what some may consider a run-down poor area, south of downtown.
- The site faces directly west with other corner views south.
- The site is currently occupied by what appears to be a place for car detailing, with a small "office" structure in the back of the site and a small Mexican food take-out restaurant (about 25 feet wide by 100 feet deep).
- Sign for the car detailer says, "Ye Olde Towne Pump."
- The site is about 100 feet wide by 100 feet deep, with an additional section in the back left behind the Mexican food place, at about 25 feet. wide by 50 feet deep, totaling 11,250 square feet for the lot.
- An alley is located directly behind the site.
- A house is located just behind the site in the upper right corner, and takes up 50 additional feet deep and 100 feet wide.
- Two large oak trees are located in the back right corner of site.
- A bus stop is located directly in front of the site.
- The site is located two blocks West from the off-ramp of the 5 Freeway South.
- East of the site (directly behind and across the alley) is an open lot with construction pending.
- South of the site (across the street) is a parking lot.
- Catty-corner (southwest) is the fairly new Family Health Clinic.
- Directly across (west) is a small market and juice stop, along with what appear to be office spaces.
- Adjacent to the left (north) is an open lot with junk cars. Beyond that are houses and a new apartment/condo building.

Most of the housing and buildings are old and somewhat run-down. There are many produce outlets, junkyards, and old housing with bars on the windows.

Some parts of the area are starting to develop and new construction, businesses, and residences are springing up.

- Down the block (south) is a large market with fresh fruits and vegetables and delicious tamales.
- Down the block (west) is a new hip bar/restaurant called The Guild that many artists frequent.
- Across from The Guild is an elementary school.
- On Cesar Chavez Boulevard, 2 large lots are being prepared for the development of the Mercado del Barrio. Currently 2 bids are under way to develop multilevel affordable housing, a large market, theatre, street venues, retail space, park, and art space directly under the bridge, further expanding Chicano Park.
- A fire station is located on the corner of National and Cesar Chavez.
- On the corner of Cesar Chavez and Main, there's a large coffee shop with a brewery of coffee in the back.
- Catty-corner from there is the famous Chewy's Restaurant.
- Next to Chewy's on Cesar Chavez and Harbor is the Trolley Stop.
- Chicano Park is directly under the bridge and is known for the murals on the columns supporting the bridge, and for the outdoor space. Much of the artwork reflects the Hispanic point of view of those living in the area for almost a century. Such notable pieces include the comment on the toxins that the industrial companies release into the air, contaminating those who live in the area.
- The bridge is massive and very much a part of the everyday view of the people who live in and frequent this neighborhood.
- Views north are directly into downtown, with a view from Main Street right into Petco Park.
- Graham Downes' Blokhaus is located down the street with a cool hair salon and restaurant nearby.

Barrio Logan does have a reputation for being a little unsavory and dangerous, as it is on the poorer side but north of the bridge. Closer to down-

Figure 11.12 Composite photo collage of a site. Courtesy interior design student Sara Plaisted.

town is a bit nicer and more ideal for this project. The City of San Diego has been working to create the redevelopment of the "City of Villages," and within the next few years the area will start to improve. For now, it is prime time to move in and invest and help to better the neighborhood and bring culture and the arts in and improve the quality of the area. (See Figure 11.12.)

Data Analysis and Interpretation

In landscape design, "the end product of the site analysis phase of the design process is a composite analysis map (sometimes referred to as an opportunities and constraints sheet). This is developed through an overlay process . . . delineating the most suitable and least suitable areas of the site for each analysis factor" (McBride, 2006).

Interior design has a few diagramming techniques especially for helping with the analytic process that precedes schematic design. It is dangerous to jump from data collection to schematic design without an intermediate step of analysis. That intermediate, analytic step is the interpretation of the data collected, which sometimes involves multiple overlays of diagrams. Using an overlay technique, begin your **Site Analysis Diagrams** with what you know; then continue to add layers of information. These layers of information will eventually become more speculative than factual. There is a moment when documentation becomes interpretation, and the diagramming will help you reach a design solution during the schematic phase.

It is important to document your findings in a visual form, through diagrams. Figure 11.13 presents illustrations of the step-by-step method interior designers can use to transition from information-gathering to analysis.

Start by identifying the structural elements (columns and walls) that would be difficult, or even structurally infeasible, to remove. You can begin to develop your own "language" through color, hatch patterns, and symbols. For example, you could mark the structural elements with a red marker. Then, identify existing plumbing locations, perhaps using a blue hatch to indicate plumbing walls and areas around piping, including the shafts and vents that contain the unseen piping. If the interior has other physical aspects that you want to document—such as condition of finishes, the feeling of the space, the view from the space—you can use color, hatch patterns, or text to communicate the site condition. The goal of these analyses is to identify the constraints or limitations of the site as well as its potential or possibilities.

In Chapter 12 we will expand on these tools and look at other diagramming techniques.

Figure 11.13 Example of a composite site analysis diagram, showing all of the layers of analysis overlaid onto the existing floor plan of a typical residential project: wet (plumbing) versus dry areas, vertical circulation (stairs), load-bearing elements (location of posts or columns and load-bearing walls), public versus private program areas, access to natural light (sunlight) (dark versus light), and the views on the existing floor plan of a typical residential project.

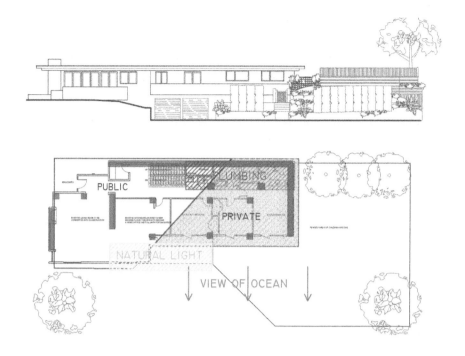

ACTIVITY 11.2 Site Analysis Diagram

Purpose: **To practice analyzing an existing condition through a series of overlays.**

Visit a local public space at your school, such as the cafeteria, student lounge, gallery, or reception area/lobby; a public commercial space, such as a grocery store or an emergency room waiting area; or a religious institution. Sketch the floor plan. Document the space with additional photographs or video.

1. Identify components of the structural systems using a red marker.
2. Identify WET VERSUS DRY AREAS (existing plumbing system elements) of the building using a blue marker.
3. Identify the areas that receive NATURAL LIGHT VERSUS ARTIFICIAL LIGHT or DARK VERSUS LIGHT with a yellow highlighter.
4. Identify QUIET VERSUS NOISY AREAS based on perceived sound levels.
5. Identify ACTIVE VERSUS PASSIVE AREAS based on kind of activity. For example, activities such as reading, writing, studying, sleeping, or listening to lectures would be passive, while activities using gross motor movements, such as running, playing, or exercising, would be active.
6. Identify PUBLIC VERSUS SEMI-PRIVATE versus PRIVATE with regard to the existing traffic patterns (visitors and staff) or program

areas. Use one color for the visitors or end users and a different color for the staff or clients.

7. Identify traffic patterns on the site, using one color for pedestrian traffic and one for vehicular traffic. Mark entry points with red arrows.

8. Identify the view(s).

9. Write a summary of what the site analysis diagrams revealed to you about the possibilities and constraints of the site.

ACTIVITY 11.3 Does the Building Fit the Program?

Purpose: **To practice describing qualitative information to determine if the existing conditions support the function of the building.**

This Activity is a great opportunity for group work, as it introduces various perspectives to the analysis process. Using your classroom building as the subject, clearly identify the program of the building, including the activities that take place within the building and a list of end users. Choose one of the following topics to focus on as you answer the question "Does the Building Fit the Program?"

1. *Feeling of the site,* inside and out (qualities of the space, including sounds, smells, safety issues, emotion)

2. *Neighborhood* and regional context (demographics, adjacent uses)

3. *Exterior and site conditions* (the style or character of the building, location of parking or pedestrian walkways)

4. *Interior configuration* (structural system and other interior building systems)

Create an existing conditions report focusing on the feeling of the site, the neighborhood, the exterior and site conditions, or the interior configuration. Use the following tips to guide the process. When you've finished, create a PowerPoint or other presentation that documents your findings. Present it to the class.

Tips:

1. Use whatever means necessary to gather information about the existing conditions of the building, focusing on the methods discussed in this book.

2. Be resourceful. Don't be afraid to interview experts such as the facilities manager, or to ask to see back-of-house areas if it will increase your understanding of the building.
3. Teach the class something new about the building that they may not have thought about already.
4. Focus on how the information gathered either supports that the building is appropriate for the program, or suggests it is not appropriate. Some students may agree with your conclusions while others disagree. Furthermore, some students may claim that the feeling of the site and building does fit the program, while the interior configuration does not. Use this as an opportunity for an open discussion.

Conclusion

Collection of data about the site concludes this portion of data collection. The next step will be to begin synthesizing all you have learned throughout the programming process. You will now be entering the schematic design phase. The schematic design phase is your opportunity to begin imposing the program onto the site and within the building shell. You will use the data that you have collected about your site and building shell to determine the ideal locations for the spaces listed in your program.

As you go on to the next chapter, keep this in mind: Although data collection has informed you about the users, the clients, the required spaces, and the elements within each space and now within the site you've chosen, the beginning of the schematic design phase is not the end of research. Research can be used at each phase to enhance the end product of that phase.

References

Fact Monster/Information Please® Database. (2007). Pearson Education. Retrieved 2008 from www.factmonster.com

Lynch, K. (1960). *The image of the city*. Cambridge: MIT Press.

McBride, S. B. (2006). *Site planning and design*. West Virginia University. Retrieved May 16, 2009, from http://www.rri.wvu.edu/WebBook/McBride/section3.html

New York City Department of City Planning (NYC DCP). (2009). *Zoning*. Retrieved May 16, 2009, from http://www.nyc.gov/html/dcp/html/subcats/zoning.shtml

Rosenberg, M. (1998). *Mental maps: How we see the world*. About.com. Retrieved May 16, 2009, from http://geography.about.com/cs/culturalgeography/a/mentalmaps.htm

Sanborn Fire Insurance Maps. (2003). The Regents of the University of California. Earth Sciences & Map Library. Retrieved May 16, 2009, from http://www.lib.berkeley.edu/EART/snb-intr.html

Part Four

Design

Part Four of *Research-Inspired Design* is a summary of the continuous information-gathering that occurs during the design process, as well as an overview of diagramming techniques, presentation techniques, and beyond. The final chapter seeks to address the cyclical nature of design: the idea that the final product, a built space, continues to be a source of feedback to inform the body of knowledge for interior design and spaces to be designed in the future.

12 Schematics

When you complete this chapter you should be able to do the following:

- Identify research techniques used in the schematic phase of design.
- Understand the role of the design concept.
- Recognize the value of finding multiple design solutions during the schematic design phase.
- Explore the diagramming techniques that interior designers use to achieve the goals of analysis and synthesis.
- Investigate organizational concepts, narrative, and circulation.

KEY TERMS

Analysis diagram

Behavioral mapping or traffic pattern diagram

Block diagram

Bubble diagram

Central circulation pattern

Charrette

Circulation diagram

Composite diagram

Corporate hierarchy diagram

Diagrams

Enfilade

Feng shui

Functional analysis diagram   Nodal circulation pattern
Functional diagram   Organization concepts
Gantt chart   Parti diagram
Hierarchy   Radial circulation pattern
Ideation   Structural analysis diagram
Linear circulation pattern   Synthesis diagram
Massing diagram   Vastu
Narrative   Work flow, activity diagram
Networked circulation pattern   Zones of use

Chapter 10 examined the tasks involved in the programming phase and the outcomes of that phase. What are the tasks involved in the next phase of the process (Figure 12.1)?

The Schematic Design Phase

The purpose of the schematics design phase is, first, for the designer to be fluid in thinking and to generate many viable solutions. Why? In a professional environment, the answer is simple: your clients have hired you for your ideas. When you generate many ideas, your flexibility in thinking allows new, previously untried solutions to emerge. Roberto Rengel, in *Shaping Interior Space* (2007), and other educators call this process **ideation**. Ideation, an active process that searches out all the ways of getting to the major goals, involves intuition and leads to alternatives (Koberg & Bagnall, 1976). The product design firm IDEO calls this process "The Deep Dive"—an immersion in the problem at hand, with all of the data gathered around them to create a collaborative state of informed chaos from which multiple ideas emerge. Dave Kelley, the founder of IDEO and of the Hasso Plattner Institute of Design at Stanford University, states, "Routinely coming up with good ideas is what leads to innovation" (Koppel, 1999). Kelley believes that you need a language, a process, and a framework in order to design (2001). He recommends reading *The Art of Innovation*, written by his brother (Kelley & Littman, 2001), which explains IDEO's unique process of

Figure 12.1 This diagram shows where the schematic design phase falls within the design process.

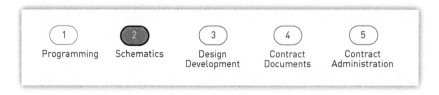

ideation. Ideation involves a highly descriptive, analytical, and speculative series of tasks: sketching, writing, building models, and talking to other designers.

The word **charrette** is used in design schools to indicate a concentrated effort to create a viable solution in a limited amount of time. Charrettes are used to get students in the practice of generating many ideas—"ideating"— as quickly as possible. Withholding judgment during this process is essential. Please refer to Chapter 4 for in-depth brainstorming techniques. To get an idea of what a charrette can be, envision this: Recently, four design schools in southern California held a charrette. Their task was to generate ideas for the design of a waiting area that would decrease anxiety and increase productivity among passengers at San Diego International Airport. Within a five-hour time limit, each student team had to produce at least one floor plan, an elevation, and a detail to illustrate their solution. The teams explored many ideas during that five-hour period. The winning solution included sleeping pods and computer workstations.

Since your thesis project will probably be a hypothetical proposal, and since school projects seek mainly to communicate the design to guest critics, the remainder of this chapter will be devoted to the tasks you are expected to undertake as part of the schematic design phase.

Revisiting the Role of the Design Concept

In Chapter 1 there was some discussion of design concepts. This chapter will focus more on the role that the design concept plays in the evolution of your design. The design concept is different from the programmatic concepts. While the program will tell you what needs to be in the space, the design concept will help you decide how to put it there. While the program will tell you the functional requirements, the design concept will help you make decisions about the aesthetics of the space. The size of the space and its relationship to other spaces are stated in the program, but the design concept will help you articulate *how* the space is configured or shaped and *how* it relates to the adjacent spaces. The design concept creates a framework for evaluation. It is the poetic image of the project, and it serves as the *basis for your design decisions*.

Your subsequent design decisions (choice and placement of lighting, flooring, wall colors, furnishings, etc.) either *will support* your concept or *not support* your concept. Every solution you come up with during the design process must be "run through" the design concept to see if that solution reinforces or sustains your concept. A strong design concept will help you answer the major questions, such as circulation pattern or overall organization, as well as address the details, such as flooring pattern, style of furnishings, or accent colors. (See Figure 12.2.)

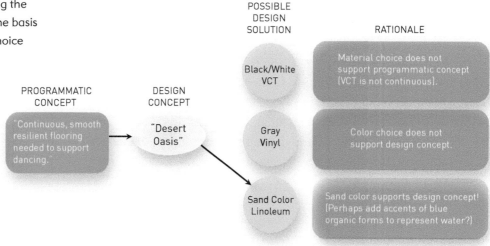

Figure 12.2 Diagram illustrating the role of the design concept as the basis for design decisions, such as choice of flooring.

PROGRAMMATIC CONCEPT

"Continuous, smooth resilient flooring needed to support dancing."

DESIGN CONCEPT

"Desert Oasis"

POSSIBLE DESIGN SOLUTION

Black/White VCT

Gray Vinyl

Sand Color Linoleum

RATIONALE

Material choice does not support programmatic concept (VCT is not continuous).

Color choice does not support design concept.

Sand color supports design concept! (Perhaps add accents of blue organic forms to represent water?)

It is important that your design concept be communicated simply and directly to the client and, if necessary, the user. Once the design concept has been accepted, making sure the design stays on course will be a much easier task, because each decision will be made in support of the design concept. The principle of *abstract thinking* applies to this task at this phase of design.

Project Management: A Way to Organize Your Tasks

The chart in Table 12.1 is a modified **Gantt chart,** which project managers use to schedule work on design or construction projects. Basically, a Gantt chart contains a list of tasks running down the left-hand column, organized by phases, and a calendar running across the top from left to right. You graphically plot (1) your due dates, or outside imposed deadlines, and (2) your internally set milestones, or personally imposed deadlines; then you estimate how much time each task will take. You can also schedule tasks to take place concurrently. For any given day, you can look at your Gantt chart and see exactly what tasks you should be working on. The chart does not reflect the actual hours to be spent on the project; you would record those on your time log or time sheet. Rather, it gives you a visual representation of the semester schedule that you and your instructor have agreed upon. It will help your instructor see that you have set reasonable amounts of time for each task and are being mindful of deadlines. In Table 12.1, the student has planned to use the three days before the diagrams are due (at the end of the first week) to "verify diagrams support concept." In the middle of the second week she has set herself a personal milestone: to build a model. She'll spend the days following this milestone getting feedback on the models, as well as doing research on color theory—two tasks that can be done concurrently.

Table 12.1

TYPICAL PROJECT SCHEDULE

PHASE/TASKS	WEEK 1 10-Jan	WEEK 2 17-Jan	WEEK 3 24-Jan	WEEK 4 31-Jan	WEEK 5 7-Feb	WEEK 6 14-Feb	WEEK 7 21-Feb	WEEK 8 28-Feb	WEEK 9 7-Mar	WEEK 10 14-Mar	WEEK 11 21-Mar
SCHEMATICS											
Analysis Diagrams/Synthesis Diagrams	★										
Verify diagrams support concept		★									
Develop several schemes											
Verify early space plan(s) fulfill program		★									
Build 3D mock-up to test concepts			★								
Seek feedback from mock-ups											
Review color theory research											
Choose preliminary color palette											
Finalize schematic design for presentation				⇨							
DESIGN DEVELOPMENT											
Research Occupancy/Life Safety Codes/ADA Compliance					★⇨		⇨				
Classroom Space Plan/Floor Plan											
Meet with Code Consultant for feedback on means of egress						★★					
Review anthropometrics for children & teachers						★	⇨				
Interior Elevations Classrooms (4)							⇨⇨⇨				
Research lighting requirements/visit lighting showroom						★★	⇨				
Draw Reflected Ceiling Plan											
Review Flammability codes for finishes											
Complete finish selection for plan							⇨⇨				
Obtain finish samples & information on maintenance/application						★★					
North/South Building Section							⇨				
East/West Building Section											
Meet with consultants structural, mech., elec., plumbing...											
Finalize Design Development Drawings for presentation											
FF&E											
Review Flammability codes for FF&E											
Review program for FF&E requirements/clearances											
Visit showroom/Collect furniture cut sheets											
Complete Classroom Furniture Plan						★★					
Select classroom furniture											
Research ADA mounting heights of equipment											
Draw Classroom Elevations											
CONSTRUCTION DOCUMENTS											
Research Green Roof components											
Isometric Roof Detail								★			
Research doors/hardware for ADA compliance											
Interior Cabinetry Detail									★		
Verify clearances for ADA compliance											⇨
Dimension all plans & elevations										★	⇨
Verify specification information with manufacturers										★	⇨
Finalize Schedules											⇨
Print 24" x 36" set and coordinate											★

LEGEND: CLASS PIN-UP   ★ MILESTONE   ⇩ DEADLINE

9/8/2009

At a site visit for the renovation of a residence, the designer noticed the long, narrow space that had a cramped kitchen at one end and a fireplace at the other (see Figure 12.3.) From her analysis of the space, she started to create a **narrative** (a story): that the fireplace (the heart/hearth of the home) and the stove (the heart/hearth of the kitchen) should have a "dialogue," from one end of the room to the other, to conceptually unify the space. She explained to the clients that placing the stove opposite the fireplace would create that dialogue spatially, and that she would further the relationship by using similar materials on both facing walls—textured slate and polished granite that would have similar proportions and bond patterns on each wall. The clients, a young couple, grasped the concept immediately, and they enthusiastically encouraged the designer to take her design in that direction. After the work was completed, at the ASID annual kitchen tour the designer overheard the couple relaying the concept of the "dialogue between the facing hearths" to their visitors! It is very rewarding to know that a concept can be appreciated and understood by non-designers, and that it will live on because they will communicate the intention of the original design to subsequent owners of the house.

Figure 12.3
"Before" plan (on the left) and design solution (on the right) of a residence in which the design concept was summarized as a "dialogue between facing hearths."

Out of research, metaphors emerge. We can derive or distill design concepts from these "stories" we create, turning a series of ideas into an abstract summary. It is best if the design concept can be distilled to its essence, to a single word or phrase. Rengel (2007) has defined the categories into which design concepts generally fall:

1. Philosophical
2. Thematic
3. Functional
4. Artistic
5. Mood-Related
6. Stylistic

In Table 12.2 this list is expanded to include a few other categories of concepts, illustrated by student examples. Remember, a good concept is one that can answer a multitude of design questions, on many levels, so a concept would be considered weak if it addressed only an artistic concern or a stylistic concern—such as only color or architectural detail.

An excellent example of a *philosophical* design concept is the Vidarkliniken in Sweden, designed by Eric Asmussen. With its first location completed in 1992, it is a place of healing based on *anthroposophical medicine*, a "philosophy of healing the body, soul, and spirit" conceived by Rudolf Steiner. This philosophy sees "illness as a gift and healing as a conscious process of self-transcending spiritual development" (Coates, 1997, p. 148).

The healing must engage the patient, as the patient is actively involved in the healing process. The design responds to the philosophy on every level of design—from the way the buildings relate to one another, interior circulation space, space plan, to the window locations, shape and detail, the furnishings, and the colors and finishes. Architecturally, the community of healing is expressed as a cluster of three buildings that complements the natural features of the site (Coates, 1997). The main circulation corridor has widened alcoves that alternately face the wild forest and the inner courtyard, a balance of the "turning inward of the life energies and a desire for isolation." The patient's gradual interest in returning to increased activity is "intentionally aroused by the corridors' rhythmically varied, naturally flowing spaces" (pp. 130–31).

The interior walls are painted by the "lazure" method, in which vegetable dyes are layered into a beeswax medium, resulting in soft, glowing walls. The color of the walls of the patient's room corresponds with the patient's illness: warm colors to balance "cold" illnesses such as sclerosis and cool colors to counteract "warm" illnesses such as inflammation (Coates, 1997, p. 131). Asmussen's placement and configuration of windows also support the mind–body–spirit connection, separating sky-viewing windows from earth-viewing windows, which emphasizes the separation of heaven from

Table 12.2 Types of Design Concepts

Design Concept	Explanation	Example
Philosophical	Based on a school of thought or practice	Rudolf Steiner's *anthroposophical medicine*, a "philosophy of healing" explored in the Vidarkliniken in Sweden
Scientific	Based on measurable or accepted principles	An aquarium based on the natural movement and physical properties of water
Process-Oriented	Based on a natural dynamic occurrence or man-made method	A fertility clinic based on the concept of growth and reproduction, or a residence that responds to the movement of the sun throughout the seasons
Formalistic	Based on the manipulation of forms (shapes), elements, and design principles	A courtroom based on symmetry and hierarchy, or a residence based on circles or circular patterns
Functional	Based on solving the functional requirements of the program as well as aesthetics	A theater based on ideal acoustics for listening to a symphony orchestra or opera.
Mood-Related	Based on the idea that interior design has the power to evoke emotion	A spiritual center that inspires occupants to feel a divine presence, or a children's museum based on mystery, discovery, and inspiring creativity
Ideological	Based on the idea of a causal relationship between a space and a social relationship or behavior	A community center based on the idea that "Art unites," or an office based on the principles of democracy, which encourages individuals to participate
Imagery	Based on a strong visual reference	A children's library based on the image of a tree house or a pirate ship
Stylistic	Based on architectural details and elements and on the principle of a particular era or genre	A theater based on Art Nouveau, or a mid-century modern residence
Thematic	Based on simulating the experience of a particular genre or architectural style	A cafeteria designed as a 1950s diner, or "Adventureland" at Disneyland
Experiential	Based on a sequence or narrative or storytelling	An outpatient clinic based on the journey of Dorothy in *The Wizard of Oz*
Juxtaposition	Based on seemingly disparate ideas put together for a unique contrast	A hotel based on "East Meets West," or a residential project based on "medieval modern"

earth. The earthbound windows are configured with deep shelves to hold flowers, plants, and artwork.

Generating Multiple Solutions

In an article titled "Lines of Inquiry" (2006), architect Alan Phillips states, "Diagrams, in whatever visual form they take, represent a threshold moment in the creation of successful architecture." In *Space Planning Basics* (Karlen, Ruggeri, & Hahn, 2004), Mark Karlen refers to a "synthesis gap": that perceptible junction or moment between the end of research (information-gathering) and the beginning of design—the conceptual leap between the known and the unknown (discussed in Chapter 10). This leap of faith at the onset of design is often a stressful moment for students. Or it can be a very exciting moment, if you are armed with the appropriate tools.

How do you go from program to space plan? How do you go from analysis to synthesis? How do you bridge the conceptual gap? The tools that designers use to go from research to design are called **diagrams**. In fact, diagrams could be considered the primitive or early *language* of design. They translate the words and phrases of the written program into visual forms. In *The Hidden Dimension,* Edward Hall (1966) sees language as a basis for perception. We often think it is the other way around, that we see things and then perceive them; but in fact learning words, even the sequence of words in our language, frames our perceptions and organizes our thoughts! For example, in the United States we name soup by the *objects* in the soup, such as clam chowder or chicken noodle. In contrast, the Japanese name their soups by what the *broth* consists of, such as miso. (*Miso* is the fermented soybean paste suspended in the broth.) If the soup contains vegetables or noodles, that information is added to the soup's name as a secondary aspect, as in "miso ramen." This also translates spatially, to the way people of different cultures experience space differently. "When Westerners think and talk about space, they mean the distance between objects . . . we are taught to perceive . . . and to think of space as 'empty.' The meaning of this becomes clear only when it is contrasted with the Japanese, who are trained to give *meaning* to spaces—to perceive the shape and arrangement of spaces; for this they have a word, *ma*" (Hall, p. 153). Diagrams are a way to perceive, analyze, and manipulate space, to give meanings to space.

The reason for bringing up the idea of language is to make a connection between diagrams and language, to increase your design "vocabulary" by introducing several different diagramming techniques, each using a different method of analyzing and configuring space.

Diagrams

"It is very difficult to think of complex things being expressed in simple terms without the use of diagrams" (Phillips, 2006, p. 68). When scientists were racing to find the form and structure of DNA, "the diagram which emerged . . . the first sketch of the double helix made by Francis Crick, is very much an architectural sketch with soft lines swimming in space, an authoritative representation of geometry, and a confidence that could easily have come from the hand of Louis Kahn or Eero Saarinen" (Phillips, p. 68). (See Figure 12.4.)

Phillips (2006) further defines architectural diagrams as either *representational* or *abstract*. A representational diagram is a sketch designed to be interpreted visually and geometrically, while an abstract diagram represents an idea. He talks about *flow* and *system*—*referential* sketches in which the designer refers to past influences or previous experience—and the *doodle*, which results from thinking about something else while drawing. He also identifies a *polemical* sketch, which is "sometimes presented as an irritable grouping of marks born of frustration . . . or awakening" (Phillips, p. 71). It is a drawing produced by the act of drawing and is not necessarily thought out first.

The "napkin diagram"—which documents communication between people in public places, at meetings, or attempts to illustrate a thought that one would have on an airplane or during a meeting—is an often underrated but valuable tool. Many designers rely on moments of inspiration that can come from meaningful conversations, or just as a result of a relaxed state of mind that encourages impromptu genius. Be prepared to put those ideas into a visual form at any moment.

> The first diagram is made in the mind of the author. . . . The beauty of the diagram "as imagination" . . . the mind-diagram contains a moral and ethical fingerprint, as to how the eventual building will provide the greatest good for the greatest number. . . . During the early stage of sketching,

Figure 12.4 Sketch of double helix by Dr. Francis Crick.

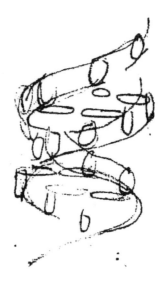

the diagram is required to fold the "self" into the drawing, so that the link between the physical work, the imagination . . . and the ethical responsibility . . . are one and the same thing (Phillips, 2006, p. 72).

Although many types of diagrams are used in science and architecture, two kinds of diagrams are used specifically for interior design:

- **Analysis diagrams**, to document and ponder existing conditions or to represent the ideal configuration as a graphic extension of the written program
- **Synthesis diagrams**, to propose something new

Analysis diagrams represent the known, while synthesis diagrams may represent the unknown. No doubt you have already been using some of these diagramming techniques. The purpose of the next few pages is to review the function of previously learned diagramming techniques, to weigh the pros and cons of each, and to introduce new ones to expand your ability to perceive and manipulate interior space. (For a summary of diagram types, see Table 12.3 on page 378.)

Diagrams Used for Analysis

Bubble Diagrams Interior design students are first introduced to the bubble diagram.

This diagram is also sometimes referred to as a *relationship diagram* or an *adjacency diagram*. Figure 12.6 provides an example of relationships and adjacencies. This family of diagrams is used to establish an understanding of relative sizes of spaces and their relationship to one another. Usually not drawn to-scale and kept separate from the base plan, these are graphic representations of programmatic requirements. A variation would be the stacking diagram, which seeks to establish relationships between vertical elements (or in a multilevel project, between spaces on different floors) that are "stacked" on top of one another. The bubble diagram puts each space in its own "bubble," showing relative sizes and adjacencies. The downside is that each of the rooms represented by a bubble is considered a separate entity. You are forced to name each one, and in doing so you will likely find it more difficult to imagine that spaces can combine or transition without full-height walls and doors. The bubble diagram is primarily analytic in nature, as it is describing programmatic concepts of relationship and relative sizes. Although some schools teach that a bubble diagram can be used for synthesis or schematic design (see Figure 12.7), it does not lend itself to easy translation to a space plan because of the curved nature of the bubbles. And what about the awkward spaces in between the bubbles?

How Can a Nine-Year-Old Girl Design a $400-Million Hospital?

The following example illustrates how a programmatic concept can lead to a design concept.

A patented process for uncovering hidden concepts and distilling information into an emerging metaphor called ZMET was used to come up with a strong design concept for a children's hospital in Pittsburgh. Architect Lou Astorino and his staff at his architecture and engineering firm turned to ZMET to conduct 90-minute interviews with representative end users (patients, staff, administration) that included sharing thoughts and feelings about a topic. The interviews with ZMET result in composite images that represent the subconscious needs and wants of the interviewees. Based on metaphors that evolved out of the extensive interviewing process, Astorino takes the information and filters it to extract design concepts and solutions that respond to the deep-seated wants and needs of the hospital end users. In this case the strongest metaphor identified was *Transformation*. Other metaphors included *Control*, *Connection*, and *Energy*.

Everyone interviewed at the hospital wanted to feel transformed in some way, not only from sick to well but also from unbalanced to balanced, and from feeling a lack of control to empowerment or the ability to manage. Astorino created a report explaining how this goal could translate to design solutions.

One of the design solutions involved the creation of a "Transformation Corridor" that begins at the garage where the family parks and carries through to ambulatory care where the patient checks into the hospital. (See Figure 12.5) The corridor literally transforms as the child and family walk through it. A mural that begins with very geometric graphics changes into a cocoon, then to a butterfly as the family reaches registration, where the three-story atrium contains butterflies hanging as artwork in the space. The corridor transformation also includes other design elements, such as lighting, textures, and floor tiles, which change to express a changing of seasons.

Furthermore, research revealed that the hospital experience does not begin when the patient walks through the doors, but instead it begins at home when the patient gets into the car to leave for the hospital. Thus, the exterior of the hospital needed to connect with the kids and avoid creating any stress. Astorino performed a color study with kids, exploring not just primary colors but also a richer (like a Mexican palette) palette that was implemented on the exterior. Because the site is on a hillside and is seen by any approach, it becomes almost iconic and can be seen by patients as they approach the hospital.

Designers then tend to draw full-height walls at the edges of bubbles and doors where the lines of adjacency intersect. A bubble diagram is best kept not-to-scale and presented independent from the base plan, solely to show relative sizes, space names, and adjacencies. This is similar to the kind of

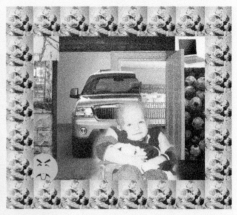

Figure 12.5
The composite graphic images resulting from the interview process, and the resulting design: Transformation Corridor (construction completed in 2009).

information represented in an adjacency matrix, but in a more visually graphic form.

Work Flow, Activity Diagrams This type of diagram seeks to establish existing or ideal relationships between people or functions in an organization, to help determine the future circulation diagram. Does work proceed in a linear fashion, from one person or area to the next, or is it a network or series of networks? Or does work revolve around a central hub, radiating in different directions, or is it arranged in a loop? Or in clusters?

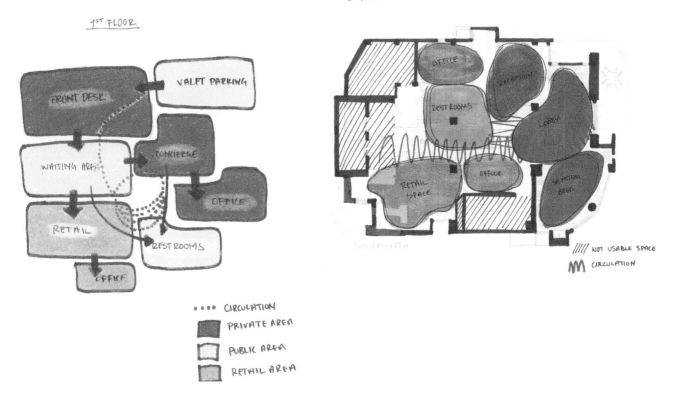

Relationship Diagram:

1ST FLOOR

BUBBLE DIAGRAM

FRONT DESK

VALET PARKING

WAITING AREA

CONCIERGE

OFFICE

RETAIL

RESTROOMS

OFFICE

•••• CIRCULATION
PRIVATE AREA
PUBLIC AREA
RETAIL AREA

OFFICE
RECEPTION
RESTROOMS
LOBBY
RETAIL SPACE
OFFICE
SHOWROOM AREA

///// NOT USABLE SPACE
CIRCULATION

Figure 12.6 (above left) This relationship diagram, drawn by student Sergio Murguia, shows the relative sizes and adjacencies of spaces on the first floor of a proposed hotel project.

Figure 12.7 (above right) This bubble diagram shows the spaces represented in Figure 12.6, overlaid on a base plan. Notice that the relationship of the spaces is in keeping with the program, and the constraints of the existing building shell are explored. In this instance, the bubble diagram is used for synthesis rather than analysis.

Corporate Hierarchy Diagrams This type of diagram graphically represents the way a company is configured, identifies the members of the organization, and illustrates the relationships among them. It is often used to identify the decision-makers during programming and the stakeholders during data collection. It is used along with the work flow diagram to inform the circulation or organization diagrams during design.

Functional Analysis, Structural Analysis Diagrams These diagrams are usually part of the site analysis when the designer is looking closely at the building shell to determine constraints and possibilities. Discussed in Chapter 11, these diagrams create a visual record of the information gathered about the site, to establish possibilities and constraints. Usually done over the existing site plan or base plan, these diagrams can analyze public space versus private space, natural light versus artificial light, quiet versus noisy. The designer might use them to highlight plumbing walls and describe the area adjacent to them as "wet," or use them to identify load-bearing elements that must remain. These diagrams can be done in sections, to make clear the structure from floor to floor or the current pattern of movement of goods and services through the existing vertical circulation. They can also be three-dimensional, mapping a building's electrical system or ventilation system.

Behavioral Mapping or Traffic Pattern Diagrams Discussed in Chapter 8, these diagrams assist the designer in observing the way people use space, which can lead to an understanding of traffic patterns. Analysis of the location of existing doors and corridors can also indicate possible traffic patterns. These diagrams are a visual record of information gathered about the way people use a space over time; they help identify conflicts and they can influence the way a space is planned during schematic design. Figure 12.8 presents first the traffic pattern in an existing home and then the re-routed and condensed path of travel in the resulting renovation.

Nontraditional Analyses (A side note about cultural analyses not necessarily taught in mainstream curricula.) In many areas of the world, culturally specific analyses need to be done before design can occur. This family of diagrams considers the invisible or metaphysical forces that may affect a project's development, as well as spiritual practices such as blessings or religious beliefs that may extend beyond the limits of scientific inquiry.

- **Feng shui** is a Chinese system of beliefs, dating back thousands of years, based on balancing the movement of energy (*chi*) throughout a space. There are two main schools or techniques: traditional, which analyzes compass directions, environmental forms, and birth charts, and the Black Hat Sect, which utilizes relational directions and a "bagua" map. The latter is more prevalent in modern Western culture. Figure 12.9 depicts an eight-sided "bagua" diagram, which is imposed

Figure 12.8 "Before" plan (on the left) and design solution (on the right) of a residence, showing main paths of travel. The remodel reduced the number of paths through the family area.

Figure 12.9 The "bagua," an eight-sided figure, may be imposed over an existing residence for a feng shui analysis.

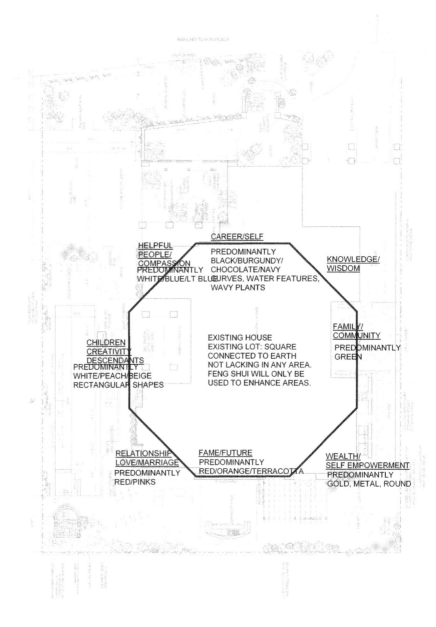

HELPFUL
PEOPLE/
COMPASSION
PREDOMINANTLY
WHITE/BLUE/LT BLUE

CAREER/SELF
PREDOMINANTLY
BLACK/BURGUNDY/
CHOCOLATE/NAVY
CURVES, WATER FEATURES,
WAVY PLANTS

KNOWLEDGE/
WISDOM

CHILDREN
CREATIVITY
DESCENDANTS
PREDOMINANTLY
WHITE/PEACH/BEIGE
RECTANGULAR SHAPES

EXISTING HOUSE
EXISTING LOT: SQUARE
CONNECTED TO EARTH
NOT LACKING IN ANY AREA.
FENG SHUI WILL ONLY BE
USED TO ENHANCE AREAS.

FAMILY/
COMMUNITY
PREDOMINANTLY
GREEN

RELATIONSHIP
LOVE/MARRIAGE
PREDOMINANTLY
RED/PINKS

FAME/FUTURE
PREDOMINANTLY
RED/ORANGE/TERRACOTTA

WEALTH/
SELF EMPOWERMENT
PREDOMINANTLY
GOLD, METAL, ROUND

on an existing residential site plan to allow analysis of the space's zones. This analysis relates to a mystical organization of trigrams representing areas of the occupant's life. Many books have been written about this cultural analysis, and one can also take steps to become a certified feng shui consultant. Sarah Rossbach and Master Lin Yun have been most successful in bringing the Black Hat Sect of relational feng shui to the attention of Western cultures. To learn more about feng shui, a good place to begin is with their book *Interior Design with Feng Shui* (Rossbach, 2000).

- **Vastu** is another system by which to analyze or organize space to accommodate varying energies. The Hindu worldview is that each material—brick, wood, steel . . . (including human beings)—radiates energies both positive and negative. Vastu aims to interface these and other terrestrial energies (our pets, us, the furniture, the electrical and other gadgets, the carpets and curtains, etc.) with the celestial energies (emanating from other planets and constellations of our universe and other universes) to make humans a part of the cosmic order and provide them with health, happiness, and contentment (Bangalore & Suprajarama, 2006).

- The diagram shown in Figure 12.10 was done by an architect for a house she designed for herself. She has done a site analysis that, as discussed in Chapter 11, includes view, solar orientation, sun path, and prevailing winds. To this she added an analysis of the existing land formations, such as the outcroppings of boulders that occur on the property. Because she and her partner have owned the property and camped there for many years, they have come to appreciate the spiritual qualities of the land and are sensitive to the existing ecosystem involving the plants and animals that live on the land. In addition, over the years they have invited their friends to create environmental art (sculpture, carvings, and other artistic "interventions" using natural and man-made materials) and embed it in the landscape. This diagram includes the names of the pieces of art by the person who created them or who they are dedicated to.

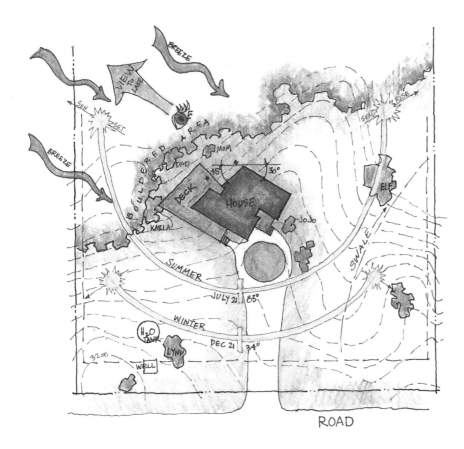

Figure 12.10 Site analysis diagram, including environmental art, for this residential project. Courtesy of architect Sandy Gramley, AIA.

Parti Diagrams "The word 'parti' passed into architecture via l'Ecole des Beaux Arts to represent that freehand sketch diagram that was at the tangent between idea and imagination. The parti is the *threshold sketch*" (Phillips, 2006, p. 73). The term comes from the French verb *partir*, which means "to separate." It is a conceptual separation of parts, distinction of areas, and intended movement through the space. It can also be conceived as a figural gesture that unifies, or a distinction of parts that makes the whole project work together. (See Figure 12.11.)

Circulation Diagrams This type of diagram focuses on the movement of people through a space. We can identify different types of **organization concepts**, conceptual plan arrangements, or circulation patterns. All plans consist of a certain series of spatial arrangements depending on work flow and **hierarchy**, meant to help determine which spaces are major destinations or are programmatically or conceptually most important. "Circulation patterns are one of the primary ways of organizing a room, an open space, or an entire interior design project. They are vital to the efficient organization of space and provide people with their strongest orientation within an environment" (Ballast, 2007). Main circulation patterns can be **linear, radial, central, networked,** or **nodal** (see Figure 12.12). Linear patterns may have variations, as in a continuous path that loops back to its origin or entry point. Networked patterns may have variations as well, as you may have to pass through one space to get to another (a French term, *enfilade*) in a linear format or in some other pattern like a triangle. In *Interior Design Reference Manual: A*

Figure 12.11 This parti diagram of a proposed museum seeks to understand the circulation of the visitor through the various spaces.

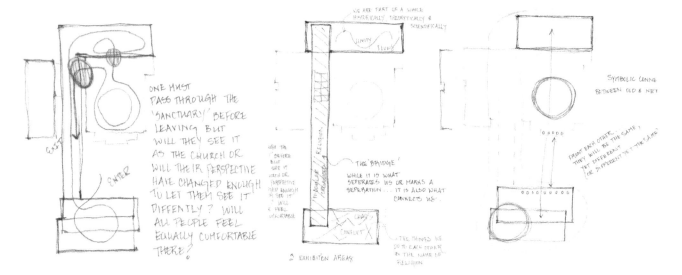

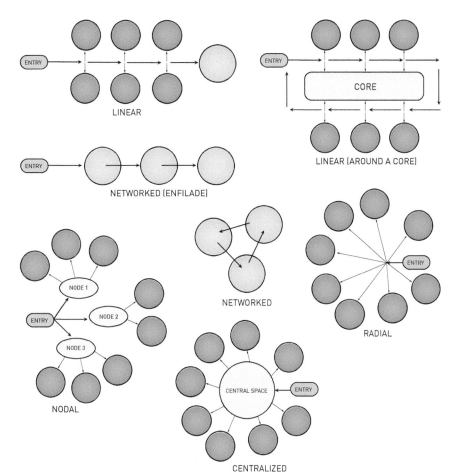

Figure 12.12 Linear, Networked, Nodal, Central, and Radial Organization Patterns.

Guide to the NCIDQ Exam, architect David Ballast also names a *grid pattern,* like the way the streets of New York City are organized, and an *axial pattern,* like the streets of Paris.

The circulation diagram can often be derived from or informed by the previously done work flow diagram. If a patient has a series of places to go on a typical doctor visit, the circulation pattern may follow as a string of destinations off of a central artery. If a visitor arrives at the entrance and has choices about which place to go, we may call upon a central or radial organization. The difference between a central circulation pattern and a radial circulation pattern is that in a central circulation pattern, the space that a person is standing in when deciding which way to go is a main space, such as an atrium or garden; and a radial circulation pattern may result from divergent corridors (which would not be a central space), as in a mall configuration that has major destinations, such as Nordstrom, Sears, and Macy's, at the end of each of the radiating main corridors.

Purpose: To apply Kevin Lynch's theory of way-finding (discussed in Chapter 11)—how people navigate through a city—to your floor plan.

Prepare a circulation diagram based on Kevin Lynch's theory of way-finding as an overlay to your base plan. Assign a different color to each element: paths, edges, nodes, districts, and landmarks. Explore how each of the elements helps people find the various destinations. In this Activity it is not important that the landmark be a brightly colored wall, a piece of artwork, or a sign hanging from the ceiling. All that matters is that you have conceptually identified the location and purpose of the landmark and have indicated its placement within the scheme. An edge can be a wall, a change in flooring material, or lighting level or ceiling height. Again, it is important to note where the change occurs. You'll be asked to further articulate the composition of the edge during design development.

Figure 12.13 Example of a block diagram by a student for an institutional project.

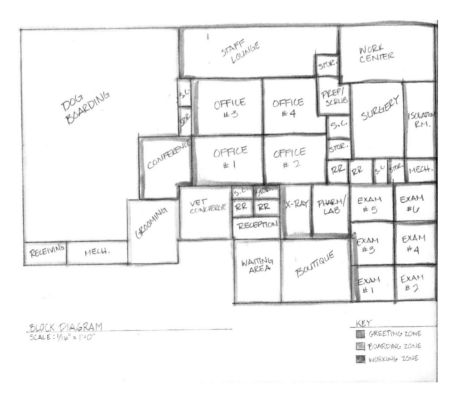

Block Diagrams A block diagram has limitations similar to a bubble diagram in that room names are assigned to each area. (See Figure 12.13.) However, it is easier to transition a block diagram into a space plan due to the straight edges and the ease of overlapping or intersecting blocks to achieve interesting spatial configurations that go one step beyond mere adjacency. Figure 12.14 makes that transition. According to Ballast (2007), there are four ways that spaces can be "adjacent" to one another: (1) they can be next to one another, (2) they can overlap one another to create an intermediary zone, (3) they can be convenient to one another through an intervening space, and (4) one space can be within the other.

Functional Diagrams This type of diagram offers a kind of flexibility that is not found in bubble or block diagrams. You are not forced to put each room

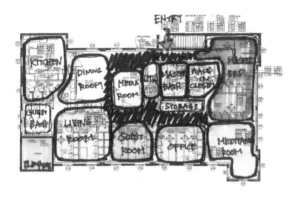

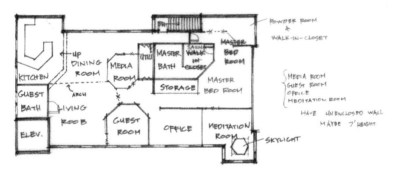

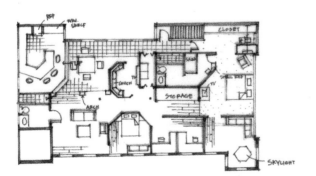

Figure 12.14 Example of a bubble diagram, block diagram, and resulting schematic floor plan by a student for a residential project.

into a bubble or a block, but can focus on a predetermined set of functions (work type) or spatial qualities and then allow the rooms to be placed in the naturally supportive locations. It divides spaces not by room names but by other aspects. These include large areas of generalization, such as program areas versus support services or core versus perimeter.

The areas can also be categorized by type of occupant: faculty versus student, adult versus children, public versus private. In a healthcare project you may want to distinguish between sterile and nonsterile, high and low ceilings, or spaces directed outward and spaces directed inward. In almost all projects, you will want to determine areas that need natural light (sunlight) and those that need to be dark, and areas that need to be quiet versus areas that can be noisy. A functional diagram may indicate areas with sound-absorptive materials and those with sound-reflective materials. In a place with a pool or other water elements, you will want to distinguish wet areas from dry areas.

This technique can apply to spaces of any size, from an 80-square-foot kitchen to a 170,000-square-foot institution. For the smaller spaces, this diagram may be thought of as **zones of use**. In kitchens designed by the zoning method, the functional spaces are designated as cook, prep, store, serve, and clean up. Thus, zones of use plans are conceived differently from those generated by the triangle method (which links a path between the three major fixtures: the refrigerator, the stove, and the sink).

Figure 12.15 is an example of a master suite planned using a zoning method that identifies the zones as sleeping, bathing, and dressing. The first

Figure 12.15 Example of parti and functional diagrams leading to a schematic floor plan of a bedroom.

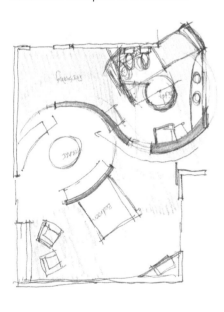
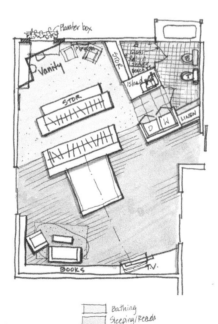

diagram is figural and represents a parti diagram that grew out of a fluid movement between the three zones. The client required individual space but no doors between the three zones. The design was achieved only through a series of diagrams that allowed for fluidity of thinking, which crystallized in the accepted design solution.

For larger spaces—such as an institutional or hospitality space, a library, a school, or a hotel—a functional diagram would correspond to your understanding and configuration of spaces on a gradation of noisy to quiet, age ranges, and active to passive. (See Figure 12.16.) In the design of a daycare center, for example, sometimes these levels of activity are listed by how much of the body is physically engaged in action—such as gross motor (running, dancing), fine motor (art, crafts), and sedentary (reading, napping).

Both zones of use and levels of activity can inform a functional diagram that would explore finish material possibilities. Flooring materials, for example, can be categorized into hard, resilient, and soft. For projects that have a "wet versus dry" functional diagram, the proposed finishes could be categorized by impervious and pervious. A functional category of seamless flooring could be an overlay on the functional areas previously marked as "sterile."

Figure 12.16 Example of a functional diagram by a student for a commercial project.

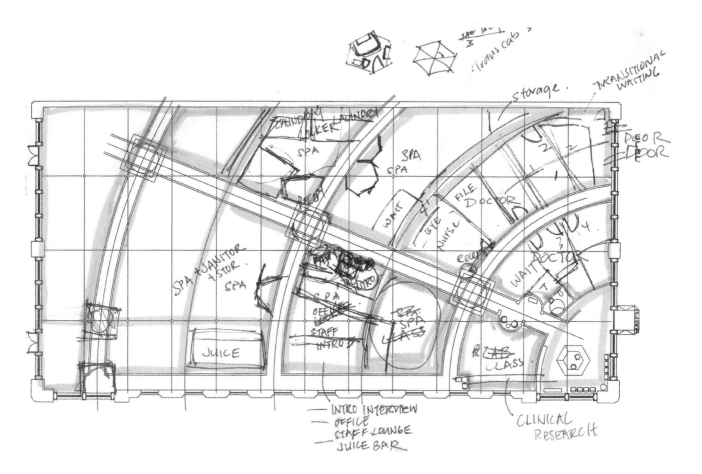

ACTIVITY 12.2 Developing a Functional Diagram Based on Flooring Materials

Purpose: **To apply a functional diagram technique to a current project.**

1. Put a sheet of trace paper over a preliminary space plan that you have begun in a studio class.

2. Assign colors or hatch patterns to three different categories of materials, such as "hard," "resilient," and "soft" or "patterned," "solid," and "directional" (or develop your own categories, such as materials that correspond with various elements: "wood," "earth," and "water," or gradations of cost, such as "very expensive," "average," and "inexpensive").

3. Define areas according to flooring material designations. Keep in mind that different materials may be used in a single room, or that many rooms may use the same material.

4. See if you can link areas conceptually by using continuous flooring, or divide a large area by introducing multiple types of flooring. Materials should respond to programmatic criteria as well as support your design concept.

One strength of a functional diagram is that you can develop your own graphic vocabulary using colors, hatches, line weights, dashes, and symbols to represent a variety of things (Rengel, 2007). The graphic vocabulary for diagramming includes graphic symbols to differentiate bubbles for hierarchy; different line types, dashes, line weights, and arrow styles to indicate movement; and special symbols to indicate entry, destination, landmarks, and exits (Rengel). Providing text labels and a key can help illustrate your thinking process and communicate that process to others. (See Figure 12.17.)

In a gym, the locker rooms can be seen as the transition between "street clothes" and "barefoot" areas. In a supermarket, areas can be categorized into "frozen," "refrigerated," and "room temperature." Alternatively, the areas can be categorized as "produce," "meat," "dairy," and "dry goods." A specialized grocery can also sort the areas by "organic," "vegetarian," "vegan," and "raw"; or "local" and "shipped." On the shelves down an aisle, how many ways can you categorize how food is organized, such as "kid's eye height"? Think about how many ways there are to separate areas at a wine retailer. You can sort by country of origin, by type of wine, by price. How many other ways can you categorize the project type you are working on? A functional diagram is unlimited in its potential to categorize, sort, and group areas to help you envision myriad spatial configurations that all correspond to programmatic requirements.

Other Types of Exploratory Diagrams

> We had prepared sketches showing the different ways of sitting . . . what came out of all this was a fairly simple system: the Chaise Longue, proceeding from the basic idea of the simple soldier, who, when he is tired, lies down on his back, puts his feet up against a tree, with his knapsack under his head (Charlotte Perriand, quoted in Phillips, 2006).

Composite Diagrams Alan Phillips sees computers as a "quicker diagram management tool, replacing hundreds of paper overlays with click-on-click-off layer process." Take advantage of the layers, the scale, and the flexibility in computer applications! The computer has its strengths, just as hand-drawn sketches do. Use a combination of both, in a back-and-forth manner, until the revolutionary, or ideal, design solution emerges. Figure 12.18 represents the use of the computer to produce a structural analysis diagram that identifies which walls must remain and the potential for expansion, as well as the scaled accuracy of the furnishings such as the bed, the depth of the hanging storage, and the toilet fixtures. The drawings done by hand explore movement, options, and functional diagram by use and flooring material (by color). Note the additional, small elevation studies for cabinets in the margins. The resulting schematic reflects the layers of information incorporated into the exploratory, composite sketch.

Massing Diagrams The massing diagram differentiates between enclosed space and open space, between objects and space, or between program space and support space. It is sometimes referred to as a *mass/void diagram*, as it shows the built space in relation to open space, or positive space in relation to negative space. In Figure 12.19, student Lorraine Tinio has successfully translated three block diagrams of her thesis project, a homeless shelter, into three three-dimensional sketches that help her decide which solution is

Figure 12.17 Example of a bubble diagram and two functional diagrams by a student for a residential project. Note the use of color and hatch patterns to distinguish areas.

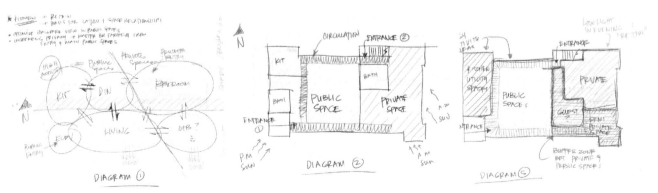

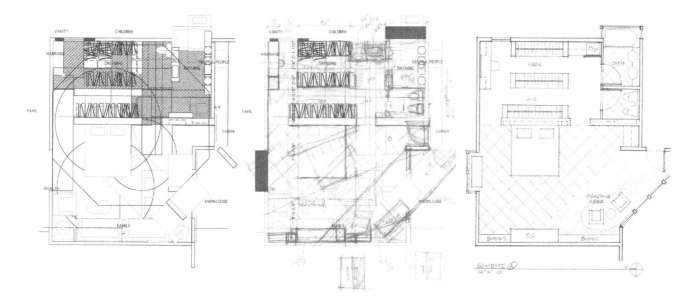

Figure 12.18 The computer can be used as a tool to layer a series of diagrams on top of one another, as you document your thinking process. This is a series of 2 exploratory composite sketches, using CAD and hand-drawing, and the resulting schematic floor plan.

best based on the resulting configurations of open space. The final solution, the third option in the series, was chosen due to the pleasing and functional shape of the outdoor space and the possibility for indoor/outdoor dining space facing south. (See Figure 12.19.)

Table 12.3 Diagram Types

Diagrams Used for Analysis	Diagrams Used for Synthesis
Bubble Diagram (independent from floor plan)	Bubble Diagram (overlaid on base plan)
Relationship Diagram	Parti Diagram
Adjacency Matrix	
Stacking Diagram	
Work Flow	Circulation Diagram
Behavioral Mapping/Traffic Patterns	Organizational Diagram
Corporate Hierarchy	
Organizational Structure	
Site Analysis	Block Diagram
Structural Analysis	Functional Diagram
Functional Analysis	Zones of Use Diagram
	Massing Diagram
Cultural or Alternative Analysis Diagram	Interpretive Diagram
	Exploratory Sketch
Composite Overlay	Composite Overlay

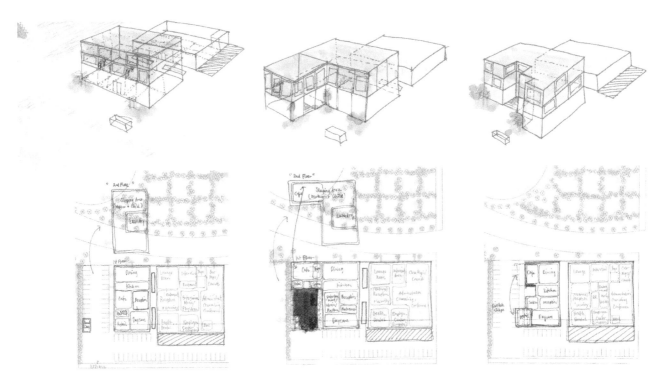

Figure 12.19 Massing diagrams and corresponding block diagrams. Courtesy student Lorraine Tinio.

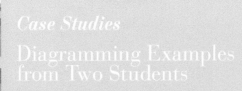

Diagramming Examples from Two Students

From Bubble to Block

The first case study is a series of diagrams produced by student Yuki Endo while exploring the relationship of spaces in a museum of Japanese art that she called *MoJa*. Yuki's bubble diagram technique was innovative. To enable her to be flexible in her thinking about relationships between spaces, she cut out circles of varying sizes and colors to represent each space in her program. Then she moved them around on a neutral piece of paper, along with cut-out arrows indicating movement and markers indicating circulation. She digitally photographed the results at different stages, generating a multitude of bubble diagrams. (See Figure 12.20a.)

Figure 12.20b is the block diagram that resulted from placing the program areas onto the building shell. Note how Yuki used a different geometry (circular spaces) to separate the exhibit spaces from other areas. The diagram also served as the basis for a preliminary codes analysis based on

Figure 12.20 In 12.20a, interior design student Yuki Endo devised a flexible system to create bubble diagrams quickly. She made paper cutouts representing each program area, and then digitally photographed them in various configurations. This allowed her to explore various adjacencies without using a lot of paper or doing multiple drawings. In 12.20b, Yuki used a block diagram to incorporate occupancy classifications in a preliminary codes analysis. In 12.20c, this schematic floor plan shows occupancy load calculations to help determine the number of exits required for the museum. Courtesy Yuki Endo.

occupancy classifications: assembly, business, mercantile. This, along with analysis of square footage, helped her to determine occupancy loads (number of people in each space), which enabled her to determine the number of exits required for each space and the number of plumbing fixtures in the resulting preliminary space plan (see Figure 12.20c).

From Functional to Parti to Block

In this next case study, student Andrew Hunsaker used a bubble diagram (Figure 12.21a) to determine adjacencies, then a functional diagram to explore the circulation as well as the presence of natural light in the existing building shell. This diagram evolved into a parti, a figural gesture that became the fundamental focus of the circulation pattern around a central atrium, shown in Figure 12.21b. Andrew then drew a block diagram that easily translated into the final schematic plan shown in Figure 12.21c.

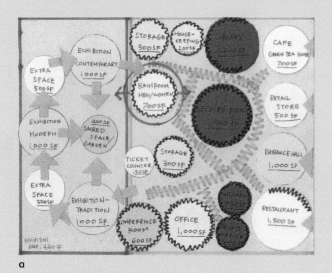

a

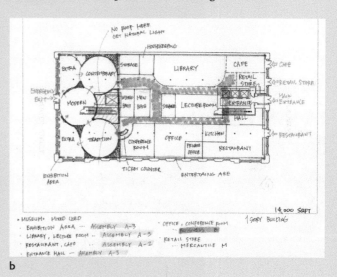

b

c

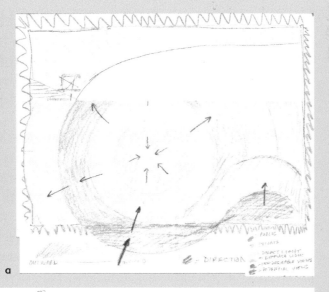

a

b

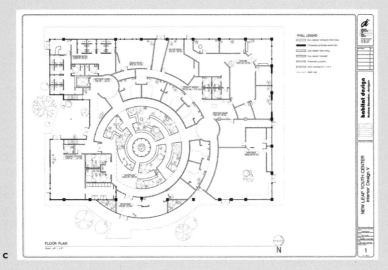

c

Figure 12.21 Interior design student Andrew Hunsaker began to impose the program onto the building shell by analyzing the qualities of the natural light and views afforded by the existing site (12.21a). In 12.21b, Andrew's resulting block diagram placed the sanctuary in the center of the centralized circulation, a diagram that emerged naturally from the analytical functional diagram. In 12.21c, the schematic floor plan drawn in CAD shows all of the circulation and program areas. The plan has benefited from the analysis and synthesis of the series of diagrams. Courtesy Andrew Hunsaker.

Conclusion

Not all projects require you to use all of the diagram types. The various diagrams covered in this chapter can serve as a menu from which to choose when you're considering the type of project and the depth of study during schematics.

Of course, the schematic phase in interior design includes many other elements—preliminary color scheme, materials direction, lighting ideas, suggestions for furnishings, and fixtures and equipment, to name a few. Each of these areas requires considerable research with regard to function, sustainable features, durability, historic aspects, etc. This chapter has focused on the translation of data into a schematic space plan rather than attempting to touch on all of the kinds of research that would occur in this phase. For a complex solution to be fully realized, research must occur at all steps. And while part of research is data collection, the other part of research is analysis: examining the data. Of course, the final part of research is to reach some sort of conclusion.

In the case of schematics, the conclusion is a design solution that visually, both in two dimensions and in three dimensions, represents the incorporation of data. Further data collection will occur when the designer presents her schemes to the client at the end of this phase. In an academic environment, your schematic designs are presented to your instructor, fellow students, or guest critics. Feedback from these individuals on your multiple design schemes is critical to helping you determine the final solution to take through to completion. In fact, a great way to look at the in-class critique is simply as another data collection method!

References

Ballast, D. K. (2007). *Interior design manual: A guide to the NCIDQ exam* (4th ed.). Belmont, CA: Professional.

Bangalore, N. B., & Suprajarama, R. (2006). *Vastu and interiors—The living room.* Retrieved May 16, 2009, from http://www.boloji.com/vastu/v14.htm

Coates, G. J. (1997). *Erik Asmussen, architect.* Stockholm: Byggforlaget.

Hall, E. T. (1966). *The hidden dimension.* New York: Anchor Books/Doubleday.

Karlen, M., Ruggeri, K., & Hahn, P. (2004). *Space planning basics.* New York: Wiley.

Kelley, D. (Producer). (2001, October 3). *The process of design* [video]. Entrepreneurship Corner. Palo Alto, CA: Stanford University. Retrieved May 16, 2009, from http://edcorner.stanford.edu/authorMaterialInfo.html?mid=683&author=25

Kelley, T., & Littman, J. (2001). *The art of innovation: Lessons in creativity from IDEO, America's leading design firm.* New York: Doubleday.

Koberg, D., & Bagnall, J. (1976). *The all new universal traveler: A soft systems guide to creativity, problem-solving and the process of reaching goals.* Los Altos, CA: William Kaufmann.

Koppel, T. (editor). (1999, July 13). Deep Dive [television series episode]. In James Goldston (executive producer), *ABC News: Nightline*. New York: American Broadcasting Corporation.

Nathan, V. (2002). Vastu purusha mandala. In K. Williams and J. Francisco Rodrigues (editors), *Nexus IV: Architecture and mathematics* (pp. 151–63). Fucecchio (Florence): Kim Williams Books. Retrieved May 16, 2009, from http://www.nexusjournal.com/conferences/N2002-Nathan.html

Phillips, A. (2006, January 1). Lines of inquiry. *The Architectural Review*. EMAP Architecture. Farmington Hills, MI: The Gale Group.

Rengel, R. (2007). *Shaping interior space*. New York: Fairchild Books.

Rossbach, S. (2000). *Interior design with Feng Shui*. Foreword by Lin Yun. New York: Penguin.

13 Design Development

When you complete this chapter you should be able to do the following:

- Fully articulate a three-dimensional interior design solution that responds to programmatic criteria.
- Gather and incorporate information about applicable codes.
- Gather and incorporate information about the Americans with Disabilities Act, the Architectural Barriers Act, and the Principles of Universal Design.
- Consider efficiency in all building systems: mechanical, electrical, heating, ventilation, air conditioning, plumbing.
- Gather and incorporate information about furniture, fixtures, and equipment.
- Gather and incorporate information about color and materials.
- Review the purpose and potential of drawings for the design development.
- Consider graphic design principles when storyboarding the final presentation.
- Be inspired to exceed expectations and take risks.

KEY TERMS

Commercial facilities
Common path of travel
Corridors
Dead-end corridor
Design intent
Exit
Exit access
Exit discharge
FF&E
Fuel load
Graphic resolution
Gross
Half-diagonal rule
Heuristic
Historic
Jurisdiction
Means of egress
Mixed use
Net
Occupancy classification

Occupant load
Occupant load factor
Orthographic
Pattern
Phenomenology
Public accommodation
Public way
Risk factors
Scoping provision
Selection
Situation
Special use
Specification
Storyboarding
Technical provision
Thumbnail
Travel distance
Universal Design
Variance

The Design Development Phase

Congratulations! Entering the design development phase means, first, that you have made a selection from among the many ideas you generated during schematics and, next, that you have embarked on the development of a single scheme. (See Figure 13.1.) The job before you is to continue to make design decisions that support your design concept as well as the programmatic criteria. The outcome of this phase will be to communicate to the client and the general public all of the elements that go into your design. If this is your thesis project, your goal is also to highlight and emphasize the *innovation* that exists in your project. The idea that your project adds to the existing body of knowledge of interior design is essential in a thesis project. Perhaps your project takes existing objects or spaces and uses them in a new way. Or perhaps you have detailed a piece of furniture that has never existed before. Whatever the innovative elements or principles in your project, they will be strongest and most successful if they emerge from the research that you have done.

Many excellent books have been written on the subject of innovation— creativity—in the design process. A few recommended texts are *The Artist's Way* by Julia Cameron, *Conceptual Blockbusting: A Guide to Better Ideas* by James Adams, and *The Art of Innovation* by Tom Kelley.

Figure 13.1 This diagram shows where the design development phase falls within the design process.

As this book has tried to show, to fully develop a single idea is not a linear process, and it requires a concentrated effort and long hours. The amount of information that you will need during just the design development phase is staggering. Plus, the information is always changing. There are always new materials, as well as new studies that render old truths obsolete. Codes are constantly being modified in response to disasters and in response to increasing knowledge about the needs of the public. As a designer in this world of information, you are required to keep abreast of changes to the codes, introduction of new materials, breakthroughs in the field of environmental psychology, and development of new technologies.

The purpose of the design development phase has these closely related parts:

- To communicate, to the best of your ability, the feeling of the interior space;
- To indicate all of the material, colors, and textures—and all of the furnishings, fixtures, lighting, and architectural elements—that make up your solution; and, ultimately,
- To get the client to approve your design and allow you to proceed to the next phase: construction documents.

In a professional environment, design development would be used for preliminary pricing (or to procure a "soft bid" from a contractor). For the client to sign off on the design development drawings indicates that the designer can proceed to construction documents: detailed, dimensioned, scaled drawings with notations and specifications that communicate to the contractor how the project is to be constructed, the precise location and size of each element, and the exact material and color to be purchased and installed.

During design development, it is essential that you clearly indicate the design intentions, the major goals of the project, and the design details—without getting too caught up in construction details. As Ballast explains it, "the **design intent** is the approach the designer and owner decide to take to satisfy the program requirements and specific need arising from these requirements" (2007, p. 242). He goes on to say that it "includes the overall appearance . . . balanced against practical considerations such as codes, cost and material limitations, the design intent is the basic starting point for developing and reviewing a detail" (p. 242). The emphasis on design intent during design

In a creative endeavor, people sometimes experience "flow." Athletes have described flow as being "in the zone," a state in which time almost ceases to exist—a kind of timeless moment or feeling of the expansion of "now" in which creative energy pours out and great things are accomplished. Richard Powell (2004) identifies three conditions that you need in order to experience "flow":

- You must be clear about your goals.
- There must be some sort of direct sensory feedback. This is essential in any visual art.
- Your "personal skills are engaged in overcoming a manageable challenge (since fear and anxiety prevent flow)."

We hope that as you read this chapter, you will discover for yourself the information you need in order to complete the design development phase so that you can set yourself up to experience flow as you pursue the development of your project.

development makes sure that the details contribute to the design concept as well as "resolve problems of connection or transition" (p. 242).

There is an important distinction between material *selection* and *specification*. Material **selection** is a recommendation you make in order to determine whether the client will accept the general idea of a material, such as a dark-stained hardwood or red linoleum. This is one step before **specification**, which "describes the quality of material and their construction or installation, information that cannot be communicated graphically" (McGowan, 2006, p. 32). In the design development phase, you are usually *selecting* the material. Material selection involves indicating the material on the design development floor plan, presenting the elevations, and showing everything in perspective, as well as providing samples (loose or mounted on a board) of the actual materials to elicit the client's approval. It is in the next phase—construction documents—that you would include written specifications.

One major goal of the design development phase is to make sure the design is viable, constructible, and code-compliant and that it protects the health, safety, and welfare of the public, supports the functions intended for the space, and achieves the programmatic requirements—all of this as well as fulfilling the conceptual and aesthetic goals.

In the schematic phase, you may have indicated the need for natural light. In design development, it is time to choose the method for introducing natural light to the space. Will it be through windows, through skylights, or via some other innovative design solution? Will the panels be opaque, translucent, or transparent? Will they be located below, above, or at eye level? What shape and size will they be? Will they be fixed or operable? What material will they be constructed of? How will the occupants control the amount of natural light? It is during this phase that all of these decisions are made, about all of the elements involved in the three-dimensional interior design solution.

ACTIVITY 13.1 Identifying "Patterns" in Interior Design

(From Professor Roberto Rengel, University of Wisconsin)

Purpose: **To help you develop trust in your own insights and intuitions as a designer.**

This Activity aims to help you develop your ability to look at the built environment (using *phenomenology*), understand design *situations*, and arrive at corresponding design criteria through the use of *heuristics*. It will help you expand your mental "design library" and develop your ability to understand and solve design problems both in general and within specific conditions.

First, some concepts to be grasped:

- **Phenomenology** is concerned with the total environment as lived experience. Phenomenological inquiry is subjective and introspective by nature. It relies on the personal interpretations of the "consciousness" subjected to the particular environment under study. The approach is intuitive, requiring non-intellectual receptivity of all the senses. It strives to get at the subjective, often unconscious, and personal nature of the way reality is experienced.
- A **heuristic** is "any principle, procedure, or other device that contributes to reduction in the search for a satisfactory solution" (Newell, Shaw, & Simon, 1967). (Be watching for examples of this in Chapter 14.)
- In addition to its ordinary meaning, the term *situation* is used to describe an inquiry based on Merleau-Ponty's idea of *situation*. A **situation** "occurs when an individual becomes totally absorbed in something, relates it to himself, and begins to understand it" (Mallin, 1980).
- The **pattern** to be identified is derived from Christopher Alexander's "Pattern Language." It uses a combination of verbal descriptions and images to "suggest a relationship between aspects of the environment and how people experience or react to them" (Kaplan, Kaplan, & Ryan, 1999, p. 3). These relationships form "the basis for recommendations or possible solutions to recurring situations" (Kaplan et al., p. 3). As

Alexander explains, "Each pattern describes a problem that occurs over and over again in the environment, and then describes the core of the solution to that problem, in such a way that you can use this solution a million times over, without ever doing it the same way twice" (Alexander, 1977, p. x).

Using *phenomenology* as a framework for the personal meaning associated with the built environment, and using *patterns* (from Alexander's Pattern Language) as a specific way to represent and share some of its meaningful qualities, complete the following steps:

1. Choose and then examine an aspect of the built environment.
2. Try to seize the reality of the experience as you, a thoughtful designer and user of the space, experience it.
3. Keep detailed notes. Draw sketches and diagrams as applicable.
4. Try to notice special qualities about the built environment, including, but not limited to, the way it embraces and shelters, the way it facilitates certain actions or behaviors, and the way it inspires, delights, or becomes meaningful in people's lives.
5. The focus of your patterns can be on many aspects of design, such as:
   - *Kinds of spaces,* such as reception areas, corridors, and classrooms
   - Special *qualities or virtues,* such as richness, clarity, and expressiveness
   - *Affordances,* or things the spaces facilitate, such as the ability to see beyond, the discovery of a nice view, or the ability to sit informally on a ledge having comfortable proportions
   - Specific *building elements,* such as stairs and benches
   - Aspects related to *design elements and principles,* such as the use of color, texture, rhythm, and focal points
   - Aspects related to *specific materials,* such as wood floors, glass, and metals
   - Anything else that seems relevant and important
6. Address all aspects of the situation and pattern in the following format:

Compelling Title:
Compelling Photo:
Summary of Situation:
Context:
Problem:
Possible Solution(s):

Therefore:
Summary of Pattern:
Additional Photos or Sketches to support summary:

Gathering Spaces

Many buildings do not offer areas for heightened activity and gathering. There is a need in academic buildings for spontaneous meetings between students and faculty. It fosters a shared sense of community and belonging.

<u>Context</u>: An academic building that is accessible by people.

<u>Problem</u>: People need a place to congregate, sit, eat, socialize or relax. Many academic buildings do not supply ample room to create this type of environment. For this reason, classrooms, labs, hallways and entryways become make-shift gathering places for faculty, students and visitors. Most of the time, these spaces do not offer the advantages present in spaces designed specifically for gathering and socialization.

In smaller settings, like classrooms and hallways, crowding may become an issue. When one's personal space is invaded, they tend to withdraw from activities and social situations. People tend to associate feelings with environments. Thus, if one feels uncomfortable within a space they will tend to dislike the environment. When a space is perceived as unpleasant, it is usually avoided as much as possible.

<u>Solution</u>: Room size and open floor plan design are important qualities in ensuring a pleasant environmental experience. Ceiling, wall color, lighting, windows and doors should all be considered. Raising the ceiling height, painting the walls a light and bright color and using lighting effects will make the room seem larger. Windows will offer novelty and visual distraction. They also extend space into the exterior environment, making the walls less constrictive.

Doors leading into and out of gathering spaces control flow of traffic. Proper gathering spaces should allow users to move freely in and out of the space. Therefore, pathways and doorways should be wide to foster fluid movement.

In carefully designed gathering spaces, one ought to be able to sit, work and socialize. Suitable seating areas are necessary to foster a sense of control when interacting with a space. Occupying a chair and/or table allows users to claim the area, at least temporarily, as their own. Providing chairs and tables that are movable is pivotal so users can change, alter or manipulate the area depending on the desired task(s).

Seating is important when considering preferred environmental experiences. Providing seating around edges and walls generate a feeling of safety and security. When a person's back is protected, they feel more secure within the environment. This also leaves front and side views into the environment where the user can choose to interact with the environment or sit back and "watch the show unfold".

As a rule, people prefer spaces that offer novelty, mystery and variation. There needs to be a reason for users to want to be in the environment. Offering something that is not available anywhere else in the building (or on campus) can create an interest to be in the space. Food, art, entertainment and technology can all bring people into environments. Novelty will also attract new visitors into the building that may have never had a reason to be in the building before.

Therefore:

Provide places large enough for people to socialize and gather without feeling crowded. Avoid narrow pathways and doorways. Produce opportunity for temporary ownership and semi-private activities. Place seating around edges and walls. Offer novelty, mystery and variation.

Mental Vacations

When people are in a place for any length of time they need to be able to refresh themselves by looking at a world different from the one they are in.

<u>Context</u>: All buildings, particularly those that house people for extended periods of time. Academic institutions, hospitals, and office buildings fall under this category.

<u>Problem</u>: Without healthy distractions, people become bored, restless, and unproductive. Attention span is the amount of time a person can concentrate on a single activity. The ability to focus one's mental or other efforts on an object is generally considered to be of prime importance to the achievement of goals. Most individuals' attention spans are 20-50 minutes in length.

Mental fatigue is the decline in the capacity to focus attention and concentrate, gradually requiring more effort. It affects cognition, actions, mood, and sociability. A person may become impatient, make errors, and show increased irritability and frustration.

To avoid getting to the point of mental fatigue and portraying this type of behavior, a person should take short breaks in order to refresh his/her attention span.

<u>Solution</u>: People should look up and rest their eyes and minds by concentrating on something farther away than what they are immediately working or focusing their attention on.

Restorative environments are settings that allow people to feel a sense of being away (most often conceptually through daydreaming), permit one to become immersed in it, fascinate, by means of directing involuntary attention toward something with innately interesting characteristics, and are compatible with the person's inclinations, purposes, and abilities. It must also be supportive through information as well as physiologically and socially.

Places like these offer relief from daily concerns, and permit rest and recovery of directed attention. Examples of things that could be included in these spaces are: people, architectural detailing, artwork such as sculptures and paintings, water features, and windows and plants.

Nature actually has benefits beyond simply providing a visual escape. Plants humanize the scale of large spaces, soften edges of hard surfaces, add complexity through color and texture, elicit relaxation, increase indoor air quality, produce positive emotional states, and improve health in general.

Therefore:

Make healthy distractions available for people to rest their directed attention upon. Artwork and plants are examples of items that should be incorporated.

Figure 13.2a (above left) Students from the University of Wisconsin identified "gathering spaces" as a pattern while completing this exercise.

Figure 13.2b (above right) A "mental vacation" is a pattern that this student identified.

Codes Research for Interior Design

The discussion about codes in this book is merely a reminder that you need to apply what you have learned in a previous or concurrent codes class. There are many excellent books that offer detailed information about the history of codes; various technical aspects, including dimensioned clearances; and other guidelines that you will need in order to complete your project. We refer you to the many books written on the subject, especially *The Codes Guidebook for Interiors* by Harmon and Kennon, and also urge you to look beyond the textbooks to the Web sites and libraries that would house the actual code itself. Often these are hard to assemble, as you may have to go to many different sources, so it is strongly recommended that you seek professional advice from an architect, or another interior designer, who is familiar with your jurisdiction and project type. For a firsthand look at codes, go to the planning or building department in the project's jurisdiction to access their records department and speak with a codes official.

The overview of codes in this chapter emphasizes the importance of further research during the design development phase to ensure that your project meets current codes. To put the issue of codes in perspective, it has been said that designing a building to code represents "the worst building you are allowed to get away with legally." It is our job as designers to understand the historical reasons behind the codes and to recognize what codes are: arbitrary minimums and maximums that have come to govern what we consider "safe." Our building codes represent a consensus, an agreement by experts, about our current hopes and fears regarding public safety and liability. It is an *ever-changing* body of knowledge that is altered by unexpected, natural, and man-made disasters and tragedies, such as hurricanes or bombs, or by changes in attitudes toward energy efficiency, land use, and population density.

Zoning

Your first task may be to find out what **jurisdiction** your project falls into. Each project must follow the codes that regulate *the area the project occupies*—codes that have been adopted by the local ordinances—as well as the overlapping series of other "zones" the project happens to find itself in. (See Figure 13.3.) There are federal, state, and local (such as county, city, or town) building regulations, areas designated as historic districts or flood plains, as well as Homeowners Associations (HOAs) or Business Improvement Districts (BIDs) that have adopted CC&Rs (covenants, conditions, and restrictions), which may regulate exterior aesthetics, landscaping, water use, parking, and many other daily activities and amenities that will impact your design.

Figure 13.3 This diagram illustrates that each site is located within a network of overlapping zones and jurisdictions. Each site is unique, and you, as the designer, must seek out the resources to determine which codes and restrictions apply to your site.

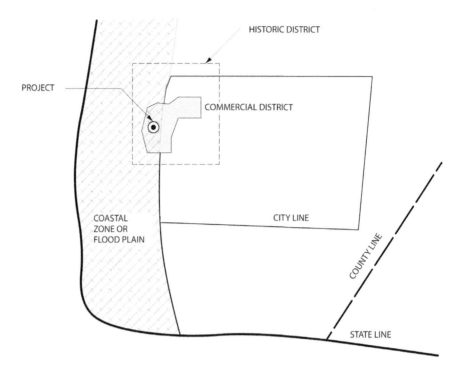

For projects that impact the public or that vary from what is currently accepted in the area (called a **variance**), there may be community board reviews or public hearings prior to a project being allowed. A designer must be aware of what is allowed in the jurisdiction, prior to the beginning of design. In the professional environment, a consult with a codes expert for that area is essential before the designer signs any agreements with a client or agrees to perform any work. A beautiful design for a restaurant will not be worth very much to a client if restaurants are not permitted in that location!

Use/Occupancy Classification

According to *The Codes Guidebook for Interiors*, the first task in determining how codes should be applied to the interior of the project is to assign **occupancy classifications** to the project as a whole as well as to the individual rooms and areas. The International Building Code (IBC) currently categorizes occupancy on the basis of the following general categories:

A	Assembly
B	Business
E	Educational
F	Factory
H	Hazardous
I	Institutional

M   Mercantile
R   Residential
S   Storage
U   Utility

There are also subcategories within each of these general categories. For the specific definition of each of these categories and in-depth discussion, refer to the International Building Code (IBC) or *The Codes Guidebook for Interiors*.

Table 13.1 helps show how codes should be applied to the interior of a project.

Risk factors are the hazardous features or situations associated with a particular use (Harmon & Kennon, 2008). "Risk factors consider the typical characteristics of both the activity that will occur in the space and the occu-

Table 13.1 Incorporating Codes into the Design Process

Code Area of Concern	What Should You Do?
Occupancy/Use	Define use or occupancy classification of project.
	Calculate the area of each space.
	Assign a function or an occupancy classification to each space.
	Find out the occupant load factor (minimum number of square feet per occupant) for each space.
	Calculate the occupant load (number of people) allowed by code for each space.
Fire and Life Safety Means of Egress	Determine the location and fire rating of fire-rated walls and partitions.
	Determine travel distances.
	Determine the number of exits from each space.
	Calculate the exit width from each space.
	Determine placement of exits (minimum distance apart).
	Determine door swing direction of exits (in direction of travel).
	Avoid dead-end corridors.
	Accommodate worst-case scenarios.
	Consider exit discharge and access to public way.
	Determine flammability ratings required for finishes/FF&E in each area.
Other . . .	Calculate the number of plumbing fixtures required.
	Determine if any areas are in a category that has additional code requirements or guidelines (for example, a commercial kitchen, a public swimming pool, a tattoo parlor, or a kennel).
	Determine if the project's jurisdiction warrants compliance with further restrictions or guidelines (for example, HOAs, historic districts, or coastal regions).

pants using the space" (Harmon & Kennon, p. 43). The strictness of the codes for each classification is directly related to the danger posed by these factors.

What makes a theater (Assembly) more dangerous than an office (Business)? First, the sheer *number of people* concentrated into one space is dangerous. If there were a fire, there would be a high degree of crowding and panic as large numbers of people funnel through the exit doors. Second is *spatial characteristics,* such as low light levels (difficulty seeing), high sound levels (occupants may not hear the fire alarm), and fixed seating (forcing evacuation through tight aisles). Third, there is a good chance that visitors are unfamiliar with the space. This may be the first time someone has been to this particular theater, and the person may not know where the exits are located. The final risk factor would be the **fuel load**, or the contents of the room that would contribute to the spread of fire—for example, the upholstered walls and seating and the hanging drapery.

The occupancy classification "Institutional" comprises subclassifications like Supervised Personal Care (Nursing Homes), Health Care (Hospitals), Restrained (Prisons), and Day Care Facilities. Question: What do these occupancies have in common? A better question is what do the *occupants* of these spaces have in common? Answer: They all need assistance getting out of a burning building. Prisoners need to be let out, while hospital patients, the elderly, and young children may need to be carried out.

The code writer originally used risk factors when determining what the minimum safety features would be for each category. And codes officials use risk factors when determining the appropriate classification of a space. Interior designers also must evaluate the risk factors of each space to determine how they will classify the room in order to determine what codes to follow. So the first step in researching codes for a new project is to determine occupancy classification(s). To accurately designate occupancy classification, consider the type of activity occurring, the types of objects or finishes in the space, and the number of occupants who could be in the space. If you are unsure, "it is always a good idea to have a code official confirm your choice of occupancy" (Harmon & Kennon, 2008, p. 45).

Each occupancy classification has a number of square feet required by code for each occupant; this is called an **occupant load factor** (OLF). In the IBC, the list of OLFs is found in "Table 1004.1.1 Maximum Floor Area Allowances Per Occupant." This information is transcribed in Table 13.2 (page 396). Keep in mind that the information in this table may not apply to your project's jurisdiction, and it is subject to change over time. It is important that you verify which codes are applicable to your particular project.

To determine how many people can safely occupy a space, divide the total square feet by the occupant load factor. This determines the **occupant load** (OL). Written as an equation, it looks like this: Total SF/OLF = OL. If a space has multiple uses, such as a multipurpose room, the occupant load for that space is determined by the use that indicates the largest concentration of people, often referred to as the *worst-case scenario*.

"The occupant load is basically the number of people that is assumed to safely occupy a space or building" (Harmon & Kennon, 2008, p. 43). Why is it important to determine the occupant load of a space? The occupant load is the *basis for many subsequent design features that are required*. The occupant load is the number that helps determine total required number of exits, total exit width, and number of plumbing fixtures (toilets, lavatories, showers, and drinking fountains).

As you can see in Table 13.2, occupant load factors are either **gross** or **net**. Gross square footage encompasses all the area within the walls, including shafts, closets, equipment, and built-ins. As noted in Table 13.2, a commercial kitchen has an occupant load factor (OLF) of 200 square feet *gross*. It makes sense that the cabinetry, appliances, and space for venting would be included in calculation of the square footage, because those items are essential to the function of the kitchen. In fact, it wouldn't be a kitchen without those things. On the other hand, a classroom has an OLF of 20 square feet *net*. Net square footage allows you to deduct those items and base your square footage on the space that a person can move around in. See Figure 13.4 for an example of the two types of square footage.

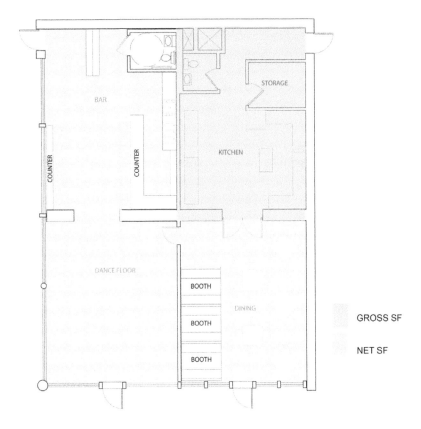

Figure 13.4 This figure shows the difference between gross square footage and net square footage. Gross square footage includes all ancillary spaces and equipment, as in the example of the kitchen on the right. Net square footage is the amount of space after you have subtracted out all of the ancillary spaces and equipment, as in the bar and dining area.

Table 13.2 Maximum Floor Area Allowances per Occupant (Occupant Load Factors)

Function of Space	Floor Area in Sq. Ft. per Occupant
Accessory Storage	300 gross
Agricultural Building	300 gross
Aircraft Terminal	500 gross
Airport Terminal	
Baggage Claim	20 gross
Baggage Handling	300 gross
Concourse	100 gross
Waiting Areas	15 gross
Assembly	
Gaming Floors (keno, slots, etc.)	11 gross
Assembly with fixed seats	Not Applicable (Number of fixed seats determines occupant load)
Assembly without fixed seats	
Standing Only	5 net
Concentrated (chairs only)	7 net
Unconcentrated (tables and chairs)	15 net
Bowling Centers	7 net
Business Areas	100 gross
Courtrooms (other than fixed seating areas)	40 net
Day Care	35 net
Dormitories	50 gross
Educational	
Classroom area	20 net
Vocational Classrooms (Wood shop, teaching kitchen, sewing, computer labs, etc.)	50 net

Mixed Use

In a mixed occupancy, two or more occupancies can occur in the same building. Having more than one occupancy usually requires separation by fire-rated walls or by partitions. Alternatively, you can have a non-separated **mixed use**, which would follow the stricter of the two classifications. Most of

Function of Space	Floor Area in Sq. Ft. per Occupant
Exercise Room and Locker Rooms	50 gross
Fabrication and Manufacturing Areas (Hazardous)	200 gross
Industrial Areas	100 gross
Institutional Areas (Health care)	
Inpatient Treatment (surgery, etc.)	240 gross
Outpatient Areas	100 gross
Sleeping Areas	120 gross
Kitchens, Commercial	200 gross
Library	
Reading Rooms	50 net
Stack Area	100 gross
Mercantile (Retail)	
Grade Floor and Basement Areas	30 gross
Areas on Other Floors	60 gross
Storage, Stock, Shipping Areas	300 gross
Parking Garages	200 gross
Residential	200 gross
Skating Rinks, Swimming Pools	
Rink and Pool	50 gross
Decks	15 gross
Stages and Platforms	15 net
Warehouses	500 gross

Source: Adapted from California Building Code. (2007). Title 24, pt. 2.

the commercial or institutional projects that you will be working on in school will be mixed use. A hotel may have a common lobby (Assembly), office areas (Business), and guest accommodations (Residential). Even a high school usually has an auditorium (Assembly), classrooms (Educational), and faculty offices (Business).

Means of Egress

There are three parts of a **means of egress** system in a building: exit access, exit, and exit discharge.

1. The **exit access** is anywhere in the building that is used for walking to an exit.
2. The **exit** is the fire-rated element that separates the exit access from the exit discharge. This is most often a door, but it can also be a fire-rated enclosure such as an exit stair or a horizontal exit passage.
3. The **exit discharge** is the area either inside the building or outside the building that is between the exit and the public way. The **public way** is an area open to the sky, usually a street or alley, that is a minimum of 10 feet wide to allow for rescue vehicles to enter it.

The two factors that most typically determine whether a room or area must have at least two exits are occupant load and **travel distance**. Codes govern how long a distance is allowed before an exit is reached. The use of sprinkler systems greatly increases the permitted distance. Consult local codes for travel distance. A **dead-end corridor** is one in which someone would have to turn around and backtrack to reach an exit. If a person can keep walking continuously until reaching an exit, the corridor is not a dead end. The IBC usually limits the length of a dead end corridor to 20 feet.

Building codes and accessibility standards require that all means-of-egress doorways provide a minimum clearance of 32 inches, which is accomplished using a 36-inch-wide door. When two or more exits are required, at least two of the exits must be a minimum distance apart, which is at least one-half the longest diagonal distance within the building or space. This is referred to as the **half-diagonal rule**.

Accessibility

As interior designers, we must be aware of the Americans with Disabilities Act (ADA), which was signed into law in 1990. (It is sometimes grouped with its forerunner, the Architectural Barriers Act [ABA] of 1968.) To protect the rights of individuals with disabilities, the ADA provides for equal accommodation and access to places of employment, public services, and businesses. The checklist of questions in Table 13.3 has been prepared to assist you in providing a plan that is accessible. Interior designers should be aware that the Department of Justice (DOJ) and the Department of Transportation (DOT) are responsible for enforcing Titles II and III of the ADA. Business owners are urged to comply to limit their *liability* (the chance that they will be sued for creating a space that is not accessible). This ADA checklist is designed to be used in full or in part, depending on the facility.

Must all interior spaces comply with ADA–ABA Accessibility Guidelines (http://www.access-board.gov/ada-aba/)? Usually, any new construction would trigger the requirement for compliance with the guidelines. However, all facilities can be divided into two types:

- Places of **Public Accommodation**
- **Commercial Facilities**

Places of public accommodation are businesses and facilities, such as a laundromat or a doctor's office, that the public enters as a regular course of business. As you may expect, these businesses need to be accessible. Commercial facilities—offices or factories that the public does not access—do not necessarily have to comply. However, owners should be made aware that if an employee is physically impaired, the office may need to accommodate that person's needs.

Table 13.3 Reviewing Your Design for ADA Compliance

ADA Area of Concern	Does your design comply?
Entrance/ Route of Travel	Is there a route of travel that does not require stairs?
	Is the route of travel stable, firm, and slip-resistant?
	Is the width of the route the minimum distance required?
	Can all of the object protruding into the circulation be detected by a person with a visual disability and a cane?
	If there is a level change in the floor, is it accomplished using an accessible sloping ramp?
	Are the doors, hinges, and hardware compliant?
	Are the heights of all fixtures and amenities compliant?
Rooms and Spaces	Are all the aisles and pathways to goods and services accessible?
	Have you shown the turning radius or area of a stationary wheelchair where appropriate?
	Are the finish materials compliant?
	Are the restroom layouts and fixture heights accessible?
	Are the spaces for wheelchair seating distributed throughout?
	Do counters and tables allow for height and knee clearances?
Way-finding and Signage	Are there visual and audio alarms for emergency egress? Are there illuminated exit signs where appropriate?
	Are signs compliant and mounted appropriately?
Other . . .	Have you considered Universal Design principles that go above and beyond ADA guidelines to accommodate the widest variety of people?

Source: Adapted from ADA–ABA Accessibility Guidelines, retrieved from http://www.access-board.gov/ada-aba/final.cfm

Whom would you consult in order to determine whether your project needs to comply with ADA? In the professional environment, you must consult with the United States Access Board (http://www.access-board.gov) and your client at the onset of a project. "If the alterations needed to meet the ADA requirements are not *readily achievable* both structurally and financially, the law allows for exceptions when the alteration could be considered an *undue burden*" (Harmon & Kennon, 2008, p. 425). Since your project is a school project, the Council of Interior Design Accreditation expects that you will produce a project that respects all humans and meets the minimum requirements set forth in the ADA.

Designated historic buildings, some federal buildings, and some religious institutions may be exempt from complying with the ADA–ABA Accessibility Guidelines. For a building to be considered **historic**, it must be "listed (or eligible to be listed) in the National Register of Historic Places" (Harmon & Kennon, 2008, p. 450). Or it may be listed by a state or local historic preservation registry. Historical significance is based on physical aspects of its design, materials, form, style, or workmanship, or the building may have been associated with important events, activities, or persons. The National Register of Historic Places can be accessed on the Internet at http://www.cr.nps.gov/nr/listing.htm.

⊛ A C T I V I T Y 1 3 . 2 Wheelchair Experiential Exercise

Purpose: **To get firsthand knowledge of the difficulty of navigating a building using a wheelchair.**

In a wheelchair, assisted by your classmates, complete the tasks below:

1. Go out the exit through the student cafeteria and enter the building through the front entrance.
2. Go into the library and check out a book.
3. Open, pass through, and close any door.
4. Enter an accessible stall in a restroom and transfer yourself to the seat, return to the wheelchair, and wash and dry your hands.
5. Come back to class and record your experience by answering the following questions:

A. This experience was valuable to me because _____.
B. What I had expected was _____

C. Problems I encountered were _____.

D. The most surprising thing I learned was _____.

ACTIVITY 13.3 ADA and ABA Guidelines Treasure Hunt

Purpose: **To familiarize yourself with the ADA–ABA Accessibility Guidelines.**

Download the pdf version of the ADA–ABA Accessibility Guidelines from http://www.access-board.gov/ada-aba/final.cfm. (Please note that you *ARE NOT REQUIRED* to print this document—it is over 300 pages!) After reviewing the document, go out and find three examples of non-compliant construction. Document the conditions with at least *one photograph and one written paragraph* describing each instance of non-compliance or non-accessibility. An example of a **scoping provision** in the new ADA–ABA Accessibility Guidelines would be the minimum number of guest rooms in a hotel that would require a roll-in shower. An example of a **technical provision** in the new ADA–ABA Accessibility Guidelines would be dimensional. Bring a tape measure (D. Stuber, personal communication, April 30, 2009).

1. Identify or paraphrase the chapter/section number of the guideline that is being violated.
2. Include any diagram or "figure" that clarifies the intent of the guideline.
3. Provide a suggestion or a solution for how the problem could be remedied.
4. Format the findings in PowerPoint slides for presentation to the class. Include all of the above. The more interesting the subject matter, the better . . .

Special Use

Areas defined as **special use** are those that require additional requirements, inspections, permits, certification, or plan review by the Department of Environmental Health (DEH). This is usually required because the planned use affects the health and safety of the public on additional levels—because it is related to food or the human body. The additional regulations are intended to help prevent unsanitary conditions or any situation that may contribute to

UNIVERSAL DESIGN

The design of products and environments to be usable by all people, to the greatest extent possible, without the need for adaptation or specialized design.

The authors, a working group of architects, product designers, engineers, and environmental design researchers, collaborated to establish the following Principles of Universal Design to guide a wide range of design disciplines, including environments, products, and communications. These seven principles may be applied to evaluate existing designs, guide the design process, and educate both designers and consumers about the characteristics of more usable products and environments.

The Principles of Universal Design are presented here, in the following format: name of the principle, intended to be a concise and easily remembered statement of the key concept embodied in the principle; definition of the principle, a brief description of the principle's primary directive for design; and guidelines, a list of the key elements that should be present in a design which adheres to the principle. (Note: All guidelines may not be relevant to all designs.)

PRINCIPLE ONE: Equitable Use
The design is useful and marketable to people with diverse abilities.

Guidelines
1a. Provide the same means of use for all users: identical whenever possible; equivalent when not.
1b. Avoid segregating or stigmatizing any users.
1c. Provisions for privacy, security, and safety should be equally available to all users.
1d. Make the design appealing to all users.

PRINCIPLE TWO: Flexibility in Use
The design accommodates a wide range of individual preferences and abilities.

Guidelines
2a. Provide choice in methods of use.
2b. Accommodate right- or left-handed access and use.
2c. Facilitate the user's accuracy and precision.
2d. Provide adaptability to the user's pace.

PRINCIPLE THREE: Simple and Intuitive Use
Use of the design is easy to understand, regardless of the user's experience, knowledge, language skills, or current concentration level.

Guidelines

3a. Eliminate unnecessary complexity.

3b. Be consistent with user expectations and intuition.

3c. Accommodate a wide range of literacy and language skills.

3d. Arrange information consistent with its importance.

3e. Provide effective prompting and feedback during and after task completion.

PRINCIPLE FOUR: Perceptible Information

The design communicates necessary information effectively to the user, regardless of ambient conditions or the user's sensory abilities.

Guidelines

4a. Use different modes (pictorial, verbal, tactile) for redundant presentation of essential information.

4b. Provide adequate contrast between essential information and its surroundings.

4c. Maximize "legibility" of essential information.

4d. Differentiate elements in ways that can be described (i.e., make it easy to give instructions or directions).

4e. Provide compatibility with a variety of techniques or devices used by people with sensory limitations.

PRINCIPLE FIVE: Tolerance for Error

The design minimizes hazards and the adverse consequences of accidental or unintended actions.

Guidelines

5a. Arrange elements to minimize hazards and errors: most used elements, most accessible; hazardous elements eliminated, isolated, or shielded.

5b. Provide warnings of hazards and errors.

5c. Provide fail-safe features.

5d. Discourage unconscious action in tasks that require vigilance.

PRINCIPLE SIX: Low Physical Effort

The design can be used efficiently and comfortably and with a minimum of fatigue.

Guidelines

6a. Allow user to maintain a neutral body position.

6b. Use reasonable operating forces.

6c. Minimize repetitive actions.

6d. Minimize sustained physical effort.

PRINCIPLE SEVEN: Size and Space for Approach and Use

Appropriate size and space is provided for approach, reach, manipulation, and use regardless of user's body size, posture, or mobility.

Guidelines

7a. Provide a clear line of sight to important elements for any seated or standing user.

7b. Make reach to all components comfortable for any seated or standing user.

7c. Accommodate variations in hand and grip size.

7d. Provide adequate space for the use of assistive devices or personal assistance.

The Principles of Universal Design address only universally usable design, while the practice of design involves more than consideration for usability. Designers must also incorporate other considerations such as economic, engineering, cultural, gender, and environmental concerns in their design processes. These principles offer designers guidance to better integrate features that meet the needs of as many users as possible.

Version 2.0 - 4/1/97

Compiled by advocates of universal design, listed in alphabetical order: Bettye Rose Connell, Mike Jones, Ron Mace, Jim Mueller, Abir Mullick, Elaine Ostroff, Jon Sanford, Ed Steinfeld, Molly Story, and Gregg Vanderheiden

Major funding provided by: The National Institute on Disability and Rehabilitation Research, U.S. Department of Education

the spread of food- and body-related bacteria or disease. DEH rulings are the reason why restrooms in restaurants have signs reminding workers to wash their hands, why the flooring in restaurants has to have a sanitary cove base (for cleaning purposes), and why bars must have a three-compartment sink (one for high-temperature water, one for bleach, and one for rinsing). The following establishments or activities are considered special use:

- Restaurants and other retail food facilities
- Special event coordinators and vendors
- Mobile food facilities (vending machines, lunch trucks, and pushcarts)
- Multi-family dwellings (apartments, condominiums, hotels, bed and breakfasts, organized camps with kitchens, jails, and detention facilities)
- Public swimming pools and spas

- Bathhouses
- Hair and nail salons
- Massage establishments
- Tattoo parlors
- Pet shops
- Animal rescue facilities and kennels

There are additional requirements to be followed if you are designing facilities for children (for example, day care centers or nursery schools).

Asking the Experts

During the design development phase, it is important to interface with the appropriate experts in order to obtain information that will help you refine the design, put the walls in exactly the right place, paint the walls the best color, choose the best equipment, lay out the furniture in the most appropriate way, and so forth. You may want to consult a book on environmental psychology to familiarize yourself with social and personal distances when laying out a reception area or a private consultation room. You may need to talk to an audio engineer when laying out the media room in a residential project, so that you know exactly where to place the speakers to achieve the best sound quality. These examples are indicative of the kind of information you can get only from experts. Tables 13.4 and 13.5 list some sources of specialized information and the kinds of questions you may want to ask those sources.

Table 13.5 lists various professionals, specialists, and craftspeople and suggests the matters these experts might be able to assist you with, given their knowledge and experience. Refer to Chapter 6 for interview techniques.

The architect Gary Leivers (personal communication, July 22–23, 2008) has some additional questions that you may want to ask an architect:

- What are the schedule, budget, and program requirements?
- What is the relationship between structure and the organization of the internal spaces?
- What is the relationship between the exterior and the local vernacular?
- How are mechanical services integrated into the building?
- What is the approach to sustainability in the design of the building envelope and the building systems?
- How does the way-finding transition between inside and out?
- What kinds of graphics are being used on the exterior?
- How does climate affect the design?

You may also want to ask about the building's fire-resistive construction type and confirm the fire-resistance rating requirements between occupancies.

Table 13.4 Experts in Design and Related Fields

Professional Consultants	Design Specialists	Related Industries, Crafts, and Trades
Architect	Lighting Designer	Fine Artist
Structural Engineer	Kitchen and Bath Designer	Developers/Financiers
Mechanical Engineer	Historic Preservationist	Contractors/Builders
Civil Engineer	Furniture Designer	Subcontractors/Installers
Plumber	Textile Designer	Property Managers
Codes Expert or Official	Graphic Designer	Real Estate Agents
Electrical Engineer	Product Designer	Product Vendors/Manufacturer Representatives
Acoustical Engineer	Event Planner	Art Dealers
Landscape Architect		Landscaper/Gardener
LEED-Certified Consultant		
Specification Writer		
Project Manager/ Owners Representative		

Furniture, Fixtures, and Equipment

Furniture, Fixtures, and Equipment (**FF&E**) are the objects in a space that help assist with the function of the space. Architects (and builders) tend to differentiate (1) items that are installed to become part of the building from (2) items that are not permanently attached. The two tend to come from different budgets. To architects, "FF&E" stands for *Furniture, Furnishings, and Equipment*: freestanding elements that are purchased separately, under separate contract by the owner and/or purchasing agency. Fixtures such as toilets and lavatories would fall under the base building budget and would be purchased by the contractor for installation by the contractor.

As an interior designer, you might not make that distinction. The information you collect about the elements that go into the interior space, the "FF&E," could be defined as *Furniture, Fixtures, and Equipment*. Fixtures are part of the total package of what you select and, later, specify. It is important, though, to remember which budget they do come out of and who is respon-

Table 13.5 Questions to Ask Design Professionals

Professional Consultant	Questions you may want to ask . . .
Architect	What jurisdiction does the project fall in?
	How does the exterior affect the interior?
Structural Engineer	What is the structural system of the building shell?
	Would you help me identify load-bearing elements?
Mechanical Engineer	What kind of Heating Ventilation and Air Conditioning (HVAC) system do you recommend?
	How do the equipment, vents, and ducting or piping affect the interior space?
Civil Engineer	How do the soil conditions, landscape elements, and site's grade affect the building?
Plumber	Where are the supply risers and drains located?
	What are the limitations or restrictions regarding the type and placement of plumbing fixtures?
Codes Expert of Official	Do you agree with my choice of occupancy classification(s) for the building?
	Would you review my drawings for code compliance?
Electrical Engineer	Would you help me calculate electrical load, locate circuits and panels, and comply with electrical code?
Acoustical Engineer	Would you help me analyze the configuration of the auditorium for its acoustical quality?
	What materials would you recommend for sound attenuation or to reduce transmission from room to room?
Project Manager or Owner's Representative	What is the budget for the project?
	What are the owner's goals for the project?
	What is the project's schedule or timeline?
Other . . .	

sible for purchasing the item during the contract administration phase. Table 13.6 presents a list of FF&E experts and some of the issues they would be able to help you with.

In addition to talking to people and looking up information in books and magazines, go to showrooms and physically sit in the chairs that you will be selecting for your project! Chapter 14 discusses mock-up and usability testing if you are designing custom furniture or you want to see how a combination of elements works in a room.

Table 13.6 Questions to Ask FF&E Experts

Furnishings, Fixtures, and Equipment Experts	Questions you may want to ask . . .
Trade Organizations	What standards exist for this product? What additional agencies provide detailed information?
Construction Specifications Institute (CSI) Certified Specification Writers	What is the product's CSI Section number? Would you help me compare product's technical information?
Testing, Rating, and Regulatory Agencies (ASTM, ANSI, UL, etc.)	How does this product compare to similar ones? What is its flammability rating? What other standard tests are performed on this product?
Furniture Designer	Is my design buildable? All questions regarding materials, fabrication, cost, joinery, function, and aesthetics.
Furniture Manufacturer	How and where is this product manufactured? What are the recommended uses of this product? What are the recommended installation procedures?
Furniture or Fixture Vendor	What are the product benefits, limitation, warranties, and cost? What are the design possibilities of this product?
Specialty Product Designers (Kitchen & Bath, Cabinetry, Fireplaces, Window Treatment, etc.)	What are projected product trends? What problems, if any, do you see with my current design? What are the costs involved with this design?
Other Product Suppliers or Installers (Doors, Windows, Railings, Hardware, Appliances, etc.)	What is involved with the installation of this product? What problems, if any, have you encountered with this product? What has been your experience with this product?

Colors and Materials

You have already determined performance criteria for the materials in your program; then, during the schematic design phase, you have selected a preliminary material palette. Now it is time to refine your selections and educate yourself about the installation, maintenance, and sustainable aspects of the materials. Now would also be an excellent time to incorporate color theory in your color selections, and to realize how color and texture interact with each other to bring your design together.

Table 13.7 will give you an idea of some of the general sources for information related to colors and materials, and some of the questions you may want to ask those sources.

Table 13.7 Questions to Ask Experts in Materials and Related Fields

Material Expert	Questions you may want to ask . . .
Trade Organizations	What standards exist for this material? What additional agencies provide detailed information?
Construction Specifications Institute (CSI) Certified Specification Writers	What is the material's or product's CSI Section number? Would you help me compare this product's technical information with the technical information of other, similar products?
Testing, Rating, and Regulatory Agencies (ASTM, ANSI, UL, etc.)	How does this material compare to similar ones? What is its flammability rating? What other standard tests are performed on this material?
Sustainability Watchdogs	How "green" is this material in terms of its impact on the earth? Is this material renewable, recyclable, biodegradable?
Product Manufacturer	How and where is this material manufactured? What are the recommended uses of this product? What are the recommended installation procedures?
Product Vendor	Can I obtain a sample? What are the design possibilities of this product?
Installer, Painter, Upholsterer	How do you achieve this texture, color, or appearance? How much raw material (paint, fabric, etc.) must I order?

In addition to interviewing experts and researching materials on the Internet, nothing beats visiting the showrooms and retail stores that sell the materials. Do not be intimidated by showrooms, and do not think that salespeople will not necessarily offer to help a student. It is essential that you establish yourself as worthy of their attention and knowledge. You are a designer (even if you are still in school). In fact, all designers are constantly learning about new things.

Showroom etiquette requires that you identify yourself as a designer, usually with a business card or, perhaps, a school identification card. Sometimes, you have to register with the company in order to gain status as a designer. Clearly state your questions from the standpoint that you have knowledge about the purpose and use of the material but want clarification on maintenance, fade resistance, appropriateness for use in certain situations, or installation (such as how the color of grout will change the look of the tile, or how to minimize the appearance of seams in wallpaper). Recognize that the showroom personnel are in business to make a profit, and don't take up their time if you don't plan to buy anything. Offer to pay for the samples or, at least, to return them after your presentation. If the store doesn't give out samples, ask if they can recommend another showroom that does give out samples. A last resort is to take a photo, although most showrooms do not allow photography, since their design installations may be proprietary. Always seek permission before you take a photograph in any store or showroom.

Incorporating Color Theory

According to professional color consultant and collage artist Anja Schoenbeck (personal communication, October 15, 2008), there are three main areas of research that you will want to focus on during design development.

1. Understand how your color choices affect peoples' perception of the size of the room(s). The technical and theoretical aspects of color, such as adding white (to make a tint) or black (to produce a shade), or adjusting the intensity of the hue, will help you to create a palette to enhance the spatial characteristics. You should also thoroughly research such theoretical aspects as harmony, proportion, and contrast.
2. Understand the physics of light and the biological or physiological impact of color on the human eye, so that you can apply the color to produce the effect you desire. The appearance of color depends on the presence of natural light and the quality of artificial light.
3. Understand the symbolic meanings of color: the cultural perceptions associated with color that may affect your users emotionally. In Chinese culture, for example, the color white is associated with death or mourning while red is associated with success and marriage. Research psychological impact, both hidden and obvious, before you present a color palette.

"Interior designers must comprehend the bigger picture and understand that all aspects are inevitably linked. The thing about color is that a designer's personal preference may be completely irrelevant to the circumstance" (A. Schoenbeck, personal communication, October 15, 2008). Color choice must be complementary to architecture, materials, style, function, and concept. If the client suggests particular colors, analyze whether those color "wishes" are appropriate. Do they suit the structure, style, function, etc.?

> Going past the materials lab, I saw a 12" × 12" piece of carpet that was a hideous red/violet color. I said to myself, "How could anyone possibly use this on the floor?" I brought it with me to class to show the students how bilious this color was. I threw the carpet sample down in the middle of the classroom floor and we all looked. Well, it was beautiful. It was the right amount of color in the right location, a jewel tone in a

large field of gray. It was somehow transformed, and my perception was changed. It was then that I realized there is no such thing as a *bad* color. It all has to do with location, proportion, and context (A. Schoenbeck, personal communication, October 15, 2008).

At this point, you should have a complete understanding of the color perceptions of your user group. Have you done research on the visual perception of colors by target audience or end users? The elderly, children, and dogs all see color differently!

Representing and Communicating Your Design

In the design development phase, it is essential that you achieve a clear level of **graphic resolution** in your drawings. The layers of information that you add depend on what you are trying to communicate to the final jury: to your instructor, to your fellow classmates, to your acting client, or to the end users. See Figure 13.5 for an effective example. With the proper use of hierarchy of line weights; appropriate size of text; readable font; subtle use of color to indicate materials, circulation, or program; and an attention to

Figure 13.5 An elegant design development floor plan of a fertility clinic called "Pod." The plan clearly shows full-height walls, built-ins, and furniture layout. At 1/8"=1'-0" scale, subtle material indications allow the viewer to clearly read the plan's circulation and functional areas. Courtesy interior design student Andrette Bugarin

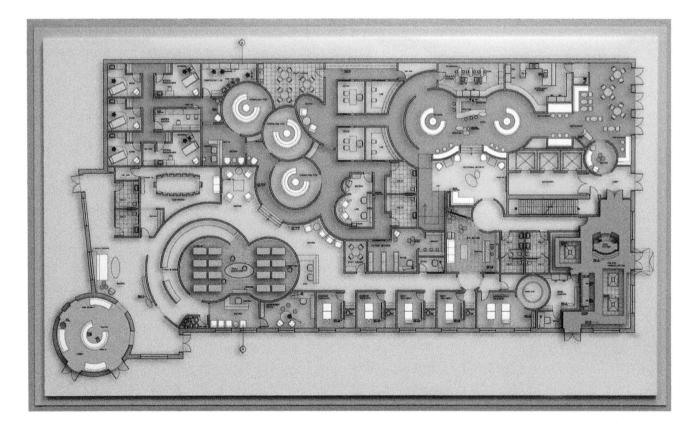

detail, the drawing can look "rich"—that is, containing and communicating a variety of information while being completely legible. Your final presentation boards and all of the components on them should be enticing to the viewer. Ultimately, when clients look at your drawings, you want them to say, "Yes! I want that!"

Conventional Drawings

> In a plan, common elements such as windows, doors, and columns, are represented as we never see them, and it requires a mind well acquainted with the gymnastics of conventional indication to understand them as windows, doors, and columns, instead of a jungle of abstract lines (Grillo, 1960, p. 194).

Grillo continues, "A plan is, in reality, a horizontal section" (1960, p. 194). It is cut four feet above the floor. But the plan represents more than just physical elements. A design development plan indicates the relationship of rooms to one another and the flow of one material or pattern into another, as well as how the rooms are broken up in concentrated areas of activity through furniture placement. "We can now understand that when we refer to a plan as a structure, it means not only its expression of purely physical construction, but [mostly] the equilibrium of the areas it defines, submitted to the many forces which control human living. We can, in the same manner, speak of the structure of a painting or of a piece of music. We can speak of a *strong* plan and a *weak* plan" (Grillo, p. 197). Because we walk around on a horizontal plane, the plan is the first place we look for circulation patterns.

The role of the reflected ceiling plan, building section, elevations, perspectives, and three-dimensional **orthographic** drawings is to express the design in conventional drawing techniques.

Unconventional Drawings

Using the computer to produce virtual models has led to less traditional drawings, such as plan perspectives (for example, a bird's-eye view). Computer software offers ease in locating the angle of the perfect isometric or axonometric view, so that we can highlight the most dynamic view before printing or plotting. The computer also allows a "surgical" precision, meaning we can cut away or remove a wall and rotate the camera view to exactly the angle needed to highlight important aspects of the design.

When it comes to presentation techniques, do your best to push the boundaries of conventional drawings. Produce composite images that cross the border between computer and hand-drawn to blur the boundary between man and machine. For an example, see Figure 13.6. Keep asking yourself, "Is there

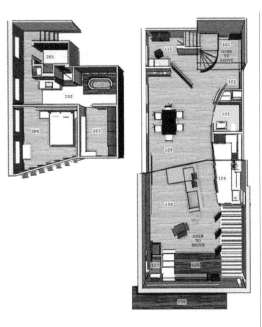

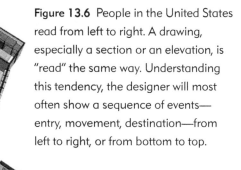

Figure 13.6 People in the United States read from left to right. A drawing, especially a section or an elevation, is "read" the same way. Understanding this tendency, the designer will most often show a sequence of events—entry, movement, destination—from left to right, or from bottom to top.

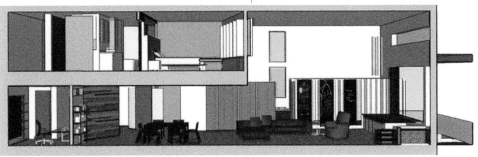

When two images are placed next to each other, it is human nature to compare them. Viewers go back and forth trying to see what is similar about the two images or how they are different. It is important to be clear about how the drawings are related to each other (if they are at all). What do you think is the relationship of the two spaces depicted in the two perspectives in Figure 13.7?

SANCTUARY PERSPECTIVE

THERAPY OFFICE PERSPECTIVE

Figure 13.7 The juxtaposition of these two perspectives allows the viewer to make an intellectual connection between the two. The drawing on the left represents a central atrium waiting area in a mental health clinic. The drawing on the right represents one of the private consultation rooms. The curved wall with the clerestory window links both drawings. On the left we see it from one side, and on the right we see it from the other side.

another way to represent this idea?" Consider using video. Entertain the idea of a full-scale mock-up or a drawing so large you feel like you could inhabit it.

Storyboarding

In the United States and other Western countries, in addition to reading from left to right, we tend to view the page from top to bottom. Contrary to this, however, is the architectural convention that floor plans be placed below reflected ceiling plans, and that first-floor plans be placed below mezzanine or second-floor plans. Architects read from bottom to top as the first-floor plan is usually placed below the second-floor plan, aligning the two floors via the vertical circulation (stairs, elevators).

When you are planning your final presentation, it is imperative to review and understand the fundamentals of graphic design. A good habit to get into is storyboarding your final presentation boards.

Thumbnails are small sketches that can literally be as small as your thumbnail, or as big as a couple of inches in width and/or height. Think of the kind of drawing that might be seen on a cocktail napkin. Thumbnails are intended to capture the basic ideas for page composition, like header placement, column structure, and text alignment, without allowing the temptation to focus on small details too early in the process. They can be quickly sketched, allowing rapid idea iteration. Don't like the one that just took 30 seconds to draw? Start another one right beside it. To keep them general, it's best to start with rather small sketches. Then slowly size them up as more details need to be worked out (Bowman, 2003).

How large should each drawing be? Which ones should be emphasized? **Storyboarding** helps you to determine hierarchy. The most important drawing could be the largest, or it could be strategically placed in the middle of the board. Storyboarding also helps you to arrange the drawings in the sequence in which you plan to address them in your verbal presentation.

Figure 13.8 was a tiny thumbnail drawing generated by a student, Nicole Rios, when she was asked to think about the series of boards for her final presentation. Her thesis project was the design of a nightclub and dance studio, so she was interested in conveying the sense of movement and rhythm. She began to explore the idea that the boards themselves would be oriented vertically to correspond to upright figures dancing, and that they could be cut to represent movement. Then, to unify the boards, she imagined that some drawings could act as connections and link the boards together. Notice too the use of white boxes and black boxes to represent a variation of night scenes and day scenes and how the placement further indicates the sense of undulation and balance. When she drew them, they reminded her of puzzle pieces—an excellent way of looking at an interior design presentation!

Interior design student Norman Reyes storyboards all of his design presentations. Figure 13.9a shows a series of sketches. The project was a firehouse conversion to an art gallery and loft. Notice how the size and color

Figure 13.8 A thumbnail sketch of an interior design student's four final presentation boards, as she seeks to convey the sense of movement and rhythm for her thesis project: a nightclub and dance school. Courtesy Nicole Rios.

Design
Development

415

Figure 13.9a (right) Interior design student storyboards his design presentation of an art gallery and loft. Courtesy Norman Reyes

Figure 13.9b (below) The student's three final presentation boards. Courtesy Norman Reyes

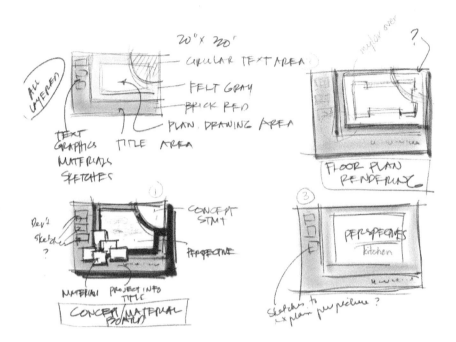

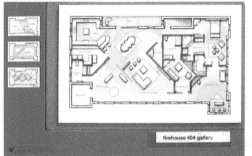

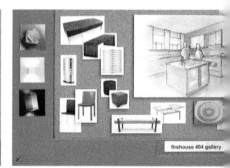

of the background board are portrayed, as well as the consistently placed, unifying elements of all the boards. This exercise helped the instructor see that Norman could consolidate all of his drawings, concept statement, and material samples onto three boards, as seen in Figure 13.9b.

Figure 13.10 shows a storyboard technique that goes one step beyond. For students who want an accurately scaled storyboard, the computer is a great sketch tool. In this example, the precision of the drawing allowed for an intricate, detailed layout. Interior design student Megan McCoy used the computer to block out a storyboard of her final presentation. All of the drawings are proportionally to-scale and labeled for clarity. The bold labels represent the main rendered drawings that she wanted to highlight.

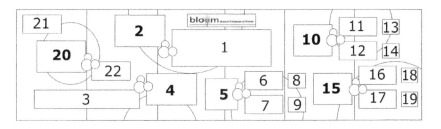

Figure 13.10 Interior design student used the computer to block out a storyboard of her final presentation. All of the drawings are proportionally to-scale and labeled for clarity. The bold labels represent the main rendered drawings that she wanted to highlight. Courtesy Megan McCoy.

1. Furniture Plan
2. **Lobby Perspective**
3. Gallery Elevation
4. **Gallery Perspective**
5. **Women of the Past Perspective**
6. Women of the Past North Wall Elevation
7. Women of the Past South Wall Elevation
8. Women of the Past Section B
9. Women of the Past Section C
10. **Women of the Present Perspective**
11. Women of the Present North Wall Elevation
12. Women of the Present South Wall Elevation
13. Women of the Present Section B
14. Women of the Present Section C
15. **Women of the Future Perspective**
16. Women of the Future North Wall Elevation
17. Women of the Future South Wall Elevation
18. Women of the Future Section B
19. Women of the Future Section C
20. **Gift Shop Perspective**
21. Gift Shop North Wall Elevation
22. Gift Shop South Wall Elevation

ACTIVITY 13.4 Storyboarding the Final Presentation

Purpose: **To graphically visualize your final presentation.**

As interior designers, we need to become familiar with some of the graphic design principles when "designing our final presentation." In fact, the final presentation may be viewed as a design project in and of itself. An exceptional interior design may be obscured by a poor presentation.

PART ONE

Summarize the main points of your presentation in a Written Summary, which includes the following:

- Thesis Statement
- Major points to be made (how you identified the problem and how you solved it)
- List of spaces where your thesis argument is made apparent
- List of drawings that will reinforce that point
- List of supplemental information to be included (case studies, research sources, statistics—presented via charts, graphs, quotes from interviews, etc.)

PART TWO

Determine how you can make your presentation unique to your project. How can your project boards "speak" to your jury before you even open your mouth?

Generate three concepts or innovative ideas for the final presentation:

1. _____

2. _____

3. _____

Now, generate thumbnails of possible final board compositions. Use these sketches to explore whether your boards are better presented vertically or horizontally, or whether certain shapes or materials should be carried through on all boards. When you have explored multiple options, storyboard one or two of them. On 11" × 17" paper, compose storyboards or scale mockups for your final presentation boards. Use color and text as necessary to show the following:

- Drawings
- Relative sizes of drawings
- Drawing placement
- Rendering style (hand-drawn versus digital) to be used
- Board format (horizontal versus vertical)
- Location of title block
- Board colors or material to be used
- Mounting technique to be used
- Any other information that would communicate your final presentation goals

Putting It All Together

The design development phase ends with a presentation to a client or a jury. Your project should be presented so that it indicates all of the information and research that has gone into the process: information collected through your literature review, interviews, surveys, observation, and case studies—as well as your analysis of the information during your design process, including your written thesis, program, site analysis, statistics, and diagrams. Your project would not be complete if your presentation did not address codes, sustainability, and other guidelines that you have spent many hours researching.

All of your hard work and research should be represented in your final presentation: the research, the program, and the design. How can you showcase your thinking process and express how much you have learned over the course of this studio project? Should you create a PowerPoint to commence your verbal discussion, set the stage, and provide a background of research? When the lights are out and the audience is focused on the images on the screen, what are the key points that you want to express about your program, your site, the information you gathered, and the preliminary sketches? You are preparing the audience to see your final rendering. How else can you present this series of experiences? In a handout or a brochure?

Presentation techniques should be researched and planned (as a design project in and of itself). Constantly refine them and look for ways to innovate, in search of the perfect way to educate your final jury about your thesis, your program, and your design solution—and your contribution to the body of knowledge of interior design.

Case Study:
An Innovative Presentation

Figure 13.11 illustrates an interactive presentation. The student had many ideas that contributed to the look of the final presentation. Her project, which she called "Project A.I.R.," had to do with using interactive retail options to enhance the waiting areas at an airport. The floor plan, lighting, and main entrance elevation that went along the top were presented first. Then, the airplane windows on the presentation board flipped up one at a time to reveal the details of her project as she verbally introduced each figure. A magnet mounted on the face held each window up. Details included sections, elevations, isometrics, and perspectives. Figure 13.11 shows the student, Morgan Greenseth, standing in front of her boards taking questions from her jury during the final presentation.

Figure 13.11 Student Morgan Greenseth standing in front of her boards, taking questions from her jury during the final presentation of her thesis project.

Conclusion

Every aspect of your project during the design development phase can be informed, enhanced, improved, and transformed through information. From the physical components such as doors and hardware, to the way the spaces are ventilated, sound is controlled, and light is manipulated, to the way that people can navigate through the space, your design solution must conform to codes, be buildable, and be economically viable. You want it to be inspiring as well. True innovation on any level comes from an intense observation, definition, and analysis of the problems to be solved, followed by an ability to absorb and utilize information from a variety of sources, and completed by a fearless resolve to take risks and propose something new.

Collecting information happens over time, which is why seasoned professionals are prized for their experience. Experience represents years of accumulated research in a specialty area. Information-gathering techniques—interviews, surveys, observation—apply to each task in the design development phase. For example, interviewing a cabinetmaker can yield information about the best wood, hardware, and installation methods. Observing a cabinet being manufactured or installed can yield information that would be essential to the planning of its use in your projects. Physically interacting with the cabinets or taking a class in woodworking will yield further understanding. There is no end to the depth of understanding that comes from research.

What motivates each decision during this phase? From the color of a wall treatment to the placement of each piece of furniture, you should always have a reason why you made that decision, and the strongest design solution comes from an informed position.

References

ADA–ABA Accessibility Guidelines. (July 23, 2004). Retrieved May 16, 2009, from http://www.access-board.gov/ada-aba/final.cfm

Alexander, C. (1977). *A pattern language.* New York: Oxford University Press.

Bowman, D. (June 2, 2003). A design process revealed. *Stopdesign.* Retrieved May 16, 2009, from http://stopdesign.com/articles/design_process

California Building Code. (2007). Title 24, part 2.

The Center for Universal Design. (1997). *The principles of universal design* (version 2.0). Raleigh: North Carolina State University.

Grillo, P. J. (1960). *Form, function & design.* New York: Dover.

Harmon, S. K., & Kennon, K. E. (2008). *The codes guidebook for interiors* (4th ed.). Hoboken, NJ: John Wiley.

International Code Council (ICC). (2006). *International building code.* Clifton Park, New York: Delmar Cengage Learning.

Kaplan, R., Kaplan, S., & Ryan, R. (1998). *With people in mind: Design and management of every-day nature*. Washington, DC: Island Press.

Mallin, S. (1980). *Merleau-Ponty's philosophy*. New Haven, CT: Yale University Press.

McGowan, M. (2006). *Specifying interiors* (2nd ed.). Hoboken, NJ: John Wiley.

Newell, A., Shaw, J. C., & Simon, H. A. (1967). The process of creative thinking. In H. Gruber (editor), *Contemporary approaches to creative thinking*. New York: Atherton.

Powell, R. R. (2004). *Wabi sabi simple*. Avon, MA: Adams Media.

14 Design as a Circular Process

CHAPTER OBJECTIVES

When you complete this chapter you should be able to do the following:

- Identify the depth of research you want to apply to your projects.
- Understand the role of the studio critique or thesis defense.
- Use methods such as heuristic evaluation and usability testing to improve your design solutions.
- Create mock-ups and prototypes to test your design solutions.
- Understand the importance of documenting and archiving your interior design project (both written and visual information) as a contribution to the body of knowledge of the interior design profession.
- Understand the role of research and information-gathering during the contract documents and contract administration phases of the Interior Design Process.

KEY TERMS

Contract document

Continuing Education Unit

Heuristic evaluation

Heuristics

Logging sheet

Mock-up

Post-evaluation questionnaire

Post-occupancy evaluation (POE)

Pre-evaluation questionnaire

Prototype

Representative user

Task scenario

Test schedule

Thesis book

Thesis defense

Usability

Usability test

Usability testing

Value engineering

You have presented your beautifully rendered drawings of your thesis project's design development phase to the jury, instructors, and fellow classmates. Does that mean your project is finished or that information-gathering has ended? No. In the academic environment, the studio critique provides yet another opportunity for information-gathering, just as in the professional environment, further testing and evaluation can continue long after the design development is complete.

Using Research as a Strategy for a Successful Presentation and Defense

In academics you have a process synonymous with the completion of the professional project: that is your final project presentation and studio critique, or, in the case of your thesis, your **thesis defense**.

Many schools have open studio critiques or juries, where all student work is pinned up simultaneously. Other schools present each student's work one at a time in a more formal presentation format. Regardless of your school's presentation style, you will likely present your design solutions with a verbal explanation that you have prepared in advance, and then you will field questions and comments from the participating jury members (Tate, 1987). The jury review can be difficult for some students, but the process is highly informative and helpful if you approach it with an appropriate attitude. In a jury review, you have the opportunity to receive the full attention of well-informed professional designers. Give them your full attention in return, taking notes if you can, for valuable information is being shared. During this process, gather the information not only from your own critics, but from critics who are reviewing the work of other students. Sometimes hearing a critique of another student's work enables you to hear comments more objectively, seeing how they might apply to your own project (Tate, 1987).

The jury presentation is, once again, about gathering information, this time from a jury that is taking time to learn about your project and offering you further information. Because the professionals are volunteering their time in the academic arena, it is up to you as the student to offer them something of value in return. You do this by using your well-researched ideas and presentation to teach the jury and other audience members something new about something they care about. Remember, now you are the expert on this one aspect of the interior design profession, and this is your opportunity to offer information back to the profession. Research, learning, teaching, and applying knowledge are all part of a reciprocal system. You take from the existing information and give back something new. As information goes in, new ideas should come out.

Responding to and Incorporating Feedback

During your thesis defense—or any design presentation, for that matter—it is a good idea to have a trusted classmate take notes, as you will likely not remember everything that was communicated in the process. In a professional environment, you would want to designate a colleague to take "meeting minutes," recording the comments made during the meeting so that there is an objective record of the proceedings.

When you are presenting, your posture tells your audience how you are responding to their feedback. Remain open and comfortable with comments. Consider the project a success if it sparks a dialogue among the jurors. Volunteer to be a part of that exchange of ideas and be open to the opportunity when it arrives. As the saying goes, "You want people to keep correcting you. When they have stopped, then you know they may have given up on you."

Although you are presenting your project in order to hear and accept criticism, there are some basic things you can and should expect from your jurors (Tate, 1987):

1. Respect
2. Common courtesy
3. Honesty
4. Willingness to answer your questions and clarify comments when asked

At the same time, as a person who has set aside time to offer help to you, there are certain things a jury member will expect from you (Tate, 1987):

1. Readiness for criticism
2. Clear explanation of your ideas

In preparation for the sharing process that is your thesis defense, begin to perfect your basic presentation skills. Interior design students sometimes struggle with this; they become so comfortable communicating through drawing that they forget that the drawings do not necessarily speak for themselves. You must be able to communicate your ideas to an audience verbally as well as visually. This is a skill you will need again and again in the professional world as you present your ideas to clients.

Especially in a thesis defense, your presentation must be well rehearsed and must contain substantial references to your research, as you will be defending your conclusions and will need to draw upon that research to support your ideas. Ideally, you should be so familiar with your thesis that you can state it clearly and concisely without referencing your notes or any other "cheat sheet." Some people call this the "elevator speech." If you had 30 seconds in an elevator to tell a stranger what your thesis is about, what would you say?

Just as for any other academic presentation, arrive early. Your presentation begins the moment you walk through the door, so take care of the messy stuff before you get there or at least before your audience gets there.

Always dress appropriately and professionally. Be careful with clothing that can distract, such as dangly jewelry or loud patterns. You do not want your attire competing with and undermining the work you have done.

During your presentation, stand up straight, face your audience, make eye contact, and speak clearly. Nothing can substitute for adequate preparation, so organize your thoughts and practice, practice, practice!

We always tell students to "own your ideas," but at the same time be willing to discuss your ideas and communicate openly without getting defensive. This is where your research is the essential factor. The quality and substance of your research should give you the confidence you need to present your ideas to a room of critics. Carefully review your research before making your presentation, so it is easier to incorporate into your thesis presentation.

3. Preparation to talk as well as listen
4. Professionalism

In addition, jurors will expect an attention to detail, clarity in your drawings and text, and a high energy level to show enthusiasm for your own project.

At some schools, the final jury for the thesis presentations is selected for the students. This has its benefits, for it ensures an objective and impartial jury and feedback. Other schools require that students recruit their own jury members in order to ensure feedback from experts specific to a student's identified problem, research, project type, and conclusions. You should be prepared to follow whatever jury selection process is required by your institution.

ACTIVITY 14.1 Selecting Your Own Jury

Purpose: **To select a jury of qualified professionals and experts.**

1. Identify someone from each of the following groups as a representative of some element of your project.
   - *Client Representative*—Based on the project client you have identified, contact an individual who could serve as a representative of that client. For example, if you have chosen a company or organization, find someone from that actual company or organization. Chances are you have already interviewed them at some point in your thesis project, so this is a great time to work on continuing that relationship. If you can contact the actual client, such as for a single-family residential project, then that would be ideal.
   - *End User Representative*—Based on the project end user you have identified, contact a representative of that user group to be a part of your jury. Make sure that the individual is qualified and is willing to offer honest and accurate feedback.
   - *Design Professional Representative*—Select an interior design professional, ideally one who specializes in your project type. For example, if you are designing a restaurant, you would want to locate a hospitality designer. If you are focusing on green design, you would want a LEED-certified professional who can focus his or her feedback in that direction. Some schools also allow interior design students to identify a professional architect for this jury member as well, so ask your instructor if this is an option.
   - *Faculty Representative*—Select a respected faculty member from your school, or from another school if you wish (and if permitted by your institution), to offer an academic perspective on your project.
2. In the spaces below, list the name and contact information for each potential jury member:

   Representative Client: _____

   Organization or Company: _____

   Address: _____

   E-mail: _____

Phone: _____

Status of Invitation: _____

Representative End User: _____

Organization or Company: _____

Address: _____

E-mail: _____

Phone: _____

Status of Invitation: _____

Design Professional: _____

Firm Name: _____

Address: _____

E-mail: _____

Phone: _____

Status of Invitation: _____

Faculty Member: _____

School: _____

Address: _____

E-mail: _____

Phone: _____

Status of Invitation: _____

3. Contact each potential jury member and invite them to join you. Out of the four people you identified, schedule at least three persons to make up your jury. (The fourth person can be contacted later, in case one of the others is not able to attend.) If this is the first time you have spoken with a person you have chosen, be sure to explain who you are, where you go to school, the nature of your thesis project, and why you have chosen to contact that person specifically. Make sure your potential jury members understand that their role in the process is to give objective feedback. Sometimes jury members are not prepared to give verbal feedback, especially if they are not designers by profession. Do your best to prepare them for the process so they are more likely to speak their mind.

4. Give your instructor the contact information for each potential juror, and keep your instructor updated on the status of your search. It is your responsibility to make sure your jury members show up for your review, so it is advisable that you contact them a day or two before your big day to confirm that they'll be attending.

5. Once the presentation is over, send each jury member a written thank-you note to express your appreciation for their attendance.

Defending your thesis to a jury is an opportunity for continuing professional relationships with jurors. It could be a great networking tool for you as you transition into the professional world. In addition to professors and other academics, your panel is likely made up of professionals, who are always looking for talent. Thank them for any and all feedback. It is appropriate to send a handwritten note or at least an e-mail to all jurors, thanking them for their time and the value of their feedback. Even if they disagreed with some of your ideas, they are there to help you learn.

Applying Research During Contract Documents and Contract Administration

At the point when you think a project is almost complete (Figure 14.1), there arise some of the greatest opportunities to measure the results of your design decisions and to inform future design.

The Consultation Process: Seeking Expertise

Chapter 13 discussed utilizing the expertise of consultants throughout design development: experts, engineers, and product representatives, to name just a few. During design development, your consultants are helping you write up your list of project parameters, identifying restrictions such as codes or zoning issues, as well as options and opportunities such as innovative new products. During the design development phase, you often use research to resolve the difference between restrictions and opportunities. For example, in a physical rehabilitation clinic, a design team wanted to use a high-density foam product to create the look of old-world wood beams in the ceiling. Up to that point, that product had not been used in this healthcare application, so the designers worked closely with the codes officials to establish whether or not the innovative product fell within the parameters for life-safety regulations. In this instance, the open dialogue with the codes official uncovered concerns about the product, and the design team was able to focus their research to better address the codes official's concerns.

In the professional arena, continue a dialogue with your experts and consultants as you move into the **contract documents** phase. These people are

Figure 14.1 Your design research will influence every stage of your design process, including the preparation of contract documents and contract administration.

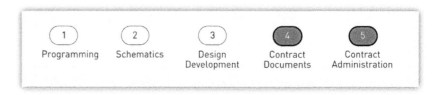

your lifeline to information you would not otherwise have. For example, on an adaptive reuse project in Washington, D.C., a client wanted to turn a historic Dupont Circle townhouse into an office space. In order to do this, the design team consulted a structural engineer about the increased weight loads on the floors, which had originally been designed for residential furniture and would now be carrying the weight of file cabinets, bookshelves, and a significant increase in occupants.

The consultation with the structural engineer told the design team two things: (1) that it could be done, and (2) that calculations would reveal the impact on the interior design, such as the impact of the new floor structure on ceiling heights, as each floor would be significantly deeper with the structural changes.

Imagine if the designers had stopped there and not spoken to the engineer again throughout the contract documents phase. Any resulting mistakes could have had legal consequences. The design team checked in with the structural engineer regularly to get feedback on exactly how the design decisions and detailing would accomplish the requirements that the engineer had established during the design development phase.

Your relationship with your consultants helps you defend your ideas—to your instructor or academic critics while in school, or to a client in a real-world situation. Imagine yourself as the design team lead in the previous example of converting a townhouse into office space. Let's say the structural engineer also noted that due to its role in structurally supporting the floor above, a certain wall should not be moved. Later, when you make your presentation, the client is displeased with this wall because it breaks up an otherwise open space, and he asks you why it is there. Your educated answers will help you to explain your reasoning to your client. The client might ask you to go back to the engineer and request that the wall be moved, at which point the engineer might give you a cost analysis that makes moving the wall prohibitive. But now you know, as you complete the contract documents, that the existing wall is a required "given" in the project and that you and the client will have to work with the wall as you complete the project.

You can also increase the effectiveness of your communication with the consultants and the client through your application of professional language, illustrating your understanding of the subject matter. In academic presentations, the students who have researched the professional terminology and can apply it confidently will impress their critics with their knowledge of the subject matter and the ease with which they talk about complicated technical details, codes terminology, and programmatic issues.

Timothy Smith, a lighting designer from the Smithsonian Institution in Washington, D.C., tells a story about the consequences of documenting your design in isolation and waiting too long to speak with an expert about the issue at hand. Specializing in museum exhibits, he shares the following:

"Professional experts, such as a lighting designer, are often not consulted or interviewed until the last minute, but they should be involved in the project from the beginning. The lighting designer is the educator of the lighting criteria since so few people are experts. Not consulting the experts results in mistakes. In the case of lighting design in museum exhibits, mistakes can result in shadows that make work illegible, or in complex nooks and spaces that are not lit. Unfortunately this kind of mistake isn't realized until installation and it is much more complicated and expensive for the lighting designer to fix the problem at that point" (personal communication, June 2008).

Value Engineering

One way in which consultants and experts are directly involved in the contract documents phase of interior design is through **value engineering**. According to the U.S. Department of Agriculture, "value engineering (VE) is a systematic, functional, and creative analysis of a construction requirement to achieve the best functional combination of cost, reliability, and performance, over the life-cycle of products, systems, equipment, facilities, services, and supplies" (U.S. Department of Agriculture, 2008).

The VE process for interior design will involve the entire design team, including the designer(s), client, contractor, and other experts such as the project manager, architect(s), and engineer(s) if relevant. The team works together to review the project costs and to identify ways to get the most value for the available budget. For example, in a public building the original design might have called for terrazzo tiles installed in various patterns on each floor of the building. After the budget is reviewed and the ratio of value to cost is evaluated, the design might be value-engineered so that the terrazzo is used on only the first floor and vinyl tiles, installed in similar patterns, are used on all subsequent floors. This solution allows the translation of the original design concept from expensive to more affordable materials as the design moves from more public spaces to more private ones.

VE usually begins in the first half of contract documents and often includes the following phases:

1. *Information Phase*—The team gathers information about the program requirements, project design, background, constraints, and projected construction costs. The team identifies high-cost areas.
2. *Speculative/Creative Phase*—The team identifies alternatives for accomplishing the functional and creative design intent.
3. *Evaluation/Analytical Phase*—The team evaluates the alternatives from the Speculative/Creative Phase to determine those with the greatest potential for cost savings and project enhancement.

4. *Development/Recommendation Phase*—The team researches the alternatives and ideas selected in the Evaluation/Analytical Phase and prepares descriptions, sketches, and life-cycle cost estimates to support VE recommendations and proposals.

5. *Report Phase*—The team presents VE recommendations to the client and other team members in a verbal presentation and written document (U.S. Department of Agriculture, 2008).

Your consultants should be involved in this process, as they can help you to research and identify the design solutions that will best solve the problem of cost and provide alternate affordable solutions. At this point, your level of research is what allows you to hold on to your creative ideas and intent through the cutting process. The more options you have to present at a VE meeting, the more likely you are to have some control over the outcome, rather than letting the contractor or another person make the decisions for you.

For example, in one hospital emergency department, the design team was told through the VE process that the organic and playful design pattern they planned for the rubber flooring was too complex and expensive, and that the contractor was recommending that the design team remove the pattern and simply choose one color of flooring and install it without the pattern. The designers knew that the pattern, which involved using different colors of rubber in different areas, was essential to the way-finding process. Also, it created a more human scale and a less institutional feel in what is otherwise a potentially intimidating space.

The design team decided to follow up by researching who was doing the installation and finding out the real reason for the high cost. Their research revealed that the contractor for the hospital was a small operation and it was the contractor's lack of tools and technology to precisely cut and install such an intricate pattern that was driving up the cost. In the end the designers recommended a simplification, rather than an elimination of the design, which turned out to be satisfactory for all parties involved. Had the designers not done their own investigation into the problem, they wouldn't have been able to suggest this better option.

Evaluating Design Decisions

You have collected evidence that informed your design decisions, but how do you use research to evaluate the success of the decisions you have made? Research can be applied throughout the later phases of the Interior Design Process to test the success of design solutions and to suggest future improvements.

Heuristic Evaluations

Recall, from Chapter 9, Roberto Rengel's definition of **heuristics** as "any principle, procedure, or other device that contributes to reduction in the search for a satisfactory solution" (Newell, Shaw, & Simon, 1967).

In a **heuristic evaluation**, you consider the characteristics of your design and determine whether the design meets the previously set criteria and requirements. This process gradually reduces the number of design solutions available to meet the set criteria and requirements. A heuristic evaluation does not yet involve your client or end users; you're still working closely with the designers and consultants as the experts. Often, it is a matter of distributing a simple checklist (such as the one shown in Figure 14.2) to multiple persons, because obtaining evaluations from multiple sources increases the chance of uncovering all potential problems with the design solution. These experts perform the evaluation independent of one another and then come together to communicate their findings (Wickens, Lee, Liu, & Gordon-Becker, 2004).

Although heuristics is about evaluating the design and, thus, could be considered part of design development, there is also a place for it in relation to contract documents, as the evaluators need some kind of design documentation in order to review the design.

The evaluation team communicates the results of the study with the design team in a group meeting, so that problems can be identified and everyone can brainstorm possible solutions (Wickens et al., 2004). This simple checklist format is often a very cost-effective way to identify and solve problems early in the design process—problems that would have been costly and difficult to change if discovered later in the process.

This is just one example of how a designer might perform a heuristic evaluation. In reality, heuristics can be any process that reduces the number of potential solutions to a problem, helping the designer to isolate and identify the right solution. In practice, heuristics should be an ongoing or "circular" process that refines your ideas throughout the entire design process. It is simply seeing your design decisions with a critical eye, using common sense, keeping the project goals and objectives in mind, and holding your design to those standards.

Mock-ups

To support interface and interaction design, usability testing and other human factors activities, product mock-ups and prototypes are built very early in the design process (Wickens et al., 2004).

A **mock-up** is a very crude approximation of the final product or space, often made in foam or cardboard, as you can see in Figure 14.3 (Wickens

Heuristic Evaluation - A Design Checklist --- **CONCEPT 1**

1. Requirements Conformance & Functionality

The system should allow the user to fully meet all high-priority requirements.

#	Review Checklist	(5) + (1) -	Comments
1.1	Does the home office concept meet the program requirements of the user?	O O O O O	
1.2	Does the home office concept meet all adjacency requirements?	O O O O O	
1.3	Does the home office concept provide a barrier-free design?	O O O O O	
1.4	Does the home office concept provide a reasonable work area adjacencies (task-related space)?	O O O O O	
1.5	Does the home office concept allow the user to perform all tasks for the specified usage scenarios?	O O O O O	
1.6	Does the home office concept allow the user to perform related tasks efficiently?	O O O O O	
1.7	Does the home office concept meet program cost guidelines	O O O O O	
1.8	Does equipment and cabinetry meet / match anthropometric constraints?	O O O O O	

2. Flexibility

Provide the most simple and efficient system for the user to accomplish a task while generating a positive affective response.

#	Review Checklist	(5) + (1) -	Comments
2.1	Has the home office concept been designed for flexible use wherever applicable	O O O O O	
2.2	Does the home office concept foster effective interpersonal use and/or communication (wherever applicable)?	O O O O O	

3. Aesthetic Potential

System should not contain information which is irrelevant or rarely needed. Every extra unit of information competes with the relevant units of information and diminishes their relative visibility.

#	Review Checklist	(5) + (1) -	Comments
3.1	Does the home office concept have a sense of visual continuity?	O O O O O	
3.2	Can the elements and principles of design be applied to achieve aesthetic excellence?	O O O O O	
3.3	Does each functional area of the home office concept (work prep, storage, clean-up) compliment other functional areas from an aesthetic potential standpoint?	O O O O O	

4. OTHER

#	Review Checklist	(5) + (1) -	Comments
4.1	Is the home office concept prototype achievable in time frame allowed ?	O O O O O	
4.2	Does the home office concept function adequately for non-impaired users?	O O O O O	
4.3	Does the concept adequately address safety concerns and provide necessary safety features	O O O O O	
4.4	Does the system meet all applicable accessibility laws and regulations?	O O O O O	
4.5	OTHER	O O O O O	

Figure 14.2 A heuristic evaluation performed in the early stages of design and construction documents can be a simple checklist that identifies the required criteria for the design. This heuristic checklist is for a home office that was intended to meet universal design criteria for a client using a wheelchair.

et al., 2004). Unlike a prototype, which will be discussed shortly, a mock-up usually comes relatively early in the design and documentation process.

Mock-ups are usually very simple and are frequently used in furniture and product design as an effective and inexpensive design tool. Although mock-ups can be rough foam core or cardboard approximations of the design, sometimes they are more extensive and realistic, such as in the example of selecting the colors for the new museum galleries at the Oklahoma City Museum of Art. After reviewing the art to be hung in each gallery, the

Figure 14.3 Students in the Human Factors course design a home office for a client using a wheelchair and test their design by building a mock-up of the space out of foam core. In their usability test, the students invite a representative end user to test the design of the space and help them identify design problems to be resolved.

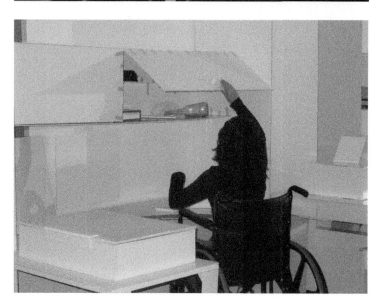

Figure 14.4 Designers began the paint selection process by painting small mobile walls in colors corresponding to the various art galleries.

design team made initial paint selections. Small mobile "walls" were used to mock up the gallery conditions. (See Figure 14.4.) The designers painted these small walls and the conservators hung the art, testing for the appropriate color selection in each gallery.

Once the paint mock-ups were complete, the curator and the design team critically evaluated the selections. It was a valuable process, for the team immediately found that once the lighting was applied, the initial color selections were too light and too washed out to appropriately enhance the artwork. (See Figure 14.5.)

Figure 14.5 Initial mock-up of gallery spaces revealed color selections that were too light and washed out for the scale of the spaces and lighting conditions.

This initial analysis allowed designers to refine the color selections, working further with lighting consultants and other team members to make final decisions. (See Figure 14.6.)

The result was art galleries that used color to create a "Wow!" experience for the museum visitor, enhancing the richness and beauty of the artwork and allowing it to be appreciated more fully. (See Figure 14.7.)

Prototypes

If budget and time permit, after preliminary issues have been identified through heuristics and the evaluation and testing of mock-ups, the next step might be to create a **prototype** of a product or space. Unlike a mock-up, which

Figure 14.6 The museum art gallery paint colors were re-selected and tested in various lighting scenarios.

Figure 14.7 The final color selections in the galleries at the Oklahoma City Museum of Art. Earlier mock-ups helped the designers refine their color selections into a more dramatic palette to complement the historical artwork. Photos courtesy of James Meeks.

can be made from foam or cardboard with glue guns and pushpins for assembly, prototypes frequently have more of the look and feel of the final product but do not yet have full functionality (Wickens et al., 2004). Similar to a mock-up, a prototype will give users and designers something to react to and use in testing design criteria (Wickens et al., 2004). (See Figure 14.8.)

In furniture design and production, for example, it is common to go through a process that might follow steps such as these: 1. Schematics, design development, and initial design documentation; 2. Rough mock-up of the furniture piece for initial evaluation; 3. Refinement and perfection of design based on information gathered through mock-up; 4. Final construction documentation; 5. Construction of a prototype, which might reveal more opportunities for refinement and later lead to mass production.

Figure 14.8 For this hospitality project, interior design students worked with graphic design and culinary students to create a restaurant. To coordinate the different teams and ensure cohesiveness in team ideas, students built a prototype of a seating area for the restaurant, including interior design, furniture, graphic elements such as signage and menus, and a sampling of menu items.

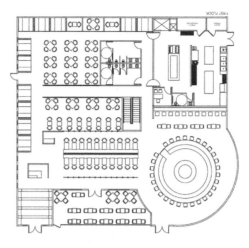

Allison, a design student, was asked to construct a piece of furniture for a furniture design studio. She identified that she needed and wanted a platform bed, but she also identified the following problems: (1) She moved frequently, so the furniture piece had to be something she could carry herself; and (2) the piece had to serve multiple functions so that it would remain usable as her living conditions changed over time.

Allison's solution to the problem of needing to be able to carry the piece herself was this: Rather than construct the furniture out of a large solid piece of material, she developed a modular system, with each module 15 inches wide and 70 inches long. Also, each module would not be made of solid wood, but instead would be made out of equally spaced slats to further reduce the weight. The idea was that multiple modules could be purchased and used in the following manner: two modules made a twin-size bed and three modules made a full-size or queen-size bed; at 18 inches high, a number of modules could be stacked up to create a shelving system. Although it was a great concept, you can see from Figure 14.9 that the initial sketches revealed a somewhat complicated design solution.

For the midterm review, Allison created a cardboard mock-up of this design. In creating it, she discovered a new design problem: that many different and complicated pieces and steps would be required to construct the design. Feedback from critics made it clear that a more elegant solution was needed, so the design was refined and construction documents were drawn up.

At the completion of the furniture studio, Allison had a prototype built in the school's wood shop. The prototype revealed even more opportunities to refine the design. For example, Allison had specified that the modules should be 18 inches high, which didn't leave much room for books or other decorative objects if the piece was stacked as shelving. If Allison were to pursue mass production of the furniture piece, constructing the prototype would have revealed the height issue. The design could be refined and the problem solved before the piece was duplicated over and over again on the assembly line—thus avoiding the risk that this problem might have limited the ability to sell the product.

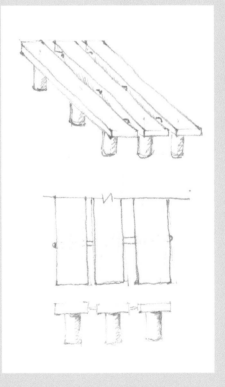

Figure 14.9 Initial design sketches for the modular furniture system reveal a complicated design solution.

In the end, it is the impact on final cost that determines how much to invest in heuristics, mock-ups, prototypes, and usability testing. Consider Figure 14.10. Similarly, if you were designing a residential kitchen, you might simply do a rough mock-up for testing design solutions. In the case of a 100-patient-bed hospital, however, the potential financial impact of a design mistake in a patient room makes building out one complete room as a prototype to be tested by nurses and doctors well worth the cost. A hospital might even build out an entire floor as a prototype, allowing it to be used for a short period of time—just long enough for issues to surface, so that designers might resolve these issues before further floors or wings are completed.

Usability Testing

Mock-ups and prototypes are commonly used to conduct **usability tests**, also called *pilot tests*. **Usability** is primarily the degree to which a design or

Figure 14.10 A prototype of a modular furniture piece allows the student to test the functionality of the pieces in a real-world situation. Issues to be resolved included adding 3 to 5 inches of height to the legs, and creating brackets to join the modular pieces together and add stability when they were used as a futon platform on hard surfaces like wood or tile. If these pieces were mass-produced, a final design solution would resolve these design problems.

space is easy to use or is "user friendly" (Wickens et al., 2004). While a heuristic evaluation identifies problems and narrows down the potential design solutions, **usability testing** evaluates those design solutions as they involve interaction with a user (Wickens et al., 2004).

A usability test replicates the Environment-Behavior interaction between your end user and the space or product with some kind of mock-up, prototype, or other realistic and interactive representation of the design. The design is evaluated for its usability, and the difficulties and frustrations the user encounters in the process are recorded: information that enables you to identify opportunities to enhance the design.

As it applies to interior design, usability is based on the following factors (Wickens et al., 2004, p. 59):

1. *Learnability*—The design should be easy to familiarize oneself with, so the user can rapidly begin getting work done.
2. *Efficiency*—The system should be efficient to use, so that a high level of productivity is possible.
3. *Memorability*—Everything should be logically placed, so that the user will easily relocate items.
4. *Errors*—The system should have a low error rate, in that the user can operate all systems or amenities without mistakes.
5. *Satisfaction*—The design should be pleasant to use, live in, work in, or look at. The user should "like it."

There is a fine line in the Interior Design Process between when it is too early for a usability test and when it is too late. A usability test must wait until the design is sufficiently documented so as to be replicated through a mock-up or prototype. However, the test should be done before the completion of contract documents, so any significant issues that are identified can be addressed. A usability test needs to be done early enough in the process that changes are still possible and affordable. Otherwise, what would be the point?

Different usability techniques can be used based on where you are in the design process. For example, in the early stages you might create a three-dimensional representation, such as a computer model, that allows you to envision the Environment-Behavior interaction and get feedback from the client. That would be a somewhat inexpensive technique and is very similar in process to a heuristic evaluation, except that it involves the feedback of the end user. Later in the process, you might build a realistic prototype of the design and ask the end user to interact physically with the prototype, allowing you and the user to identify problems that must be addressed before the project can move forward. This is especially important in spaces such as a hospital nurse's station or a patient room, where the principles of usability are literally a life-or-death matter.

The cast of a usability test includes the following: at least one representative end user, and often more than one; a test host who oversees the process; at least one of the designers as an observer; and often at least one business representative, also as an observer. For example, in the case of a hospital patient room, you might have a collection of nurses, doctors, and other healthcare providers, the design team, the host who oversees the process, and various administrative staff to observe the process.

At times you might be conducting your own usability test, both formally and informally. The following steps will help you to conduct this type of research in a professional manner. Similar to scientific experiments, usability tests have a typical protocol to be followed to achieve the most reliable results.

To prepare the usability test, first you must clearly establish what "usability" is in this situation and identify the **task scenario**, or representative tasks to help you establish whether the criteria for usability have been accomplished. (See Figure 14.11.) You must also have a clear definition of when a task has been completed. You will then prepare a **test schedule**, or *agenda*, which will serve as the script that all parties involved will follow. Finally, you will need to identify and arrange a location and time for the usability test to take place, then identify your **representative users** and invite them to attend. It is usually better to schedule "too much time" for the testing process rather than "just enough," as having extra time leaves more time between sessions for you or your team to take notes and discuss issues.

The following is a list of supplies you will need in order to conduct the usability test:

1. Videotaping equipment or camera, and release or consent forms if applicable
2. A test schedule or formal script, so that all participants involved have equal experiences
3. A **pre-evaluation questionnaire** or other means of checking that your participants match the required profile of your end user
4. Your **task scenario** or list of tasks, together with clear criteria for measuring whether they have been successfully completed
5. **Logging sheets** on which to record timing, events, participant actions, concerns, and comments
6. A **post-evaluation questionnaire** to measure user satisfaction and understanding and to glean any additional information that participants may want to provide
7. Compensation, an appropriate "thank-you" gift, or a thank-you card for each of your user representatives

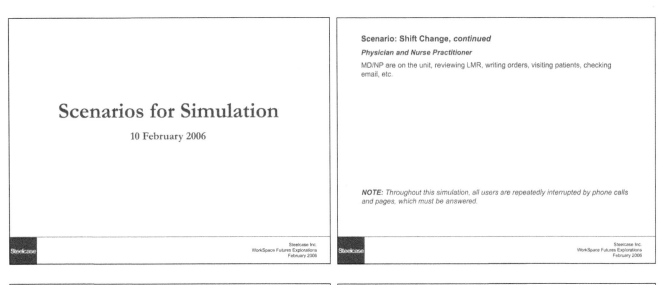

Scenarios for Simulation

10 February 2006

Steelcase Inc.
WorkSpace Futures Explorations
February 2006

Scenario: Shift Change, *continued*

Physician and Nurse Practitioner

MD/NP are on the unit, reviewing LMR, writing orders, visiting patients, checking email, etc.

NOTE: *Throughout this simulation, all users are repeatedly interrupted by phone calls and pages, which must be answered.*

Steelcase Inc.
WorkSpace Futures Explorations
February 2006

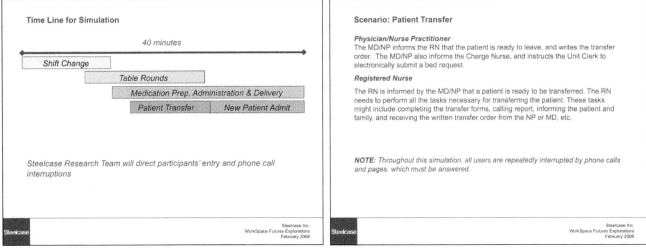

Time Line for Simulation

40 minutes

Shift Change

Table Rounds

Medication Prep, Administration & Delivery

Patient Transfer | New Patient Admit

Steelcase Research Team will direct participants' entry and phone call interruptions

Steelcase Inc.
WorkSpace Futures Explorations
February 2006

Scenario: Patient Transfer

Physician/Nurse Practitioner
The MD/NP informs the RN that the patient is ready to leave, and writes the transfer order. The MD/NP also informs the Charge Nurse, and instructs the Unit Clerk to electronically submit a bed request.

Registered Nurse

The RN is informed by the MD/NP that a patient is ready to be transferred. The RN needs to perform all the tasks necessary for transferring the patient. These tasks might include completing the transfer forms, calling report, informing the patient and family, and receiving the written transfer order from the NP or MD, etc.

NOTE: *Throughout this simulation, all users are repeatedly interrupted by phone calls and pages, which must be answered.*

Steelcase Inc.
WorkSpace Futures Explorations
February 2006

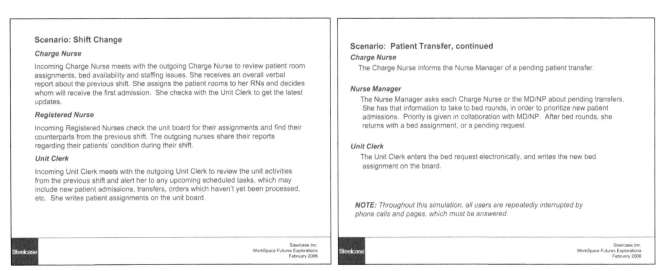

Scenario: Shift Change

Charge Nurse

Incoming Charge Nurse meets with the outgoing Charge Nurse to review patient room assignments, bed availability and staffing issues. She receives an overall verbal report about the previous shift. She assigns the patient rooms to her RNs and decides whom will receive the first admission. She checks with the Unit Clerk to get the latest updates.

Registered Nurse

Incoming Registered Nurses check the unit board for their assignments and find their counterparts from the previous shift. The outgoing nurses share their reports regarding their patients' condition during their shift.

Unit Clerk

Incoming Unit Clerk meets with the outgoing Unit Clerk to review the unit activities from the previous shift and alert her to any upcoming scheduled tasks, which may include new patient admissions, transfers, orders which haven't yet been processed, etc. She writes patient assignments on the unit board.

Steelcase Inc.
WorkSpace Futures Explorations
February 2006

Scenario: Patient Transfer, continued

Charge Nurse
The Charge Nurse informs the Nurse Manager of a pending patient transfer.

Nurse Manager
The Nurse Manager asks each Charge Nurse or the MD/NP about pending transfers. She has that information to take to bed rounds, in order to prioritize new patient admissions. Priority is given in collaboration with MD/NP. After bed rounds, she returns with a bed assignment, or a pending request.

Unit Clerk
The Unit Clerk enters the bed request electronically, and writes the new bed assignment on the board.

NOTE: *Throughout this simulation, all users are repeatedly interrupted by phone calls and pages, which must be answered.*

Steelcase Inc.
WorkSpace Futures Explorations
February 2006

Figure 14.11 When conducting a usability test for a hospital nurse's station, Steelcase focused on nurse travel distance and issues related to the effectiveness of the nurse's station. The scenario for simulation, or script, was based on Steelcase's knowledge of how hospitals and nurse's stations work.

Scenario: New Patient Admission (from OSH/ER)

Charge Nurse

The Charge Nurse is informed by the Nurse Manager that a new patient is to be admitted. Activities might include (but are not limited to) verifying that the room is clean, and informing the appropriate nurse (assigned to 'first admit') of the new admission.

Registered Nurse

The RN needs to perform the activities involved when a new patient is admitted to the floor. Such activities might include (but are not limited to) greeting the patient or family in the room, making sure the chart is in order, reviewing the patient's case with the MD/NP, making/documenting the first neurologic/medical assessment. The RN might also take the patient to CT/angio PRN, and assist the MD/NP with procedures.

MD/NP

The MD/NP examines the new patient, and if they are not already written, writes admission orders. S/he also writes the H&P, and makes appropriate calls to Neurology/Neurosurgery/Interventional Neuroradiology. If required, the MD/NP obtains central access.

Scenario: Medication Preparation, Administration & Delivery, *continued*

Registered Nurse

The RN reviews the charts for the latest orders after the Unit Clerk has finished processing them. She calls the pharmacy for quick delivery of 'stat' medications. She goes to the medication prep area and retrieves the prescribed medication from the Pyxis machine, refrigerator or cabinets. She logs the drugs and dosage in the Medication Administration Record (MAR) and then brings the drugs to patient. She then records her actions in the patient's chart.

NOTE: *Throughout this simulation, all users are repeatedly interrupted by phone calls and pages, which must be answered.*

Scenario: New Patient Admission (from OSH/ER), *continued*

Unit Clerk

The Unit Clerk needs to perform all the tasks necessary for receiving this patient. Such tasks might include (but are not limited to) making sure the room is clean, making the change on the unit board, starting a new chart, checking the patient in when s/he arrives, etc.

CNA

The CNA works with the RN to take care of the new patient. Tasks might include assisting with patient transfer to the bed, checking the patient's temperature and blood sugar, and making sure the patient is comfortable.

NOTE: *Throughout this simulation, all users are repeatedly interrupted by phone calls and pages, which must be answered.*

Scenario: Table Rounds

Physician, Nurse Practitioner, Pharm.D and RN

The Medical Team gathers in the meeting space to review charts of current patients. Activities may include looking at scans, accessing patient records, writing orders in the chart, using the phone, etc.

NOTE: *Throughout this simulation, all users are repeatedly interrupted by phone calls and pages, which must be answered.*

Scenario: Medication Preparation, Administration & Delivery

Medical Team

The MD/NP reviews the patient chart and medication log book before visiting the patient. Based on his/her assessment s/he writes the new orders in the chart and hands off the chart to the Unit Clerk.

Unit Clerk

The Unit Clerk pulls the copy of the medication orders from the charts, sends them to the pharmacy and enters lab test orders directly into the system. If the medication needs to be administered immediately, she gives the order form directly to the RN for quick delivery from the pharmacy. The medications are tubed directly to the unit if they are 'stat', and placed in a bin by the Pharmacy Tech if they are routine.

Pharmacist

Throughout the shift, the Pharm. D gives advice to the clinical staff regarding medication questions and the plan of care.

Ongoing Activities during the Simulation
Role players will be going in and out of the nurses' station, per the research team's instructions.

CNA

Throughout the shift, the CNA responds to patient call alerts. Activities might include taking temperatures, emptying the foley bags, taking blood sugars, assisting with turning/suctioning, delivering trays, bathroom assistance, meeting with the RN, etc.

Registered Nurse

Throughout the shift, the RN responds to patient call alerts and speaks with patients' families. She consults with physicians and therapists.

Physician/Nurse Practitioner

Throughout their time on the unit, MDs and NPs check on their patients, write notes/orders, call consults, dictate, and may be interrupted at any point by pages, staff questions, or patient emergencies.

Unit Clerk

Throughout the shift, the Unit Clerk answers the phone and relays messages. She greets outside visitors and internal staff to the unit and directs them to the appropriate room.

Figure 14.11 (continued)

Unless your usability test is very simple and informal, run a test scenario to ensure that the process runs smoothly. This test doesn't require real users, just a means of running through the tasks with any available person. In all other respects, the test run should be as close to realistic as possible. During the test, make sure your participants are put at ease. Also, unless absolutely necessary, do not prompt your participants during the test as it might influence the results. Finally, record the events in as much detail as possible, as well as proposing inferences as to why events occurred as they did. Your notes do not have to contain a solution to the issue or problem, because you and your team will be generating options after the testing is complete. Rather than focusing on solutions, focus on gathering information to inform the design process later. (See Figure 14.12.)

Being a participant in a usability test for a space or product can be a fun learning experience. At some point in your career, you may be called upon to be a representative user yourself. For example, one paint company in Washington, D.C., calls on interior designers to test new packaging ideas for its paint samples. Interior designers evaluate the product design in terms of aesthetics, ease of transportation, and convenience of paint swatch sizes for color selection, as well as documentation in both client presentations and specification binders. If an opportunity like this arises, take advantage of it as a chance to participate in another's research process, as well as an opportunity to meet other interior designers or related professionals in your area.

Post-Occupancy Evaluations

A **post-occupancy evaluation (POE)** is performed shortly after the client and/or users move into the space. The evaluation allows the designer to gather information on users' satisfaction with the space, and it can give the designer a chance to educate him- or herself for future projects—identifying successes and uncovering problems to avoid in the future. There are various ways to conduct a POE. It can be as simple as an informal conversation or as formal as a questionnaire submitted to the end users in a space or direct observation of users of a space. (See Figure 14.13.)

Sometimes, a third party conducts the POE of a project as an objective participant or as part of a larger study of similar project types. It is common to conduct POEs in order to test complex building systems and energy consumption to inform future projects. Depending upon the scale of the evaluation, a public presentation might be made to audiences of other designers to share the results, promote the use of the design interventions, and invite designers' feedback on how the usefulness of the information from the POEs could be enhanced. Participating designers can make suggestions for improvements, which might be incorporated into subsequent design decisions.

There are some common mistakes you can avoid when conducting a usability test. Often a design team might conduct the test prematurely, testing a design that already has several significant, readily identifiable usability issues. Postpone the test until those issues are addressed; otherwise, valuable time during the usability test will be devoted to discussing problems you have already identified.

Another common mistake is to do the usability testing with insufficient time—or insufficient willingness—to make improvements and implement recommendations. This lack of time is often due to budgetary constraints. If it is likely that no changes can be made anyway, the testing is a waste of time and money.

Always be sensitive to your users, and maintain an attitude of professional neutrality. Avoid using qualitative remarks like "Good" or "Well done," which imply that the person, not the system, is being tested. Avoid finishing participants' sentences for them or verbalizing what you think is on their minds. Testers often provide users with too much information, making recommendations along the way. Recall from Chapter 2 that as the observer you want to avoid influencing what is being observed. Instead, just watch, listen, be attentive, be patient, and objectively record what you observe. (Figure 14.12 is an example of the document you might use to record your observations.)

Documenting and Archiving Your Work

The documentation of your project research, design, presentation, and subsequent conclusions is essential to continuing the circular nature of interior design. At some point, another designer might reference the collection of information you have compiled, in order to inform his or her own research process. There are multiple ways to document and archive your work. The most common are the bound book and the project binder.

From the beginning of the thesis process, document everything, keeping a record of your research, your casual notes and formal writing, and all sketches, drawings, and presentation materials. Keep and scan all process work, including sketches, diagrams, and trace paper work, even if you think it is likely not valuable. If the image on the paper has some kind of message or meaning toward the development of your design, then keep it. You might be surprised how important that information is for cohesively presenting your ideas. Professionals repeatedly comment that while the polished portfolio pieces are nice, they are more interested in a potential employee's personal style and how he or she thinks and problem-solves. These skills are more evident in your process work.

USABILITY TEST EVALUATION FORM

PARTICIPANT NO:_____
PG #:_____

Project or Product:	
Facilitator:	
Notetaker:	
Testing Date & Time:	
Notes:	

User Experience Legend	
Experience Related :	**Task Related:**
R: Reattempted Task	TC: Task Completed
Q: Question Asked PartialCompletion	PC:
C: Comment Made	NC: Not Completed
F: Frustration/Confusion	
Severity Code:	
1: Severe 2: High 3: Medium 4: Low	

Task#/Time	UEC	Participant Comments	Notetaker Insight & Ideas	SC

Figure 14.12 During a usability test, there must be a systemized method of recording information and annotating the results, such as this logging sheet or usability test evaluation form. Notice that the document includes a legend for recording information quickly and interpreting the annotations used.

Figure 14.13 Steelcase assesses the impact and success of their design for a hospital infusion center by submitting a Post-Occupancy Questionnaire to end users of the space.

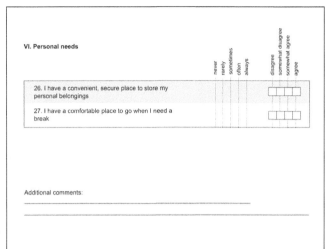

Upon completion of your presentation, photograph your boards and all presentation materials, such as models and material selections, in high resolution, using a tripod to help display your work and obtain well-presented images. You might also have someone photograph or videotape your presentation for you. Scan all original work at a minimum of 300 dpi for incorporating into both your thesis documentation and your academic portfolio.

The Thesis Book: Elements, Organization, Formats

The **thesis book** will become the permanent archive of your work, showing your initial thesis proposal as well as research, development, design process, and final conclusions. Frequently, students use velo binding or spiral binding to create their book. Both are common binding techniques offered at many print shops. Another option is to simply use a three-ring binder, creating a cover page and carefully organizing the sections. However, because you will want to keep a record of your thesis for a long time, book binding is strongly recommended. It is more durable, compact, and professional-looking than other methods. It can also be duplicated easily, which is important if your school requires that you submit a copy for the library archives. Institutions often have specific requirements for the documentation and archiving process, so you should check with your instructor before deciding how to proceed.

The thesis book should be carefully formatted and organized. You can even use the concept of your thesis project to aid you in paper selection and the design of section dividers. Often, sections or chapters are chronologically organized by semester or quarter or by review schedule. Other times they are organized by subject matter. Either way, the result is a summary of all that you have accomplished in your academic career, and it is a document you have earned with your persistence and hard work. Give it the same care you have given the entire project. Make it a symbol of your accomplishments and something to be proud of.

What Kind of Researcher Are You?

According to Hamilton (2003), there are four levels of commitment and methods in design research:

- *Level 1 practitioners* make a careful effort to base their design decisions on available evidence. By staying current with literature in the field, they attempt to follow the evolving research related to the physical setting. They interpret the meaning of the evidence as it relates to their projects, and they make judgments about the best design for specific circumstances.
- *Level 2 practitioners* take the next important step. Based on readings, they hypothesize the expected outcomes of their design decisions and subsequently measure and evaluate the results. These designers must understand the research, interpret the implications, and build a chain of logic connecting the design decision to a measurable outcome, reducing arbitrary decisions. The potential for bias in gathering and reporting results means they must resist the temptation to report success and downplay failure.
- *Level 3 practitioners* follow the literature, hypothesize intended outcomes of design, and measure results—and then go further by reporting their results publicly. Writing or speaking about results moves information beyond the firm or client team. These practitioners are taking a chance, as it subjects their research methods and results to scrutiny from others who may or may not agree with the findings. Level 3 practitioners should seek advanced education to enable greater rigor in the research process.
- *Level 4 practitioners* are scholar–practitioners who perform the same tasks: following the literature, hypothesizing outcomes of design decisions, measuring results, and reporting their findings. These designers go further by publishing their findings in peer-reviewed journals or collaborating with other academics. They subject their work to the highest level of rigorous review.

According to Hamilton, there are also "level-zero practitioners" (2003). These are designers who understand that the environment has an effect on its end users in every situation and that there is evidence to support various conclusions about those effects. These designers might take isolated comments from an article, make a personal interpretation that fits their design bias, and claim that the subsequent design is evidence-based. A level-zero practitioner likely has not read the original research and might misinterpret important principles.

What kind of researcher are you? What kind of researcher do you want to be? Whether you are a student or a professional, your opportunities to impact the direction of the interior design field increase as the depth of your research methods increases. If you strive to make design decisions that are inspired by the best-known evidence in the field, you will benefit yourself as a professional as well as benefitting the people who will experience the spaces you design.

Design as a Circular Process

Although this book is written with an academic audience in mind, there is really no difference between the information communicated here and the tools you will use every day in your professional experience. We all know people who are perpetual students, never seeming to move beyond the walls of their schools. For your own future, take on the heart not of a perpetual student, but of a habitual learner as you make your transition into the interior design profession.

Essential to an interior designer's success is the process of constant self-education and evaluation, through all kinds of research and information-gathering. In fact, once you pass your professional exams, such as the NCIDQ (National Council for Interior Design Qualification) or LEED (Leadership in Energy and Environmental Design) or join our various professional organizations, such as ASID (American Society of Interior Designers) or IIDA (International Interior Design Association), you will be required to complete a certain number of **Continuing Education Units** (CEUs) each year.

Conclusion

Table 14.1 is a review of the most significant points covered throughout the book and how the chapters all fit together. In this table, the underlying premise of each chapter is identified, and you will see the methods relevant to that premise and the application of the methods to your design process. Use this table as a quick reference, but remember that although it is presented in a step-by-step manner, like design itself each topic is fluid and flexible in its relationship to you and how research will inspire your design process.

Use the circular nature of interior design to your advantage, enjoying the evolution of your ideas and feeling the sense of satisfaction when you learn something new or discover a body of research that reveals how design has the power to change the human experience. Relish the excitement on a client's face when they see how you listened to them and how you fulfilled their wishes in a way they couldn't have imagined. Do not be frustrated when your design changes or requires revisions. Know the relief when you realize a major mistake was avoided because you took the time to mock up your ideas and uncover a significant problem to be solved now, rather than after it was too late.

References

Hamilton, K. (2003, November). The four levels of evidence-based design practice. *Healthcare Design*, 18–26.

Newell, A., Shaw, J. C., & Simon, H. A. (1967). The process of creative thinking. In H. Gruber (Ed.), *Contemporary approaches to creative thinking.* New York: Atherton.

Tate, A. (1987). *The making of interiors: An introduction.* New York: Harper & Row.

U.S. Department of Agriculture. (2008). *Engineering design & construction.* Retrieved July 26, 2008, from http://www.afm.ars.usda.gov/engineering/value.htm

U.S. Department of Health and Human Services. (2008). *Learn about usability testing.* Retrieved July 26, 2008, from http://www.usability.gov/refine/learnusa.html

Wickens, C. D., Lee, J. D., Liu, Y., & Gordon-Becker, S. E. (2004). *An introduction to human factors engineering.* Upper Saddle River, NJ: Prentice Hall.

	Key Point #1: Basis	Key Point #2: Method	Key Point #3: Application
Chapter 1: Why Research?	The keys to design excellence: knowledge, creativity, exploration	Define a problem, gather information, and analyze data.	Be a creative problem solver.

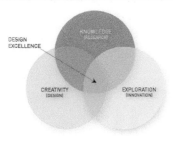

Figure 1.1

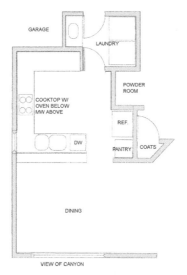

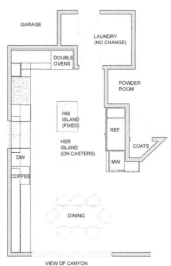

Figures 1.7 and 1.8

Figures 1.8 and 1.10

	Key Point #1: Basis	Key Point #2: Method	Key Point #3: Application
Chapter 2: Systems of Inquiry	Identify your assumptions and value systems.	Understand the relationship between subjectivity and objectivity.	Blend the creative and subjective nature of art with the logical or objective nature of science.

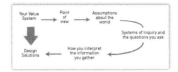

Figure 2.3

Figure 2.7

Figure 2.8

continued

	Key Point #1: Basis	Key Point #2: Method	Key Point #3: Application
Chapter 3: Meaningful Influences	What is design theory?	Challenge existing paradigms and propose a paradigm shift.	Develop your personal design philosophy.

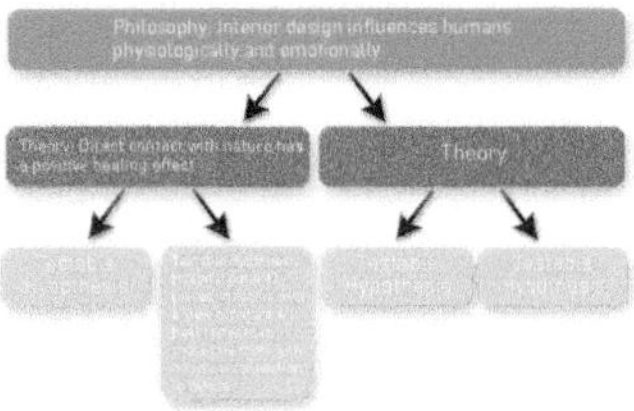

Figure 3.1

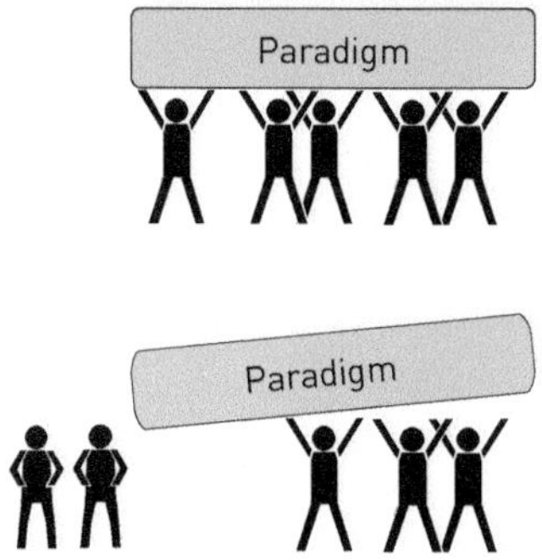

Figure 3.12

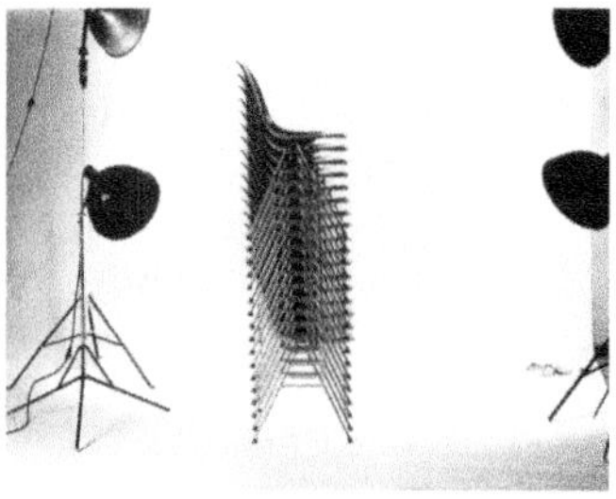

Figure 3.6 (partial)

	Key Point #1: Basis	Key Point #2: Method	Key Point #3: Application
Chapter 4: Brainstorming	Identify a research question.	Develop creative brainstorming techniques.	Use research as a source of inspiration.

Figure 4.2

Figure 4.3 (partial)

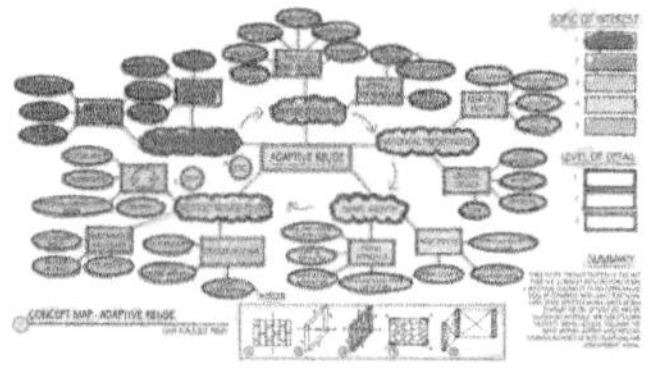

Figure 4.4

	Key Point #1: Basis	Key Point #2: Method	Key Point #3: Application
Chapter 5: Identifying Information Sources	Conduct a thorough literature review.	Understand the basic information-gathering strategies.	Evaluate the value and validity of your information sources.

	Key Point #1: Basis	Key Point #2: Method	Key Point #3: Application
Chapter 6: **Interviews**	Who has the information you need? Identify interviews that need to take place.	Format and prepare an interview.	Conduct and record the interview using various techniques and innovative approaches.

Figure 6.1

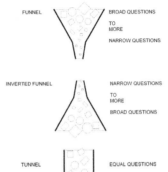

Figure 6.4

Figure 6.7

Chapter 7: **Surveys**	Identify a sample population.	Develop a standardized questionnaire with a clear goal.	Analyze, represent, and communicate your data.

Figure 7.2 (partial)

Figure 7.3

Figure 7.7

	Key Point #1: Basis	Key Point #2: Method	Key Point #3: Application
Chapter 8: Observation	Identify observation techniques.	Record and document your observations.	Develop a case study to share your conclusions.

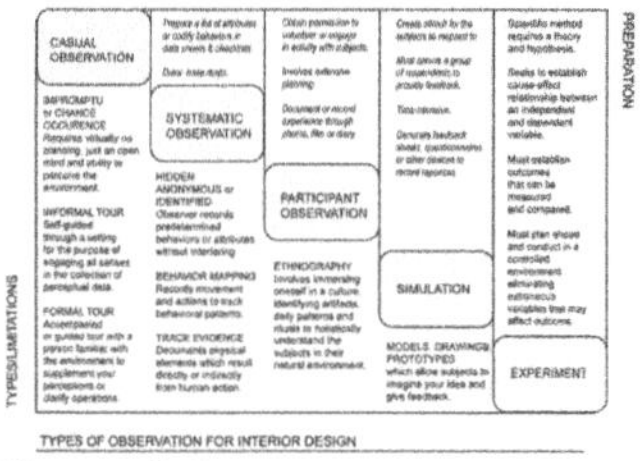

Figure 8.1

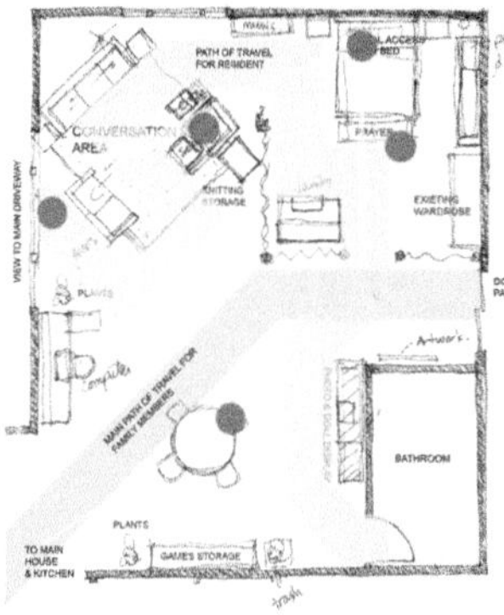

Figure 8.3

Figure 8.10

	Key Point #1: Basis	Key Point #2: Method	Key Point #3: Application
Chapter 9: Research-Inspired Design	Create an interior design thesis statement, taking a side of the fence on the topic.	Identify the issues common to your project type.	Declare your intentions and goals in the thesis proposal.

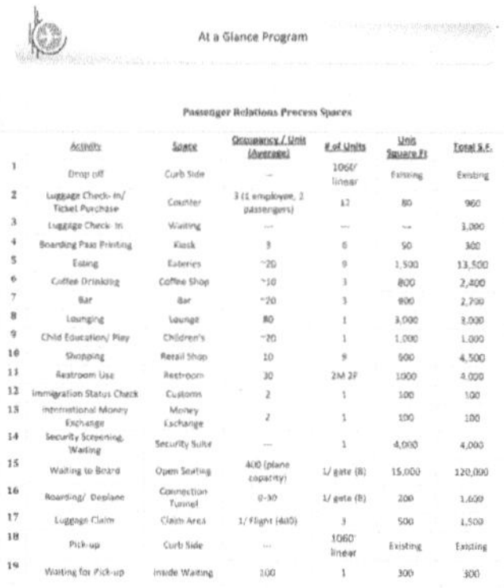

Figure 9.2

Figure 9.3

Figure 9.8

	Key Point #1: Basis	Key Point #2: Method	Key Point #3: Application
Chapter 10: The Written Program	Define project goals and the problems to be solved through design.	Navigate the five steps of the programming process.	Synthesize your information into an organized and detailed project program.

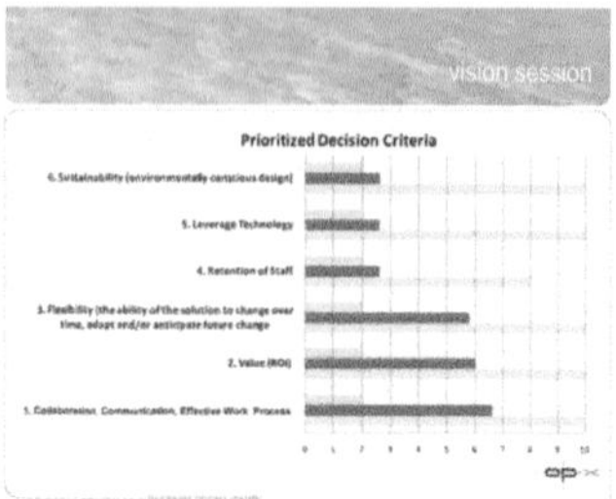

Figure 10.7

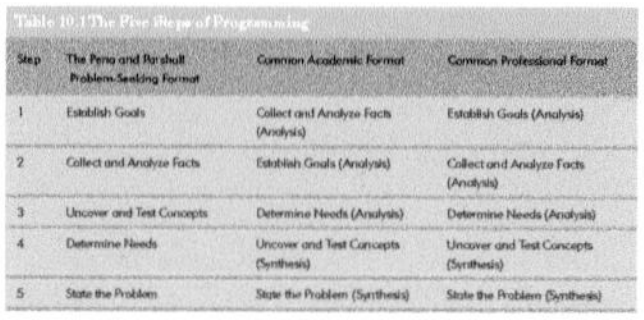

Table 10.1

Figure 10.12

	Key Point #1: Basis	Key Point #2: Method	Key Point #3: Application
Chapter 11: **Site Selection** **and Analysis**	Understand the site on multiple levels and from a variety of sources.	Collect data on the existing conditions.	Analyze the site in terms of physical possibilities and constraints: Does the building fit the program?

Figure 11.3

Figure 11.11

Figure 11.13

	Key Point #1: Basis	Key Point #2: Method	Key Point #3: Application
Chapter 12: **Schematics**	Translate the written program into design solutions.	Use diagramming techniques to investigate concepts and explore options.	Generate many schematic design solutions.

Figure 12.2

Figure 12.20a

Figure 12.16

	Key Point #1: Basis	Key Point #2: Method	Key Point #3: Application
Chapter 13: **Design** **Development**	Design Development: articulate a three-dimensional interior design solution.	Incorporate information from expert sources.	Storyboard your final presentation.

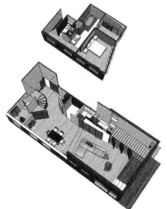

Figure 13.6 (partial)

Figure 13.4

Figure 13.11

continued

	Key Point #1: Basis	Key Point #2: Method	Key Point #3: Application
Chapter 14: Design as a Circular Process	Identify what kind of researcher you are.	Use evaluation techniques to refine your design decisions.	Allow information to inspire your design process . . .

Figure 14.2

Figure 14.5

Figure 14.7 (partial)

Figure 14.3 (partial)

Credits

Chapter 1

1.1 Illustration re-created by Andrea Lau, original by the authors

1.2 Illustration re-created by Andrea Lau, original by the authors

1.3 Illustration re-created by Andrea Lau, original by the authors

1.4 Jain Malkin, Inc.

1.5 Courtesy of the authors

1.6 Courtesy of the authors

1.7 Courtesy of Lily Robinson

1.8 Courtesy of Lily Robinson

1.9 Courtesy of Lily Robinson

1.10 Courtesy of Lily Robinson

Chapter 2

2.1 Courtesy of Alexandra Parman

2.2 Illustration re-created by Andrea Lau, original by the authors

2.3 Illustration re-created by Andrea Lau, original by the authors

2.4 Courtesy of the authors

2.5 Courtesy of the authors

2.6 Courtesy of Brad Brown

2.7 Illustration re-created by Andrea Lau, original by the authors

2.8 Illustration re-created by Andrea Lau, original by the authors

2.9 Courtesy of the authors

2.10 Courtesy of the authors

2.11 Courtesy of the authors

2.12 Courtesy of the authors

Chapter 3

3.1 Illustration re-created by Andrea Lau, original by the authors

3.2 Illustration re-created by Andrea Lau, original by the authors

3.3 © James Leynse/CORBIS

3.4 Courtesy of the authors

3.5 © Francis G. Mayer/CORBIS

3.6 Courtesy of Eames Office Resources

3.7 © Eric Laignel

3.8 Courtesy of LTL Architects

3.9 Courtesy of the authors

3.10 Courtesy of the authors

3.11 Courtesy of the authors

3.12 Illustration re-created by Andrea Lau, original by the authors

Chapter 4

4.1 Illustration re-created by Andrea Lau, original by the authors
4.2 Courtesy of Fathom
4.3 Courtesy of Lily Robinson
4.4 Courtesy of Rain Perry
4.5 Courtesy of the authors
4.6 Courtesy of the authors
4.7 Courtesy of Adam Kalkin
4.8 Illustration re-created by Andrea Lau, original by the authors
4.9 Illustration re-created by Andrea Lau, original by the authors

Chapter 6

6.1 Courtesy of the Salk Institute
6.2 Courtesy of Dalia Feldman
6.3 Illustration re-created by Andrea Lau, original by the authors
6.4 Illustration re-created by Andrea Lau, original by the authors
6.5 Courtesy of Edith Cherry
6.6 Courtesy of Edith Cherry
6.7 Courtesy of Edith Cherry
6.8a–c Courtesy of Fathom

Chapter 7

7.1 Courtesy of Define Design
7.2 Illustration re-created by Andrea Lau, original by the authors
7.3 Courtesy of the authors
7.4 Courtesy of the authors
7.5 Courtesy of National Center for Education Statistics
7.6 Courtesy of National Center for Education Statistics
7.7 Courtesy of National Center for Education Statistics

Chapter 8

8.1 Courtesy of the authors
8.2 Courtesy of Define Design, Annahi Barce
8.3 Courtesy of the authors
8.4 Courtesy of Define Design, Leanna Duncan
8.5 Courtesy of Define Design, Leanna Duncan
8.6 Courtesy of Edith Cherry
8.7 Courtesy of the authors
8.8 Courtesy of Design Share
8.9 Courtesy of Design Share
8.10 Courtesy of Design Share

Chapter 9

9.1 Illustration re-created by Andrea Lau, original by the authors
9.2 Illustration re-created by Andrea Lau, original by the authors
9.3 Courtesy of the authors
9.4 Courtesy of the Smithsonian Institution
9.5 Courtesy of Fathom, C. Berdik
9.6 Courtesy of Fathom, C. Berdik
9.7 Courtesy of Fathom, L. Conley
9.8 Courtesy of Fathom, L. Conley
9.9 Courtesy of Fathom, L. Conley
9.10 Courtesy of Fathom

Chapter 10

10.1 Illustration re-created by Andrea Lau, original by the authors
10.2 Courtesy of WDG, Washington DC
10.3 © OPX, pllc 2008, all rights reserved
10.4 © OPX, pllc 2008, all rights reserved
10.5 © OPX, pllc 2008, all rights reserved
10.6 Courtesy of WDG, Washington DC
10.7 © OPX, pllc 2008, all rights reserved
10.8 Illustration re-created by Andrea Lau, original by the authors
10.9 Courtesy of the authors
10.10 Courtesy of the authors
10.11 Courtesy of Michelle Hill
10.12 Courtesy of Kelly Powell
10.13 Courtesy of Morgan Greenseth
10.14 Courtesy of Morgan Greenseth

Chapter 11

11.1 Courtesy of the authors
11.2 Courtesy of the authors
11.3 Illustration re-created by Andrea Lau, original by the authors
11.4 Courtesy of the authors
11.5 Courtesy of OkSolar and Home Building Clinic
11.6 Courtesy of San Diego Fire Department
11.7 Courtesy of NYC DOB
11.8 Courtesy of Heather Williams
11.9 Courtesy of the authors
11.10 Courtesy of the authors
11.11 Courtesy of the authors
11.12 Courtesy of Sara Plaisted
11.13 Courtesy of the authors

Index